CW00957037

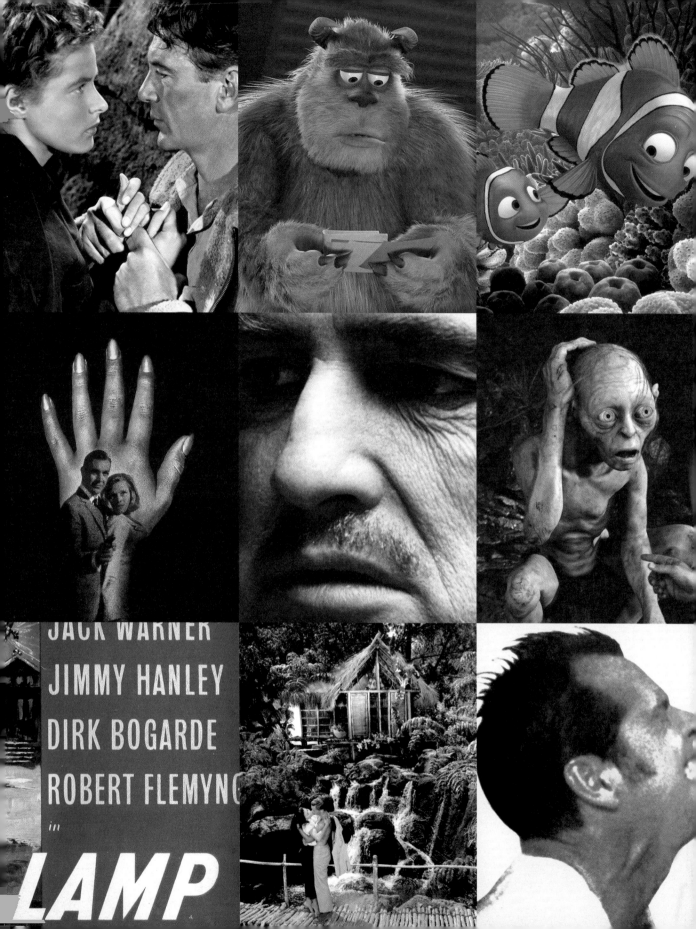

THE
ULTIMATE FILM

The UK's 100 most popular films

Foreword by Jonathan Ross

Edited by Ryan Gilbey

bfi

First published in 2005 by the
BRITISH FILM INSTITUTE
21 Stephen Street
London
W1T 1LN

The British Film Institute's purpose is to champion
moving image culture in all its richness and diversity
across the UK, for the benefit of as wide an audience
as possible, and to create and encourage debate.

British Library Cataloguing-in-Publication Data
A catalogue record for this book is available from
the British Library

ISBN 1–84457–105–X (pbk)

Project Editor: Keith Mansfield
Design: Ashley Western

Printed in the UK by Scotprint, Haddington,
East Lothian

CONTENTS

THE ENTRIES EXPLAINED

An abridged listing of the people who made the film and those that starred in it, taken from the BFI database

The rank in *The Ultimate Film* chart

Basic filmographic data, including the estimated attendance

A contemporary view by a film critic. For very recent films, the 'WHAT THEY SAID THEN…' and 'WHAT THEY SAY NOW…' sections have been combined into a single 'WHAT THEY SAY…' entry

A description of an outstanding scene

Anecdotes from the production of the film

66

Dir: Frank CAPRA / USA
Released in Britain: 1937
Running Time: 132 minutes
Colour: Black and white
Estimated Attendance: 9.2 million

are excellently blended to suggest atmosphere. The acting is good: Ronald Colman and E. E. Horton are admirable, and H. B. Warner as Chang achieves natural sincerity and an outstanding performance; Thomas Mitchell is excellent as the company promoter; Isabel Jewell is equally convincing. Capra is not so happy with this vast canvas: there is little opportunity for the subtle humour which has marked his previous films. But the skill of the opening and the final sequences is unforgettable, and the film is an outstanding essay in the epic class.

SCENE STEALER
Despite her denial of the life-prolonging properties of Shangri-la, Maria begins to age rapidly as soon as she and the Conway brothers have left its boundaries. Before the eyes of the hysterical, desperate George, she withers into unnatural old age and dies.

BEHIND THE SCENES
Columbia's cheapskate philistine Harry Cohn so hated Sam Jaffe's performance that he insisted on an expensive re-shoot, on a new set, with Walter Connolly (Claudette Colbert's father in *It Happened One Night*). He hated that more, so Jaffe was brought back for another re-shoot. Capra's original print ran six hours, cut to 132 minutes for release. The current restored version runs 128, with lost footage replaced with stills over the soundtrack.

Frank Capra is best known for cherished favourites like *It Happened One Night* (1934) and *It's a Wonderful Life* (1946). But neither of those are on the Ultimate Film list. No, the Capra movies that really drew the crowds are *Mr Deeds Goes to Town* (1936, at number 90) and this moving drama about the search for inner peace.

LOST HORIZON

Director/Producer **Frank Capra**
Screenplay **Robert Riskin, adapted from the novel by James Hilton**
Director of Photography **Joseph Walker**
Editors **Gene Havlick, Gene Milford**
Art Director **Stephen Goosson**
Music **Dimitri Tiomkin**

Robert Conway • Ronald Colman
Sondra Bizet • Jane Wyatt
George Conway • John Howard
Maria • Margo
Henry Barnard • Thomas Mitchell
Alexander P. Lovett • Edward Everett Horton
Gloria Stone • Isabel Jewell
Chang • H. B. Warner
High Lama • Sam Jaffe
Prime Minister • David Torrence
Lord Gainsford • Hugh Buckler
Talu • Val Duran
Fenner • Milton Owen
Shanghai Airport Official • Richard Loo
Bandit Leader • Willie Fung
Bandit Leader • Victor Wong
Wynant • John Burton
Carstairs • John Milterm
Meeker • John T. Murray
Aviator • Dennis D'Auburn

THE STORY
Robert Conway, a British diplomat, is evacuating the small white population from a revolution at Baskul. On the last plane to leave, Conway travels with his brother George; Barnard, an absconding company promoter; Lovett, a fossil-hunter; and Gloria Stone, a consumptive girl. Kidnapped by the Tibetan pilot, they are taken miles beyond civilisation to Shangri-la, a kind of secular monastery, situated on a high plateau above the secluded and fertile Blue Valley, where Chang, the intellectual administrator of Shangri-la welcomes them. The little kingdom is an Erewhon – a combination of a millionaire's playground, an economist's paradise and Nirvana. Absence of causes for worry makes men and women in their sixties appear in their twenties.

Gradually Conway and his friends, but not his brother, find contentment and a new non-commercial outlet for their talents. The High Lama, 200 years old, the founder and spiritual leader of Shangri-la, announces his approaching death to Conway. Dying, he bestows his mantle on him. But persuaded by his brother, Conway leaves for home with George and with Maria, an apparently young girl from Shangri-la. The perilous journey ends in tragedy: Maria turns old before their eyes and George commits suicide. Conway is discovered by missionaries and sent back to England; but en route the urge to return to Shangri-la is too strong and he leaves the ship at Singapore. Years afterwards, we are given to understand, he at last rediscovers Shangri-la.

WHAT THEY SAID THEN …
The story is Utopian fantasy on a grand scale. But inordinate length has disadvantages. The fundamental difficulty is that once Shangri-la is achieved the long passages of philosophical dialogue are not equal to the stupendous excitement of the kidnapping. The contrast between the Tibetan storm at 20,000 ft. and the sunny peace of Shangri-la is perfectly achieved, and the sound effects

WHAT THEY SAY NOW …
Although it has a naivety and innocence that show its age, and the sojourn in Shangri-la is talkative and languid, there are sequences in this epic adaptation of James Hilton's 1933 bestseller that are still thrilling the China hijacking sequence that brings the Conway brothers, the con man, the palaeontologist and the dying floozy to the hidden paradise in Tibet) and haunting (the sequence of desperate events after leaving the enchanted valley). Its delicate beauty and atmosphere justify its seven Academy Award nominations at the time, and its restored reputation as a gem of Hollywood's golden age.

CLASSIC QUOTE
Lord Gainsford: 'Gentlemen, I give you a toast. Here's my hope that Robert Conway will find his Shangri-la. Here's my hope that we all find our Shangri-la.'

IN THE CHAIR
Frank Capra is celebrated as the purveyor of idealised small town American values in comedy fables about ordinary Joes, such as *It's a Wonderful Life*. But his two extraordinary classics, 1933's sensuous *The Bitter Tea of General Yen* (arguably his masterpiece of mood) and *Lost Horizon*, are complex works to which the adjective 'Capraesque' is not applicable.

OSCARS
7 Nominations **2 Winners**
Outstanding Production
Actor in a Supporting Role: H. B. Warner
Art Direction: Stephen Goosson
Assistant Director: C. C. Coleman, Jr.
Film Editing: Gene Havlick, Gene Milford
Music (Scoring): Morris Stoloff, Dimitri Tiomkin
Sound Recording: John Livadary

WHAT WON THAT YEAR
Outstanding Production: *The Life of Emile Zola*
Director: Leo McCarey, *The Awful Truth*
Actor: Spencer Tracy *Captains Courageous*
Actress: Luise Rainer *The Good Earth*

BAFTAS
Not awarded until 1947

Right The scent of paradise: George Conway (John Howard) softly around Maria (Margo) in Shangri-la

An edited version of the synopsis of the film from a BFI publication at the time of release: either *Monthly Film Bulletin* (up until 1991) or *Sight & Sound* (from 1991 onwards)

A memorable piece of dialogue

An edited version of the review of the film from a BFI publication at the time of release: either *Monthly Film Bulletin* (up until 1991) or *Sight & Sound* (from 1991 onwards)

Nominations and winners for each film are given for both the Oscars and the Baftas. In addition, the winners of the major awards from that year are also given to help place the film in context with its contemporaries. Due to limitations of space, names are only given when three or fewer people have been cited for an award

A passage about a key protagonist, in this case the Director

FOREWORD

Spies, soldiers, sharks, aliens, nannies, wizards, soldiers, strippers, hooligans, heroes, villains, insects, dinosaurs and doctors …

It would be impossible not to enjoy this fascinating book. The BFI has found the top 100 films that people have gone to see in Britain – ever. It's the only list based on bums on seats instead of box-office receipts. It's the only list that's chosen by the people and not by the critics.

And of course, what's popular isn't always the critics' choice. While *The Third Man*, which topped the BFI's own poll of the best British films ever made, is on the list, it is joined by unlikely bedfellows such as *Carry on Nurse* and *Bridget Jones: The Edge of Reason*. Although Bridget's charms have never really won me over, if people want to see Renée Zellweger perform Madonna's 'Like a Virgin' in a Thai prison then who am I to spoil their fun?

So here they are, the 100 most popular movies. Each entry is illustrated from the BFI stills collection – the largest such archive in the world – with reviews for each film from when it was released, allowing you to compare what critics said at the time with what they think now. There are classic quotes, scenes that stand out and snippets of gossip about the films that always leave you wanting more.

Just as the book is a celebration of British cinemagoing, it is also a celebration of British cinema talent – six of the top ten films have British leading ladies. For the men it's not just Roger Moore keeping the British end up. Alec Guinness and Green Cross Man David Prowse are there in the top five, but the actor with most appearances of all is Bernard Lee – best known and loved for his role as Bond's M but appearing in several more besides. Behind the camera David Lean and Lewis Gilbert prove themselves to be great and popular British Directors.

The 1940s dominate the list with twenty films, while the introduction of video in the 1980s sees only four from that decade scraping into the lower echelons. The times though are a-changing. We're only halfway through this decade yet already eighteen films have made the top 100. The new golden age of cinemagoing is *now* and I'm delighted to be involved in it.

The most recent addition is *Star Wars Episode III: Revenge of the Sith*. The original *Star Wars* is sometimes said to have saved the film industry back in the late 1970s. The sequels and prequels haven't always saved George Lucas from the wrath of reviewer, myself included. The intelligentsia may mock, but old friends Scorsese and Coppola still turn up at Skywalker Ranch most Wednesdays for a hearty breakfast – and if that isn't a seal of approval from the industry's great and good, you tell me what is.

So have the hobbits beaten Harry Potter? Is *Mary Poppins* more popular than *The Wicked Lady*? Everything is here from Azkaban to Doctor Zhivago, via South Pacific, Arabia, Middle Earth and Tatooine. Read on if you want to know what the most popular film, *The Ultimate Film*, of all time in the UK is. And if you've got money on it being *Confessions of a Window Cleaner* I'll warn you now – it was close, but sadly not to be.

Jonathan Ross

INTRODUCTION

Welcome to *The Ultimate Film* – the only comprehensive record of the most widely seen films screened in British cinemas. And thank you for all your hard work in doing the groundwork for the book that you are now holding in your hands. No, really – you should congratulate yourself. You put in the hours (and weeks and months and years) and a good deal of the effort too, though hopefully the enjoyment outweighed the suffering. For this is the first time that a tally of filmgoing in Britain has been compiled using the bare facts of how many people actually bought a seat in the stalls (or, for anyone not weaned exclusively on multiplexes, in the circle too). If you have ever seen a film at a British cinema then you have played your part in making this book possible. Whether you went to the pictures on a romantic date one Saturday night, a family outing on a Sunday, or a 'sick day' on an otherwise dreary Monday, you can consider yourself to be one of the authors of this book. Clearly this is going to be problematic when it comes time to hand out the royalties, but you take the point.

At the end of the book, two BFI researchers, Phil Wickham and Matt Ker, reveal exactly how the list was pieced together from around seventy years of data. But before you come to that, there is the list itself, which plots in detail the tastes of four generations of cinemagoers. As much as you played your part in choosing the titles assembled here, so too did your relatives, distant or otherwise. You can blame your family if there are movies here of which you do not approve. If you are a hip young thing, and the whimsy of *The Bells of St Mary's* turns your stomach, blame your grandparents for propelling it onto the list. Alternatively, perhaps you have been going to the cinema since it was all fields around here, and wish to have a quiet word with your great-grandchildren about all three *Star Wars* prequels muscling in on the rundown.

The point is that, unlike a tally of critical favourites, or worldwide hits, *The Ultimate Film* list belongs to everyone in Britain; it is a record of how we spent, and continue to spend, our leisure time. I hope that, as well as supplying comprehensive information about each movie, *The Ultimate Film* will also provide unexpected access to this country's memories of cinemagoing. Perhaps you queued around the block for *Gone with the Wind*? Maybe you preceded your trip to see *Jaws* with a stiff drink around the corner from the Regal? Did you sob into your handkerchief during *Random Harvest*? Pretend to be sixteen in order to get past the usher tearing tickets for *A Clockwork Orange*? Buy a snazzy white suit on the walk to the bus stop after *Saturday Night Fever*? You didn't – did you?

Anyone for whom cinema has been important cannot fail to find this list peculiarly evocative. The titles here can conjure a lifetime of filmgoing memories; for my own part, I was strangely excited to see that my late grandmother's favourite film, *The Best Years of Our Lives*, had made the top ten. And I picture my other grandmother, an Italian immigrant to East London, catching the number 123 bus to the now-derelict Granada cinema to see some of the other films here and, by the by, brush up on her English. *The Jungle Book* and *Pinocchio*, which she took me to as a boy, are listed alongside those I've since watched with my own children, with our buckets of popcorn and outsized cups of tooth-rotting cola.

What about the films themselves? The delightful thing about the Ultimate Film list is that it includes genuine surprises alongside the usual suspects. Admittedly there is a high proportion of blockbusters (*Titanic*, *Independence Day*) and sequels (the *Harry Potter* and *Lord of the Rings* series) and children's films. Disney is responsible for a massive twelve titles in the list, four of them co-productions with the mighty Pixar. (Two Disney titles – *Cinderella* and another Pixar effort, *The Incredibles* – missed the list by a whisker.) This dominance, along with the high placings for other family-oriented films like *Shrek 2* or the *Harry Potter* series, can obviously be explained by the filmgoing habits associated with U and PG (or, pre-1983, A-rated) pictures. The entire family chooses to go together, possibly more than once, thus maximising ticket sales. It takes a colossally successful 15 (AA) or 18 (X) rated picture, then, to notch up the sort of admissions necessary to compete with a Disney classic.

Consequently, with the exception of *The Wicked Lady*, the only non-comedic 'adult' movies that feature here – that is, those to which children would not be admitted – are those that tick the box marked 'cultural phenomenon': *The Godfather*, *A Clockwork Orange*, *One Flew Over the Cuckoo's Nest*, *The Exorcist*. All date from the early or mid-1970s, substantiating the claim that mainstream adult filmmaking was effectively phased out by Hollywood after the success of *Star Wars*. This is only one sense in which the list charts the trends, positive or otherwise, which have influenced the films we have paid to see. Throughout the book, you will also be able to read about other factors – the onset of war, the rise of video – that have had an impact on the list, as well as pondering such questions as why there are no non-English language titles here.

It was to be expected that James Bond would feature significantly in the chart (though who thought that *Thunderball* would be the most successful entry of the series?) And it's no shock to find Steven Spielberg making his presence felt (four movies here, plus one as producer). Rather it's the oddities, the eccentric hits, the snapshots of former popular favourites now rarely mentioned, that really piques the interest. It must say something about Britain as a nation that the smoulderingly sadistic cads played by James Mason proved popular enough to feature twice in the top ten (in *The Seventh Veil* and *The Wicked Lady*). And while it is unusual for Anna Neagle's name to crop up in a discussion of hit movies, here she is starring in four of the nation's most-seen films, one of which – *Spring in Park Lane* – drew more than 20 million adoring viewers. That's nearly three times as many as Keanu Reeves in *The Matrix Reloaded*, though it should be up to readers to decide who's the coolest, Anna or Keanu.

Comparisons between admissions for old and new films is a little unfair, since the number of screens now available to movies has been reduced dramatically; the spectre of opening weekend – that Friday to Sunday period where success or failure is measured in the US, thereby dictating which films will be given the hard sell when they open in Britain – has also cramped significantly the commercial chances of many movies. In this paranoid marketplace, if a film isn't a hit within a day or two of opening, then it is effectively a failure. That's rather different to the climate in which, say, *The Sound of Music* or *The Jolson Story* were released; in those days, a film trickled out from London to the suburbs and across the country, allowing time for its popularity to grow.

The sheer disparity between the number of cinemas back in 1940, when *Gone With the Wind* was released, and now, makes it unlikely that the titles here will be much disturbed from their placings, though there will surely be new entries from any film bearing the prefix *Harry Potter and the . . .*, or the credit 'Written by Richard Curtis and starring Hugh Grant.' But who knows? If enough of you out there express sufficient enthusiasm for a movie, it will show up in future editions of this book. It is, in the most literal sense, up to you. Happy viewing. **Ryan Gilbey**

Dir: Victor FLEMING / USA
Released in Britain: 1940
Running Time: 220 minutes
Colour: Technicolor
Estimated Attendance: 35 million

Rhett Butler might not have given a damn, but 35 million Britons certainly did. The undisputed Ultimate Film is a 24-frames-per-second definition of epic melodrama: sweeping, passionate, over-the-top and brimming with classic sequences that still take the breath away.

GONE WITH THE WIND

Director **Victor Fleming**
Producer **David O. Selznick**
Screenplay/Story **Sidney Howard**, based on the novel by Margaret Mitchell
Director of Photography **Ernest Haller**
Editor **Hal C. Kern**
Production Designer **William Cameron Menzies**
Music **Max Steiner**

Rhett Butler • Clark Gable
Scarlett O'Hara • Vivien Leigh
Gerald O'Hara • Thomas Mitchell
Ellen O'Hara • Barbara O'Neil
Suellen O'Hara • Evelyn Keyes
Carreen O'Hara • Ann Rutherford
Stuart Tarleton • George Reeves
Brent Tarleton • Fred Crane
Mammy • Hattie McDaniel
Pork • Oscar Polk
Prissy • Butterfly McQueen
Jonas Wilkerson, the Overseer • Victor Jory
Big Sam • Everett Brown
John Wilkes • Howard Hickman
India Wilkes • Alicia Rhett
Ashley Wilkes • Leslie Howard
Melanie Hamilton • Olivia de Havilland
Charles Hamilton • Rand Brooks
Frank Kennedy • Carroll Nye
Aunt 'Pittypat' Hamilton • Laura Hope Crews

THE STORY

Drama set in Civil War-era Georgia. Scarlett O'Hara, the tempestuous daughter of a Southern landowner of Irish descent, is in love with quiet Ashley Wilkes, who is to marry the gentle Melanie. Suddenly war begins, and all the young men ride off. Scarlett marries one of them, out of spite, but he is soon killed. She has already met, attracted, and been attracted by, Rhett Butler, a wild Southerner with a bad reputation. War goes on, and the South is defeated. In a welter of bloodshed and devastation, Scarlett and Melanie nurse the wounded, the former bitter, the latter compassionate. Competently but angrily, Scarlett delivers Melanie's baby and, with Rhett's help, takes her on the perilous journey back to Tara. There she finds desolation, but sets to work to restore her home and make the land fertile again. She shoots a Yankee deserter, and robs him before burying his body. Ashley returns, but Scarlett cannot win him away from Melanie. She marries her sister's beau because he has money. He is killed, and she marries Rhett, as he too has money. Melanie dies, and only then does Scarlett realise she never loved Ashley. Disgusted, Rhett leaves after the death of their child, and Scarlett remains at Tara, alone.

WHAT THEY SAID THEN …

This breathtaking, overwhelming picture has marvellous settings, photographed in colour as beautiful as anything yet seen on screen. It is, however, a matter for regret that a film conceived on such epic proportions should deal only with the life-story of a hussy. It is a tribute to producer, director and cast alike that, though interest is not equally sustained, it only flags and is never lost. The director has handled a large cast with skill and intuition. He has had the courage to deglamorise war, creating a picture of slaughter and desolation not quickly forgotten.

Vivien Leigh as Scarlett is beautiful, cruel, sly, demure when she wants to be, with kitten-like grace, and sudden outbursts of fury. Clark Gable makes a dashing if rather obvious and superficial Rhett, and Leslie Howard gives a thoughtful study of Ashley, never quite seeming at ease. As Melanie, Olivia de Havilland is gentle without being insipid. Hattie McDaniel is unforgettable as the nanny.

Tara had survived ... to face the hell and famine of defeat ...

Top *The horror of war is spelt out* **Above** *Fire! Atlanta burns* **Above right** *'If we'd had that many soldiers we would have won the war!'* **Below** *Is there room on your horse for two?*

WHAT THEY SAY NOW ...

The meticulously spectacular *Gone With The Wind*, the Technicolor mother of all romantic historical epics, changed the way movies are marketed forever. It generated unprecedented hyperbole, from the battle for Margaret Mitchell's blockbuster novel to the movie's coronation-like world premiere and the Academy Awards night christened by its host Bob Hope as 'a benefit for David O. Selznick'.

Having cost a then-colossal $4 million to make, it has attracted more viewers globally than any other picture. It is dated, its depiction of slavery cringe-makingly false, its glorification of the Old South's 'pretty world' ('a civilization gone with the wind ...') baldly sentimentalised. But *Gone With The Wind* remains the most gorgeous chunk of melodrama committed to celluloid, and a blueprint for grand-scale storytelling. The showcase images continue to pack a wallop. Scarlett, draped in mourning black for the boy she married in pique, troops with Rhett Butler like a merry crow through a shocked, pastel assemblage at a fundraising ball. Scarlett's search for the doctor during the siege of Atlanta takes her to the train depot where the camera cranes up and retreats from her stunned face to reveal a sea of wounded men, the faded grey of the awful scene ironically accentuated by the gay colours of a tattered Confederate flag in the foreground (a shot that provoked Mitchell's husband to drawl, 'If we'd had that many soldiers we would have won the war!'). Rhett and the women's hair-raising flight through the burning of Atlanta (for which Selznick employed every Technicolor camera in Los Angeles – all seven of them – and torched 30 acres of backlot) is still thrilling. Rhett's first and farewell kiss as he abandons Scarlett still weakens the knees.

What makes the film such a treat apart from the classic set pieces (immeasurably enhanced by production designer William Cameron Menzies's groundbreaking use of colour) are its unflagging passion, the range of great

OSCARS
13 nominations, **8 winners/2 special awards**

Outstanding Production
Directing: Victor Fleming
Actor: Clark Gable
Actress: Vivien Leigh
Actress in a Supporting Role: Olivia de Havilland
Actress in a Supporting Role: Hattie McDaniel
Interior Decoration: Lyle Wheeler
Cinematography: Ernest Haller, Ray Rennahan
Film Editing: Hal C. Kern, James E. Newcom
Music (Original Score): Max Steiner
Sound Recording: Thomas T. Moulton
Special Effects: John R. Cosgrove, Fred Albin, Arthur Johns
Writing (Screenplay): Sidney Howard

SPECIAL AWARDS:

William Cameron Menzies for outstanding achievement
 in the use of color for the enhancement of dramatic mood
Scientific or Technical Award (Class III)

WHAT WON THAT YEAR?
Actor: Robert Donat *Goodbye, Mr. Chips*

BAFTAS NOT AWARDED UNTIL 1947

characters and the precision, intensity and wit with which they are propelled through life. The script still works like a fine Swiss watch. In the early, delightful scenes of introductions and confrontations, the self-absorption of the heroine is instantly conveyed. Scarlett's compulsive flirtations are eternally amusing, as is the first, heart-stopping sight of Rhett, sizing up Scarlett.

The tone turns hushed and grim as the devastation of the war reaches Atlanta, exuberant again with Scarlett's resurrected fortunes, and moody when love does not conquer all but is blasted by pragmatism, misunderstanding and tragedy. Gable is fabulous: sexy, sardonic, proud, tender and disgusted by turns with a lift of a brow or a sneering curl of his lip. Olivia de Havilland's sweetly brave Melanie, Leslie Howard's gallant, thin-blooded dreamer Ashley, and all the secondary characters are excellent foils to Leigh, none more so than Hattie McDaniel's indomitable Mammy. America's most famous movie likely always will be.

CLASSIC QUOTE
Rhett: 'Frankly, my dear, I don't give a damn.'

SCENE STEALER
The great turning point for Scarlett is also the moment when the audience discovers real sympathy and admiration for her. After the harrowing journey to Tara, Scarlett has found her mother dead, her father out of his mind, the Yankees have taken everything, and the frightened little band remaining are starving. Reduced, sobbing and retching, to grubbing in the soil for a root, she lifts herself silhouetted against a fiery sky to shake her fist at heaven and make the unforgettable vow that, whatever it takes, 'As God is my witness, I'll never be hungry again!'

BEHND THE SCENES
Driving at least fifteen hapless writers (including F. Scott Fitzgerald) and three directors mad, leaving open the ongoing debate on who did what, Selznick finally arrived at a filmable screenplay. This was credited to Sidney Howard, a Pulitzer Prize-winning playwright who died before production was completed, making his the first posthumous Academy Award.

IN THE CHAIR
Ten days in, 'women's director' George Cukor was fired by Selznick, to the distress of the principal actresses, who continued to consult with him. His replacement, Victor Fleming, was more craftsman than artist but one of quality, particularly deft at action pictures and at a pinnacle of success after directing *The Wizard of Oz* (1939). Fleming's Academy Award for *Gone With The Wind* was his last real hurrah. Of his five subsequent pictures only *Dr Jekyll and Mr Hyde* (1941) and *A Guy Named Joe* (1943) were successes, while Cukor recovered quickly from humiliation with smash hits *The Women* (1939) and *The Philadelphia Story* (1940).

Opposite above Oscar winners Vivien Leigh (left) and Hattie McDaniel **This page** Handsome couple: Rhett (Clark Gable) and Scarlett (Vivien Leigh) in each other's arms

Dir: Robert WISE / USA
Released in Britain: 1965
Running Time: 172 minutes
Colour: Deluxe
Estimated Attendance: 30 million

It went from Broadway musical to Hollywood film to camp London singalong. But *The Sound of Music* has always been as rousing as it is ridiculous, as adored as it is reviled. The UK's second most popular film of all time continues to divide opinion. So: how *do* you solve a problem like Maria?

THE SOUND OF MUSIC

Director/Producer **Robert Wise**
Screenplay/Story **Ernest Lehman**, based on the musical
  by Richard Rodgers and Oscar Hammerstein II
Director of Photography **Ted McCord**
Editor **William H. Reynolds**
Production Designer **Boris Leven**
Music **Richard Rodgers**

Maria Augusta Kutschera • Julie Andrews
Captain Gaylord von Trapp • Christopher Plummer
Max Detweiler • Richard Haydn
Mother Abbess • Peggy Wood
Sister Margaretta • Anna Lee
Sister Berthe • Portia Nelson
Herr Zeller • Ben Wright
Rolfe • Daniel Truhitte
Frau Schmidt • Norma Varden
Sister Sophia • Marni Nixon
Franz • Gil Stuart
Sister Bernice • Evadne Baker
Baroness Ebberfeld • Doris Lloyd
Liesl von Trapp • Charmian Carr
Friedrich von Trapp • Nicholas Hammond
Louisa von Trapp • Heather Menzies
Kurt von Trapp • Duane Chase
Brigitta von Trapp • Angela Cartwright
Marta von Trapp • Debbie Turner
Gretl von Trapp • Kym Karath
The Baroness • Eleanor Parker

THE STORY

Maria, a tomboyish postulant at the Abbey in Salzburg, is told by the Abbess that she should try to resolve her feelings about her vocation, and is sent off as governess to the Trapp family. Arriving at the family villa, she discovers that Captain von Trapp, a retired naval officer and widower, rules his seven children with strict discipline. The atmosphere is initially chilly, but Maria gains the confidence of the children, takes them on picnics and teaches them to sing. Although the stern Captain is at last won over, he refuses the request of his friend, Max, to enter them in the Salzburg Festival. At the same time, he begins to take an interest in Maria. This upsets his new love, a Baroness from Salzburg, who senses that Maria is also infatuated. After talking with the Baroness, the confused Maria returns to the Abbey, but the Abbess consoles her and sends her back to find her true love. The Captain and the children are delighted, the Baroness makes a graceful withdrawal, and the wedding takes place in Salzburg Cathedral. Their honeymoon coincides with the Anschluss and, on their return, the Captain (who is a strong anti-Nazi) finds himself in opposition to the local Gauleiter. When ordered to join a navy unit, he realises the family must flee. When the Germans intercept the party, Max persuades them that the family is on the way to the Festival. After giving a performance and winning the first prize, they slip out through the crypts behind the Abbey. Rolf, a Hitler Youth who was courting one of the Trapp girls, gives the alarm, but the Germans are thwarted when the nuns remove the distributor caps from their cars. The Captain, Maria and the children make their way over the mountains to a new life.

WHAT THEY SAID THEN …

To say that this version of the stage success contains everything one would expect should serve as sufficient warning to those allergic to singing nuns and sweetly innocent children. It is, in fact, an exceedingly sugary experience, full of good thoughts and religious feelings and as wholesome as the well-scrubbed face of its heroine, with her beautiful articulation and pure singing tone. Even these ingredients might have been bearable if the songs had been better; alas, this is one of Rodgers and Hammerstein's less memorable scores (although the film tries to disprove this by repeating everything three or four times), and the plot's serious overtones fit uneasily into the paper-thin fabric, especially when Robert Wise directs these scenes as if they came from some anonymous B feature.

Being a big-budget 70mm enterprise, the film partially comes into its own when it gets outdoors. Although the exteriors sometimes look like cuts from a Cinerama travelogue on Austria, the views of Salzburg and its environs are very eye-catching, especially the aerial shots at the beginning (photographed by Paul Beeson), culminating in a great downward sweep on to a hill as Julie Andrews appears, to fling herself into her first ditty. The introductions to the other songs are very awkwardly manoeuvred, and there is little to suggest that Wise will ever become a great musical director. The most one can say is that his handling is tactful and efficiently smooth.

Faced with daunting opposition from nuns and children, the other players have a rather thankless task, although Eleanor Parker makes the most of her few acid lines and Christopher Plummer appears unnaturally stiff and sinister, as if he were preparing to play Count Dracula. Julie Andrews looks good enough to eat but, this being *The Sound of Music*, she is spared that fate.

Above *Maria full of grace: Julia Andrews reaches her peak*

WHAT THEY SAY NOW ...

So many of the titles in the Ultimate Film list have now been passed down affectionately from generation to generation, like family keepsakes, and *The Sound of Music* is perhaps the best example of this. It is wheeled out on British television whenever there is a bank holiday, and has been the subject of seemingly endless 'Where Are They Now?' specials detailing the subsequent careers of the young performers who played the von Trapp children (one appeared in a pornographic film; another played Spiderman in the 1978 TV movie). The movie is as much a part of our social and cultural fabric as it was when it flooded onto cinema screens in 1965.

It might be clumsily directed and inelegantly staged, enlivened by protracted singalong sequences that use melody and repetition as a blunt instrument to batter the viewer into submission, and untroubled by the dark material that makes its presence felt at the edges of the frame. But it has proved oddly durable. The film's sincere faith in the goodness of Julie Andrews is still charming after all these years, and it's hard to suppress delight at her scenes with Christopher Plummer, who appears to be trying not to laugh.

He would have to try much harder were he to witness what *The Sound of Music* has turned into today. Without affecting its status as a family favourite, the film has become the latest audience participation phenomenon, with *SingalongaSoundofMusic* events mounted on a weekly basis. The craze began in the late 1990s when the London Lesbian and Gay Film Festival showed the film with subtitles to enable the audience to join in with the songs. From there, the idea exploded, and now screenings are attended by fans in full uniform – lederhosen, stormtrooper outfits, snazzy two-pieces cut from curtains or just a good old-fashioned wimple.

OSCARS
10 nominations, **5 winners**

Best Picture
Directing: Robert Wise
Actress: Julie Andrews
Actress in a Supporting Role: Peggy Wood
Art Direction/Set Decoration (Color): Boris Levin, Walter M. Scott, Ruby Levitt
Cinematography (Color): Ted McCord
Costume Design (Color): Dorothy Jeakins
Film Editing: William Reynolds
Scoring of Music (adaptation or treatment): Irwin Kostal
Sound: James P. Corcoran, Fred Hynes

WHAT WON THAT YEAR?
Actor: Lee Marvin *Cat Ballou*
Actress: Julie Christie *Darling*

BAFTAS
1 nomination

British Actress: Julie Andrews (jointly for *The Sound of Music* and *The Americanization of Emily*)

WHAT WON THAT YEAR?
Film: *My Fair Lady*
British Film: *The Ipcress File*
British Actor: Dirk Bogarde *Darling*
Foreign Actor: Lee Marvin *The Killers/Cat Ballou*
British Actress: Julie Christie *Darling*
Foreign Actress: Patricia Neal *In Harm's Way*

Opposite top SingalongaSoundOfMusic: These are a few of my favourite things Opposite middle Maria draws a veil over her habit Opposite bottom It's curtains for the Von Trapp children Above Baron Von Trapp (Christopher Plummer) and his brood climb every mountain

CLASSIC QUOTE

Mother Abbess: 'Maria, these walls were not meant to shut out problems. You have to face them. You have to live the life you were born to live.'

SCENE STEALER

Nothing in the film quite has the same impact as the grand opening shot, as the camera swoops down to capture a twirling, ecstatic Julie Andrews, flanked by mountains and blue sky, before she bursts into her opening song: 'The hills are alive with the sound of music …' It's all downhill from there. Literally.

IN THE CHAIR

Robert Wise, director of *West Side Story* (1961), took on *The Sound of Music* after the departure of the original choice, William Wyler. Wise never had such a big hit again, specialising in stodgy mainstream fare like the 1968 *Star!* (again with Julie Andrews) and *Star Trek: The Motion Picture* (1979).

Dir: David HAND / USA
Released in Britain: 1938
Running Time: 83 minutes
Colour: Technicolor
Estimated Attendance: 28 million

The third most popular film for British audiences is animated. But then this is no mere cartoon: this is Disney at his best. The film is simplicity itself, yet the devil is in the details: the affectionate characterisation of the seven dwarfs, the enduring songs and a journey through the enchanted forest that turns out to be no picnic.

SNOW WHITE AND THE SEVEN DWARFS

Director **David Hand**
Producer **Walt Disney**
Screenplay/Story **Ted Sears, Richard Creedon, Otto Englander, Dick Rickard, Earl Hurd, Merrill De Maris, Dorothy Ann Blank, Webb Smith**
Director of Photography **Maxwell Morgan**
Music **Frank Churchill, Leigh Harline, Paul Smith**

Voice of Snow White • Adriana Caselotti
Voice of Prince Charming • Harry Stockwell
Voice of the Wicked Queen • Lucille Laverne
Voice of the Magic Mirror • Moroni Olsen
Voice of Sneezy • Billy Gilbert
Voice of Happy • Otis Harlan
Voice of Sleepy/Grumpy • Pinto Colvig
Voice of Bashful • Scotty Mattraw
Voice of Doc • Roy Atwell

THE STORY

A Wicked Queen is jealous of the beauty of her stepdaughter, Snow White, and plans to have her killed. The huntsman who is charged with the deed cannot bring himself to do it, and Snow White escapes, terrified, into the forest. She flees through the dim wood – which in her fear, she peoples with clutching hands, glowing eyes and evil beasts of prey – to fall, sobbing, on the ground. And then the sun strikes through the trees and the little forest creatures come out to welcome her. They lead her to the miniature, dishevelled home of the Seven Dwarfs, who work in a diamond mine. Snow White, with the help of the animals, tidies the house before they return. With the coming of evening the little bearded men – Grumpy, Sneezy, Happy, Bashful, Dopey, Doc and Sleepy – arrive home. After some hesitation they agree to allow Snow White to stay with them, although they fear the vengeance of the Wicked Queen.

Informed by her magic mirror of Snow White's escape, the Queen disguises herself as an old woman and takes poisoned fruit to the dwarfs' cottage. Snow White bites an apple and falls to the ground in the sleeping death to which the only antidote is love's first kiss. The dwarfs, warned by the animals, return too late and chase the Queen through a thunderstorm and over a precipice. The men build a shrine for Snow White in the woods where they keep watch through the seasons. A Prince who loved Snow White and had been seeking her hears of the sleeping maiden. He visits the shrine, recognises the Princess and kisses her. Snow White awakes, the dwarfs' tears turn to joy and 'they live happily ever after'.

WHAT THEY SAID THEN …

It is difficult to find any flaws in this lovely film; there is beauty here and tenderness, fantasy and humour and, above all, a perfect understanding of a young child's dreams. The animation is almost perfect, giving, except on very rare occasions, the illusion of life. Snow White herself and the Prince are perhaps

Opposite Snow White gets to the core of the problem
Top Hi-Ho, Hi-Ho, it's off to work they go… Middle Snow White adjusts to domestic life with her new housemates
Bottom A bird in the hand: no Disney animation would be complete without a supporting cast of cute and attentive wildlife

a little doll-like, but the gay little Disney animals, the Wicked Queen and the Seven Dwarfs are real 'living' creatures. There are certain incidents in the picture nevertheless which make this film unsuitable for young and nervous children. For older children and adults, however, it is impossible to imagine a film that can be more highly recommended.

WHAT THEY SAY NOW …

The picture labelled 'the greatest film ever made' by the brilliant Russian director Sergei Eisenstein contains reserves of sweetness and horror that cannot be found in such potent quantities anywhere else in the Disney canon. Certainly the death of Bambi's mother, and to a lesser extent the murder of Simba's father in *The Lion King*, are traumatic for a young audience, but *Snow White and the Seven Dwarfs* retains the power to astonish and unnerve young and old alike.

From the moment Snow White sings 'I'm wishing …' into a well, you know the songs will be enchanting, and they don't disappoint. The Queen is suitably dreadful, her old-hag alter-ego even more so. The poisonous apple, like Snow White's blood-red lips, throbs with Freudian overtones. The tomfoolery of the Seven Dwarfs is delightful without being cloying, and the activities of the woodland creatures keep the frame lively, and the eye busy. Only the Prince is blandness personified, but then he's just there to be Snow White's saviour, and her arm-candy.

CLASSIC QUOTE

Grumpy: 'Angel, ha! She's a female! And all females is poison! They're full of wicked wiles!'

SCENE STEALER

Snow White's expedition through the enchanted forest, with its tree branches that seem to grab at her, is one of the most disturbing sequences in Disney's work, and introduces genuine jeopardy into the largely whimsical atmosphere. Indeed, the power of the film lies in the constant friction between humour, represented by the Seven Dwarfs, and horror, as embodied by this sequence, and the appearances of the Wicked Queen, who suggests Joan Crawford on a bad day. The BBFC was so concerned that it slapped an 'A' certificate on the film, requiring all children to be accompanied by an adult. You can now discern the influence of the forest sequence on everything from *The Night of the Hunter* to *Repulsion* to *The Evil Dead*.

BEHIND THE SCENES

Walt Disney's first full-length animated feature – also the first US animated feature – employed 32 animators, 20 layout artists, 25 artists specialising in watercolour backgrounds, 65 effects animators, and 158 inkers and painters; 1,500 shades of paint were deployed to complete 2,000,000 illustrations.

Dir: George Lucas / USA
Released in Britain: 1977
Running Time: 121 minutes
Colour: Technicolor
Estimated Attendance: 20.76 million

A long time ago, in a galaxy far, far away, one man set out to claim the hearts, minds and pocket money of children young and old. His marriage of pantomime thrills and cutting-edge special effects captured imaginations, launched a franchise and changed cinema forever.

STAR WARS

Director **George Lucas**
Producer **Gary Kurtz**
Screenplay/Story **George Lucas**
Director of Photography **Gilbert Taylor**
Editors **Paul Hirsch, Marcia Lucas, Richard Chew**
Production Designer **John Barry**
Music **John Williams**

Luke Skywalker • Mark Hamill
Han Solo • Harrison Ford
Princess Leia Organa • Carrie Fisher
Grand Moff Tarkin • Peter Cushing
Ben (Obi-Wan) Kenobi • Alec Guinness
See-Threepio (C-3PO) • Anthony Daniels
Artoo-Detoo (R2-D2) • Kenny Baker
Chewbacca • Peter Mayhew
Lord Darth Vader • David Prowse
Voice of Lord Darth Vader • James Earl Jones
Uncle Owen Lars • Phil Brown
Aunt Beru Lars • Shelagh Fraser
Chief Jawa • Jack Purvis
General Dodonna • Alex McCrindle
General Willard • Eddie Byrne
Red Leader • Drewe Henley
Red Two (Wedge) • Denis Lawson
Red Three (Biggs) • Garrick Hagon
Red Four (John 'D') • Jack Klaff
Red Six (Porkins) • William Hootkins

THE STORY

In a distant time and galaxy, where a benevolent republic has been replaced by an oppressive empire, Princess Leia Organa, a member of a rebel movement, attempts to escape with the plans of the Empire's deadly new weapon, the Death Star. She is captured by Grand Moff Tarkin, Governor of the Imperial Outland Regions, and his evil henchman Darth Vader, but her two robots, C-3PO and R2-D2, escape to the barren planet Tatooine, where they are picked up by desert scavengers and sold to farmer Owen Lars and his nephew Luke Skywalker. R2-D2 projects the plea for help that Leia has recorded for a man called Ben Obi-Wan Kenobi. In the desert, Luke finds Ben, a former Jedi knight of the Republic, who talks of the old ways and of the mystical 'Force', which was an article of faith with the knights. Reluctant at first to join Ben in rescuing Leia, Luke changes his mind when he finds that imperial stormtroopers have destroyed his home and killed his uncle and aunt. With the robots, he and Ben hire a mercenary space pilot, Han Solo, and his ape-like companion Chewbacca. Captured by Tarkin and taken aboard the Death Star, they succeed in rescuing Leia. Ben is killed in a laser duel with Vader, but the others escape and head for the rebels' stronghold. Rebel fighters then launch an assault on the Death Star. Almost all are destroyed before Luke, inspired by Ben's spiritual presence and faith in the Force, makes the decisive bombing run. With the Death Star destroyed, the friends return to Leia and a triumphant reception.

WHAT THEY SAID THEN …

Star Wars has pulled off a feat of spiritual legerdemain more impressive than all the religious connotations of 'the Force' within the film. Whatever its qualities as a piece of film-making, it is interesting primarily as an exercise in programming: the Pavlovian machinery which has gone into action to capture more people than the last great blockbuster of audience participation, *Jaws* (1975). Both films are a product of new generation Hollywood, made by directors who have already been film buffs, and whose grasp of movie lore and magic is of a simpler but more

Left Han Solo (Harrison Ford) and Chewbacca (Peter Mayhew) strike a deal with Obi-Wan Kenobi (Alec Guinness) and Luke Skywalker (Mark Hamill) **Below left** Desert droids: R2-D2 (Kenny Baker), C-3PO (Anthony Daniels) **Below right** The world's first sighting of Darth Vader (David Prowse) **Bottom left** Vader and Kenobi: the duel that launched a million playground games **Bottom right** Han Solo and Princess Leia (Carrie Fisher) escape the Death Star

OSCARS
10 nominations, **6 winners/1 Special Award**

Best Picture
Actor in a Supporting Role: Alec Guinness
Art Direction
Costume Design: John Mollo
Directing: George Lucas
Film Editing: Paul Hirsch, Marcia Lucas, Richard Chew
Music (Original Score): John Williams
Sound
Visual Effects
Writing (Screenplay written directly for the screen): George Lucas

SPECIAL ACHIEVEMENT AWARD:
**Benjamin Burtt, Jr. for the creation of the alien, creature and
robot voices**

WHAT WON THAT YEAR?
Directing: Woody Allen *Annie Hall*
Best Picture: *Annie Hall*
Actor in a Leading Role: Richard Dreyfuss *The Goodbye Girl*
Actress In A Leading Role: Diane Keaton *Annie Hall*

BAFTAS
6 nominations, **2 winners**

Best Film
Production Design (John Barry)
Costume Design (John Mollo)
Film Editing (Paul Hirsch/Marcia Lucas/Richard Chew)
Sound Track
Anthony Asquith Award for Original Film Music: John Williams

WHAT WON THAT YEAR?
Film: *Julia*
Direction: Alan Parker *Midnight Express*
Actor: Richard Dreyfuss *The Goodbye Girl*
Actress: Jane Fonda *Julia*

overpowering kind than that of, say, Hitchcock, the past master
of building audience responses into his films. *Star Wars* offers
more varied pleasures of this kind than *Jaws*, but is less cleanly
engineered and executed. *Jaws* is based on one compelling
premise – fear of the deep, the unknown – where *Star Wars* is
empty, based on not a single idea but a variety of conceits.

Most of these are recognition effects, for *Star Wars* may be
the first movie to appeal to film buffs who would never dream of
calling themselves that, drawing as it does on a host of popular
movie types. It could scarcely be termed science fiction at all –
at least not as it has been practised for twenty years – but, as
Lucas has indicated in naming *Flash Gordon* (1936) and Edgar
Rice Burroughs as his inspiration, a simple space adventure, now
overlaid with sterile nostalgia and multilevelled movie puns.

Lucas's specific references point straight to the more
contradictory, even self-destructive, aspects of the project. There
is an homage to *The Searchers* (1956) when Luke Skywalker
returns from his meeting in the desert with Obi-Wan Kenobi
and finds his guardians' settlement ablaze, and one to *Triumph
of the Will* (1935) in the final victory march of the champions of
republican right. But as the first has little emotional resonance,
and the second no political application in this world of feudal
struggle, they seem rather dislocated gimmicks, and lead one
to question why Lucas needs such hints of sophistication, and
such a complicated technological apparatus, to reach back to
the tatty serials and comic-lore of his childhood.

The discrepancy between the naivety the film pretends to
and the know-how (and knowingness) that went into its making
results in a resounding emptiness overall. Despite the amount
of hardware on display, and the up-to-date technology that went
into the design and special effects, Lucas never lets us into the
workings of this world except in terms of the comic-book
oppositions of good and evil. The film is thus deprived of the
purpose of most science fiction: to provide the 'culture shock' of
showing the present transformed, or extended, into the future.

This flight into atavistic fantasy is successful on some
levels, but the recreation is less than half convincing,
particularly in the concept of 'the Force' – the mystical
power exercised by the Jedi knights which once bound the
galaxy in sweetness and light. Without the simple spiritual
convictions of his predecessors, or the philosophical
speculations of his contemporaries, Lucas has rather left
his audience out in the cold, with only regularly administered
shots of special effects to keep them warm.

WHAT THEY SAY NOW …

The years have not been kind to the first *Star Wars* film. As a franchise, the series has no equals in the movie world, and that situation will remain unchanged as long as the sequels and prequels and computer games and toys keep on coming. The films represent a cause for celebration in the marketplace, and a cause for consternation among those who believe in the limitless potential of cinema. It isn't just that *Star Wars* has dated abominably while Lucas's earlier films *THX-1138* (1971) and *American Graffiti* (1974) show no sign of losing their zing. The real problem is that its imagination is so meagre. After an iconic opening, in which the full magnitude of a space-cruiser roaring into view is conveyed in one long, awestruck shot, Lucas's vision deserts him. Unlike his friend Steven Spielberg, he loses sight of the characters within his epic frame, thereby depriving the action of consequence. Audiences flocked to see the special effects (retouched vainly by Lucas in a 1997 reissue). Their nostalgia, passed on to their children, has bestowed upon this dead film an artificial longevity.

CLASSIC QUOTE

The best line isn't in the film. It was uttered on set by Harrison Ford when he was called upon to deliver more of Lucas's stiff dialogue: 'You can type this crap, George, but you can't say it.'

SCENE STEALER

The Cantina on the planet Tatooine bustles with bad-tempered representatives from countless slimy species. A band of rubber-faced musicians toot a nagging refrain on their intergalactic clarinets while Luke Skywalker is rescued from the bar-room bullies by one judicious stroke of Ben's light sabre. Over in the snug, Han Solo shoots an alien assassin and drops the bartender a few bills to pay for the damage – just like James Stewart in *Destry Rides Again* (1939).

BEHIND THE SCENES

Lucas's closest friends and family all believed that the film was doomed. After an early screening for his director buddies, where war-movie footage was inserted where the battle scenes would eventually go, Brian De Palma is reputed to have stood up afterwards and posed a pertinent question: 'What is this shit?' Even Lucas was nervous about opening the film so close to Martin Scorsese's picture, *New York, New York* (1977).

The success of *Star Wars* didn't silence all the doubters. Alec Guinness, who played Ben, once signed an autograph for a fan on the proviso that the child promised never to watch the film again.

Dir: Herbert WILCOX / UK
Released in Britain: 1948
Running Time: 90 minutes
Black and white
Estimated Attendance: 20.5 million

Herbert Wilcox directed Anna Neagle in more than thirty features. But it was this witty upper-class farce about a footman who falls for his employer that gave audiences a warm glow in the chilly post-war climate. *Miss Julie* it ain't …

SPRING IN PARK LANE

Director/Producer **Herbert Wilcox**
Screenplay/Story **Nicholas Phipps, from the story 'Come Out of the Pantry' by Alice Duer Miller**
Director of Photography **Max Greene**
Editor **Frank Clarke**
Art Director **William C. Andrews**
Music **Manning Sherwin**

Judy Howard • Anna Neagle
Richard • Michael Wilding
Uncle Joshua • Tom Walls
Basil Maitland • Peter Graves
Rosie • Lana Morris
Mildred Howard • Marjorie Fielding
Marquis of Borechester • Nicholas Phipps
Perkins • G. H. Mulcaster
Kate O'Malley • Josephine Fitzgerald
Mr Bacon • Nigel Patrick
Lady Borechester • Catherine Paul
Higgins • H. R. Hignett
Antique Dealer • Cyril Conway
Bates • Tom Walls Jnr

THE STORY

Judy Howard, secretary and niece to Joshua Howard, a wealthy diamond merchant and art collector, returns to her Mayfair home after a shopping trip and is surprised to find an unfamiliar face opening the door. Perkins, the butler, introduces Richard, whom he has employed as footman. Judy finds Richard to be lacking the expected deference, while displaying unusual cultural sophistication.

The art thief Bacon arrives at the Howard house with a letter from Judy's uncle asking for a cheque to be handed to him. Judy is suspicious; Richard escorts Bacon from the premises.

At a dinner party marking his return from Cape Town, Joshua is annoyed to hear that Bacon was sent packing. He blames Richard, but Judy defends him. Joshua later explains that he knew Bacon was crooked but wanted to use the cheque as a trap to trace the theft of his Gauguin. Also at the party is Judy's suitor George, a Marquis struggling financially at his country seat, Borechester Towers. At dinner, Borechester mentions his brother Richard, missing with family assets. Richard, serving, skilfully avoids being recognised by his brother.

On his afternoon off, Judy joins Richard on the bank of the Serpentine. She asks him about his background, but he is evasive. They visit a nightclub, where Richard challenges one of the art thieves. Judy spots Borechester at an adjoining table, and they make a quick exit to the Lyceum Ballroom, where they dance together. Arriving at Judy's house, they are glimpsed kissing by a private detective hired by Borechester.

Borechester arrives and informs Judy that her 'footman' is his errant brother. Richard has meanwhile gone to London airport, leaving a note revealing that the missing Gauguin is with a crooked dealer. Joshua recovers his picture, and the dealer is arrested.

Judy finds Richard at the airport and he relates his story: he sold the family pictures in America, but received a telegram saying he had been given a dud cheque. Leaving the ship in hiding to avoid his waiting brother, he wandered the streets. At London Zoo, he met Perkins, a former retainer and now the Howards' butler, and asked if he could lay low for a time. Perkins explained there was a

Above Richard (Michael Wilding) and Judy (Anna Neagle) come dancing **Below** Famous face: Anna Neagle stars in four entries in The Ultimate Film chart **Overleaf** Richard and Judy on the bank of the Serpentine

footman vacancy at the house, but it required experience. When the doorbell rang, Richard seized the initiative and dashed upstairs to answer it. It was Judy.

Richard returns home with Judy. He takes another envelope – unopened – from his pocket. It is a telegram saying that the cheque was good after all. Richard is in the clear, and Joshua is delighted that his Gauguin is safe. Judy tells Joshua that she and Richard are to marry.

WHAT THEY SAID THEN ...

Here an old and sorely tried story has been taken and transformed by Nicholas Phipps into a brilliant script bubbling over with gaiety and wit. It is an invitation to sit back and relax; there are no inhibitions, high ideas or psychiatry. Phipps himself contributes the perfect sketch of a bore telling an unfunny story in the funniest way. Anna Neagle is charming as Judy, and Peter Graves gives a recognisable performance as an overbearingly conceited film star. Tom Walls, Marjorie Fielding and the rest of the cast give the impression they are thoroughly enjoying themselves. Each character deserves merit, but it is really Michael Wilding's film. With the lightest of touches he makes full use of every line of his script. He is tender, audacious and lovable, with the indefinable quality of charm.

OSCARS

WHAT WON THAT YEAR?
Best Motion Picture: *Hamlet*
Directing: John Huston *The Treasure of the Sierra Madre*
Actor: Laurence Olivier *Hamlet*
Actress: Jane Wyman *Johnny Belinda*

BAFTAS

WHAT WON THAT YEAR?
Best Film: *Hamlet*
British Film: *The Fallen Idol*

Left *Richard (Michael Wilding) avoids being recognized while serving dinner* **Opposite above** *Everyone loves a happy ending: Joshua's (Tom Walls') Gaughin is safe and Richard and Judy get engaged* **Opposite below** *All smiles as Anna Neagle leans on Michael Wilding to sign autographs for two young soldiers*

WHAT THEY SAY NOW ...

Spring in Park Lane appeals to nostalgia for the pre-war social order when (for the middle classes) domestic servants were widespread. In this world, hierarchy and rituals are important – Judy is suspicious of Richard because he breaks the rules. In an ordered society, one is expected to 'know one's place'.

The film is also concerned with decorum governing sexual relations. The influence of this is evident in the psychology of the mistress/servant relationship, in which Judy is exalted and all-powerful, with Richard prostrate before her (literally so when he is at Judy's feet). He is also humiliated when a vain film star arrives to take her to his latest film premiere, forced to observe them at a social distance. Judy is always assured, confident and in control. At the conclusion, convention would dictate that Richard ask Joshua if he might marry Judy, but it is Judy who *tells* her uncle that she and Richard are to marry.

But such modes of behaviour, speech and conduct are for those 'above stairs'. Compare this with the directness of the maid Rosie, whose healthy interest in the opposite sex is indicated by a nudge, a wink and a dancehall encounter.

Among the Wilcox/Neagle regulars are two figures who were no strangers to high society and its rituals – actor Peter Graves (a real-life Lord and West End musical star) and well-connected actor/screenwriter Nicholas Phipps (Phipps also wrote the crisp, self-referential screenplay). The Wilcox 'family'

also includes Tom Walls, cinematographer Max Greene, and Robert Farnon, whose luscious arrangements include English traditional melodies ('Early One Morning') and 'The Moment I Saw You' (from a 1945 stage revue).

This was the third in the Neagle/Wilding 'Mayfair cycle'. All performed well financially, but this was 1948's top moneymaker, and the top-rated wholly British film of all time in this list. It gave audiences what they craved – 90 minutes of escapism and glamour. It was so successful that the same territory was mined again, in *Maytime in Mayfair* (1949), with many of the same sets and cast.

IN THE CHAIR

From the early 1920s to the 1950s, Herbert Wilcox produced more than one hundred films, and directed around half of them. His long-term collaboration with Anna Neagle, which resulted in more than thirty films together, began in 1932 with *Goodnight Vienna* and went on to include the racy 1934 remake of *Nell Gwyn*, a pair of hagiographic accounts of Queen Victoria (*Victoria The Great*, 1937, and *Sixty Glorious Years*, 1938) and the subdued and serious *They Flew Alone* (1942). Wilcox and Neagle spent the early years of the war in America making musical comedies for RKO. After Wilcox directed a section of the pro-British pageant, *Forever and a Day* (1943), they returned to Britain, where he directed her in *They Flew*

Alone, based on the life of the aviator Amy Johnson, and *The Yellow Canary* (1943), an espionage thriller with Neagle daringly cast as a seemingly pro-Nazi society lady who is shipped out to Canada as a security risk.

An earlier collaboration, *The Courtneys of Curzon Street* (1947), appears on the Ultimate Film list at number 17; two of their later films , *I Live in Grosvenor Square* (1945) and *Piccadilly Incident* (1946), appear at numbers 51 and 43 respectively. But it was the lavish, champagne-soaked escapism of *Spring in Park Lane* that audiences cherished most. By contrast, *Odette* (1950), a surprisingly authentic account of the experiences of the SOE agent Odette Sansom in occupied France, dealt convincingly with the dangers and discomforts of life as a resistance fighter and showed scenes of torture and cruelty that still seem harrowing.

Dir: William WYLER / USA
Released in Britain: 1947
Running Time: 182 minutes
Black and white
Estimated Attendance: 20.4 million

Post-war audiences looked to cinema for comfort and reassurance about the fragmented world they were piecing back together. And few films addressed ordinary people in the late 1940s as sensitively as William Wyler's account of the battles that remain once the fighting is over.

THE BEST YEARS OF OUR LIVES

Director **William Wyler**
Producer **Samuel Goldwyn**
Screenplay/Story **Robert E. Sherwood**, based on the novel *Glory For Me* by MacKinlay Kantor
Director of Photography **Gregg Toland**
Editor **Daniel Mandell**
Art Directors **Perry Ferguson, George Jenkins**
Music **Hugo Friedhofer**

Milly Stephenson • Myrna Loy
Al Stephenson • Fredric March
Fred Derry • Dana Andrews
Peggy Stephenson • Teresa Wright
Marie Derry • Virginia Mayo
Wilma Cameron • Cathy O'Donnell
Butch Engle • Hoagy Carmichael
Homer Parrish • Harold Russell
Hortense Derry • Gladys George
Pat Derry • Roman Bohnen
Mr Milton • Ray Collins
Mrs Parrish • Minna Gombell
Mr Parrish • Walter Baldwin
Cliff Scully • Steve Cochran
Mrs Cameron • Dorothy Adams
Mr Cameron • Don Beddoe
Woody Merrill • Vic Cutler
Luella Parrish • Marlene Aames
Prew • Charles Halton
Mr Mollett • Ray Teal

THE STORY

World War II has just ended, and all over America servicemen are returning to civilian life. Recently discharged from the US airforce, bombardier Captain Fred Derry is in Portland trying to catch a flight back to his home in Boone City. Hitching a ride on a USAF transport plane, he meets fellow veterans sergeant Al Stephenson and naval engineer Homer Parrish. On the flight, the three men confess to being anxious about their homecoming, especially Parrish who lost his hands in battle and has since been coping with artificial limbs.

Al and Fred drop Homer at his parents' house, and see him react coolly to his sweetheart Wilma's welcome home. Al also finds his first night back with his family difficult, and takes his wife Milly and daughter Peggy out on the town to mark his return. At the bar owned by Homer's uncle Butch, Al runs into Fred, who has been searching the local nightclubs where he's been told his glamorous young wife Marie now works. The two ex-servicemen get drunk and are driven back to Al's flat. The next morning Fred has breakfast with Peggy – with whom he establishes an easy rapport – before at last tracking down Marie. She seems pleased to see him.

The three veterans struggle to adjust to life outside the service. Former banker Al gets a new position with his old employer assessing loans to ex-GIs, but is drinking heavily. Self-conscious about his artificial hands, Homer continues to reject Wilma's advances. Fred gets a job in the drugstore where he worked before the war; but he squabbles with Marie, who is bored by their new life together. Meeting Peggy one lunchtime, he kisses her. Peggy arranges to go on a double date with the Derrys, convinced that meeting Marie will stop her from falling for Fred. Instead she realises that the shallow Marie is unsuitable for Fred and tells her parents she is determined to break up their marriage.

Shocked by his daughter's behaviour Al makes Fred promise not to see Peggy. Fred loses his job when he punches a customer who attacks Homer's war record. After urging Homer to marry Wilma, Fred returns home where Marie tells him she wants a divorce. Fred decides to leave Boone City, but

Above Peggy (Teresa Wright) tries to shake some sense into Fred (Dana Andrews) **Left** I do. As Homer (Harold Russell) and Marie (Virginia Mayo) marry, best man Fred realizes his love for Peggy **Below** Director of Photography Greg Toland (left) surveys a shot with William Wyler

at the last moment takes a job turning decommissioned bomber aircraft into prefabricated houses. Homer marries Wilma. At the wedding Fred and Peggy kiss.

WHAT THEY SAID THEN ...

With a good script, this is probably the most efficient film that Hollywood has made in years: smooth, observant, human. Edited to a leisurely tempo, it interweaves these three stories of readjustment into a true and moving picture of small-town life. But it is the theme of the armless soldier which establishes it above mere efficiency. This theme grabs the attention immediately and is handled throughout with correct emphasis and restraint. Much of its success is due to an amateur but not amateurish actor, Harold Russell, who did lose his arms in the war. The simplicity of gesture and expression by which he conveys his emotional struggle is truly remarkable. The climax comes when he shows his sweetheart the intricacies of the harness which operates his metal claws – and his helplessness without the harness. Apart from Russell's contribution, the acting is of a polished standard with March, particularly, in one of his best roles of recent years.

WHAT THEY SAY NOW ...

The Best Years of Our Lives must have had huge emotional resonance for the audiences of 1946, who had just endured long years of conflict. And even today this is poignant, stirring stuff – thanks in no small part to the performances of the three leads. Fredric March is quietly affecting as a former sergeant who turns to drink to cope with his return to family life. As the

decorated bombardier, Dana Andrews is as upright as you would expect from a war hero; but he brings an appealing vulnerability also. And, in a turn that anticipates Tom Cruise's acclaimed performance in *Born on the Fourth of July* (1989), real-life amputee Harold Russell rightly won an Oscar as the invalided veteran who finds the condescending treatment of his family more disabling than his physical war-wound.

A studio favourite in the late 1930s, director William Wyler shot combat documentaries during the war and shows real empathy for the returning GIs. The low-key approach, loose dramatic structure and frank appreciation for the difficulties

OSCARS
8 nominations, **7 winners/1 Special Award**

Best Motion Picture
Directing: William Wyler
Actor: Fredric March
Actor in a Supporting Role: Harold Russell
Film Editing: Daniel Mandell
Music (Dramatic or Comedy Picture): Hugo Friedhofer
Sound Recording: Gordon Sawyer
Writing (Screenplay): Robert E. Sherwood

SPECIAL AWARD:
Harold Russell, for bringing hope and courage to his fellow veterans

WHAT WON THAT YEAR?
Actress: Olivia de Havilland *To Each His Own*

BAFTAS
1 nomination, **1 winner**

Film

facing ex-servicemen – only in the fevered urban nightmares of film noir do we find American cinema more anxious about the consequences of peace – stops the film from tipping into sentimentality. The film's melancholy undertow may have represented a risk for producer Sam Goldwyn, but his production values remained typically high: this expensive film paid lavish attention to detail and its running time was a then-unthinkable 165 minutes. And yet Goldwyn's instincts proved canny: the film's sensitive handling of a subject relevant to many filmgoers touched a nerve; acclaimed by critics, *The Best Years of Our Lives* was also a worldwide hit. It even did well in Germany.

CLASSIC QUOTE
Butch [breaking off from playing the piano to give his nephew Al a pep talk]: 'You know your folks will get use to you, and you'll get used to them. Then everything will settle down nicely. Unless we have another war. Then none of us have to worry because we'll all be blown to bits the first day.' [He resumes his piano playing] 'So cheer up.'

SCENE STEALER
Despite the film's often downbeat realism, it ends on a joyful note with Homer at last marrying his sweetheart Wilma. As they embrace on one side of the frame, Homer's best man Fred spots Peggy, the woman he was reluctantly persuaded to give up, on the other side of the room. Fred and Peggy exchange a look. He walks across to her, and the two fall into one another's arms. All this is done in one blissful, unbroken take – and only the most stony-hearted will fail to be moved.

BEHIND THE SCENES
A climactic scene where Derry relives his wartime trauma in the bombardier's post of a wrecked B-17 came about when Wyler spotted a vast 'graveyard' containing countless decommissioned USAF aircraft in a stretch of desert near Los Angeles. The filming of Derry inside this grounded craft as if he were in the air is not in the original script and was one of Wyler's late inventions during production.

BEHIND THE CAMERA
Director of photography Gregg Toland's cinematography is outstanding. Toland pioneered a form of photography known as 'deep focus'. Shooting specially lit sets with a wide-angle lens, Toland was able to keep in sharp focus objects in the foreground, middle-ground and background of the same shot. Towards the end of *The Best Years of Our Lives*, for example, we can see Homer and his uncle playing the piano directly in front of the camera, while in the background the smaller figure of Fred makes an important phone call, watched anxiously by Al, who is midway between these two bits of (crystal-clear) action. Toland used this technique to stylised effect in Orson Welles's *Citizen Kane* (1941); here, prompted by Wyler's desire for realism, he employed 'deep focus' in a more unobtrusive, naturalistic way, enabling the viewer to scan the image for himself or herself and select areas of interest. For influential French film critic André Bazin, 'deep focus' was a cornerstone of cinematic realism, and he found it put to exemplary use in *The Best Years of Our Lives*.

Dir: Wolfgang REITHERMAN / USA
Released in Britain: 1968
Running Time: 78 minutes
Colour: Technicolor
Estimated Attendance: 19.8 million

The second most popular Disney film in the list had nothing to do with Rudyard Kipling. Bright and breezy where Kipling was murky and tangled, this was an excuse for zany gags, memorable singalongs and 1960s exuberance. As Baloo the Bear puts it: 'Man, that's what I call a swinging party ...'

THE JUNGLE BOOK

Director **Wolfgang Reitherman**
Producer **Walt Disney**
Screenplay/Story **Larry Clemmons, Ken Anderson, Ralph Wright, Vance Gerry**, adapted from the novel by Rudyard Kipling
Editors **Tom Acosta, Norman Carlisle**
Music **George Bruns**

Voice of Baloo the Bear • Phil Harris
Voice of Bagheera the Panther • Sebastian Cabot
Voice of King Louie of the Apes • Louis Prima
Voice of Shere Khan the Tiger • George Sanders
Voice of Kaa the Snake • Sterling Holloway
Voice of Colonel Hathi the Elephant • J. Pat O'Malley
Voice of Mowgli the Man Cub • Bruce Reitherman
Voice of Elephant • Verna Felton
Voice of Elephant • Clint Howard

THE STORY

Mowgli has been raised in the jungle by wolves, who look on him with affection as the Man Cub. But when it is learned that the ferocious tiger Shere Khan is returning to his hunting ground, the wolves fear for the boy's life and decide that he must be returned to his own kind. Bagheera the Panther volunteers to escort the protesting Mowgli through the jungle. After successfully avoiding the hypnotic designs of Kaa the Snake, the travellers next encounter the elephant herd, led in military style by Colonel Hathi, who is outraged by Mowgli's attempt to join the troop. Exasperated, Bagheera temporarily deserts Mowgli, who strikes up a friendship with the genial Baloo the Bear. But he is kidnapped by monkeys and taken to the ape king, who hopes to obtain from him the secret of fire. Mowgli is rescued by Bagheera and Baloo, before straying into the hangout of a trio of beatnik vultures who at first tease him and then make friends with him.

When Shere Khan arrives, it seems that Mowgli must face him alone. Brave Baloo tackles the tiger, but is beaten and left for dead. Mowgli is saved by the vultures, and Shere Khan is scared off by fire when lightning strikes a tree. Baloo turns out to have survived, and Mowgli is overjoyed to think he can remain in the jungle after all. But a chance meeting with a Girl Cub proves a stronger attraction, and Bagheera and Baloo depart in the knowledge that Mowgli is best left with his own kind.

WHAT THEY SAID THEN ...

Kipling enthusiasts may recoil in horror, and those constitutionally allergic to the Disney cartoon remain stubbornly unconvinced, but this animated feature is in its way surprisingly engaging. Certainly it is far and away the best of its kind to emerge for some time. The standard of design remains the same as before, but the film scores with an inventive and often witty script and some highly entertaining vocal characterisations. George Sanders in particular is very funny as a suavely sinister Shere Khan. This is Disney at his most imaginative, with even the sentimentality kept well in check.

WHAT THEY SAY NOW ...

Despite being adapted from Kipling, Disney's film of *The Jungle Book* is very much a product of the era in which it was made – the Swinging Sixties. Baloo is clearly a laid-back beatnik figure who finds himself put upon by 'the Man', as represented by the uptight Bagheera and, more menacingly, Shere Khan. Baloo tries to induct Mowgli into the joys of beatnik life in a jungle where the population includes a snake whose eyes and enunciation suggest some kind of narcotic influence, and a quartet of moptopped Liverpudlian vultures modelled on the Beatles. Baloo doesn't succeed entirely; he might open Mowgli's mind, but in the end the child deserts him for the lure of a young woman with goo-goo eyes and a clay pot on her head.

It is a seminal, poignant moment in Disney storytelling, even if the film itself isn't quite as spick and span as you might remember it. There is too much repetition in the animation, too many shortcuts taken, to place it in the same league as *Snow White and the Seven Dwarfs* (1937) or *Pinocchio* (1940). But the songs are a blast. And they've endured, even after 'Trust In Me' was covered by Siouxsie and the Banshees, and 'I Wanna Be Like You' aped by Los Lobos.

BEHIND THE SCENES

The Jungle Book was the last film overseen by Walt Disney. Early in its making, he is reported to have told his animators to discard the Rudyard Kipling source material because it was too dark. A live action version, with Jason Scott Lee as Mowgli, was released in 1995; it wasn't animated in either sense of the word. Some thirty-five years after the release of Disney's original, a tardy animated sequel – *The Jungle Book 2* – was released, to little impact and even less acclaim. Scarcely more than a facsimile of the first picture, it had John Goodman as the voice of Baloo, and even featured 'The Bare Necessities'. Again.

OSCARS
1 nomination

Music (Song): 'The Bare Necessities', Music and Lyrics by Terry Gilkyson

WHAT WON THAT YEAR?
Best Picture: *In the Heat of the Night*
Directing: Mike Nichols *The Graduate*
Actor: Rod Steiger *In the Heat of the Night*
Actress: Katharine Hepburn *Guess Who's Coming to Dinner*

BAFTAS

WHAT WON THAT YEAR?
Film: *The Graduate*
Direction: Mike Nichols *The Graduate*
Actor: Spencer Tracy *Guess Who's Coming to Dinner?*
Actress: Katharine Hepburn *The Lion in Winter/Guess Who's Coming to Dinner?*
Animated Film: Norman McLaren *Pas de Deux*

Opposite *Life is a long quiet river: Mowgli (top) and Baloo go boating*
This page *An extract from the Jungle Book storyboards shows Shere Khan failing to fall under the spell of Kaa the snake*

KAA. "LET ME SHOW YOU HOW IT WORKS!"

8

Dir: James CAMERON / USA
Released in Britain: 1998
Running Time: 195 minutes
Colour: Deluxe
Estimated Attendance: 18.91 million

Hollywood expected *Titanic* to sink. Instead, the most expensive film of all time sailed on to Oscar-laden glory, making superstars of Leonardo DiCaprio and Kate Winslet, and giving Celine Dion a hit single. The film's popularity goes on. As does its running time.

TITANIC

Director **James Cameron**
Producers **James Cameron, Jon Landau**
Screenplay **James Cameron**
Director of Photography **Russell Carpenter**
Editor **Conrad Buff, James Cameron, Richard A. Harris**
Production Designer **Peter Lamont**
Music **James Horner**

Jack Dawson • Leonardo DiCaprio
Rose DeWitt Bukater [young] • Kate Winslet
Cal Hockley • Billy Zane
Molly Brown • Kathy Bates
Ruth DeWitt Bukater • Frances Fisher
Captain Smith • Bernard Hill
Bruce Ismay • Jonathan Hyde
Fabrizio • Danny Nucci
Spicer Lovejoy • David Warner
Brock Lovett • Bill Paxton
Rose DeWitt Bukater [old] • Gloria Stuart
Thomas Andrews • Victor Garber
Lizzy Calvert • Suzy Amis
Lewis Bodine • Lewis Abernathy
Bobby Buell • Nicholas Cascone
Anatoly Milkailavich • Dr Anatoly M. Sagalavitch
Tommy Ryan • Jason Barry
First Officer • Murdoch Ewan Stewart
Fifth Officer Lowe • Ioan Gruffudd
Second Officer Lightoller • Jonny Phillips

THE STORY

The Atlantic Ocean, the present day. Brock Lovett explores the Titanic wreck, secretly looking for a famous diamond, the Heart of the Ocean, fabled to have sunk with the ship. In a safe, he finds sketch of a young woman. After the discovery is reported, an elderly woman named Rose DeWhitt Bukater contacts him, explaining that she is the woman depicted in the drawing and that she knows he's looking for the diamond. Rose is then airlifted to the ship, where she relates her experience of the disaster.

The year 1912. The Titanic is boarded by the young Rose, her mother and her wealthy fiancé, Cal Hockley. Jack Dawson, an artist, wins his steerage passage in a poker game. That evening, Rose almost throws herself over the rail but Jack talks her out of it. Cal promises to give Rose the Heart of the Ocean diamond. Meanwhile, Ismay, the Chairman of the White Star Line, demands the ship go faster. The next day, Rose confesses her happiness to Jack. He dines with the first-class passengers, then invites Rose to a raucous party in steerage. She asks him to draw her in the nude and leaves the sketch in Cal's safe. The two lovers flee, pursued by Cal's valet, Lovejoy. They make love in a car in storage. The lookouts sight an iceberg, but attempts to evade it fail and it collides with the ship.

Rose and Jack are captured, and Lovejoy plants the diamond on Jack, who is arrested and handcuffed to a pipe. Andrews, the ship's designer, tells the Captain that the ship will sink. The crew distributes lifejackets and begins loading an inadequate number of lifeboats with women and children. Panic ensues. Rose rescues Jack. Cal bribes and lies his way to a lifeboat. The ship breaks in half, and sinks entirely. Jack and Rose find some driftwood that will only support Rose. She is rescued after he dies from cold, and once ashore she hides from Cal, changing her name.

Back in the present, the elderly Rose sneaks up to the deck and tosses the Heart of the Ocean diamond overboard. She dies and joins Jack and the other deceased crew and passengers of the Titanic.

WHAT THEY SAY ...

James Cameron heads for old-fashioned Hollywood epic territory with *Titanic*, reputedly the most expensive film ever made at over $200 million. Using computer-generated imagery, he succeeds at capturing the visceral terror and awe of the legendary maritime disaster. The minutes when the ship splits in half, its stem tilts upward, exposing its enormous propellers, and the desperate passengers cling to the suddenly perpendicular deck or plummet from its heights into the icy water are particularly effective.

Likewise, Cameron is in his element during the action sequences of the film's second half, in which the characters race through rapidly flooding passages and make several narrow escapes from drowning. *Titanic* is ostentatious in its fidelity to the material aspects of its subject, presenting in detail the handsome staterooms, decks and swankily appointed first-class atrium with its famous staircase. Many of the establishing shots have an air of the guided tour about them, carefully displaying a production design so meticulously created that it has won the approval of minutia-obsessed Titanic buffs – no small feat. Cameron even commissioned his own underwater footage of the wreck.

Nevertheless, *Titanic* rarely feels like anything more than the most impressive movie money can buy. What grandeur and pathos the film possesses belong to the mythic story of the shipwreck itself, a fantastic confluence of history and the stuff that ballads are made from (as well as several films already, including the modest but superior *A Night to Remember* of 1958).

Cameron adds precisely nothing to the sum if you calculate his many gaffes against his commitment to a strict, methodical standard of authenticity.

Above Club-class Rose (Kate Winslet) is charmed by economy traveller Jack (Leonardo DiCaprio), but the deck is stacked against them

This page Women and children first: the few lifeboats are lowered into the water **Opposite above** Cameron recreates the departure of Titanic from Southampton in sepia tones **Opposite below** DiCaprio and Winslet; the former later referred to the lengthy, arduous shoot as 'hell'

And even that standard disintegrates when it comes to Cameron's own screenplay, a vulgar, cliché-ridden, anachronistic effort that entirely fails to capture the rigidly stratified manners of the era, despite Cameron's apparent interest in class relations. In fact, what Jack, Rose and Cal most resemble are the teens in John Hughes's high-school dramas of the 1980s in which noble, if brash, poor boys win the prettiest girls in class away from arrogant, bullying football stars. Having Rose drop vapid references to Picasso and Freud, and Jack reel off a list of stock bohemian adventures (drawing nude prostitutes in Paris, working a shrimp boat in Monterey) only compound the aura of phoniness.

Cameron's appealing young leads do struggle to bring vigour to their thin, cartoonish characters. Winslet often looks stiff and lost, as if affronted by her lines. While DiCaprio mostly just coasts on his insouciant movie-star charm; he's still a bit too unripe to make a convincing leading man.

While the film's first half, focused as it is on Rose and Jack's budding romance and the nastiness of Cal (who lacks only a handlebar moustache to twirl), seems overlong, Titanic is more crude than inept. The movie works as a simple-minded entertainment that provides a setting for spectacular visual effects, and many audiences will find it adequately enjoyable.

That everything about Titanic – from its stereotyped characters to its bright lighting and an overbearing score by James Horner (which gives way to the trite Celine Dion number 'My Heart Will Go On') – feels ersatz and obvious may only trouble the kind of people who dislike the immaculate, synthetic re-creations of real places in Disney theme parks. Not everyone who sees Titanic will yearn for the movie it might have been had it been made by a film-maker with imagination, and intelligence, rather than just raw ambition. But those who do will find the movie littered with missed opportunities as well as demonstrations of conspicuous spending. There were many complex and fascinating grown-ups aboard the Titanic, and several dozen true stories more compelling than Jack and Rose's teenage love. In addition, there are deep veins of tragedy and mystery in the tale of the star-crossed ship that James Cameron lacks the sensitivity to tap.

CLASSIC QUOTE
Jack: 'I'm the king of the world!'

BEHIND THE SCENES
Gossipmongers had spread the word that *Titanic* was destined to sink as swiftly as the ship after which it was named. The signs were not good. The initial budget of £135 million was exceeded by £65 million when the film went two months over schedule. Post-production work on the special effects in turn nudged the film past its release date of summer 1996 (it opened in the US in December 1997, and in the UK a month later). But the film defied these omens to become an all-round record-breaker, making more than $1 billion worldwide. It tied with *Ben Hur* (1959) by winning 11 Oscars, though 2003's *The Lord of the Rings: The Return of the King* later equalled this record.

IN THE CHAIR
James Cameron may have hit it big with *Titanic*, but he began with some quirky, likeable B-movie-style exploitation flicks: the silly *Piranha II: Flying Killers* (1981) and the sinister thriller *The Terminator* (1984). *Aliens* (1986) was crude and noisy, but effective; thereafter, his ego and bluster almost overwhelmed the honest spectacles of *Terminator 2: Judgment Day* (1991) and *True Lies* (1994). It may have been embarrassing when Cameron borrowed a line from his own screenplay to declare 'I'm the king of the world!' on the night of his Oscar success for *Titanic*. But you couldn't say he didn't sound sincere.

OSCARS
14 nominations, **11 winners**

Best Picture
Directing: James Cameron
Actress in a Leading Role: Kate Winslet
Actress in a Supporting Role: Gloria Stuart
Art Direction/Set Decoration: Peter Lamont, Michael Ford
Cinematography: Russell Carpenter
Costume Design: Deborah L. Scott
Film Editing: Conrad Buff, James Cameron, Richard A. Harris
Makeup: Tina Earnshaw, Greg Cannom, Simon Thompson
Music (Original Dramatic Score): James Horner
Music (Original Song): 'My Heart Will Go On', Music by James Horner; Lyrics by Will Jennings
Sound
Sound Effects Editing: Tom Bellfort, Christopher Boyes
Visual Effects

WHAT WON THAT YEAR?
Actor In A Leading Role: Jack Nicholson *As Good As It Gets*
Actress In A Leading Role: Helen Hunt *As Good As It Gets*

BAFTAS
10 nominations

Film
Direction: James Cameron
Film Music: James Horner
Cinematography: Russell Carpenter
Production Design: Peter Lamont
Costume Design: Deborah Scott
Editing: Conrad Buff, James Cameron, Richard A. Harris
Sound
Special Visual Effects
Make Up/Hair

WHAT WON THAT YEAR?
Film/British Film: *The Full Monty/ Nil By Mouth*
Direction: Baz Luhrmann *William Shakespeare's Romeo and Juliet*
Actor: Robert Carlyle *The Full Monty*
Actress: Judy Dench *Mrs Brown*

Dir: Leslie ARLISS / UK
Released in Britain: 1946
Running Time: 104 minutes
Black and white
Estimated Attendance: 35 million

Melodramas pitched by the Gainsborough studio at a predominantly female audience were big business in the 1940s. But when sex, violence and wanton immorality were added to the mix in *The Wicked Lady*, cinemagoers queued up in their millions to be scandalised.

THE WICKED LADY

Director **Leslie Arliss**
Producer **R. J. Minney**
Screenplay/Story **Leslie Arliss**, adapted from the
   novel by Magdalen King-Hall
Director of Photography **Jack Cox**
Editor **Terence Fisher**
Art Director **John Bryan**
Music **Hans May**

Lady Barbara Skelton • Margaret Lockwood
Captain Jerry Jackson • James Mason
Caroline • Patricia Roc
Sir Ralph Skelton • Griffith Jones
Kit Locksby • Michael Rennie
Hogarth • Felix Aylmer
Lady Kingsclere • Enid Stamp-Taylor
Lord Kingsclere • Francis Lister
Aunt Moll • Beatrice Varley
Aunt Doll • Amy Dalby
Cousin Agatha • Martita Hunt
Martin Worth • David Horne
Ned Cotterill • Emrys Jones
Mistress Betsy • Helen Goss
Mrs Munce • Muriel Aked
Doctor • Aubrey Mallalieu
Clergyman • Ivor Barnard
Hawker • Peter Maddon

THE STORY

Wealthy landowner Sir Ralph Skelton is due to marry Caroline, the orphan who has grown up as his ward, when he is seduced by the latter's oldest school friend, Barbara. The unlikely pair are married, and one guest at their wedding is the architect Kit Locksby, who instantly falls in love with Barbara. Married life quickly bores Barbara, which is not lost on Caroline, who has stayed to keep house. When Ralph's sister and brother-in-law, Lady and Lord Kingsclere, arrive from London, Barbara sits up late with them at cards and gambles away all her possessions, including a ruby brooch given her by her dying mother. Regretting her action, and provoked by Lady Kingsclere wearing the brooch, Barbara disguises herself as a highwayman (inspired by stories of the legendary Captain Jackson) and steals it back.

But Barbara is now thrilled to have discovered a new pastime; one night she encounters the real Captain Jackson, and after escaping pursuit together they become lovers. Subsequently learning from one of her husband's ex-tenants of the passage of a bullion coach, Barbara persuades Jackson to ambush it, and in the affray shoots one of the guards. This causes widespread alarm, and Ralph is anxious to do something to protect his people.

Barbara takes no interest in these proceedings and is chided by Caroline who, having realised that she is in fact deeply in love with Ralph, departs for London when she discovers that Ralph feels the same way. Barbara now overhears a plan to apprehend Jackson and sets off to warn him. She discovers him in bed with another woman in an inn and, still disguised as a highwayman, throws a note revealing his whereabouts into Ralph's drawing room.

Jackson is caught and taken to London for trial. But Barbara's secret has been discovered by Ralph's old servant Hogarth, and she determines to dispose of him by slow poisoning. Caroline is summoned back to restore order to the house, but is too late to save Hogarth, who dies before he can reveal Barbara's secret. Realising that she has no hope of living with Ralph, Caroline returns to London having decided to marry Kit Locksby in the knowledge that she does not love him, nor he her. On the gallows, Jackson sees Barbara in her coach and understands that she has betrayed him. A fight breaks out which allows the highwayman to be cut down before he dies, and make an escape. Back in the country, he turns up one night in Barbara's room determined to strangle her, and in the ensuing struggle rapes her.

She now realises that she loves Kit but despairs of ever being able to marry him. She again disguises herself as a highwayman, bent this time not on robbery but murder. She encounters Jackson, and shoots him dead when he tries to stop her, but her attempt on Ralph's life goes wrong and she is herself fatally wounded. Confessing all her misdeeds, she dies in Kit's arms, which leaves Caroline and Ralph free to marry at last.

WHAT THEY SAID THEN ...

With excellent photography from Jack Cox, lavish costuming and rich settings, this resembles a novelette on high-quality art paper. Nobody, surely, is expected to believe in its naive manner of narrative, its dialogue which wanders uncertainly

This page Stand and deliver: James Mason, as Captain Jerry Jackson, is the dandy highwayman, with Margaret Lockwood as Lady Barbara Skelton his equal in criminality

between seventeenth- and twentieth-century idiom. And some of the sequences – notably those on the frozen Thames – are as false as ye olde teashoppe. From a box-office point of view these shortcomings will no doubt be proved negligible, but it is hardly surprising that, with the exception perhaps of Mason and Griffith Jones, none of the cast manages to be convincing. Mason swashbuckles through without a care whether his part is credible or not, and Jones attempts some quiet work with patent sincerity. The Hays office, and its counterpart in many private homes, will perhaps find much to object to in the display of décolletage and in the sexual situations that begin with wanton trading and culminate in rape.

WHAT THEY SAY NOW ...

The most commercially successful of all the Gainsborough melodramas, and arguably the best known, *The Wicked Lady* is in many ways the definitive example of the formula. While its predecessors had featured strong female roles, as befitting

Opposite above Give him enough rope:
Jerry Jackson cuts loose from the noose
Opposite below Costume drama: impressive
outfits for Sir Ralph (Griffith Jones), Lady Barbara
(Margaret Lockwood) and Caroline (Patricia
Roc) *Right* Kit (Michael Rennie) and Caroline
go shopping

films aimed at largely female audiences, the characters were for the most part straitjacketed by the society that produced them, with even the villainesses like Hester in *The Man in Grey* (1943) or Alicia in *Fanny by Gaslight* (1944) conforming to type.

However, Lady Barbara Skelton (Margaret Lockwood) is clearly pushing at the barriers right from the start, as she steals her best friend's fiancé, marries him and, after belatedly discovering married life to be somewhat dull, turns to gambling, highway robbery, murder and every social transgression under the sun. Totally rejecting any conventional image of 'femininity', she spends much of the film challenging stereotypes head-on, running rings around her male counterparts, whether they be the dull but essentially good Sir Ralph (Griffith Jones), the wickedly sexy highwayman Jerry Jackson (James Mason), the stern, high-minded puritan Hogarth (Felix Aylmer) or the vivacious Kit (Michael Rennie), the man she really loves but who she never seems to meet at the right time.

What unites the men is that they all have at least some kind of moral code – even Jackson baulks at killing – whereas Barbara rejects anything that might conveniently pigeonhole her (her dead mother is the only person towards whom she remains unswervingly loyal). But by rejecting society, she's playing a dangerous game – as society in turn rejects her to the point of degradation and death, leaving her utterly alone awaiting her fate. The ending, while undoubtedly motivated at least partly by the British Board of Film Censors' moral code regarding criminals getting their comeuppance, is tragically inevitable – transgression may be hugely entertaining, but there's an unmistakable price to pay.

CLASSIC QUOTE

Lady Barbara: 'I could never resist anything that belonged to someone else.'

BEHIND THE SCENES

Margaret Lockwood as Lady Barbara Skelton was the talk of British cinemagoers, but American audiences weren't given the opportunity to see what all the fuss was about: the film was expensively reshot for the American edition after Lockwood's cleavage was considered too prominent to meet the moral strictures laid down by the Hays Code. Even by today's standards, *The Wicked Lady* is startlingly racy, and it must have seemed thrillingly subversive to 1945 audiences. Michael Winner's 1983 remake, on the other hand, with Faye Dunaway in the role of Barbara, featured nudity in abundance, and failed to raise a slither of the controversy whipped up by the fully clothed original.

IN THE LEAD

Of the four lead actors in the first 'official' Gainsborough melodrama, *The Man in Grey* (also directed by Leslie Arliss), Margaret Lockwood was the only one who was already an established star, having previously played the female lead in Hitchcock's internationally successful *The Lady Vanishes* (1938) for the same studio. But the melodramas made during the 1940s established her reputation, and in 1945 and 1946 she was unarguably the most popular homegrown female star in British cinema, although her appeal had waned by the end of that decade.

10

Dir: Compton BENNETT / UK
Released in Britain: 1945
Running Time: 94 minutes
Black and white
Estimated Attendance: 35 million

Few things thrilled British cinema audiences of the late 1940s as much as a generous portion of over-wrought melodrama and the spectacle of James Mason being perfectly beastly. *The Seventh Veil* offered both, set to an intoxicating classical soundtrack.

THE SEVENTH VEIL

Director **Compton Bennett**
Producer **Sydney Box**
Screenplay **Sydney Box, Muriel Box**
Director of Photography **Reginald Wyer**
Editor **Gordon Hales**
Art Director **James A. Carter**
Music **Benjamin Frankel**

Nicholas • James Mason
Francesca Cunningham • Ann Todd
Dr Larson • Herbert Lom
Peter Gay • Hugh McDermott
Maxwell Leyden • Albert Lieven
Susan Brooks • Yvonne Owen
Dr Kendal • David Horne
Dr Irving • Manning Whiley
James • John Slater

THE STORY

Francesca Cunningham is a celebrated pianist whose hands have been burned in a car accident and who is suffering from acute depression. She attempts suicide, and afterwards becomes silent and lifeless. A psychiatrist, Dr Lassen, places her under narco-hypnosis, during which she reveals the truth of her past life, episode by episode. Each stage in her life has led to her depression: the headmistress who canes her on the hands the day before an important music examination, the guardian who tyrannises over her in order to force the pace of her training and career, the collapse of her adolescent and mature love affairs.

Above *'Trust me I'm a doctor,' says Dr Larson (Herbert Lom) to Francesca (Ann Todd)* **Right** *'Play it again, Ann,' as Nicholas, the 'scowling and devilishly handsome' James Mason looks on* **Opposite** *Francesca on the concert stand before the fall*

OSCARS

1 nomination, **1 winner**

Writing (Original Screenplay): Muriel Box, Sydney Box

WHAT WON THAT YEAR
Best Motion Picture: *The Best Years of Our Lives*
Directing: William Wyler *The Best Years of Our Lives*
Actor: Fredric March *The Best Years of Our Lives*
Actress: Olivia de Havilland *To Each His Own*

BAFTAS NOT AWARDED UNTIL 1947

WHAT THEY SAID THEN ...

James Mason plays his usual role – sardonic, brooding, the man to whom wealth and a mysterious past permit a romantic licence for ill manners and egocentric behaviour. Yet the film has distinct virtues and cinematic power; the opening is beautifully and brilliantly handled, haunting and tense. The music is a delight to hear (Chopin, Mozart, Rachmaninoff, Grieg, Beethoven). The psychological theme – the neurosis of a talented girl whose thwarted emotional life culminates in an acute regard for her hands, which she wrongly believes injured beyond healing – seems correctly conceived, and the psychiatrist is well played by Herbert Lom. James Mason is an excellent actor with a fine face for screen-work. Why must he always play a Victorian maidservant's conception of a rich, romantically overbearing lord?

Ann Todd's performance is sensitive and true to the character. She performs the difficult task of being completely satisfying and convincing in her portrayal of a great artist in another sphere of art. The audience experiences fully the artist's agony of public appearance at concerts that demand the highest standards of discipline and execution. The pity is that all this fine work should have been given to what is only, after all is said, another rather obvious story of luxury and the romantic yearnings of the poor little rich girl.

WHAT THEY SAY NOW ...

The Seventh Veil was shot on the cheap in Riverside Studios in west London. The director, Compton Bennett, was a first-timer. The star Ann Todd was far from a household name. Nonetheless, the film's 'rich, portentous mixture of Beethoven, Chopin, kitsch and Freud' (as Pauline Kael later put it) was exactly what audiences in austerity-era, post-war Britain craved. It is lurid and wildly enjoyable, with a whiff of eroticism and sadism that still carries a charge today. Todd plays a suicidal concert pianist. Herbert Lom is the purring, sinister psychiatrist trying to 'strip' her mind. James Mason (as Todd's music-loving guardian) limps around, scowling and looking devilishly handsome. There are moments when the production creaks – the flashbacks in which the thirtysomething Todd is required to play a teenage girl are some distance from convincing – but the film-makers attack their material in such a full-blooded way that it seems churlish to complain about the odd duff note.

SCENE STEALER

James Mason beating Ann Todd's hands with a walking stick. In the 1940s, Mason specialised in playing bullies and cads. He thrashed Margaret Lockwood with a poker in *The Man in Grey* (1943) and tormented his wife in *They Were Sisters* (1945), but the worse he behaved, the more audiences seemed to love him.

BEHIND THE SCENES

Betty Box recalls that her brother Sydney, who wrote and co-produced *The Seventh Veil*, had seen Ann Todd in theatre. 'Theatre was his first love,' she said. 'He liked Ann very much. I personally didn't think she was a brilliant actress. She did two or three films for David Lean, which were about the worst films he ever made. She was a little temperamental. *The Seventh Veil* was such an unexpected success. I remember the night it opened in Leicester Square. You couldn't move. They had to bring out the mounted police. Ann Todd was absolutely taken aback, as we all were. She came into the office the next day and cried, and said, "It has come too late, I am too old." She was about 35. Everybody had had chunks out of their life with the war really; this was a time when she might have been much more at the top of her profession.'

In February 1896,

weeks after Louis and Auguste Lumière had shown their projected films to a paying audience in Paris, the French brothers displayed their invention at the Polytechnic Hall, Regent Street, London. The impact was sensational. Soon the Lumière Cinématographe was part of the bill at the Empire, Leicester Square, London's leading variety theatre.

For the first few years of its life cinema was a novelty attraction. There were no stories, merely views

of waves crashing on the shore, trains entering stations, streets bustling with horse-drawn traffic. Films were shown in fairground tents, in music halls, later in temporarily empty shops, known as 'penny gaffs'. The first exhibitors were literally showmen. The name stuck and was still being used in the trade press until relatively recently.

With the emergence of more sophisticated films, newsreels, stories and effects, the purpose-built theatre, with room for two or three musicians, started to appear, eventually driving out the penny gaffs. Disastrous fires caused by careless handling of nitrate film stock, and denunciations from the pulpit on the corrupting

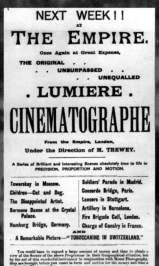

influence of cinema, led to official regulation and licensing, and the creation of the BBFC (British Board of Film Classification).

By the First World War every town had at least one film theatre, but further expansion was placed on hold. In the 1920s huge super-cinemas sprouted up, usually in city centres, with some capable of housing full orchestras. Exhibition interests consolidated, and a handful of big circuits dominated the business. When talking pictures arrived at the end of the decade it was they who won the race to wire up for sound, and many older, independent theatres

closed. Imposing buildings were soon springing up in every suburb, led by Oscar Deutsch's Odeon circuit with its calculated use of Moderne architecture, and Sidney Bernstein's Granadas, blending Moorish and Gothic to create cathedrals of filmgoing.

The Second World War terminated building for a decade, at a time when audiences had peaked to record levels. Exhibition was now dominated by a duopoly of Rank, which controlled the Odeon and Gaumont circuits, and ABC. By the 1950s, when restrictions were eased, the growth of television had severely eroded the level of admissions, and in the middle of the decade substantial closures began. By the late 1960s many large towns no longer had any cinemas at all, and the filmgoing habit was lost. Numerous large cinemas were hastily converted into three smaller auditoriums, while the rest became bingo halls or were razed for development.

Each year until the mid-1980s audience figures diminished. Then the tide turned. The reason was the advent of the multiplex, the first ten-screener opening at Milton Keynes in 1985. During the next 20 years multiplexes became the dominant force in exhibition, offering a range of programmes and parallel leisure activities. Small, independent cinemas declined further, in spite of attempts to establish art-houses in upmarket locations. By mid-2005 the effect of DVD sales and improved home viewing systems had seriously affected admissions in the United States, forcing exhibitors to think anew, and to plan the second multiplex generation, a trend that inevitably will cross the Atlantic.

Opposite above The Majestic Leeds, 1922
Opposite below The Lumière brothers top the bill at The Empire, Leicester Square
Above The Odeon, Harlow, in 1960 before it was divided into three smaller auditoriums
Below The Odeon, Leicester Square, 1937

Dir: Chris COLUMBUS / USA, UK
Released in Britain: 2001
Running Time: 152 minutes
Colour: Technicolor
Estimated Attendance: 17.56 million

HARRY POTTER AND THE PHILOSOPHER'S STONE

Director **Chris Columbus**
Producer **David Heyman**
Screenplay **Steve Kloves**, adapted from the novel
 by J. K. Rowling
Director of Photography **John Seale**
Editor **Richard Francis-Bruce**
Production Designer **Stuart Craig**
Music **John Williams**

Harry Potter • Daniel Radcliffe
Ron Weasley • Rupert Grint
Hermione Granger • Emma Watson
Nearly Headless Nick • John Cleese
Rubeus Hagrid • Robbie Coltrane
Uncle Vernon Dursley • Richard Griffiths
Albus Dumbledore • Richard Harris
Professor Quirrell/Voldemort • Ian Hart
Mr Ollivander • John Hurt
Professor Snape • Alan Rickman
Aunt Petunia Dursley • Fiona Shaw
Professor McGonagall • Maggie Smith
Sean Biggerstaff • Oliver Wood
Goblin Bank Teller/Professor Flitwick • Warwick Davis
Mrs Weasley • Julie Walters
Madame Hooch • Zoe Wanamaker
Mr Filch • David Bradley
Draco Malfoy • Tom Felton
Baby Harry Potter • Saunders Triplets
Dudley Dursley • Harry Melling

The publishing phenomenon of the late 1990s became the movie smash of 2001, though it was never certain that Harry Potter's film debut would triumph over the first *Lord of the Rings*, which opened just a month later. In the end, Harry beat the hobbits by a wand, securing nearly 2 million more admissions at UK cinemas.

THE STORY

Somewhere in Britain, the infant Harry Potter survives an attack by the evil wizard Voldemort, though his parents are killed. He is left with his vindictive 'muggle' (non-wizard) relatives, Aunt Petunia and Uncle Vernon. On his eleventh birthday, Harry is removed by the giant Hagrid, caretaker of Hogwarts School for wizards. Hagrid retrieves a mysterious package from Gringotts Bank.

On board the Hogwarts Express, Harry encounters Hermione and Ron; later all three are enrolled in Gryffindor House. By accident they stumble upon a room in which a huge three-headed hound guards a trapdoor. When a troll finds its way into the school, the three suspect Professor Snape of seeking whatever it is the hound is guarding, especially as Snape appears to be muttering incantations at Harry during his first, victorious game of the school sport, Quidditch.

The three children are given a detention for visiting Hagrid at night. They realise that the giant hound is guarding Hagrid's mysterious package, the Philosopher's Stone, which could restore Voldemort's power. Searching the woods for a wounded unicorn, Harry is attacked by Voldemort but saved by a centaur.

Finding the hound lulled to sleep, the children pass tests required to reach an inner sanctum. Harry enters alone and manages to repel Voldemort – who has been inhabiting the form of Professor Quirrell, not Snape – before they get the stone. The children's bravery is rewarded with extra points which ensure that Gryffindor win the school cup.

Opposite Dinner in the Great Hall at Hogwarts
Above A lost Harry (Daniel Radcliffe) asks for platform 9¾ ***Below*** *'It does not do to dwell on dreams, Harry, and forget to live'*

WHAT THEY SAY ...

Those who applaud J. K. Rowling's success in selling Harry Potter books to children may miss the point that it has as much to do with multimedia merchandising, brand-name exploitation and the saleability of nostalgia as with any deep-rooted return to literature. It may be that the books' reader base is exceptionally wide, but it is also shallow, made up of children and adults who read sparingly but enjoy Rowling's boarding-school fantasy world as a gratifying version of burgeoning adolescence. Anyone who knows the darker hue of comparable children's fiction – Susan Cooper, Roald Dahl, Philip Pullman, J. R. R. Tolkien – may be less impressed with Hogwarts and a central character who, though orphaned, is a major celebrity among wizards, heir to a vaultful of gold, the best natural Quidditch player ever known, possessed of a cloak of invisibility and a phoenix-feather wand, protégé of the headmaster and centre of a close-knit circle of friends. The proportion of whimsy to brutality in the Harry Potter books is high.

This first film adaptation is clearly conscious of a vast international market. Eccentric cameos from British comics seem curtailed (or, in the case of Rik Mayall's, apparently cut). John Cleese has only a few lines as a semi-decapitated ghost; Zoe Wanamaker is notable mainly for her yellow contact-lenses. The motto seems to have been: keep it bland. Only Alan Rickman bucks the general trend by camping it up to the rafters as Professor Snape, Master of Potions.

OSCARS

3 nominations

Art Direction/Set Decoration: Stuart Craig, Stephenie McMillan
Costume Design: Judianna Makovsky
Music (Original Score): John Williams

WHAT WON THAT YEAR?
Best Picture: *A Beautiful Mind*
Directing: Ron Howard *A Beautiful Mind*
Actor in a Leading Role: Denzel Washington *Training Day*
Actress in a Leading Role: Halle Berry *Monster's Ball*

BAFTAS

7 nominations

Outstanding British Film of the Year
Actor in a Supporting Role: Robbie Coltraine
Production Design: Stuart Craig
Costume Design: Judianna Makovsky
Sound
Special Visual Effects
Make Up and Hair: Amanda Knight, Eithné Fennell, Nick Dudman

WHAT WON THAT YEAR?
Film: *The Lord of the Rings*
British Film: *Gosford Park*
Direction: Peter Jackson *The Lord of the Rings*
Actor: Russell Crowe *A Beautiful Mind*
Actress: Judi Dench *Iris*

As for the young leads, Daniel Radcliffe is genial and inoffensive as Harry, yet he manages to hold the film together. Rupert Grint is very good as Ron, a set-jawed Artful Dodger to Harry's Oliver Twist, but Emma Watson as Hermione is shrill and prim, reminiscent of the disagreeable little girls who come to nasty ends in Dahl stories.

Escape is a central theme: the film is full of doorways and portals, each leading to a more magical place. Harry's initial view of the world is through an air vent in the door of the cupboard where his aunt and uncle keep him locked up. A wall unbricks itself to reveal a secret passageway to shops selling potions, broomsticks and wands. Another magic wall in King's Cross Station conceals the entrance to platform nine-and-three-quarters, where Harry boards the Hogwarts Express. While exploring Hogwarts under cover of his invisibility cloak, Harry sneaks through a door to find a magic mirror that shows whomever looks into it that which their heart most desires.

The journey towards magic is also a journey into the past. When Harry looks through the cupboard vent, he sees a 1950s suburban interior. There is a Victorian inn and bank populated by wizened shopkeepers and goblin-bankers wearing capes or half-moon spectacles. The Hogwarts Express steam-train bisects a landscape where no sign of modem technology can be seen. And Hogwarts itself is a dreamworld, a mixed-sex multiracial Eton for magicians. Each setting adds something to a kaleidoscope of imagined Englands: a heritage theme park kept scrubbed and shiny. The film is like that magic mirror. It shows a wished-for world – a world without machines, a public school without bullying or sexual tension, a childhood where abusive adults can be outwitted.

There are still moments of terror and grief. Harry is frozen by the sight of Voldemort drinking a dead unicorn's blood. Earlier, Harry sits cross-legged and very quiet, staring into the mirror that shows his parents flanking him. His vigil is interrupted by the headmaster, Professor Dumbledore, after which the film moves to the next minor escapade, leaving the feeling spent and Harry's brooding unexplored.

The best thing about the book may be the jokes, and the film retains many, such as the wizards' confectionery, Bertie Botts' Every Flavour Beans, which occasionally come in vomit or ear-wax flavour. Rowling's more visual gags – newspapers with moving pictures, 'wizard chess' with violently active pieces – also transfer well to the screen.

Harry Potter and the Philosopher's Stone will captivate younger children, but overall it's oddly anticlimactic. It has cuteness in plenty but neither epic sweep nor any edge of emotional conflict. Harry Potter may battle all manner of monsters but – barring some extraordinary volte-face on Rowling's part – he will continue his well-adjusted adolescence inside a closed and essentially unthreatening world. At the end

of *Harry Potter and the Philosopher's Stone*, John Williams's music soars, recalling his score for *Star Wars*. But an evil empire hasn't been hobbled – instead, Harry's house, Gryffindor, has won the school cup.

CLASSIC QUOTE

Dumbledore: 'It does not do to dwell on dreams, Harry, and forget to live.'

BEHIND THE SCENES

In the US, the film's title was changed to the more mall-friendly *Harry Potter and the Sorcerer's Stone*. Consequently, each scene in which the Philosopher's Stone is referred to required an additional take for the US version, so that the actors could call it the Sorcerer's Stone.

IN THE CHAIR

Chris Columbus is known for his undistinguished, anonymous treatment of other people's material, and his work on the first two *Harry Potter* films has done little to alter this. It has been remarked that he won the coveted directing job because of the financial success of his earlier movies, such as *Mrs Doubtfire* (1993) and the first two *Home Alone* films (1990 and 1992), or his experience with child actors. What made him a likely candidate was his innocuous style: he would impose no personality on Rowling's material. Also rumoured to be in the running were Terry Gilliam, Steven Spielberg and Brad Silberling (director of the film of a superior series of children's books, *Lemony Snicket's A Series of Unfortunate Events*, 2004).

Above Neville Longbottom (Matthew Lewis) demonstrates his (lack of) flying skills *Below* Anyone for quidditch?

Dir: Randal KLEISER / USA
Released in Britain: 1978
Running Time: 110 minutes
Colour: Metrocolor
Estimated Attendance: 17.2 million

The boys wore leather jackets and quiffs dripping with Brylcreem. The girls had starburst smiles and puffball skirts. There was rock'n'roll on the jukebox and milkshakes in the diner. This was the 1950s, *Grease* style, and audiences went crazy for it. But did it ever really exist?

GREASE

Director **Randal Kleiser**
Producers **Robert Stigwood, Allan Carr**
Screenplay **Bronte Woodard**, adapted by Allan Carr
  from the musical by Jim Jacobs and Warren Casey
Director of Photography **Bill Butler**
Editor **John F. Burnett**
Production Designer **Philip M. Jefferies**
Music Supervisor **Bill Oakes**

Danny Zucco • John Travolta
Sandy Olsson • Olivia Newton-John
Betty Rizzo • Stockard Channing
Kenickie • Jeff Conaway
Doody • Barry Pearl
Sonny • Michael Tucci
Putzie • Kelly Ward
Frenchie • Didi Conn
Jan • Jamie Donnelly
Marty • Dinah Manoff
Principal McGee • Eve Arden
Teen Angel • Frankie Avalon
Vi • Joan Blondell
Vince Fontaine • Edward Byrnes
Coach Calhoun • Sid Caesar
Mrs Murdoch • Alice Ghostley
Blanche • Dody Goodman
Johnny Casino and The Gamblers • Sha-Na-Na
Patty Simcox • Susan Buckner
Tom Chisum • Lorenzo Lamas

THE STORY

On a summer visit to California with her parents, Australian teenager Sandy Olsson meets Danny Zucco at the beach, and they fall for each other. When her parents decide not to return to Sydney, Sandy enrols in the senior class at Rydell High, where she discovers that her summer suitor is the leader of the school's tough-guy gang. Fearful of losing status, Danny is off-hand with Sandy; she subsequently dates one of the school's cleaner-cut athletes. A jealous Danny starts training secretly as an athlete in the hope of regaining Sandy's respect; he also wins a hot-rod race against the leader of the delinquent Scorpions, whose moll, Cha Cha, starts to show a predatory interest in him. At the graduation dance, Sandy loses Danny to Cha Cha, but is later transformed into a sexy temptress for the end-of-term carnival, to which a contrite Danny comes dressed for her benefit as a sober athlete. The two re-affirm their love.

WHAT THEY SAID THEN ...

Even in these days of blanket nostalgia, when cinema fashions have all but eclipsed the present tense, *Grease* arguably achieves a new low in retro styles. Not that the 1950s of Randal Kleiser's *Grease* is – or ever was – a specifically locatable historic era. It is a compound of motley artefacts, styles, rhythms, sounds and movie references, bound together by the fact that they are perceived through the wrong end of a telescope.

Beneath its remorseless and aggressive façade of twitching adolescent energy, the film is actually celebrating a state of middle-class adulthood. Even middle age. Insidiously, it congratulates its audience on having achieved a stable perspective from which it can view with amused tolerance the turbulent times of its supposed teenage traumas. By drawing its archetypal teen crises from screen classics rather than first-hand experience, it seduces its audience into believing that they have lived more recklessly and glamorously than they had supposed.

The lines between the years – even the decades – appear unusually blurred. The film opens with its young lovers embracing on a deserted beach in a chaste

OSCARS
1 nomination

Music (Original Song): 'Hopelessly Devoted To You',
  Music and Lyrics by John Farrar

WHAT WON THAT YEAR?
Best Picture: *The Deer Hunter*
Directing: Michael Cimino *The Deer Hunter*
Actor in a Leading Role: Jon Voight *Coming Home*
Actress in a Leading Role: Jane Fonda *Coming Home*

BAFTAS

WHAT WON THAT YEAR?
Film: *Julia*
Direction: Alan Parker *Midnight Express*
Actor: Richard Dreyfuss *The Goodbye Girl*
Actress: Jane Fonda *Julia*

Opposite *Life's a beach: Sandy (Olivia Newton-John) and Danny (John Travolta) say goodbye in the film's prologue* **Right above** *The young-ish lovers overcome their differences and look forward to a life together in matching leather* **Right below** *Go greased lightning: Danny and friends take a break from repairs*

variation on *From Here to Eternity* (1953), to the strains of 'Love is a Many Splendoured Thing'; next, to the sound of a reggae-beat rock tune, the animated credits present each of the principal characters as cartoon figures, surrounded by such nostalgic items as a volume of *Sick, Sick, Sick* and a vintage *Mad* magazine; then term begins and a leather-jacketed gang that seems to have strayed in from *West Side Story* joins with some of the pert virgins from the *Beach Party* cycle to deliver original songs whose expository refrains remind us of *Hair* and the Sixties, while the choreography seems to have grown out of Jerome Robbins via *Saturday Night Fever* (1977).

Ultimately, the most oppressive thing about *Grease* is not so much its wholesale pirating of incompatible sources as its insistent knowingness. Travolta's strutting performance as Danny matches the script and direction in this respect. Only Olivia Newton-John performs as if she believed that there really was a period when teenagers were young and spent more time looking over the rainbow than over their shoulders at the box-office trends.

WHAT THEY SAY NOW ...

If *Grease* looked dated when it was first released, it has now become something stranger. It's a kind of karaoke party movie, though it will never have the cult cachet of *The Sound of Music* (1965) or *The Rocky Horror Picture Show* (1975), both of which have been transformed and improved by their latter-day, event-style screenings. *Grease* cannot benefit from that treatment because it's so resolutely square in its conception. Like a 'Hits of the 1950s' CD cover-mounted on a mass-market tabloid, it tries to sell to its audience a manufactured, airbrushed version of their past. Only now, those children who were taken to the film in 1978 by their own nostalgic parents are showing *Grease* to their children, who can have no possible emotional connection to it beyond learning the clunking dance steps.

CLASSIC QUOTE

Sonny: 'When a guy picks a chick over his buddies, something's gotta be wrong.'

BEHIND THE SCENES

The senior class at Rydell High are played by such relatively veteran performers as Stockard Channing, who was the best performer in the cast and, at 34, the oldest. John Travolta, fresh from the success of *Saturday Night Fever* and *Carrie* (1976), was 24, while Olivia Newton-John, for whom *Grease* was the single pinnacle of her film career, was 29. She was reunited with Travolta in the 1983 flop, *Two of a Kind*.

13

Dir: Joshua LOGAN / USA
Released in Britain: 1958
Running Time: 177 minutes
Colour: Technicolor
Estimated Attendance: 16.5 million

There is nothing like a dame, or a good Rodgers and Hammerstein musical. Two movie versions of the duo's stage hits make it into *The Ultimate Film* top thirty. *South Pacific* might lag behind *The Sound of Music* (1965) in camp appeal (though not by much), but it has unforgettable tunes and lavish locations in abundance.

SOUTH PACIFIC

Director **Joshua Logan**
Producer **Buddy Adler**
Screenplay **Paul Osborn**, adapted from the play
   by Richard Rodgers, Oscar Hammerstein II and
   Joshua Logan
Director of Photography **Leon Shamroy**
Editor **Robert L. Simpson**
Art Direction **John DeCuir, Lyle R. Wheeler**
Music **Richard Rodgers**

Emile de Becque • Rossano Brazzi
Nellie Forbush, Ensign, USN • Mitzi Gaynor
Lt Joseph Cable, USMC • John Kerr
Luther Billis • Ray Walston
Bloody Mary • Juanita Hall
Liat • France Nuyen
Captain 'Iron Belly' Brackett • Russ Brown
Commander Harbison • Floyd Simmons
Lt Buzz Adams • Tom Laughlin
The Professor • Jack Mullaney
Stewpot • Ken Clark
Native Chief • Archie Savage
Ngana, Emile's Daughter • Candace Lee
Jerome, Emile's Son • Warren Hsieh
Henry, Emile's Servant • Francis Kahele
Communications Man • Robert Jacobs
Radio Man • John Gabriel
Co-pilot • Richard Harrison
Navigator • Ron Ely
Seabee Dancer • Steve Wiland

THE STORY

In 1943 Nellie Forbush, a young American Navy nurse stationed on a South Pacific island, falls in love with Emile de Becque, a rich French planter. Lt Joseph Cable arrives on the island with orders to find de Becque, whom he hopes to persuade to be his guide on a reconnaissance of the Japanese-held islands in the area. On the strange island of Bali Ha'i, Cable meets and falls in love with Liat – the beautiful daughter of Bloody Mary, a rumbustious native trading woman; but, because of her skin colour, he refuses to marry her. Then Nellie learns that de Becque has two Eurasian children by a previous marriage to a Polynesian woman. Deeply shocked, she breaks off her engagement with him and, in the mood of dejection that follows, he agrees to guide Cable through the islands. Together the two men are able to radio back to the Americans vital information about Japanese troop movements. When Nellie hears that de Becque has gone with Cable she realises how foolish her prejudices were. Cable is killed by the Japanese, but de Becque manages to escape back to the American island. At his hill-top home he finds Nellie, and his two children, waiting for him.

WHAT THEY SAID THEN ...

As an attraction, it must be readily granted that *South Pacific* is the biggest of the cinema's blockbusters in the battle against television. A mammoth of a film, packed with colourful entertainment values, it is also, alas, a crashing bore. Joshua Logan's direction is portentous, lacking in surprise and vitality; and his attempts to create mood and atmosphere by the use of colour are banal. During key scenes the screen is bathed in deep tints – yellow, red, gold – to produce a weird, magic-lantern effect; one scene gives the principals charcoal complexions and cement-coloured lips. This method also results in nerve-racking moments when the colour tries to return to normal – which it does in a series of violent jerks.

THERE IS NOTHING YOU CAN NAME THAT IS ANYTHING LIKE

RODGERS & HAMMERSTEIN'S

SOUTH PACIFIC

starring

ROSSANO BRAZZI · MITZI GAYNOR · JOHN KERR · FRANCE NUYEN

featuring
RAY WALSTON   JUANITA HALL

Produced by
BUDDY ADLER

Directed by
JOSHUA LOGAN

Screenplay by
PAUL OSBORN

Colour by **Technicolor**

A MAGNA Production
Released by 20th Century-Fox

"DITES-MOI" · "A COCKEYED OPTIMIST" · "SOME ENCHANTED EVENING" · "BLOODY MARY" · "MY GIRL BACK HOME" · "THERE IS NOTHIN' LIKE A DAME" · "BALI HA'I"
"I'M GONNA WASH THAT MAN RIGHT OUTA MY HAIR" · "A WONDERFUL GUY" · YOUNGER THAN SPRINGTIME · "HAPPY TALK" · "HONEY BUN" · "CAREFULLY TAUGHT" · "THIS NEARLY WAS MINE"

Below *Mitzi Gaynor's going to wash that man right out of her hair*

The chief pleasure to be had from the film is, of course, the music – a superior Rodgers and Hammerstein score. The sound is first-class, with particularly good balance between chorus and orchestra in the playing over the credit titles; with five loudspeakers along the top of the screen, and twenty-seven more scattered around the auditorium, it remains the best sound system yet heard in the cinema. In general the acting is routine and lacklustre. Mitzi Gaynor has a brave but unsuccessful try at the skittish Nellie Forbush. Rossano Brazzi borders on a caricature of mannered romantic charm. The best performance is given by Ray Walston, whose vigorous playing of the conniving Luther Billis is highly enjoyable.

WHAT THEY SAY NOW …

Shot largely on Hawaii, doubling for the Polynesian islands on which it's set, *South Pacific* helped usher in a vogue for musicals that boasted lavish location filming. But while director Joshua Logan includes many gorgeous vistas of this Pacific idyll (enhanced by colour filters), he lacked the flexibility and fluidity of movement that filming in a studio allows. The result is an often static movie with pedestrian dance numbers – it's hard to shake a leg when you're sinking in sand. Lacking the delirious inventiveness of Hollywood-made musicals such as

Singin' in the Rain (1952), *South Pacific* feels like a 'straight' adaptation of an existing stage success, an impression heightened by the film's theatrical structure, complete with intermission breaks and an overture.

But despite its lack of cinematic flair, *South Pacific* has in plentiful supply that key ingredient for all successful musicals: beautifully sung renditions of beautifully written songs. Rodgers and Hammerstein's score features some of their best work: 'There is Nothing Like a Dame', 'Happy Talk' and 'You've Got to be Carefully Taught' (which, unusually for a musical of the time, touched on the issue of racism and miscegenation, although the stage musical's liberal treatment of this is compromised by the film's condescending portrayal of the native inhabitants). *South Pacific* may at times be as 'corny as Kansas in August' (as Mitzi Gaynor sings), but it sounds wonderful.

CLASSIC QUOTE
Nellie, singing 'A Cock-eyed Optimist': 'I hear that the human race / is falling on its face / And hasn't very far to go.'

SCENE STEALER
Frustrated by the lack of available women on the island where they are stationed, US Navy sailors, led by the irrepressible Luther Billis, bemoan their lot in song. Cue a fun, beachside rendition of 'There is Nothing Like a Dame'.

BEHIND THE SCENES
Acting in his capacity as executive producer, Oscar Hammerstein called for an expensive reshoot of the scene in which Mitzi Gaynor sings 'I'm Gonna Wash That Man Right Out of My Hair', convinced that it wasn't as good as the stage version. Logan clashed with Hammerstein, but eventually relented and later said of the lyricist's decision: 'He was right.'

HOLDING THE BATON
Composer Richard Rodgers had already enjoyed a hit Broadway career with Lorenz Hart before collaborating in 1943 with lyricist Oscar Hammerstein II (whose writing partners had included Jerome Kern and George Gershwin) on the stage show *Oklahoma!* The success of that show began a run of blockbuster productions on Broadway, a successful track record that only Andrew Lloyd Webber has ever neared equalling. Rodgers and Hammerstein were also able to maintain this popularity and reputation for quality in their movie adaptations. With films such as *Oklahoma!* (1955), *Carousel* (1956) and *The King and I* (1956) doing huge box office, their partnership became a byword for lavish, expensive musicals, often filmed outside the confines of the studio. Their most popular movie in Britain, *The Sound of Music* (1965) – credited with helping save its studio 20th Century Fox from ruin – was also their last collaboration: Hammerstein died soon after its release.

OSCARS
3 nominations, **1 winner**

Cinematography (Color): Leon Shamroy
Music (Scoring of a Musical Picture): Alfred Newman, Ken Darby
Sound: Fred Hynes

WHAT WON THAT YEAR?
Best Motion Picture: *Gigi*
Directing: Vincente Minnelli *Gigi*
Actor: David Niven *Separate Tables*
Actress: Susan Hayward *I Want To Live!*

BAFTAS

WHAT WON THAT YEAR?
Film/British Film: *Room at the Top*
British Actor: Trevor Howard *The Key*
Foreign Actor: Sidney Poitier *The Defiant Ones*
British Actress: Irene Worth *Orders to Kill*
Foreign Actress: Simone Signoret *Room at the Top*

Opposite *The South Pacific Officer's Club*
This page *It's in his kiss: Lt Joseph (John Kerr)
sweeps Liat (France Nuyen) off her feet*

14

Dir: Steven SPIELBERG / USA
Released in Britain: 1975
Running Time: 125 minutes
Colour: Technicolor
Estimated Attendance: 16.2 million

Out of the blue it came, as lean and mean as a Great White, sinking its fangs into box-office records, and inventing the modern blockbuster. Beside this witty, wicked breakthrough hit from some kid called Spielberg, most other Hollywood thrillers are just plankton.

JAWS

Director **Steven Spielberg**
Producers **Richard D. Zanuck, David Brown**
Screenplay/Story **Peter Benchley, Carl Gottlieb,**
    Howard Sackler, John Milius
Director of Photography **Bill Butler**
Editor **Verna Fields**
Production Designer **Joe Alves**
Music **John Williams**

Chief Martin Brody • Roy Scheider
Captain Quint • Robert Shaw
Matt Hooper • Richard Dreyfuss
Ellen Brody • Lorraine Gary
Mayor Larry Vaughn • Murray Hamilton
Ben Meadows, The Editor • Carl Gottlieb
Lenny Hendricks • Jeffrey C. Kramer
Chrissie, First Victim • Susan Backlinie
Tom Cassidy • Jonathan Filley
Estuary Victim • Ted Grossman
Michael Brody • Chris Rebello
Sean Brody • Jay Mello
Mrs Kintner • Lee Fierro
Alex Kintner • Jeffrey Voorhees

THE STORY

Convinced that the remains of a girl found on the shore indicate a shark attack, Martin Brody – chief of police in the Long Island resort of Amity – decides to close the beaches. Pressured by prominent citizens including Mayor Vaughn, who argue that the victim might have been mangled by a boat and point out the disastrous consequences of a shark scare on the tourist trade (the Fourth of July influx is imminent), Brody reluctantly agrees to post guards and warning signs instead. The shark kills a small boy and, with the beaches now closed, local sportsmen set out on a shark hunt. They return triumphant, but Brody is assured by Hooper, an oceanographic expert, that the dead shark is not the Great White that perpetrated the attacks.

The distraught town council agrees to pay the $10,000 demanded by Quint, an experienced shark-killer, to do the job for them. Despite Brody's pathological fear of the sea – increased when he and Hooper find the deserted wreck of a fishing boat attacked by the shark – he forces himself on the sneering Quint as an assistant along with Hooper. After a prolonged chase in which the shark seems to have become the hunter, Hooper is lost when he goes over the side in a diving cage to try a tranquillising dart; and Quint, rejecting any advice in his obsessive vendetta (he was one of the few survivors when his ship was torpedoed in shark-infested waters after delivering the Hiroshima bomb), is killed when the shark succeeds in demolishing the boat. Clinging despairingly to the wreckage, Brody contrives to blow the shark to bits with a compressed oxygen tank from Hooper's diving equipment. Hooper reappears unharmed, and Brody exultantly discovers that he has lost his fear of the sea.

WHAT THEY SAID THEN …

Jaws is a perfectly acceptable, and sometimes genuinely exciting, entry in the disaster stakes. The Ibsenish first act, in which the police chief finds himself an enemy of the people because his action threatens prosperity and his inaction threatens security, would have been much more effective had a brilliant opening

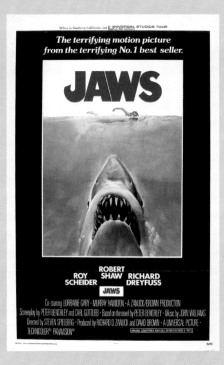

sequence (a solitary moonlit bathe by the first victim) not made the shark's presence so unequivocally evident that the dignitaries who try to argue otherwise are merely uninteresting straw dummies.

Nevertheless the plot is much improved by ruthless trimming of Peter Benchley's original novel. The resulting streamlining allows Spielberg to make some effective gestures towards setting the teeth on edge (quite literally as Quint, making his first appearance at a turbulent council meeting, imposes silence by suddenly scraping his fingernails down a blackboard). The sense of edgy unease is beautifully transmitted in a series of tiny, throwaway moments like the one on the crowded beach where Brody is politely listening to an importuning citizen but really trying to see past his obstructing body for any signs of alarm at the water's edge (and we suddenly realise we haven't heard a word the speaker is saying either); or when, just as a lookout gives the all-clear for swimmers, we seem to catch a momentary glimpse of a dark shadow he has missed.

Once the trio of shark-hunters head out to sea in their boat (where they remain for the rest of the film), *Jaws* finds itself on firmer ground with a brisk narrative that neatly blends documentary (the fascinating details of equipment, skills and mystique required for a shark-killer) and fiction (the exciting duel with a monster whose size and cunning gradually inflate in the mind) with a just measure of unpretentious psychological insight (initially hostile, the trio are gradually drawn together, but only by the euphoria of their communal effort).

This page In the swim: the shark claims its first victim

'You're gonna need
a bigger boat.'

OSCARS
4 nominations, **3 winners**

Best Picture
Film Editing: Verna Fields
Music (Original Score): John Williams
Sound

WHAT WON THAT YEAR?
Best Picture: *One Flew over the Cuckoo's Nest*
Directing: Milos Forman *One Flew over the Cuckoo's Nest*
Actor: Jack Nicholson *One Flew over the Cuckoo's Nest*
Actress: Louise Fletcher *One Flew over the Cuckoo's Nest*

BAFTAS
7 nominations, **1 winner**

Film
Direction: Steven Spielberg
Screenplay: Peter Benchley, Carl Gottlieb
Film Editing: Verna Fields
Sound Track: John R. Carter, Robert Hoyt
Actor: Richard Dreyfuss
Anthony Asquith Award for Original Film Music:
  John Williams (also for *The Towering Inferno*)

WHAT WON THAT YEAR?
Film: *Alice Doesn't Live Here Anymore*
Direction: Stanley Kubrick *Barry Lyndon*
Actor: Al Pacino *The Godfather Part II/Dog Day Afternoon*
Actress: Ellen Burstyn *Alice Doesn't Live Here Anymore*

Here, with the battleground boldly staked out by the marker buoys trailing behind the harpooned shark, but suddenly and alarmingly abandoned as strategically placed shots suggest a guerrilla warfare in which the shark steals up to reconnoitre the enemy or retreats to contemplate attack on the placidly vulnerable boat isolated in the middle of nowhere, Spielberg almost manages to invest the shark – like the nightmarish petrol-tanker in his earlier *Duel* (1971) – with the quality of a Jungian archetype. His good work, unfortunately, is partially undone by a script straining to become Herman Melville and ending the portentous profundities delivered by Robert Shaw's Quint (more Old Man of the Sea than Captain Ahab) by projecting him, not unexpectedly, into the jaws of his own unconvincing, mechanical Moby Dick.

WHAT THEY SAY NOW ...

As the first movie ever to reach the $100 million mark at the US box office, *Jaws* is routinely cited as the monster hit which ushered in the era of the high-concept summer blockbuster. But not even the grumpiest critic of the Hollywood money-making machine would deny that Spielberg's masterpiece earned this status on pure technical merit; the film remains such a watertight thrill ride it even manages to get away with that pesky mechanical shark on viewing after viewing.

Spielberg understood that establishing the reality of the broader scenario was key to making it work, and Amity Island is, from top to bottom, the most real-feeling, lived-in place in any of his pictures. With the sole exception of Robert Shaw's oversalted sea dog Quint, the characters here

Above left The making of a claustrophobic blockbuster ***Above*** A grizzled Robert Shaw as Quint ***Opposite left*** Young buck Steven Spielberg listens in on the action ***Opposite right*** Roy Scheider as Chief Brody

seem to breathe Earth air, not movie air; the witty economy of the script is matched only by the improvised comic and dramatic grace notes Spielberg accommodates both in the Brody household and on the boat. A lesser director would have made a hateful corporate stooge out of Murray Hamilton's character, instead of the anxious, vacillating master of ceremonies we actually get; and look how skilfully Roy Scheider and Lorraine Gary suggest latent fault-lines in their marriage with just the odd loaded glance. Given the movie's notoriously chaotic genesis, it's remarkable how controlled and meticulous *Jaws* has always seemed in its portrait of a community imperilled – not just the trailblazing prototype for your high-stakes event movie, but the absolute model for how to do it right.

CLASSIC QUOTE

Brody: 'You're gonna need a bigger boat.'

SCENE STEALER

The opening: Chrissie (Susan Backlinie) dives out to sea and faces a hideous, thrashing ordeal as the shark's first course. Still one of the most brilliantly unnerving scene-setting overtures in modern cinema.

BEHIND THE SCENES

Robert Shaw – Spielberg's third choice for Captain Quint, after Lee Marvin and Sterling Hayden – wrote Quint's speech about the fate of the USS Indianapolis himself, with uncredited help from screenplay writers Howard Sackler and John Milius.

The scene where Hooper finds Ben Gardner's head was shot and added in post-production when Spielberg decided the film needed one more big shock. On his next projects Spielberg switched editors, reportedly aggrieved that Oscar-winning veteran Verna Fields received so much insider credit for *Jaws*'s success.

IN THE CHAIR

Only a handful of times in his subsequent career has Spielberg come close to matching the all-round tautness and resonance of *Jaws*. *Raiders of the Lost Ark* (1981) achieved the former but only the former, *E.T. The Extra-Terrestrial* (1982) a good deal more of the latter. He would soon abandon the primal themes of these early films in favour of weighty liberal Oscar bids, but not even the garlanded *Schindler's List* (1993) completely exorcised a nagging preachiness and sentimentality in his output. Returns to genre material, notably the back-to-back sci-fi diptych *A.I.: Artificial Intelligence* (2001) and *Minority Report* (2002), have been terrific ideas compromised by treacly endings.

15

Dir: Steven SPIELBERG / USA
Released in Britain: 1993
Running Time: 127 minutes
Colour: Deluxe
Estimated Attendance: 16.17 million

Modern audiences are increasingly blasé about the mirages conjured up on screen by computer-generated imagery; awe has become almost extinct. But the technology was still in its infancy in 1993, when Steven Spielberg brought horror and wonderment to the blockbuster movie, as he had done nearly two decades earlier with *Jaws* (1975).

JURASSIC PARK

Director **Steven Spielberg**
Producer **Kathleen Kennedy, Gerald R. Molen**
Screenplay/Story **Michael Crichton, David Koepp, Malia Scotch Marmo**, adapted from the novel by Michael Crichton
Director of Photography **Dean Cundey**
Editor **Michael Kahn**
Production Designer **Rick Carter**
Music **John Williams**

Dr Ellie Sattler • Laura Dern
John Hammond • Richard Attenborough
Dr Alan Grant • Sam Neill
Ian Malcolm • Jeff Goldblum
Ray Arnold • Samuel L. Jackson
Robert Muldoon • Bob Peck
Donald Gennaro • Martin Ferrero
Dr Wu • B.D. Wong
Tim • Joseph Mazzello
Lex • Ariana Richards
Dennis Nedry • Wayne Knight
Harding • Jerry Molen
Rostagno • Miguel Sandoval
Dodgson • Cameron Thor

THE STORY

When one of his workers is killed, leisure tycoon John Hammond is advised by lawyer Donald Gennaro to have outside experts survey and endorse his latest venture, Jurassic Park. Palaeontologist Alan Grant, palaeobotanist Ellie Sattler and chaos theoretician Ian Malcolm are taken to an island off the coast of Costa Rica and given a tour of facilities where dinosaurs have been genetically engineered. With Hammond's grandchildren Tim and Alexis, the team are sent on an automated 'ride' through areas in which various species of dinosaur are penned. It soon becomes apparent that, beyond the successful re-creation of the dinosaurs, the park is rife with design flaws, with the animals stubbornly refusing to conform to Hammond's plans.

As a storm hits, Dennis Nedry, who designed and operates the park's computer systems, shuts down the security programmes so that he can steal a selection of dinosaur embryos he intends to sell to a rival corporation. The ride breaks down and Gennaro is eaten by a tyrannosaurus rex which tries to get at the children, who are rescued by Alan while Ian is wounded distracting the beast. Nedry, lost in the storm, is blinded and killed by a venom-spitting dilophosaurus while Hammond is forced to shut down the power to get around blocks Nedry has integrated into the control systems.

Ellie, accompanied by Robert Muldoon, a game warden who has always distrusted dinosaurs, ventures out to reactivate the power from a generator, while Alan and the children make their way back to the control centre. Muldoon is killed by velociraptors; Ellie turns the power on just as Tim is clambering over an electric fence. Alan manages to save Tim, but the survivors discover that the velociraptors have breached the control centre. Alan, Ellie and the children are menaced by the velociraptors, who are only defeated when the tyrannosaurus intervenes and kills the smaller beasts. The survivors flee the island.

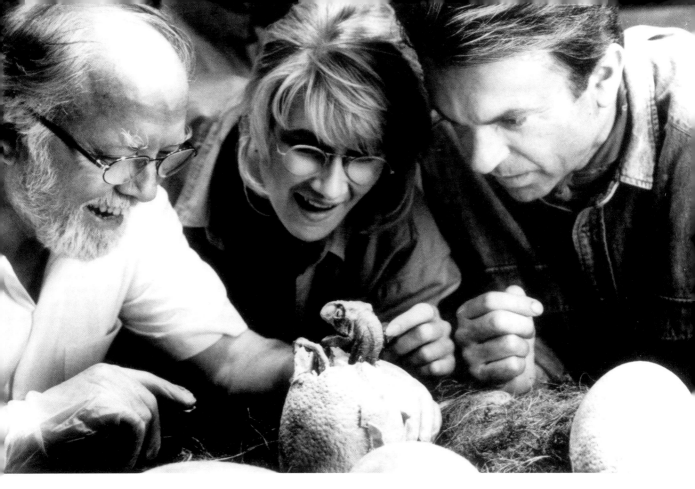

WHAT THEY SAID THEN ...

The narrative motor of *Jurassic Park* is the overlap of irreconcilable agendas: the creation and ultimate failure of the theme park requires the input of caring palaeontologists, wide-eyed children, Frankensteinian genetic engineers, chaos doomsayers, 'bloodsucking lawyers', ferocious predators and a fatherly multimillionaire. Similarly conflicted and contrasting motives power the conversion of Michael Crichton's bestselling novel into an 'event' movie by Steven Spielberg. The stresses between the plot and the circumstances of its depiction are what make this blockbuster at once an all-but-infallible entertainment and a demonstration of its character Ian Malcolm's theory that things go wrong exponentially.

The film will be seen by millions for its effects alone, and the combination of puppetwork and animation certainly goes beyond the previous high water marks of Willis H. O'Brien's *King Kong* (1933) or Ray Harryhausen's *The Valley of Gwangi* (1969). However, just as a group of diverse experts under the direction of a showman are responsible for the genetic engineering here, lone visionaries like O'Brien and Harryhausen have been replaced by teams of multiskilled employees whose collective achievement lacks the individual heart of Kong.

The most significant change between Crichton's novel and Spielberg's film is the transformation of John Hammond from an unsympathetic capitalist into a cuddly cod-Scots visionary played by Attenborough (irresistibly recalling Dr Dolittle). While the novel is an Awful Warning with a 'gosh-wow-dinosaurs!' undercurrent, the film is quite properly in love with these beasties. Spielberg

Above It's a ... dinosaur: John Hammond (Richard Attenborough), Ellie (Laura Dern) and Alan (Sam Neill) oversee an unusual birth
Below Face to face with a Tyrannosaurus Rex

OSCARS
3 nominations, **3 winners**

Sound
Sound Effects Editing: Gary Rydstrom, Richard Hymns
Visual Effects

WHAT WON THAT YEAR?
Best Picture: *Schindler's List*
Directing: Steven Spielberg *Schindler's List*
Actor in a Leading Role: Tom Hanks *Philadelphia*
Actress in a Leading Role: Holly Hunter *The Piano*

BAFTAS
2 nominations, **1 winner**

Sound
Special Effects

WHAT WON THAT YEAR?
Film: *Schindler's List*
British Film: *Shadowlands*
Direction: Steven Spielberg *Schindler's List*
Actor: Anthony Hopkins *The Remains of the Day*
Actress: Holly Hunter *The Piano*

Left above *A safari with a difference, as a dinosaur rears up on its hind legs*

takes his prehistoric animals seriously, employing advisers to ensure that the dinosaurs act more like real ones than the *Jaws* shark did a real Great White.

Many annoying things about the film probably constitute survival traits in the international marketplace. The softening of the novel so that only secondary characters are killed; the switch from nightmare horror to clean chase; the downplaying of any critique of entertainment capitalism and the pointless science; the inclusion of Laura Dern in shorts – all these factors compromise the film as drama but widen its appeal.

Like Jurassic Park, *Jurassic Park* is ultimately unable to safely contain its attractions, but the dinosaurs are magnificent: the tyrannosaurus attack during a night storm and the game of velociraptor hide-and-seek must stand as definitive. However, the most deeply felt and emotionally complex shot of the film – a pan from a rack of now-unsaleable dinosaur merchandise to the dejected Hammond – raises issues that the media monolith of a 1990s studio blockbuster could never address.

WHAT THEY SAY NOW ...

After a mixed run in the late 1980s and early 1990s, Steven Spielberg here made a triumphant return to the blockbuster event movie he himself pioneered with *Jaws*. Indeed *Jurassic Park* was, in many respects, a self-conscious retread of the earlier picture's monster-movie formula. As with that 1975 film, this was based on a hugely successful novel (by Michael Crichton) and featured scenes of consummately crafted suspense involving defenceless humans stalked by toothy carnivores. The key difference was that whereas *Jaws* depended for much of its impact on not seeing the shark, here Spielberg made use of advances in computer-generated imagery (CGI) and animatronics to show, in glorious detail, long-extinct dinosaurs brought to life. The photo-real CG herbivores we see in the film's early moments were as much a cause of awe for audiences as for the movie's amazed characters.

In the same year that Spielberg made his dinosaur film, he completed his harrowing Holocaust drama *Schindler's List*. The serious and darkened sensibility of that movie runs through his subsequent output, too, even *Jurassic Park*'s 1997 sequel *The Lost World*. *Jurassic Park* marks a return to the old-style 'fairground' thrills of *Jaws* but only to bid them farewell.

CLASSIC QUOTE

Alan Grant: 'We're the ones that are extinct now.'

SCENE STEALER

A storm has cut the power to the island which has been stocked with genetically engineered dinosaurs by tycoon John Hammond. Hammond's grandchildren and palaeontologist Alan Grant are stranded in their electrically controlled car. The ground shakes – faintly at first, then more vigorously – and appearing before the immobilised vehicle is a huge, fanged tyrannosaurus rex.

Dir: Peter JACKSON / USA, New Zealand
Released in Britain: 2001
Running Time: 178 minutes
Colour: Deluxe
Estimated Attendance: 15.98 million

Left *The New Zealand landscape, one of the many stars of* The Lord of the Rings

Everyone from John Boorman to the Beatles had toyed with the idea of filming J. R. R. Tolkien's enduring adventure. But following an underwhelming 1978 animated version, it was decreed that a low-budget horror director should be the one to risk the wrath of generations of fans.

THE LORD OF THE RINGS: THE FELLOWSHIP OF THE RING

Director **Peter Jackson**
Producers **Barry Osborne, Peter Jackson, Fran Walsh, Tim Sanders**
Screenplay/Story **Fran Walsh, Philippa Boyens, Peter Jackson**, adapted from the novel by J. R. R. Tolkien
Director of Photography **Andrew Lesnie**
Editor **John Gilbert**
Production Designer **Grant Major**
Music **Howard Shore**

Frodo Baggins • Elijah Wood
Gandalf • Ian McKellen
Arwen • Liv Tyler
Aragorn, 'Strider' • Viggo Mortensen
Samwise 'Sam' Gamgee • Sean Astin
Galadriel • Cate Blanchett
Gimli • John Rhys-Davies
Peregrin Took, 'Pippin' • Billy Boyd
Meriadoc Brandybuck, 'Merry' • Dominic Monaghan
Legolas • Orlando Bloom
Saruman • Christopher Lee
Elrond • Hugo Weaving
Boromir • Sean Bean
Bilbo Baggins • Ian Holm
Gollum • Andy Serkis
Celeborn • Marton Csokas
Haldir • Craig Parker
Lurtz • Lawrence Makoare
Voice of the Ring • Alan Howard
Everard Proudfoot • Noel Appleby

THE STORY

A village in the Shire, Middle-earth. After his uncle Bilbo vanishes, hobbit Frodo Baggins inherits a magic ring. The wizard Gandalf determines that this is the One Ring, forged centuries ago by Sauron, the Dark Lord of Mordor, and used to rule most of Middle-earth. Sauron now knows where the ring is and has sent his Black Riders after it; if he recovers it, the Free People of Middle-earth (elves, dwarves and men, along with hobbits) are doomed.

Gandalf entrusts Frodo to carry the ring out of the Shire to the village of Bree, where he and his three hobbit companions are attacked by the Black Riders but sheltered by a human named Strider. Strider leads the group onward; on a nearby hilltop they are again attacked by the Riders. Drawn by the power of the ring, Frodo puts it on and is grievously wounded by one of the Riders. Strider, also known as Aragorn, enlists the aid of Arwen, an elvish woman (and his betrothed) who carries the injured Frodo to the elvish retreat of Rivendell. There he is reunited with Bilbo and Gandalf, who meanwhile has escaped the clutches of the wizard Saruman, who has come under Sauron's power.

At a conference, it is decided that the ring must be carried into the land of Mordor and thrown into the Cracks of Doom where it was forged. Frodo volunteers for this desperate mission and is sent on his way with a fellowship of eight others: hobbits Sam, Merry and Pippin; Legolas the elf; Gimli the dwarf; the men Aragorn and Boromir; and Gandalf. The fellowship travels under the Misty Mountains through the Mines of Moria where it is beset by armies of Sauron's orcs. Gandalf is dragged into a chasm in a battle with the Balrog, an ancient evil spirit.

The others escape and make it to the enchanted wood of Lórien, ruled by the elvish queen Galadriel. From there they travel south by boat on the Great River. Boromir wants the ring to help his own people fight Sauron and tries to take it from Frodo. Frodo slips on the ring and escapes towards Mordor, followed by Sam. Merry and Pippin are seized by orcs; the repentant Boromir dies trying to save them. Aragorn, Legolas and Gimli decide to follow the orcs, allowing Frodo and Sam – and the ring – to travel eastward on their own.

WHAT THEY SAY ...

Perhaps the secret ingredient in Peter Jackson's extraordinary film interpretation of the first volume of J. R. R. Tolkien's *The Lord of the Rings* is New Zealand itself. The director's temperate homeland, much of it still wild and little affected by industrial development, may be the best available substitute for the pre-modern landscapes of northern Europe so compellingly imagined in Tolkien's epic. By dragging his enormous assemblage of actors and technical staff to this remote

Above left The Black Riders are washed away at the borders of Rivendell *Above right* Middle Earth mapped out *This page* Ring, ring: Frodo Baggins (Elijah Wood) reaches out *Opposite* Small but perfectly formed: Gimli (John Rhys-Davies) wields the axe

"Nobody tosses a dwarf."

location for an eighteen-month shoot, Jackson transformed his film-making process into a real-life quest narrative, one nearly as foolhardy as Frodo Baggins's journey into Mordor.

For all its models and computer animation – the most massive of the special-effects sequences is surely the battle in the Great Hall of Moria, a vaulted grand-opera set teeming with orcs – *The Lord of the Rings The Fellowship of the Ring* has an untamed human roughness, a feeling of damp ground and dirty clothing that it's difficult to imagine Spielberg or Lucas replicating at any price. When Frodo (played by the cherubic Elijah Wood, who darkens and seems to age appreciably as the story progresses) opens his hand to display the One Ring of Power, we see that his fingernails are filthy, the whorls of his palm caked with grime.

If Wood's Frodo is the Alice in this Wonderland, and his coming of age is inescapably the central focus, Jackson's adroitly chosen cast provides other pleasures. As the wizard Gandalf, who is both a kindly old geezer and a semi-angelic power, Ian McKellen serves to connect the film's two narrative spheres: the great mythopoetic narrative of Sauron and the ring on one hand and the rustic comedy of the domestic-minded hobbits confronting a wider world on the other. Jackson even locates a tragic hero whom Tolkien only

half-notices in the conflicted figure of Boromir, played by Sean Bean as a man struggling against the corrosive power of the ring. Bean's performance nearly overshadows that of Viggo Mortensen, who plays the saga's human hero, Aragorn, as a brooding Hamlet type.

Jackson and his co-writers, Fran Walsh and Philippa Boyens, have significantly reordered and reshaped Tolkien's narrative, which widens its focus and quickens its pace gradually, requiring a hundred pages to get the hobbits out of the Shire. But they have tremendous respect for the linguistic and mythic density of Tolkien's creation. (Tyler and Mortensen even play portions of two scenes in Quenya, the Finnish-like language of the High Elves.) In subsequent instalments of the trilogy, it became clear just how much of Tolkien's mournful, elegiac tone Jackson captured. With this first film, and the trilogy as a whole, the best-loved fantasy novel of our age has been translated into a commanding screen adventure, one with a sense of human terror and danger and grit under its nails, one that makes Harry Potter and Luke Skywalker look like the feeble wraiths they are.

CLASSIC QUOTE
Gimli: 'Nobody tosses a dwarf.'

OSCARS

13 nominations, **4 winners**

Best Picture
Directing: Peter Jackson
Actor In A Supporting Role: Ian McKellen
Art Direction: Grant Major, Dan Hennah
Cinematography: Andrew Lesnie
Costume Design: Ngila Dickson, Richard Taylor
Film Editing: John Gilbert
Makeup: Peter Owen, Richard Taylor
Music (Original Score): Howard Shore
Music (Original Song): 'May It Be', Music and Lyric by Enya,
   Nicky Ryan, Roma Ryan
Sound
Visual Effects
Writing (Adapted Screenplay): Fran Walsh, Philippa Boyens, Peter Jackson

WHAT WON THAT YEAR?
Best Picture: *A Beautiful Mind*
Directing: Ron Howard *A Beautiful Mind*
Actor in a Leading Role: Denzel Washington *Training Day*
Actress in a Leading Role: Halle Berry *Monster's Ball*

BAFTAS

12 nominations, **4 winners**

Film
Direction: Peter Jackson
Adapted Screenplay: Fran Walsh, Philippa Boyens, Peter Jackson
Actor: Ian McKellen
Music: Howard Shore
Cinematography: Andrew Lesnie
Production Design: Grant Major
Costume Design: Ngila Dickson, Richard Taylor
Editing: John Gilbert
Sound
Special Visual Effects
Make Up and Hair: Peter Owen, Peter King, Richard Taylor

WHAT WON THAT YEAR?
Actor: Russell Crowe *A Beautiful Mind*
Actress: Judi Dench *Iris*

Above *Beware the Balrog*

SCENE STEALER

Despite the stunning shots of Peter Jackson's native New Zealand, the film's finest scene takes place entirely underground, in the Mines of Moria, a once-opulent dwarf dwelling now over-run with orcs. Reluctantly passing through this labyrinth, whose huge chambers are occasionally illuminated by Gandalf's stave, the fellowship are pursued by swarms of orcs, and, in the film's most thrilling moment, Gandalf does battle with an ancient, many tentacled creature called the Balrog on a narrow stone causeway that is the only exit. A finely crafted cliffhanger moment that was unresolved until the release of the second *Lord of the Rings* instalment a year later.

BEHIND THE SCENES

All three films in the *Lord of the Rings* saga were shot back-to-back over a mammoth fifteen-month schedule. Some 350 sets were constructed, and as many as seven different units were filming on a single day. To save time during the production Jackson cycled between different sets in the Wellington studio.

HOLDING THE BATON

Howard Shore was rightly acclaimed for his music for the *Lord of the Rings* trilogy, a rich, strings-heavy score whose many musical references included Wagner, New Age mood pieces and Celtic folk. It was a typically astute work from this classically trained former rock musician, whose eclectic CV includes the eerie, atmospheric soundtracks to fellow Canadian David Cronenberg's movies, the emotive, operatic score to *The Silence of the Lambs* (1991) and the 1950 B-movie stylings of his work for *Ed Wood* (1994). Unusually for a Hollywood music composer, Shore orchestrates his own work – most of his contemporaries delegate this time-consuming job – and pays meticulous attention to the tonal detail of his soundtracks. Conceiving of the score for all three films as a two-and-a-half hour 'opera', Shore's score for *The Fellowship of a Ring* won him an Oscar.

Dir: Herbert WILCOX
Released in Britain: 1947
Running Time: 120 minutes
Black and white
Estimated Attendance: 15.9 million

Left 'Edward meet Edward Jr!' Catherine (Anna Neagle) introduces Michael Wilding to the son he didn't know he had (Michael Madwin)

The London settings of Herbert Wilcox's romantic dramas of the 1940s – all starring Anna Neagle – suggested a cinematic Monopoly board, taking in Park Lane, Piccadilly, Grosvenor Square. It was on to Curzon Street for the second film in this unofficial series, which became the biggest homegrown hit of 1947.

THE COURTNEYS OF CURZON STREET

Director/Producer **Herbert Wilcox**
Screenplay/Story **Nicholas Phipps**, adapted from a story by Florence Tranter
Director of Photography **Max Greene**
Editors **Flora Newton, Vera Campbell**
Art Director **William C. Andrews**
Music **Anthony Collins**

Catherine O'Halloran • Anna Neagle
Sir Edward Courtney • Michael Wilding
Cynthia • Daphne Slater
Teddy Courtney • Jack Watling
Edward Courtney Jr • Michael Medwin
Sir Edward Courtney Sr • G. H. Mulcaster
Valerie • Coral Browne
Lady Courtney • Gladys Young
Mary Courtney • Helen Cherry
Maud, Stage Dresser • Thora Hird
Mr R • Edward Rigby
Colonel Gascoyne • Bernard Lee
Sir Frank Murchison • Percy Walsh
Algie Longworth • Max Kirby
Singer • Gene Crowley
Phipps • Nicholas Phipps
Pam • Terry Randall
Theatre Manager • Kenneth Warrington
Irish Priest • James Kavanagh

THE STORY

In 1900, Sir Edward Courtney, a baronet's son, falls in love with and marries his mother's Irish maid, Catherine O'Hallaran, against the advice of his mother. Later ostracised by the Victorians, who consider her to be beneath them, Catherine leaves him so that he and the 'Regiment' should not be parted. Unbeknown to him she bears him a son while he is endeavouring to forget in India. Catherine goes on to become a singer and dancer to enable their child to attend Sir Edward's old school. Suddenly, at an entertainment for troops in the 1914–18 war, Catherine and Sir Edward meet again and life is resumed happily and devotedly. Their grandson in his turn marries a factory worker in 1944, in a mirror-image of Catherine and Sir Edward's class-crossing relationship.

WHAT THEY SAID THEN …

Here are all the ingredients for a popular money-making film. It may be a pot-boiler, but it is a pleasant and, for many, a nostalgic one where the audience can laugh, cry, suffer and hum the well-known songs of three wars. It is far from being a brilliant film and mistakes are numerous. Though British, the dignity of Curzon Street is Hollywoodised, and it is rare, in 1945, that people in their sixties look as if they have one foot in the grave. But Michael Wilding is at his best, and Anna Neagle, with her usual charm, proves that she knows all the tricks of the trade. Definitely a 'Cavalcade' of incident and sentiment.

WHAT THEY SAY NOW …

Released in the US under the less parochial title *The Courtney Affair*, this is the second most popular of the Wilcox–Neagle–Wilding–Phipps romantic dramas, but remains the least-loved among critics. What does it lack that *Spring in Park Lane* (1948) and *Piccadilly Incident* (1946) possess? Deftness, grace, gentle wit. But a more pertinent question might be: what off-putting element does it possess that serves to undermine enjoyment? To which the

OSCARS

WHAT WON THAT YEAR?
Actor: Ronald Colman *A Double Life*
Actress: Loretta Young *The Farmer's Daughter*
Directing: Elia Kazan *Gentleman's Agreement*
Best Motion Picture: *Gentleman's Agreement*

BAFTAS

WHAT WON THAT YEAR?
Film: *The Best Years of Our Lives*

This page *Anna Neagle is carried aloft in another blockbuster performance, this time as all singing and dancing Irish girl Catherine O'Halloran*

only reasonable answer could be: Anna Neagle's Irish accent, which is almost as lethal to the ears as Dick Van Dyke Cockney.

But it would be unfair to blame the low opinion of *The Courtneys of Curzon Street* solely on Anna Neagle's vocal chords. There is something patronising in the contrived machinations of the plot that had been smoothed out by the time of *Spring in Park Lane*. Perhaps it is merely the fact that the film objects to the values of the upper-class characters, who snipe and sneer at Neagle's poor-but-jolly maid, while displaying palpable reverence for their wealth, clothes and accoutrements. Some interest lies in the supporting cast, with early appearances by Coral Browne and Thora Hird.

SCENE STEALER

The German cinematographer Max Greene (his name Anglicised from the original Mutz Greenbaum) had shot films in his native country since 1916, before coming to England in the early 1930s. A regular collaborator with Herbert Wilcox, it is Greene's crisp camerawork that captures subtly the social demarcations in the best scene in *The Courtneys of Curzon Street*, when Catherine overhears Sir Edward's friends and

relatives making disparaging remarks about her during a private function attended by Queen Victoria. From that moment we know that, no matter how strong their love is, it will be thwarted, at least temporarily, by class and custom.

IN THE LEAD

The partnership of Anna Neagle and Michael Wilding proved magnetic to 1940s audiences; indeed, they have two other titles – *Spring in Park Lane* (at number 5) and *Piccadilly Incident* (number 43) – in the Ultimate Film list, both directed by Herbert Wilcox and scripted by Nicholas Phipps. That quartet could do little wrong throughout the decade, though Wilding's name has not perhaps endured in the way that Neagle's has, except in his most taxing role as Elizabeth Taylor's second husband. Wilding had started out as an extra in the 1930s before appearing in notable roles in *Secret Mission* and *In Which We Serve*, both in 1942. But it was his run of hits with Wilcox, Neagle and Phipps – ending with *Maytime in Mayfair* (1949) – that really established him. Thereafter, he worked twice with Hitchcock in *Under Capricorn* (1949) and *Stage Fright* (1950) before finding modest but fleeting success in Hollywood.

The glory years of the Bond movie, which lasted until Sean Connery bowed out for the first time in 1967, were in full swing when *Thunderball* opened. The most popular Bond escapade of all time is a genuine romp high on suspense, gadgetry, cool sets and outrageous implausibility.

Dir: Terence YOUNG / UK
Released in Britain: 1966
Running Time: 130 minutes
Colour: Technicolor
Estimated Attendance: 15.6 million

Director **Terence Young**
Producer **Kevin McClory**
Screenplay/Story **Richard Maibaum, John Hopkins**,
   adapted from the book by Ian Fleming
Director of Photography **Ted Moore**
Editor **Ernest Hosler**
Production Designer **Ken Adam**
Music **John Barry**

James Bond • Sean Connery
Dominique 'Domino' Derval • Claudine Auger
Emilio Largo • Adolfo Celi
Fiona Volpe • Luciana Paluzzi
Felix Leiter • Rik Van Nutter
'M' • Bernard Lee
Paula Kaplan • Martine Beswick
Count Lippe • Guy Doleman
Patricia • Mollie Peters
'Q' • Desmond Llewelyn
Miss Moneypenny • Lois Maxwell
Foreign Secretary • Roland Culver
Pinder • Earl Cameron
Angelo Palazzi/Major François Derval • Paul Stassino
Madame Boitier • Rose Alba
Vargas • Philip Locke
Ladislav Kutze • George Pravda
Janni • Michael Brennan
Group Captain Pritchard • Leonard Sachs
Air Vice-Marshal Sir John • Edward Underdown

THUNDERBALL

THE STORY

SPECTRE, the International Crime Syndicate, plans to hijack two atomic bombs from NATO, promising Whitehall not to wipe out two cities so long as a ransom of £100 million is paid. The signal for Whitehall's acceptance is that Big Ben should strike seven at six o'clock. The operations are begun at a health clinic near the NATO airfield, when Count Lippe tries to kill Agent 007, James Bond, on an exercising machine. Bond is rescued by a therapist, Patricia, and retaliates by stepping up the heat in Lippe's steam bath. Meanwhile Fiona, of SPECTRE, suborns Major Derval, of NATO, and has him murdered by a bandaged man at the clinic. The bandages cover the results of plastic surgery: SPECTRE man Palazzi has become his victim's double.

Palazzi now flies off with the bombs in a plane which sinks to the ocean floor. He is in turn murdered by SPECTRE executive Largo, who takes the bombs in a submarine to a secret underwater cave. Despatched to Nassau, Bond meets

Right *The winner takes it all: Bond (Sean Connery) faces up to Largo (Adolfo Celi) over a game of chemin de fer*

Derval's sister, Domino, who is living with Largo. After losing to Bond at chemin de fer, Largo invites him to Palmyra, his secluded palatial estate. Bond falls into Largo's steel-lidded, shark-infested swimming pool, but escapes.

He returns to his hotel to find Fiona in his bathtub. They make love, after which Fiona betrays him to Largo's men. Though shot in the leg, Bond makes a getaway under cover of a local carnival. Fiona follows the trail of blood to a crowded dance floor, where Bond dances with her before manoeuvring her into the path of a bullet meant for him. With the help of Domino, who is shocked to learn that Largo killed her brother, Bond manages to locate the bombs and eliminate Largo and his army of frogmen.

WHAT THEY SAID THEN ...

Thunderball is all gargantuan sets, paintbox blood, sexless blondes and gadgetry. There is absolutely nothing memorable about it. It is simply there for the moment, to be superficially enjoyed if you like that kind of thing, and if you can condone the vast cost of such a toyshop trifle.

What does it offer? More polish than usual, for one thing. Terence Young's direction is nothing if not taut, whisking the narrative along with the speed and precision of a jet plane, defying you to express boredom. To achieve this, he has wisely thrown away most of Bond's character detail, the drinks-and-cars expertise, and stripped Bond down to a kinky-looking Superman in red rubber, an outline Sean Connery fills admirably and with ease. The gadgets are splendid – hydrofoil, radioactive pill, underwater jet-harness, a health-clinic rack which threatens to rattle Bond's bones to pulp, a black-leather clad motorcyclist whose machine fires rockets and who turns out under her crash-helmet to be the delectably treacherous Luciana Paluzzi.

John Hopkins has been brought in on the screenplay to provide some insolent, amatory wit; the post-*Strangelove* sets are by Ken Adam; Ivan Tors has provided some eerily effective underwater sequences, including a long climactic battle which looks like Agincourt fought with submarines instead of horses. In other words the film is all of a piece, cunning, heartless, extravagant, shamelessly mid-1960s.

Above *Sean Connery displaying the physique that won him third place in the 1950 Mr Universe contest* **Below left** *The climatic underwater battle with SPECTRE agents* **Below right** *SPECTRE command centre: Largo and his henchmen plot world domination* **Overleaf** *Head to head: Largo versus 007*

OSCARS
1 nomination, **1 winner**

Special Visual Effects: John Stears

WHAT WON THAT YEAR?
Best Picture: *The Sound of Music*
Directing: Robert Wise *The Sound of Music*
Actor: Lee Marvin *Cat Ballou*
Actress: Julie Christie *Darling*

BAFTAS
1 nomination

British Art Direction (Colour): Ken Adam

WHAT WON THAT YEAR?
Film: *My Fair Lady*
British Film: *Ipcress File*
British Actor: Dirk Bogarde *Darling*
Foreign Actor: Lee Marvin *The Killers/Cat Ballou*
British Actress: Julie Christie *Darling*
Foreign Actress: Patricia Neal *In Harm's Way*

WHAT THEY SAY NOW ...

The fourth official screen outing for James Bond, *Thunderball* reveals a franchise in confident, rousing form. With a budget that was five times Bond's 1962 debut *Dr No* and exotic location filming in France and the Bahamas, the film provided the lavish spectacle we now take for granted from Bond movies. Director Terence Young arguably makes too much of the gizmos Q entrusts to Bond, but when the hardware includes a portable jet-pack, a Geiger-counter watch and a further outing for *Goldfinger*'s Aston Martin DB5, who's complaining? (Tellingly a range of *Thunderball*-related toys followed the film's release.)

With its opening scenes set in a health spa and a sultry villainess in the form of Fiona Volpe, there was also plenty of opportunity for characterful one-liners from Sean Connery's Bond. Although it never was used as the title track, the song 'Mr Kiss Kiss Bang Bang' was recorded for this film – and its suggestive double nod towards action-driven spectacle and sexual innuendo defined the series from here on.

A huge box-office success, the film's popularity arguably marks the point where audiences ceased to think of Bond as author Ian Fleming's creation, instead viewing the spy purely as a movie icon. In a curious presage of this, the story's roots were more cinematic than literary, with Fleming basing his 1961 novel on a screenplay he had collaborated on with producer Kevin McClory. The two subsequently fell out, prompting a dispute over copyright which, in 1983, saw elements of the plot reworked for Sean Connery's comeback in the 'unofficial' entry *Never Say Never Again*.

CLASSIC QUOTE

Bond: 'That looks like a woman's gun.'
Largo: 'Do you know a lot about guns, Mr Bond?'
Bond: 'No, but I know a little about women.'

BEHIND THE SCENES

The director of the film's underwater sequences was Ricou Browning, whose past credits included playing the gill-man in 1954's *Creature from the Black Lagoon*.

AT THE DRAWING BOARD

A veteran of seven Bond movies, production designer Ken Adam's outlandish sets were one of the franchise's key ingredients. The massive, sci-fi-like lairs he fashioned for Bond's villains – the SPECTRE HQ inside a volcano for *You Only Live Twice* (1967); the oil-rig base of the criminal mastermind of *Diamonds Are Forever* (1971); even the space-station abode of *Moonraker* (1979) – were memorable settings for the films' climaxes, and were usually demolished in a riot of gunfire and explosions.

The extent to which these designs have been parodied – in *Casino Royale*, for example, or the *Austin Powers* movies – testifies to their influence, but these pastiches also rather miss the point, since Adam's spirited style (a kind of pop-art futurism) was itself inclined towards self-parody.

As well as his Bond work, Adam also collaborated with Stanley Kubrick, on the immaculate period detail of *Barry Lyndon* (1975) and *Dr Strangelove* (1963), which boasted a Bond-like war-room set.

Dir: Peter JACKSON / USA, New
   Zealand, Germany
Released in Britain: 2003
Running Time: 201 minutes
Colour: Deluxe
Estimated Attendance: 15.22 million

Hopes were high for the first *Lord of the Rings* film.
For the third, they were through the roof. Delivering
the ring to Mount Doom would have been easier
than making a final chapter to surpass audiences'
expectations. So did Peter Jackson manage it?

THE LORD OF THE RINGS: THE RETURN OF THE KING

Director **Peter Jackson**
Producers **Barry Osborne, Peter Jackson, Fran Walsh**
Screenplay/Story **Fran Walsh, Philippa Boyens, Peter
   Jackson**, adapted from the novel by J. R. R. Tolkien
Director of Photography **Andrew Lesnie**
Editor **Jamie Selkirk**
Production Designer **Grant Major**
Music **Howard Shore**

Frodo Baggins • Elijah Wood
Gandalf • Ian McKellen
Arwen • Liv Tyler
Aragorn, 'Strider' • Viggo Mortensen
Samwise 'Sam' Gamgee • Sean Astin
Galadriel • Cate Blanchett
Gimli • John Rhys-Davies
Peregrin Took, 'Pippin' • Billy Boyd
Meriadoc Brandybuck, 'Merry' • Dominic Monaghan
Legolas • Orlando Bloom
King Theoden of Rohan • Bernard Hill
Elrond • Hugo Weaving
Eowyn, Theoden's Niece • Miranda Otto
Faramir • David Wenham
Eomer, Eowyn's Brother • Karl Urban
Denethor, Steward of Gondor • John Noble
Smeagol, 'Gollum' • Andy Serkis
Bilbo Baggins • Ian Holm
Boromir • Sean Bean
The Witch-king of Angmar/Gothmog • Lawrence Makoare

THE STORY

Two hobbits find a ring while fishing and are seized with an urge to own it; one, Smeagol, murders his friend and degenerates into the creature known as Gollum. Currently, Gollum is guiding Frodo Baggins, the ringbearer, and his friend Sam into the dark land of Mordor (where Frodo intends to destroy the ring) but he is plotting to have the hobbits killed. In the aftermath of the battle of Helm's Deep and the defeat of the wizard Saruman, the remainder of the Fellowship of the Ring – wizard Gandalf, human Aragorn (possible heir to the kingdom of Gondor), elf Legolas, hobbits Pippin and Merry, and dwarf Gimli – are allied with King Theoden of Rohan and his niece Eowyn. The orcish armies of Sauron continue to wage war against mankind, now turning their attack from Rohan to Gondor.

Gandalf insists that Theoden aid Gondor in the war and sets out with Pippin to persuade Denethor, steward of Gondor, to mount a strong defence to keep the forces of evil occupied so that Frodo can get to Mount Doom, the only place where the ring can be destroyed. Denethor, maddened by the death of his son Boromir, sends his less-loved son Faramir off in a futile battle. In Mordor, Gollum turns Frodo against Sam; the ringbearer tries to send his friend back, only to be led by Gollum into the lair of Shelob, a giant spider who paralyses him and wraps him in her web. Sam finds Frodo and, thinking him dead, takes the ring. Frodo later revives and is reunited with his friend, to press on to Mount Doom.

The hordes of Sauron attack Gondor and the forces of good resist. Eowyn and Merry defeat Sauron's most fearsome lieutenant and the orcish hordes are broken. In Mount Doom, Frodo hesitates to destroy the ring and Gollum makes a last grab for it, dying in a vain attempt to preserve it from destruction. With the

Opposite *Former horrormeister Peter Jackson gives his orders on set* **Above** *The duplicitous Gollum (Andy Serkis) faces the accusations of Sam (Sean Astin)* **Below** *Sam and sword facing Shelob*

ring melted, the power of Sauron is broken and an age of magic comes to an end. Aragorn is crowned king of Gondor and the hobbits return to the Shire. With the age of men upon Middle-earth, the elves depart in a boat, taking Frodo and his uncle Bilbo, once a ringbearer himself, with them.

WHAT THEY SAY ...

As if realising that the third part of his *Lord of the Rings* triptych will be concerned with such momentous business that tiny felicities are liable to get squeezed, Peter Jackson opens *The Return of the King* with its smallest denizen, a wriggling worm destined to be impaled on a fish-hook. It's almost a joke at the expense of the remembering-who-everybody-is phase of the picture that the cheery hobbit fisherman turns out not to be one of the four 'halflings' among the Fellowship but Andy Serkis as Smeagol, the previously unseen, pre-corruption incarnation of Gollum.

The major challenge here is that the meat of the story and the emotional involvement are with Frodo, Gollum and Sam while all other business – far more conventionally spectacular – is essentially a side-issue orchestrated to keep the villains busy while victory is won by throwing a trinket into molten lava. Whereas Tolkien had to interleave whole chapters on his various strands, Jackson can punctuate the central quest with snippet-like asides that keep us updated on what everyone is doing. Nevertheless, all the cutting back and forth does undermine the momentum and sometimes gives the picture the air of a soap opera.

There is a great deal of bitty material to get through, as all the characters have to do something to justify their presence: the elf Legolas, for instance, gets one sustained heroic sequence as he single-handedly boards and brings down a lumbering war-elephant before taking a well-earned bow. Jackson, confident in his effects team and post-production skills, puts on screen images that would

THE LORD OF THE RINGS
THE RETURN OF THE KING

have defeated any pre-CGI film-maker: vast chunks of masonry catapulted from the ramparts of a besieged city to squash dozens of photo-realistic orc goons, answered by equally devastating missiles from the attacking armies.

A point comes when it's hard to tell whether praise or criticism is due to Jackson for his adaptation or Tolkien for his original text, which presents at least as many traps as opportunities. The side of the novel that seems twee and arch is kept in check until the epilogue, when it is unleashed along with the complex, hard-to-dramatise bitter pill that the heroic triumph of the story which brings about 'the Age of Men' also means an end to the age of appealing magic that is the setting.

Also problematic is that all richness of character is on one side (Gollum, though ultimately corrupted, is not a minion of Sauron), and so we see how the forces of good are riven by personality conflicts, misjudgments and prejudices while the hordes of evil are monolithically rotten. History suggests that societies like Nazi Germany or Stalinist Russia collapse because it's impossible for self-seeking bad men to make common cause, but the armies of Mordor march as one.

Considered as a stand-alone film, *The Return of the King* plays least well of the three: it is three-quarters climax and one-quarter straggling epilogue. The reintroduction of Ian Holm's Bilbo comes well after business has satisfyingly been concluded and demands a shift of attention when audiences will be reaching for their coats. However, as the last act of a nine-hours-plus movie, it fits perfectly. The entire production must take its place in film history: it exposes the shortcomings of the initial *Star Wars* trilogy and stands as the most successful filming of a monumental bestseller since *Gone With The Wind* (1939). The sense of what's possible in mainstream cinema has been changed by Jackson's achievement in ways that will take decades to assimilate.

CLASSIC QUOTE

On the battlefield of Gondor, armour-clad Rohan princess Eowyn faces off the feared Lord of the Nazgûl.
Lord of the Nazgûl: 'Fool! No man can kill me. Die now!'
Eowyn, removing her helmet and felling the Nazgûl: 'I am no man!'

SCENE STEALER

Desperate to have the ring again, Gollum leads Frodo into the lair of giant spider Shelob, where the creature paralyses and binds the hobbit in her sticky web. Not for arachnophobes.

BEHIND THE SCENES

The Return of the King received its premiere in Wellington, and the trilogy was embraced by New Zealand authorities keen to exploit growing tourist interest in the films' locations. The customs desk at Wellington airport featured a check-in for orcs and the government even appointed a minister for *Lord of the Rings* to maximise movie-related revenue.

BEHIND THE PIXELS

Of the three films, *The Return of the King* made the most use of Gollum, a computer-generated creation integrated into the real-life action. In an unusual move, Andy Serkis 'performed' Gollum's movements against a green screen, and his interpretation of the role was the basis for computer animators' design of Gollum. Also providing the voice for Gollum, Serkis won an MTV best-actor award for this CG-assisted performance (a first). He appears as himself in the prologue to *The Return of the King* when playing Gollum's uncorrupted former self Smeagol. The collaboration with Jackson proved so successful that the director later cast Serkis as *King Kong* in a remake that deployed similar technology.

OSCARS
11 nominations, **11 winners**

Best Picture
Directing: Peter Jackson
Art Direction/Set Decoration: Grant Major, Dan Hennah, Alan Lee
Costume Design: Ngila Dickson, Richard Taylor
Film Editing: Jamie Selkirk
Makeup: Richard Taylor, Peter King
Music (Original Score): Howard Shore
Music (Original Song): 'Into the West', Music and Lyric by Fran Walsh, Howard Shore, Annie Lennox
Sound Mixing
Visual Effects
Writing (Adapted Screenplay): Fran Walsh, Philippa Boyens, Peter Jackson

WHAT WON THAT YEAR?
Actor in a Leading Role: Sean Penn *Mystic River*
Actress in a Leading Role: Charlize Theron *Monster*

BAFTAS
12 nominations, **4 winners**

Film
Direction: Peter Jackson
Adapted Screenplay: Fran Walsh, Philppa Boyens, Peter Jackson
Supporting Actor: Ian McKellen
Music: Howard Shore
Cinematography: Andrew Lesnie
Editing: Jamie Selkirk
Production Design: Grant Major
Costume Design: Ngila Dickson, Richard Taylor
Sound
Special Visual Effects
Make Up and Hair: Richard Taylor, Peter King, Peter Owen

WHAT WON THAT YEAR?
Direction: Peter Weir *Master and Commander: The Far Side of the World*
British Film: *Touching the Void*
Actor: Bill Murray *Lost in Translation*
Actress: Scarlett Johansson *Lost in Translation*

Dir: Leo McCAREY / USA
Released in Britain: 1947
Running Time: 127 minutes
Black and white
Estimated Attendance: 15.2 million

Reprising his role as Father O'Malley, the singing priest from *Going My Way* (1944), gave Bing Crosby his second Oscar nomination in two years, and the adoration of audiences on both sides of the Atlantic. But what seemed like an endorsement of human goodness in 1946 can look different to jaded modern eyes.

THE BELLS OF ST MARY'S

Director/Producer **Leo McCarey**
Screenplay **Dudley Nichols**, from a story by Leo McCarey
Director of Photography **George Barnes**
Editor **Harry Marker**
Art Director **William Flannery**
Music Robert **Emmett Dolan**

Father Chuck O'Malley • Bing Crosby
Sister Mary Benedict • Ingrid Bergman
Horace P. Bogardus • Henry Travers
Joe Gallagher • William Gargan
Sister Michael • Ruth Donnelly
Patsy Gallagher • Joan Carroll
Mrs Gallagher • Martha Sleeper
Dr McKay • Rhys Williams
Eddie Breen • Richard Tyler
Mrs Breen • Una O'Connor
Nun • Aina Constant
Nun • Gwen Crawford
Nun • Eva Novak
Workman • Joe Palma
Clerk in Store • Matt McHugh
Luther • Jimmy Crane
Tommy • Bobby Frasco
Blind Man • Peter Sasso
Elderly Woman • Cora Shannon
Truck Driver • Dewey Robinson

THE STORY

Father O'Malley comes to St Mary's mid-city school when it is threatened with a demolition order for lack of repair funds. While he and the school superintendent Sister Benedict indulge in friendly rivalry about how the children should be handled in work and play, they join in prayer and machination to persuade the owner of the new building next door to give it to the school. When Father O'Malley learns that Sister Benedict is ill, he arranges for her transfer. It is a great disappointment to her as her school moves into its new building, but her prayers that bitterness shall be removed from her heart are answered.

WHAT THEY SAID THEN …

Inevitably there is strong emphasis on star values here, but the merits of direction are not inconsiderable. McCarey's style is plain but well-spoken prose. He favours the framed picture and the symmetrical design, and within those conventions he builds some effective patterns with white starch and dark habit, to swamp and dissolve them in rich piling up of velvet blacks. Deservedly, with this and *Going My Way*, Crosby looks like making Father O'Malley a hardy annual. Bergman produces the requisite mixture of liveliness and religious calm. Joan Carroll, as a nervous adolescent, and Henry Travers, as a worried businessman, are effective in the supporting cast.

WHAT THEY SAY NOW …

The post-war era in US cinema was dedicated predominantly to maintaining faith in the American way of life. *The Bells of St Mary's* fits perfectly into this trend, alongside other box-office successes of the time, such as *The Jolson Story* (1946, which features in the Ultimate Film list at number 42), *Easter Parade* (1948), *Jolson Sings Again* (1949), *Show Boat* and *An American in Paris* (both 1951).

Its emphasis on unity, compassion and optimism must have been a considerable balm to British audiences too when it opened here in 1946; unfortunately, the means by which it promotes those values can appear suspect to a modern audience less willing to tolerate the passages of unadulterated schmaltz. Where a film like *It's a Wonderful Life* (1946) has survived the intervening years due to its cinematic and narrative skill, not to mention its complex undertones, *The Bells of St Mary's* has no comparable qualities to insulate it against changing trends in cinema and society.

The movie gets by as far as it does on the undeniable chemistry between Bing Crosby and Ingrid Bergman. The latter is reported to have lobbied for the part of Sister Benedict in the face of opposition from David O. Selznick, who saw little point in loaning her out to a production in which she would be required to provide little more than reaction shots to Crosby's warbling. But it is precisely the understatement of Bergman's performance that makes Crosby bearable for those viewers with a low tolerance of his rather self-satisfied, weirdly distant acting style.

Crosby's musical interludes are a real impediment now to the film's modest momentum, as well as to the audience's enjoyment. The narrative is a patchwork of sub-plots, each one designed to highlight the pleasing friction between Father O'Malley and Sister Benedict, but the songs tend to emphasise the scattershot structure of the movie. Which is not to say that even the hardiest viewer will remain dry-eyed by the time Sister Benedict learns that she is in the early stages

of tuberculosis, and Father O'Malley arranges for her transfer. But any tears are likely to be tinged with embarrassment.

CLASSIC QUOTE

Father O'Malley: 'Dial "O" for O'Malley.'

BEHIND THE SCENES

Bing Crosby received an Oscar nomination for this, his second outing as Father O'Malley – the first time an actor has been nominated for playing the same character in two different films.

AT THE TYPEWRITER

Dudley Nichols was a former New York journalist who took Hollywood by storm when he arrived there in the early 1930s to make his name as a screenwriter. The Talkies were the talk of the town, and Nichols was in his element, crafting high-calibre scripts for regular collaborators like John Ford (*The Informer*, 1935, for which Nichols won an Oscar, and *Stagecoach*, 1939), Howard Hawks (*Bringing Up Baby*, 1938, and *Air Force*, 1943) and Fritz Lang (*Man Hunt*, 1941, and *Scarlet Street*, 1945). He made a handful of directorial ventures, but it was writing at which he excelled. He was as dexterous as he was prolific, effortlessly crossing genre lines to great success before his death in 1960.

OSCARS
8 nominations, **1 winner**

Actor: Bing Crosby
Actress: Ingrid Bergman
Directing: Leo McCarey
Film Editing: Harry Marker
Music (Dramatic or Comedy Picture): Robert Emmett Dolan
Music (Song): 'Aren't You Glad You're You?', Music by
    James Van Heusen; Lyrics by Johnny Burke
Best Motion Picture
Sound Recording: Stephen Dunn

WHAT WON THAT YEAR?
Best Motion Picture: *The Lost Weekend*
Directing: Billy Wilder *The Lost Weekend*
Actor: Ray Milland *The Lost Weekend*
Actress: Joan Crawford *Mildred Pierce*

BAFTAS NOT AWARDED UNTIL 1947

Opposite Father Chuck (Bing Crosby) and Sister Mary (Ingrid Bergman) seek divine intervention to stop the demolition **Left above** The nuns enjoy a singalong with Bing **Left below** Director/Producer Leo McCarey ignores advice to work with children and animals

Scan the titles on the

Ultimate Film list and what immediately jumps out is how few were reliant on stars for their box-office appeal. One of the curiosities about the screen career of Vivien Leigh is that her single major box-office hit was in *Gone with the Wind* (the number one film). Producer David O. Selznick famously spent years searching for his Scarlett. Leigh was perfect for the role, but never again matched her success as the Southern belle. Kate Winslet also inspired devotion among fans for her role in James Cameron's *Titanic*, but if not exactly a one-hit wonder, she is yet to have another popular success on anything like the same scale.

Given that the 1940s marked the peak in British cinemagoing (in 1946 alone, UK admissions were at 1,640 million), it is only to be expected that so many films from that decade feature on the list. What may surprise contemporary readers is how many were homegrown. Anna Neagle has *Spring in Park Lane* and *The Courtneys of Curzon Street* nestling high up the polls. As journalists noted, her filmography in the late 1940s began to read like a smart address book. For austerity-era audiences, starved of glamour, the appeal of such upscale projects was self-evident. Neagle was also helped in having a husband and producer, Herbert Wilcox, with a Harvey Weinstein-like relish for press and marketing.

Margaret Lockwood, meanwhile, benefited from audiences' enthusiasm for 'wicked ladies'. After the restraint and self-sacrifice of the war years, the British public clearly relished an

actress who could play sulky, selfish and mischievous types. Still, as if to provide a counterweight, the ever-virtuous Phyllis Calvert (the yin to Lockwood's yang, so often the heroine to her wicked ladies) is there with *Fanny by Gaslight*. Underlining the streak of masochism that 1940s audiences

clearly felt, Ann Todd became an overnight star as the long-suffering pianist in *The Seventh Veil*.

Few of the most popular films yielded much in the way of opportunity for leading ladies. Lockwood apart, the Brits seemed to like their actresses wholesome. Julie Andrews's performances in *Mary Poppins* and *The Sound of Music* were hugely cherished; a similar reaction greeted Olivia Newton-John in *Grease*. Back in the 1940s, Greer Garson was the Home Counties über-heroine in *Mrs Miniver*. The presence on the list of *Random Harvest* underlines her popularity. Even Renée Zellweger's Bridget Jones was a good lass at heart.

You'll look in vain in the higher reaches of the list for any sign of the greatest (or at least the spikiest) actresses in Hollywood: Katharine Hepburn doesn't feature. Neither does Joan Crawford nor Greta Garbo. Ingrid Bergman wriggles in at 60 with one of her less memorable features, *For Whom The Bell Tolls*. Julia Roberts secures her place courtesy of *Notting Hill*. In fact, there is a surprising absence of what used dismissively to be referred to as 'women's pictures'. *Rebecca*, with Joan Fontaine, chimes in at 75. The classy Grace Kelly is there with *High Society* and Hollywood's favourite gamine Audrey Hepburn with *My Fair Lady*, but these were popular musicals already, rather than showcases for their female stars. And where, oh where, is Marilyn Monroe?

21

Dir: Cecil B. DeMILLE / USA
Released in Britain: 1957
Running Time: 222 minutes
Colour: Technicolor
Estimated Attendance: 15 million

Equal parts innovator, visionary, circus ringmaster and charlatan, Cecil B. DeMille was renowned for his fire-and-brimstone epics. But he outdid himself with *The Ten Commandments*, in which authenticity came a distant second to bombastic spectacle. It was to be his last film – and no one could claim he didn't go out with a bang.

THE TEN COMMANDMENTS

Director/Producer **Cecil B. DeMille**
Screenplay **Aeneas MacKenzie, Jesse L. Lasky Jr,**
  Jack Gariss, Fredric M. Frank
Director of Photography **Loyal Griggs**
Editor **Anne Bauchens**
Art Directors **Hal Pereira, Walter Tyler, Albert Nozaki**
Music **Elmer Bernstein**

Moses • Charlton Heston
Nefretiri • Anne Baxter
Sephora • Yvonne De Carlo
Joshua • John Derek
Bithiah • Nina Foch
Memnet • Judith Anderson
Aaron • John Carradine
Jannes • Douglass Dumbrille
Oentaur • Henry Wilcoxon
Mered • Donald Curtis
Amminadab • H. B. Warner
Rameses • Yul Brynner
Dathan • Edward G. Robinson
Lilia • Debra Paget
Sethi • Cedric Hardwicke
Yochabel • Martha Scott
Baka • Vincent Price
Miriam • Olive Deering
Abiram • Frank De Kova
Jethro • Eduard Franz

THE STORY

Adopted as a child and given Egyptian nationality by the Princess Bithiah, the Hebrew Moses is the favourite and apparent heir of the Pharaoh Sethi. Moses's love for the hereditary Princess Nefretiri antagonises Sethi's son, the powerful Prince Rameses. He is betrayed by Dathan, a court official, who reveals the secret of his origins, and asserts that Moses plans to lead his people out of Egyptian bondage. Disowned by Sethi, Moses is exiled to the desert, to be eventually rescued by Jethro, Sheik of Midian. He learns from Jethro's daughter Sephora (whom he subsequently marries) of the mysterious Mount Sinai. Here the voice of God from a burning bush commands Moses to return to Egypt and free the enslaved Hebrew peoples.

Rameses, now Pharaoh and married to Nefretiri, refuses Moses's entreaties, whereupon a disastrous series of plagues descends on the land. Rameses relents; Moses leads the slaves, and Dathan, his prisoner, out of Egypt. A miracle enables them to cross the Red Sea, while Rameses's pursuing army is drowned. Reaching Mount Sinai, Moses hears the voice of God and receives the tablets of the Ten Commandments. Meanwhile Dathan has led the people into idolatry and revolt. When Moses confronts them with the tablets, however, the earth opens up and swallows up the unrepentant. After forty years of expiation, spent wandering in the wilderness, an aged Moses leads his faithful survivors to the promised land.

WHAT THEY SAID THEN ...

This enormous film (not, in fact, a remake of DeMille's own 1923 *The Ten Commandments*) is less of a brash, pseudo-Biblical charade than might have been expected. The scriptwriters adopt an air of heavy reverence towards their central character. What is missing, though, despite the magnificent costumes and the lavish pictorial values, is any evidence of even an elementary historical sense.

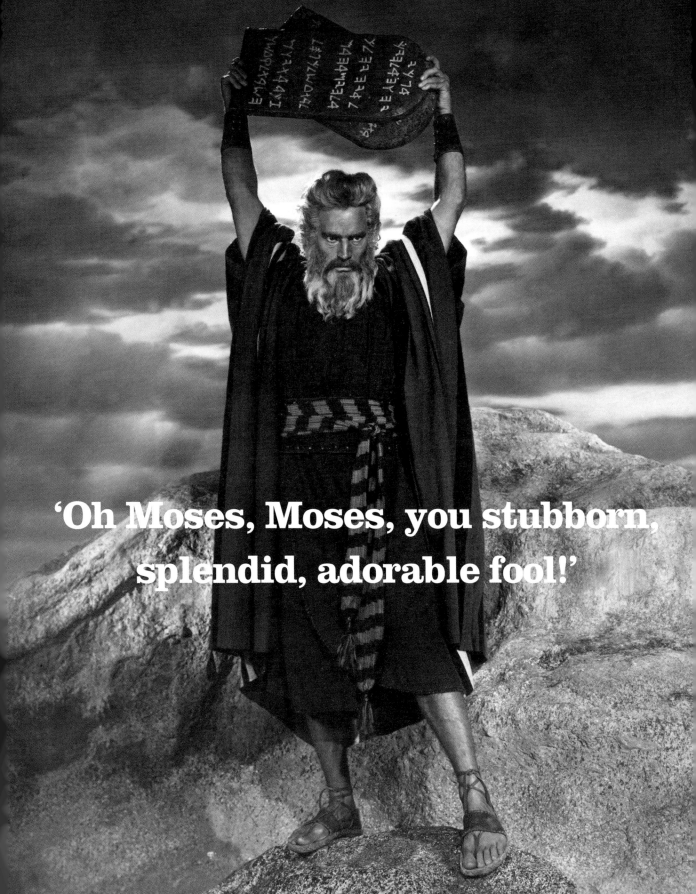

'Oh Moses, Moses, you stubborn, splendid, adorable fool!'

Above 'Let my people go!' Moses (Charlton Heston) demands of an uninterested Rameses (Yul Brynner)
Below Pharoah's favourite, Moses, before his exile
Opposite The original Moses basket

(This despite intentions to the contrary; there are copious acknowledgments to scholarly authorities besides a fulsome and earnest introduction by DeMille himself.) It is all presented like a Drury Lane spectacle of 1900.

Most unsatisfactory is the film's inadequate approach to character. Moses is a beef-and-brawn comic strip hero; Yul Brynner's Rameses has stature but no novelty; Edward G. Robinson makes Dathan heavily theatrical; Anne Baxter is a glacial, intermittently fiery Nefretiri. And so on.

Save for the sequences involving Jethro's man-hungry daughters and the protracted orgy of the golden calf, DeMille's characteristic preoccupations are restrained. The worst moments of *The Robe* (1953) are recalled, though, in the scenes of the burning bush and the giving of the Ten Commandments – a melodramatic pot pourri of portentous voices, sepulchral music and lightning flashes. In contrast, the exodus and the parting of the Red Sea are well staged. These episodes give temporary impetus and drama to a film which is for the most part lacking in both these qualities.

WHAT THEY SAY NOW ...

Subtlety was not in Cecil B. DeMille's vocabulary, but his second go at the Book of Exodus, made when he was 75, shows the vigorous, vivid storytelling that makes his work so skilfully and shamelessly entertaining. This grand hokum has an almost touching charm in the pomposity of its performances. The highly melodramatic tableaux vivants trace the life of Moses from baby in a basket through Charlton Heston's upbringing as a prince of Egypt (well pitted against Yul Brynner's imperious Rameses and Anne Baxter's vamping tramp princess Nefretiri) to his exile and selection by God, becoming the righteous patriarch booming, 'Thus sayeth the Lord God of Israel: Let my people go!'

OSCARS
7 nominations, **1 winner**

Best Motion Picture
Art Direction/Set Decoration (Color)
Cinematography (Color): Loyal Griggs
Costume Design (Color)
Film Editing: Anne Bauchens
Sound Recording: Loren L. Ryder
Special Effects: John Fulton

WHAT WON THAT YEAR?
Best Motion Picture: *Around the World in 80 Days*
Directing: George Stevens *Giant*
Actor: Yul Brynner *The King and I*
Actress: Ingrid Bergman *Anastasia*

BAFTAS

WHAT WON THAT YEAR?
Film/British Film: *The Bridge on the River Kwai*
British Actor: Alec Guinness *The Bridge on the River Kwai*
Foreign Actor: Henry Fonda *Twelve Angry Men*
British Actress: Heather Sears *The Story of Esther Costello*
Foreign Actress: Simone Signoret *The Witches of Salem*

The Oscar-winning special effects represent a triumph of ingenuity in the era of smoke and mirrors: God appearing to Moses as a burning bush, the Nile turning blood red, the creeping green mist that brings death to Egypt's first born, the burning of the commandments onto the stone tablets, and the unforgettable parting of the Red Sea.

Such wonders could never suffice for DeMille, for whom no epic was complete without fetching slave girls and a highly choreographed orgy. Here the kitsch ballet is performed around the golden calf to greet Heston's outraged Moses when he comes down from the mountain with the commandments.

CLASSIC QUOTE
Nefretiri: 'Oh Moses, Moses, you stubborn, splendid, adorable fool!'

SCENE STEALER
A big moment in the Old Testament, the parting of the Red Sea is tough to top. A host of hams bewail their certain doom, Heston's formidable Moses rebukes them and invokes the terrible power of God: 'The Lord of Hosts will do battle for us. Behold his mighty hand.' Even though the sequence now looks fuzzy around the edges, the rescue of the Hebrews pinned down at the shore is an iconic scene of awesome cinematic magic. The effect was achieved by dumping 300,000 gallons of water into two huge basins, creating a roiling froth, then running the film in reverse.

BEHIND THE SCENES
DeMille supposedly cast Heston because he reminded him of Michelangelo's statue of Moses, changing Heston's career path from rugged tough guy to premier epic hero. DeMille himself was damaged by the production. He had a heart attack after climbing the giant gate through which the departing Israelites would pass. He resumed work within days, but his health steadily deteriorated once he'd finished the picture.

IN THE CHAIR
Cecil Blount DeMille was the first showman director whose name on a marquee meant more than those of the stars. Flamboyant in personal style and film-making, he pioneered feature-length pictures (and Hollywood as their capital), made stars and shaped tastes. A storyteller of shrewdness, sentiment, vulgarity and power in large, equal measures, he is remembered most for the gargantuan scale, extravagance and sometimes spectacular absurdity of his Biblical and historical epics. But he worked in – or in some cases invented – every genre. As late as 1952 he pulled off an Oscar for Best Picture for circus saga *The Greatest Show On Earth*, an apt analogy for his *oeuvre*; that movie makes it onto the Ultimate Film list at number 32. He appeared as himself in Billy Wilder's *Sunset Boulevard* (1950), immortalised as the archetypal autocratic director in the line, 'Ready when you are, C.B.' As well as being DeMille's last film, *The Ten Commandments* was the biggest hit of his phenomenal career.

22

Dir: Peter JACKSON / USA,
   New Zealand, Germany
Released in Britain: 2002
Running Time: 179 minutes
Colour: Deluxe
Estimated Attendance: 14.4 million

With scene-setting out of the way, the middle entry in the *Lord of the Rings* trilogy was free to concentrate on rousing action. But amid the sprawling battle scenes, the limelight was stolen by the unlikeliest of stars – a slimy creature with bug eyes, cadaverous skin and a split personality ...

THE LORD OF THE RINGS: THE TWO TOWERS

Director **Peter Jackson**
Producers **Barry Osborne, Peter Jackson, Fran Walsh**
Screenplay/Story **Fran Walsh, Philippa Boyens, Stephen Sinclair, Peter Jackson**, adapted from the novel by J. R. R. Tolkien
Director of Photography **Andrew Lesnie**
Editor **Michael Horton, Jabez Olssen**
Production Designer **Grant Major**
Music **Howard Shore**

Frodo Baggins • Elijah Wood
Gandalf • Ian McKellen
Arwen • Liv Tyler
Aragorn, 'Strider' • Viggo Mortensen
Samwise 'Sam' Gamgee • Sean Astin
Galadriel • Cate Blanchett
Gimli • John Rhys-Davies
Peregrin Took, 'Pippin' • Billy Boyd
Meriadoc Brandybuck, 'Merry' • Dominic Monaghan
Legolas • Orlando Bloom
King Theoden of Rohan • Bernard Hill
Elrond • Hugo Weaving
Eowyn, Theoden's Niece • Miranda Otto
Faramir • David Wenham
Eomer, Eowyn's Brother • Karl Urban
Grima Wormtongue • Brad Dourif
Smeagol, 'Gollum' • Andy Serkis
Haldir • Craig Parker
Voice of Treebeard • John Rhys-Davies
Hero Orc • Victoria Beynon-Cole

THE STORY

Middle-earth. After the disappearance of the wizard Gandalf, the Fellowship of the Ring has split up. The hobbit Frodo Baggins, intent on taking the ring to Mordor to be destroyed, travels towards Sauron's realm with his loyal companion Sam, guided by Gollum, a creature who once possessed the ring and is now obsessed with getting it back. The human Aragorn, the elf Legolas and the dwarf Gimli enter the Kingdom of Rohan, searching for hobbits Merry and Pippin, who have been captured by the Uruk-hai, soldiers in the orc armies amassed by the turncoat wizard Saruman in the service of his alliance with Sauron.

King Theoden of Rohan, possessed by Saruman and badly advised by Saruman's ally Wormtongue, is in no position to resist Saruman's hordes. Wormtongue ensures the death of Theoden's son and heir Theodred and the banishment of his nephew Eomer. Sam distrusts Gollum, but Frodo has sympathy with the former ringbearer. Aragorn's party encounters Eomer, who has slaughtered the Uruk-hai party who took Merry and Pippin, but the hobbits have escaped into the Forest of Fangorn, where they encounter Treebeard, an ent (giant sentient tree), who resists getting involved in the coming war.

Gandalf reappears, transformed into the equal of Saruman, and exorcises Theoden, who decrees that his people should retreat to the keep of Helm's Deep to take a stand against the armies of Saruman. Though Aragorn disagrees with Theoden's tactics, he pledges himself to the cause of Rohan, surviving a battle in which he is feared dead. Frodo and Sam are captured by Faramir, who forces Frodo to lure Gollum into a trap. Though an elven army joins with the forces of

Opposite The Riders of Rohan **Above left**
Eomer (Karl Urban), rescuer of hobbits
Above right *Inside Helm's Deep, setting
of the dramatic final battle* **Below** *'Gissa job!'
Bernard Hill looks for something to occupy
him as King Theoden*

Rohan to defend Helm's Deep, the Uruk-hai lay siege and are only defeated
when a human army, gathered by Gandalf, come to their aid. After an attack on
Gondor by the Nazgûl, a dragon in the service of Sauron, Faramir lets Frodo and
the ring go to Mordor. As Frodo and Sam walk on, Gollum plots to betray the
hobbits and take back his 'precious'.

WHAT THEY SAY ...

Just as J. R. R. Tolkien's *Lord of the Rings* was initially published as three
separate novels with nearly-year-long intervals between volumes but is now
generally seen as a single continuous narrative, the definitive form of Peter
Jackson's trilogy is likely to be marathon day-long sessions (or, more likely,
DVD box sets) that run the three parts together into one very long film. To
that end, *The Two Towers* makes only a token attempt at getting newcomers
up to speed. Generally speaking, Jackson assumes you not only saw the first
film but have total recall of it.

Ian McKellen's Gandalf returns from the dead in *The Two Towers*. But
it is Gollum, barely glimpsed in the first film, who steals the show. A CGI
creation, albeit with more than vocal input from British actor Andy Serkis,
Gollum inhabits a live-action film as more than an equal of his unaugmented
co-stars; the baser instincts of the cruel Gollum argue with the finer being he
once was about the goodness of Frodo, until in a chilling culmination the two
shattered halves of a personality agree with each other that further treachery
is the best course. His non-human face has at least the expressive range of
any other actor in the film, and techies will gasp at the illusion when Gollum
and the hobbits are splashing in the same stream. Others will accept the
perfect mimesis and not realise what has been achieved – another step
towards the moment when CGI becomes so invisible that it ceases to be
recognised even subconsciously as effects trickery.

OSCARS
6 nominations, **2 winners**

Best Picture
Art Direction/Set Decoration: Grant Major, Dan Hennah, Alan Lee
Film Editing: Michael Horton
Sound
Sound Editing: Ethan Van der Ryn, Michael Hopkins
Visual Effects

WHAT WON THAT YEAR?
Best Picture: *Chicago*
Directing: Roman Polanski *The Pianist*
Actor in a Leading Role: Adrien Brody *The Pianist*
Actress in a Leading Role: Nicole Kidman *The Hours*

BAFTAS
9 nominations, **2 winners**

Film
Direction: Peter Jackson
Cinematography: Andrew Lesnie
Production Design: Grant Major
Costume Design: Ngila Dickson, Richard Taylor
Editing: Michael Horton
Sound
Special Visual Effects
Make Up and Hair: Peter Owen, Peter King, Richard Taylor

WHAT WON THAT YEAR?
Film: *The Pianist*
British Film: The Warrior
Direction: Roman Polanski *The Pianist*
Actor: Daniel Day-Lewis *Gangs of New York*
Actress: Nicole Kidman *The Hours*

The Lord of the Rings trilogy stands among the best adaptations of a major work of fantasy ever managed by the cinema. But it remains an adaptation rather than an original, in the manner of a John Huston who could take perfect books like *The Maltese Falcon* and make great films by shooting what was on the page rather than that of a Howard Hawks who saw in novels like *The Big Sleep* a foundation for even greater films. Jackson's films are exciting cinema, but his hitherto vital personality seems invisible here, as if the sacred task of filming *The Lord of the Rings* involved channelling Tolkien rather than transforming the source material from one medium to another.

CLASSIC QUOTE
Gollum on the ring: 'They stole it from us. My precioussss. Curse them. We hates them. It's ours, it is, and we wants it.'

SCENE STEALER
A 10,000-strong army of orcs – most of them digitally created by the film's effects team – stage an assault on Helm's Deep, where the people of Rohan have retreated. Using a mix of real-scale sets, model work and CGI, Jackson orchestrates this battle with epic flair. Despite their valiant defence work – skilfully picked out amid the clash of crowd scenes – it looks bad for the outnumbered armies of Rohan. But as day breaks Gandalf appears from over the brow of a hill together with reinforcements, who rout the orcs.

BEHIND THE SCENES
To create the sound of a vast army of orcs rallying around the wizard Saruman's call to war, Peter Jackson used the specially recorded roar of a 25,000-strong crowd at a New Zealand cricket match.

IN THE CHAIR
Although few who knew Peter Jackson's work prior to *The Lord of the Rings* could have anticipated the series's scope and spectacle, his earlier films lay the foundation for the trilogy's success. An obsession with fantasy runs through all his films, from the horror spoof of his 1987 debut *Bad Taste* to the self-deluding heroines of his acclaimed 1994 drama *Heavenly Creatures* (whose sympathetic account of a terrible crime looks forward to the moral complexity surrounding Gollum). Jackson's effects-heavy direction of the puppet black comedy *Meet the Feebles* (1989) and zombie flick *Braindead* (1992) was valuable preparation for the extensive model work and creature creation of *The Lord of the Rings*. And his introduction to then-developing computer-generated imagery on *The Frighteners* (1996) convinced the director that the technology was in place to realize Tolkien's vision.

Dir: Peter CATTANEO / USA, Great Britain
Released in Britain: 1997
Running Time: 91 minutes
Colour: Metrocolor
Estimated Attendance: 14.19 million

Left Gaz (Robert Carlyle) gets shirty

Unemployment. Suicide attempts. Broken families. Custody battles. Not the typical ingredients for a feelgood phenomenon to wow the homegrown crowds and woo Hollywood. But against the odds, this chirpy comedy put disco in the dole queue and proved that it can, on occasion, be glam up North.

THE FULL MONTY

Director **Peter Cattaneo**
Producer **Uberto Pasolini**
Screenplay **Simon Beaufoy**
Director of Photography **John de Borman**
Editors **Nick Moore, David Freeman**
Production Designer **Max Gottlieb**
Music **Anne Dudley**

Gaz • Robert Carlyle
Gerald • Tom Wilkinson
Dave • Mark Addy
Jean • Lesley Sharp
Mandy • Emily Woof
Lomper • Steve Huison
Horse • Paul Barber
Guy • Hugo Speer
Linda • Deirdre Costello
Reg • Bruce Jones
Nathan • William Snape
Barry • Paul Butterworth
Alan • Dave Hill
Terry • Andrew Livingstone
Sharon • Vinny Dhillon
Bee • Kate Layden
Sheryl • Joanna Swain
Louise • Diane Lane
Dole Clerk • Kate Rutter
Lomper's Mum • June Broughton

THE STORY

Gaz and Dave are young, unemployed Sheffield steelwelders. Gaz needs money to retain joint custody of his son Nathan; Dave's loss of self-respect is making him fat and impotent. When the male stripping group the Chippendales visit the city, Gaz, Dave and a reluctant Nathan gatecrash, and Gaz is impressed by the reaction of the hysterical female audience to the strippers. Gaz and Dave foil fellow-steelworker Lomper's attempt to gas himself. The three men persuade their former foreman, Gerald, an expert ballroom dancer who has not told his wife that he has been unemployed for six months, to help them form a strip act. Reinforcements include an ageing man named Mr Horse and Guy, who can run up walls like Donald O'Connor in *Singin' in the Rain* (1952). The group realise they have only one chance of drawing a lucrative crowd: to go 'the full monty' and completely undress. Anxieties soon set in. Gerald is afraid of becoming aroused on stage; Dave, worried he may never get it up again, backs out of the act. The dress rehearsal goes ahead, but a policeman stops by to investigate. Gaz, Gerald and Mr Horse are arrested for indecent exposure. Gerald returns home and his wife, incensed by his deception, throws him out. When Dave's wife Jean finds red leather knickers in his drawer, he is forced to confess that he is a failed stripper. Her love restores his confidence and the group's sixth member. The publicity from the police arrest boosts ticket sales. On the big night, Gaz crumbles, claiming he can't go on. Nathan's dressing-down forces him on stage, where the six finally bare all to the crowd's roar of approval.

WHAT THEY SAY ...

Unemployment may be no joke, but *The Full Monty*'s rich, consistent humour derives from showing that losers who make their own luck do indeed have the last laugh. Peter Cattaneo takes the British tradition that includes *Trainspotting* and *Brassed Off* (both 1996) to its logical conclusion: the requisite group of male friends (ex-steelworkers) are stripped physically as well as emotionally. Gaz, Dave, Lomper and Co. have an excess of free time and an absence of

Six men. With nothing to lose. Who dared to go...

THE YEAR'S MOST REVEALING COMEDY.

THE FULL MONTY

OSCARS
4 nominations, **1 winner**

Best Picture
Directing: Peter Cattaneo
Music (Original Musical or Comedy Score): Anne Dudley
Writing (Original Screenplay): Simon Beaufoy

WHAT WON THAT YEAR?
Best Picture: *Titanic*
Directing: James Cameron *Titanic*
Actor in a Leading Role: Jack Nicholson *As Good As It Gets*
Actress in a Leading Role: Helen Hunt *As Good As It Gets*

BAFTAS
11 nominations, **3 winners**

Film
Outstanding British Film of the Year
Direction: Peter Cattaneo
Actor: Robert Carlyle
Original Screenplay: Simon Beaufoy
Supporting Actor: Mark Addy
Supporting Actor: Tom Wilkinson
Supporting Actress: Lesley Sharp
Editing: David Freeman, Nick Moore
Music: Anne Dudley
Sound: Alastair Crocker, Adrian Rhodes, Ian Wilson

WHAT WON THAT YEAR?
Direction: Baz Luhrmann *William Shakespeare's Romeo + Juliet*
Actress: Judi Dench *Mrs Brown*

Right (from left to right) Nathan (William
Snape), Dave (Mark Addy), Gaz (Robert Carlyle),
Lomper (Steve Huison) and Gerald (Tom Wilkinson)
Opposite All the right moves: the amateur
Chippendales, including Guy (Hugo Speer, second
right), in action

funds or future, all of which force them to look more closely
at themselves. They discover the truism of humour – laugh
at yourself and the whole world laughs with you – and take
it one step further: expose yourself on stage and the whole
world will pay to laugh at you.

In a sense, this is a coming-of-age film. Unemployment
is shown as an emasculating, claustrophobic but above all
childlike state. The job centre is identical to a classroom, with
the slouching, rebellious men resembling reluctant schoolboys.
(They contrast with Gaz's son Nathan, who maturely rejects his
father's usually illegal and always irresponsible ideas of 'fun',
such as gatecrashing football matches or forming a Chippendales
of the North.) These man-children spend a lot of time sitting
awkwardly on swings or in playrooms. Everywhere has become
a playground for them: the strippers' rehearsals in a disused
steel plant are incongruous and very funny, but serve to highlight
that they no longer have any place in which to be grown-ups.

Women, here mostly wives and mothers or a leering mob,
are very much secondary characters. Yet the way *The Full
Monty* reverses the gender roles is startlingly effective: women
urinate standing up and men strip for money. These women
have power over men's self-image, but they are easily fooled
by costumes of various kinds: Gerald's suit blinds his wife to his
unemployment. Lomper and Dave are both insecure security
guards, with macho costumes that disguise the former's
homosexuality and the latter's impotence. When police disrupt
the dress rehearsal, Lomper and Guy flee, snatching negligees
from a washing line to cover themselves up. In a superbly
understated scene, the two silk-clad men discover that they are
in love with each other. Because clothes don't make the man,
these boys strip so that their women – or their men – will see

them properly. It is no coincidence that the strippers' swiftly removed costumes in the grand finale are police uniforms.

The men's vulnerability supplies the film with an odd, aching humour that complements the uproariousness of the strip scenes. Dave, Gaz and Lomper sitting on a hill discussing suicide is funny-sad soul-baring, *Last of the Summer Wine* by way of *Gregory's Girl* (1981). But there is also a more complex undertone – the wide green vistas with Sheffield in the distance contrast with the claustrophobic homes, closed-down shops and deserted steel plants – that recalls *The Boys From the Blackstuff* (1982).

In some ways, *The Full Monty* is about group therapy, in both visual and narrative terms. Conversation, admission of need and collective action provide the only solutions to these men's situation. Talking, training, attending funerals or stripping, they are framed and filmed as a cohesive (if volatile) unit. The group's ability to turn weakness into strength by stripping off all the layers provides the redemptive finale so essential to any feelgood film. The posters advertise the act as 'Hot Metal' (subtitle: 'We dare to be bare!') and *The Full Monty*'s final positive message is that these men are not the scrap which they initially feel themselves to be, but hot and malleable material indeed. By using their unwanted skills to weld themselves into a unit, these six unattractive anti-heroes succeed in reinforcing their self-esteem. When Gaz first tries stripping – in car headlights, cigarette in mouth, to the strains of Hot Chocolate's 'You Sexy Thing' – the audience laughs at him, not with him. By the final, euphoric scene, complete with *Top of the Pops*-style zooms and cheers, the characters have gained acceptance on their own terms.

CLASSIC QUOTE

Dave: 'Anti-wrinkle cream there may be, but anti-fat-bastard cream there is not.'

AT THE TYPEWRITER

Simon Beaufoy's career since writing the most successful British comedy of the latter half of the 20th century has largely been spent trying to shake off all memories of the movie that made his name. While *The Full Monty* was reborn as a smash-hit Broadway musical, Beaufoy's screenplays became increasingly gritty, taking in the revenge thriller *This Is Not A Love Song* (2002) and *Yasmin* (2004), a post-9/11 study of racial tension in Britain. But the influence of that likeable debut persisted, and could be felt most strongly in *Billy Elliot* (2000), which followed to the letter *The Full Monty*'s formula (gritty subject matter + escapist overtones = international success and lucrative stage transfer).

24

Dir: Chris COLUMBUS / USA, UK, Germany
Released in Britain: 2002
Running Time: 160 minutes
Colour: Technicolor
Estimated Attendance: 14.18 million

HARRY POTTER AND THE CHAMBER OF SECRETS

Director **Chris Columbus**
Producer **David Heyman**
Screenplay **Steve Kloves**, adapted from the novel
   by J. K. Rowling
Director of Photography **Roger Pratt**
Editor **Peter Honess**
Production Designer **Stuart Craig**
Music **John Williams**

Harry Potter • Daniel Radcliffe
Ron Weasley • Rupert Grint
Hermione Granger • Emma Watson
Gilderoy Lockhart • Kenneth Branagh
Nearly Headless Nick • John Cleese
Rubeus Hagrid • Robbie Coltrane
Uncle Vernon Dursley • Richard Griffiths
Albus Dumbledore • Richard Harris
Professor Snape • Alan Rickman
Aunt Petunia Dursley • Fiona Shaw
Lucius Malfoy • Jason Isaacs
Mrs Weasley • Julie Walters
Moaning Myrtle • Shirley Henderson
Professor McGonagall • Maggie Smith
Professor Flitwick • Warwick Davis
Madam Pomfrey, School Nurse • Gemma Jones
Professor Sprout • Miriam Margolyes
Mr Weasley • Mark Williams
Dudley Dursley • Harry Melling
Voice of Dobby, the House Elf • Toby Jones

Christmas 2002 saw a familiar battle being staged at cinemas everywhere. In the blue-blooded corner, squeaky clean Harry Potter and the whimsical world of boarding school wizardry. In the red-blooded corner, the more grimy, nightmarish milieu of hobbits and orcs. So who won? Seconds out, round two …

THE STORY

Harry Potter, an adolescent wizard, finds a house elf named Dobby in his Surrey home who warns him not to return to his school Hogwarts. Harry's friends, the Weasley family, rescue him from the house in a flying car. At Hogwarts an inscription appears in blood one night announcing that the Chamber of Secrets has been opened. Soon staff and students become petrified by unexplained means. Harry and his friends Ron Weasley and Hermione Granger investigate, and learn that the school co-founder Slytherin had a monster sealed up in the chamber a thousand years ago. The chamber has been opened now, as it was a generation ago, by the arrival at the school of Slytherin's direct descendent. Suspicion falls on Harry, especially when he reveals a sinister ability to talk to snakes.

In a remote bathroom the friends meet the ghost Moaning Myrtle, a one-time Hogwarts student. There they cook up a potion to transform themselves into the friends of fellow student Draco Malfoy, whom they wrongly suspect of either being or knowing who is Slytherin's heir. Later, Hermione is petrified. Harry finds a magic diary of a former student, Tom Riddle. By 'entering' it, Harry learns how the school caretaker Hagrid was accused of opening the Chamber of Secrets when he was a student, and expelled. In the present, Hagrid is arrested and the headmaster Dumbledore is relieved of his post. Harry and Ron discover that the monster Hagrid hid years ago was a giant spider Aragog who now lives in the woods.

Eventually Harry and Ron deduce that Myrtle was killed by the chamber's monster, a massive basilisk (snake). The basilisk has captured Ron's little sister Ginny. Accompanied by Dark Arts teacher Gilderoy Lockhart, they enter the chamber via the bathroom. There Harry meets Tom Riddle, who turns out to be Voldemort, the evil wizard who tried to kill Harry as a baby and is the heir of Slytherin. Harry defeats Voldemort, slays the basilisk and rescues Ginny. The petrified people are restored to normal, Dumbledore is reinstated and Hagrid is cleared. Harry tricks Dobby's owner, Draco's father Lucius (who planted the diary), into freeing Dobby.

WHAT THEY SAY …

You could have many gripes about the first two *Harry Potter* movies, but you could never accuse them of being unfaithful to the books. Following slavishly close to its J. K. Rowling source novel, each film clocks in at a demanding two

Top 'If it wasn't for you pesky kids', Lucius Malfoy (Jason Isaacs) might have gotten away with it **Above** Armed and dangerous, Harry (Daniel Radcliffe) and Ron (Rupert Grint) corner Gilderoy Lockart (Kenneth Branagh)

hours plus, proving that younger audience members will sit still for that long provided you give them plenty of what they want. Which, in this case, seems to be a steady supply of digital monsters and snowy owls, magic candles and shifting staircases, threaded together by a hero so wholesome he makes Prince William look like Harmony Korine.

As was the case with the first *Harry Potter* movie, 2001's *Harry Potter and the Philosopher's Stone*, this one was up against the second *Lord of the Rings* venture at the box office, though unlike in the first round of that battle, Tolkien triumphed over Rowling. Still, the competition evidently forced the makers of *Harry Potter and the Chamber of Secrets* to keep up their game.

They were lucky that *The Chamber of Secrets* is a better book. Less burdened with explication, the film plunges right into a rich plot. Endowed with a meatier cast of supporting characters, it affords an opportunity for such character actors as Kenneth Branagh and Shirley Henderson to let rip. As in the book, the narrative takes steps to temper the privileged smugness of the boarding-school setting by introducing a PC subplot that condemns racism against human-born wizards.

The ropey-looking CGI monsters from the first film are smoother and more nuanced here, though there's still something cold about them. The house elf Dobby, for instance, has well-animated facial expressions but his movements are too studied and liquid-like. He might have been more endearingly tactile if someone as talented as the late Jim Henson had jimmied the creature together from rubberised cloth and glass eyes, like Yoda in the early days of *Star Wars*. By contrast some of the children's performances might have been better rendered by pixels, as director Chris Columbus fails to elicit any discernible improvements in the work of his leads. Luckily pleasant surprises were in store for the third instalment, when the director Alfonso Cuarón was shipped in to spruce up a series that was in danger of looking old before its time.

CLASSIC QUOTE
Dumbledore: 'It is not our abilities that show what we truly are. It is our choices.'

OSCARS

WHAT WON THAT YEAR?
Best Picture: *Chicago*
Directing: Roman Polanski *The Pianist*
Actor in a Leading Role: Adrien Brody *The Pianist*
Actress in a Leading Role: Nicole Kidman *The Hours*

BAFTAS
3 nominations

Production Design: Stuart Craig
Sound
Special Visual Effects

WHAT WON THAT YEAR?
Film: *The Pianist*
Direction: Roman Polanski *The Pianist*
Actor: Daniel Day-Lewis *Gangs of New York*
Actress: Nicole Kidman *The Hours*

Dir: Robert STEVENSON / USA
Released in Britain: 1964
Running Time: 139 minutes
Colour: Technicolor
Estimated Attendance: 14 million

A magical nanny brings a dose of music and laughter into the lives of two bored London children in this much-loved adaptation of the popular books. But has time been kind to Mary Poppins? Is the film still supercalifragilisticexpialidocious, or as charmless as Dick Van Dyke's Cockney accent?

MARY POPPINS

Director **Robert Stevenson**
Producer **Walt Disney**
Screenplay **Don Da Gradi**, adapted from the books
  by P. L. Travers
Director of Photography **Edward Colman**
Editor **Cotton Warburton**
Art Directors **Carroll Clark, William H. Tuntke**
Animation Art Director **McLaren Stewart**
Songs **Richard M. Sherman, Robert B. Sherman**

Mary Poppins • Julie Andrews
Bert • Dick Van Dyke
Mr Banks • David Tomlinson
Mrs Banks • Glynis Johns
Ellen • Hermione Baddeley
Jane Banks • Karen Dotrice
Michael Banks • Matthew Garber
Katie Nana • Elsa Lanchester
Constable Jones • Arthur Treacher
Admiral Boom • Reginald Owen
Uncle Albert • Ed Wynn
Mrs Brill • Reta Shaw
Mr Dawes • Arthur Malet
The Bird Woman • Jane Darwell

THE STORY

Rigid disciplinarian George Banks, enraged by the rapid turnover of nannies for his two children Jane and Michael, relieves his wife of further responsibility in the matter and places in *The Times* an advertisement for the sort of nanny who will stand for no nonsense. The next morning a queue of suitably severe-looking women forms outside 17 Cherry Tree Lane; but the children's own specification for the new nanny, written on a piece of paper which their father had torn up and thrown into the fireplace, has floated out of the chimney and reached sympathetic eyes.

A great wind sweeps all the nasty nannies out of the street, and in on her umbrella sails Mary Poppins, who has every possible attraction including magic powers. On their first walk together she takes the children into a picture of the countryside that her friend Bert has chalked on the pavement. Another day they visit her Uncle Albert, who floats laughing around the ceiling of his living room.

Unimpressed by what he hears of these frivolities, Mr Banks takes the children to visit the bank where he works. There, an incident arising from Michael's refusal to open an account with his tuppence is misconstrued by a customer and starts a run on the bank. The children run away, and are taken home by a chimney sweep who turns out to be Bert. Mr Banks is fired from the bank, but seized by sudden frivolity quotes a joke that his children learned in the company of Mary Poppins. Later, seeing the point, the aged Chairman of the Board dies of laughter. A new and carefree Mr Banks is asked to fill the vacancy on the Board. Mary Poppins, her good work completed, flies off.

WHAT THEY SAID THEN ...

It seems that the best bits of this film spring from the imagination of author P. L. Travers. Walt Disney's musical, despite or maybe because of its songs and dances, carefully chosen cast and highly competent trick work, simply circumscribes that imagination. With the kind of film the Disney team makes, when everything happens according to a well-established formula and without

OSCARS

13 nominations, **5 winners**

Best Picture
Directing: Robert Stevenson
Actress: Julie Andrews
Art Direction/Set Decoration (Color)
Cinematography (Color): Edward Colman
Costume Design (Color): Tony Walton
Film Editing: Cotton Warburton
Music Score (substantially original): Richard M. Sherman, Robert B. Sherman
Music (Scoring of Music—adaptation or treatment): Irwin Kostal
Music (Song): 'Chim Chim Cher-ee', Music and Lyrics by Richard M. Sherman, Robert B. Sherman
Sound: Robert O. Cook
Special Visual Effects: Peter Ellenshaw, Eustace Lycett, Hamilton Luske
Writing (Adapted Screenplay): Bill Walsh, Don DaGradi

WHAT WON THAT YEAR?
Best Picture: *My Fair Lady*
Directing: George Cukor *My Fair Lady*
Actor: Rex Harrison *My Fair Lady*

BAFTAS

1 nomination, **1 winner**

Most Promising Newcomer: Julie Andrews

WHAT WON THAT YEAR?
Film/British Film: *Dr Strangelove*
British Actor: Richard Attenborough *Guns at Batasi/Séance on a Wet Afternoon*
Foreign Actor: Marcello Mastroianni *Yesterday, Today and Tomorrow*
British Actress: Audrey Hepburn *Charade*
Foreign Actress: Anne Bancroft *The Pumpkin Eater*

any surprises, this is perhaps inevitable. Like the good, clean joke that kills the Chairman of the bank, the Disney world is nonetheless enjoyable on its own level.

Fitting neatly into Mary Poppins's description of herself as 'practically perfect in every way', Julie Andrews cuts a pretty figure as the nicest of all nannies; so, as the sentimentalised little mother, does Glynis Johns. David Tomlinson is covered with gloom as the stereotyped city gent, and Dick Van Dyke full of noise as the equally stereotyped stage Cockney. Apart from a few complacent reminders – like the bird woman selling bread outside St Paul's – of the town made familiar by *My Fair Lady* (1964), the London settings, especially the street in which the Banks live, have a genuine Edwardian charm. It is really when the film is at its most fanciful that it pleases least; when, for instance, the children step into Bert's picture to move among a host of animated cartoon animals against luridly colourful backdrops or through floating flower petals. Basic Disney perhaps, but not somehow the stuff that dreams are made of.

WHAT THEY SAY NOW ...

Despite a successful rebirth as a stage musical in 2005, *Mary Poppins* no longer glimmers with its old magic. Partly this is the fault of Dick Van Dyke and his incredible, strangulated, hear-it-to-believe-it Cockney accent; so notorious has his assault on the dialect become that it is now the first thing that springs to the collective memory when the film is mentioned. That's a pity because it does have another warm turn from Julie Andrews, playing against the stiffness of David Tomlinson much as she would a year later with Christopher Plummer in *The Sound of Music* (1965). What the film lacks, despite its gravity-defying heroine, is the levity of the most fleet-footed daydreams.

CLASSIC QUOTE

Mary Poppins: 'In every job that must be done, there is an element of fun. You find the fun and – "Snap!" – the job's a game.'

BEHIND THE SCENES

Walt Disney had various tussles with the novelist P. L. Travers, first over the script, which she wanted to change, and then over the casting of the lead, of which Dick Van Dyke has said she failed to approve. But the film went on to provide Disney with his biggest ever win come Oscar night – five prizes out of a possible thirteen.

Opposite Life is tweet: Mary Poppins (Julie Andrews) *Above* Soots you, Sir: Bert (Dick Van Dyke), Jane (Karen Dotrice), Michael (Matthew Garber), Mary *Overleaf* Chim Chim Cher-ee: Dick Van Dyke with his grubby fellow sweeps

26

Dir: Carol REED / UK
Released in Britain: 1949
Running Time: 104 minutes
Black and white
Estimated Attendance: 14 million

A recent BFI poll concluded that *The Third Man* is the best British film ever made. But exactly how British is it? Who is lurking in those shadows? Whatever happened to Harry Lime? And where is that zither music coming from?

THE THIRD MAN

Director **Carol Reed**
Producers **Alexander Korda, David O. Selznick, Carol Reed**
Screenplay/Story **Graham Greene**
Director of Photography **Robert Krasker**
Editor **Oswald Hafenrichter**
Set Designer **Vincent Korda**
Music **Anton Karas**

Holly Martins • Joseph Cotten
Anna Schmidt • Alida Valli
Harry Lime • Orson Welles
Major Calloway • Trevor Howard
Harry's Porter • Paul Hoerbiger
'Baron' Kurtz • Ernst Deutsch
Dr Winkel • Erich Ponto
Popescu • Siegfried Breuer
Anna's Landlady • Hedwig Bleibtreu
Sergeant Paine • Bernard Lee
Crabbin • Wilfrid Hyde White
Porter's Wife • Annie Rosar
Hansl • Herbert Halbik
Brodsky • Alexis Chesnakov
Hall Porter at Sacher's • Paul Hardtmuth
Hansl's Father • Frederick Schreiber
Winkel's Maid • Jenny Werner
Kurtz's mMother • Nelly Arno
Barman at Casanova • Leo Bieber
British Policeman • Geoffrey Keen

THE STORY

Holly Martins, an American writer of western stories, arrives in Vienna to work for his friend, Harry Lime, but is shocked to discover that he was killed in a car accident. He is told by the British police officer Major Calloway that Lime was a notorious racketeer involved in selling diluted penicillin. Martins begins to track down all those who knew his friend: the lonely, frightened actress Anna Schmidt who was in love with Lime; two acquaintances, Kurtz and Popescu, who witnessed the accident; his porter and his doctor. These investigations lead him to the heart of corruption in Vienna, to the discovery that Lime is still alive, to a struggle with his conscience which ends with the pursuit of his friend, who retreats to the sewers of the city. There, Lime is shot dead by Martins.

WHAT THEY SAID THEN ...

Although much of the film was shot on location in Vienna, it does not give an intimate picture of the city. The dead-looking streets with their piles of bombed masonry, the interiors with relics of splendour, the half-empty cafés and the enormous, glistening sewers, seem to exist in a decaying no-man's-land. The melancholy scene is heightened from the first by the brilliant use of zither music with its relentless, jangling tunes.

By the side of this dislocated city, the human beings with their shabby intrigues and miseries are almost insignificant. At the end, they fade back into the shadows and are gone completely. But the impression left by the film is lasting and powerful, because the characters are sharply created and well-acted: Trevor Howard particularly good as the British officer, Orson Welles magnetic in the small role of Lime, Joseph Cotten catching exactly the moodiness and uncertainty of Martins. Only Alida Valli, as the actress, is rather negative, and one feels her relationships with both Lime and Martins are too thinly conveyed.

By the very nature of its settings and story, there are occasional reminiscences of Lang and Hitchcock, but there is nothing borrowed or imitated. Stylistically, *The Third Man* is Reed's most impressive film: as an analyst of mood and situation, he is practically unequalled today.

WHAT THEY SAY NOW ...

British cinema flourished in the years immediately after the Second World War. Never before or since has there been such a glut of high quality, commercially successful movies produced in this country. Between 1944 and 1949, British-made films included *Henry V* (1944), *Brief Encounter* (1945), *A Matter of Life and Death*, *Great Expectations* (both 1946), *Brighton Rock* (1947), *The Red Shoes*, *Hamlet*, *Oliver Twist*, *The Fallen Idol* (all 1948) and *Kind Hearts and Coronets* (1949). This was the UK's one and only cinematic 'golden age'.

What's striking is how many of these famous and accomplished films were associated with literary prestige. Alongside the adaptations of Dickens and Shakespeare were films written, or based on stories by, rising literary stars – Noël Coward in the case of *Brief Encounter*, Graham Greene in the case of *Brighton Rock*, *The Fallen Idol* and *The Third Man*. These films were edgy and complex in tone, reflecting all the flux and uncertainty of a country recovering from war and adjusting to a new era.

The Third Man is a case in point. At the time of its release, some regarded the movie as simply a superior thriller. Now it's considered possibly the finest

Opposite *The spotlight falls on Orson Welles as Harry Lime finally steps out of the shadows*
Below *Paul Hoerbiger is coached by Elizabeth Montagu – the Austrian director Paul Martin (left) assists with translation*

British film ever made. The irony is that it remains the most cosmopolitan of pictures, with a production that ignored the national boundaries dividing Vienna at the time.

The film's producer, Alexander Korda, was a Hungarian long since settled in Britain. Working with his producing partner, the American David O. Selznick, he decided to set his latest picture in Austria to free up finances tied to the local currency. The film's star Joseph Cotten was American (and contracted to Selznick); so too was Orson Welles, while the Yugoslav actress Alida Valli was his love interest. And the whole thing was set at the other end of Europe from Blighty, among the ruinous beauty of post-war Vienna, caught at tilted angles by the Australian Robert Krasker's photography as if his camera were sinking into the sewers where the climax is staged.

And yet there's something characteristically British about this enterprise. With a screenplay by England's foremost novelist Graham Greene, the film follows a tradition of espionage mysteries

Above *Filming in a Viennese square* **Right** *The secret passage into the sewers*

that begins with John Buchan and anticipates Ian Fleming and John le Carré. The film's black humour, its imperious urbanity and sophisticated wit also evoke Hitchcock, but director Carol Reed tempers that director's gothic tendencies with a feel for the everyday suffering of the Viennese citizens. Excessively stylised, with baroquely staged exterior sequences that make real-life locations look like expressionistic movie sets, yet also a fascinating time-capsule portrait of a city in historical turmoil, *The Third Man* is an inspired compromise between cinema's competing urges towards fantasy and documentary – and who does compromise better than the Brits?

CLASSIC QUOTE

Harry Lime: 'In Italy for thirty years under the Borgias they had warfare, terror, murder, bloodshed, but they produced Michelangelo, Leonardo da Vinci and the Renaissance. In Switzerland they had brotherly love, 500 years of democracy and peace, and what did that produce? The cuckoo clock.'

SCENE STEALER

Holly Martins has just left the apartment of Anna Schmidt, the lover of his dead friend Harry Lime. It's night, the cobbled streets are glossy with rainfall, and Holly – drunk, in love with Anna, still grieving his old pal – stumbles forward. A cat slips into a dark doorway, caresses the shoes of an unknown figure. Holly hears a noise, thinks he's being followed, and challenges his pursuer. Disturbed by this yell, a neighbour swings open her window. The light from her flat illuminates the doorway. Holly can't believe his eyes: there in the doorway, in the ghostly light of an upstairs apartment, is Harry Lime.

BEHIND THE SCENES

Arriving at the last moment to film his sequences in Vienna, Orson Welles refused, on the grounds of hygiene, to work in the sewer, where much of the film had been shot. A replica was then built at Shepperton Studios in London, where Welles completed his scenes.

IN THE PRODUCER'S CHAIR

It is telling that on *The Third Man*, one of his most well-known films, Alexander Korda should have been paired with the influential US producer David O. Selznick because Korda had the energy, the ambition, the flair and the determination of the best of the Hollywood moguls. He started out as a director in his native Hungary, arriving in Britain in the early 1930s where he founded London Productions: his 1933 film *The Private Life of Henry VIII* was the first British Oscar success.

But it was in the role of producer that Korda's astute showmanship was best applied. Often working with his brothers Zoltan (as director) and Vincent (as art director), Korda gravitated towards big projects with prestige literary credentials – H. G. Wells is credited for the screenplay for the spectacular *Things to Come* (1936) – and the cream of British acting talent, including Charles Laughton, Laurence Olivier and Robert Donat.

However, Korda's decisions weren't always the most financially sound – Denham Studios, which he built on the back of his first international successes, collapsed in debt. But in the often drab world of British cinema there is no doubt that Alexander Korda stood out.

27

Dir: Guy HAMILTON / UK
Released in Britain: 1964
Running Time: 109 minutes
Colour: Technicolor
Estimated Attendance: 13.9 million

He's the man – the man with the Midas touch. The highest-rated Bond movie on *The Ultimate Film* list may be *Thunderball*, but *Goldfinger* is indisputably the most stylish. Sean Connery in his prime, a blood-and-thunder theme song, menacing villains and *that* car. Does it get any better than this?

GOLDFINGER

Director **Guy Hamilton**
Producer **Harry Saltzman, Albert R. Broccoli**
Screenplay **Richard Maibaum, Paul Dehn**, adapted
   from the novel by Ian Fleming
Director of Photography **Ted Moore**
Editor **Peter Hunt**
Production Designer **Ken Adam**
Music **John Barry**

James Bond • Sean Connery
Pussy Galore • Honor Blackman
Auric Goldfinger • Gert Fröbe
Jill Masterson • Shirley Eaton
Tilly Masterson • Tania Mallet
Oddjob • Harold Sakata
'M' • Bernard Lee
Solo • Martin Benson
Felix Leiter • Cec Linder
Simmons • Austin Willis
Miss Moneypenny • Lois Maxwell
Midnight • Bill Nagy
Kisch • Michael Mellinger
Johnny • Peter Cranwell
Bonita • Nadja Regin
Smithers • Richard Vernon
Mr Ling • Burt Kwouk
'Q' • Desmond Llewelyn
Mei-Lei • Mai Ling
Swiss Gatekeeper • Varley Thomas

THE STORY

En route to London after a successful Caribbean operation, James Bond stops off at Miami. There he is asked to keep an eye on the wealthy and mysterious Auric Goldfinger, whose current pastime is the systematic cheating of a wealthy American at cards. Bond calls a halt to this by suborning Goldfinger's secretary and accomplice, Jill Masterson. In revenge, Goldfinger has Jill murdered – suffocated under a thin coating of gold paint.

Back in London, Bond learns that the Bank of England wants to find out just how Goldfinger is contriving to smuggle bullion out of the country. He tracks Goldfinger's Rolls-Royce across Europe to his Alpine headquarters, encountering on the way Tilly Masterson, sister of the murdered Jill, who is hunting Goldfinger with a shotgun. But Tilly is killed by a lethal blow from the stiffened bowler which Oddjob, Goldfinger's Korean henchman, hurls like a discus; and Bond himself, having identified the smuggling technique (a solid gold Rolls), is captured. He is flown out by Pussy Galore, Goldfinger's private pilot, to the Kentucky ranch where the master criminal is assembling the cast for his greatest coup – operation Grand Slam, a raid on Fort Knox. His plan: to paralyse the defences by a lethal nerve gas sprayed from the planes of Pussy's flying circus; then to blow the place up with an atomic device borrowed from Red China, so making the entire American gold reserve radioactive.

Under Bond's influence Pussy changes sides and puts through a call to Washington. Bond is rescued from the vaults of Fort Knox, where he has been left handcuffed to the bomb. He survives a final encounter with Goldfinger, who has boarded a US airforce jet wearing general's uniform, and finally parachutes to safety with Pussy.

WHAT THEY SAID THEN ...

A seagull bobs on a night sea; slowly it rises from the waves, and from under it emerges 007 in frogman's kit. He scales a wall, throttles a guard, plants a dynamite charge, hops back over the wall; the frogman's suit is stripped

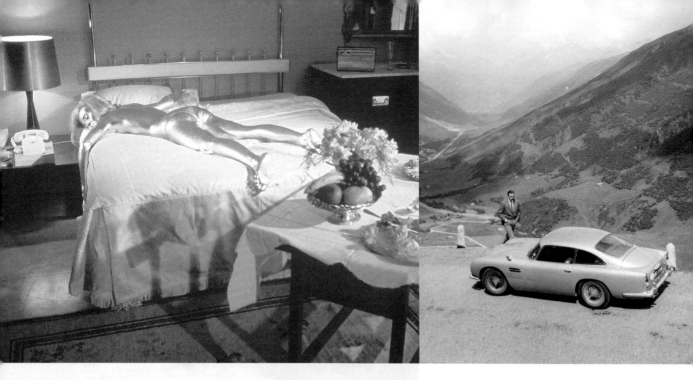

Above left All that glitters: Jill (Shirley Eaton) is painted out of the picture *Above right* Bond's silver Aston Martin DB5 (later stolen from Boca Raton airport and, sadly, never recovered) *Left* Here, kitty, kitty: Pussy Galore (Honor Blackman) *Below* 'Do you expect me to talk?' 'No, Mr Bond, I expect you to die'

OSCARS
1 nomination, **1 winner**

Sound Effects: Norman Wanstall

WHAT WON THAT YEAR?
Best Picture: *My Fair Lady*
Directing: George Cukor *My Fair Lady*
Actor: Rex Harrison *My Fair Lady*
Actress: Julie Andrews *Mary Poppins*

BAFTAS
1 nomination

British Art Direction (Colour): Ken Adam

WHAT WON THAT YEAR?
Film/British Film: *Dr Strangelove*
British Actor: Richard Attenborough *Guns of Batasi/Séance on a Wet Afternoon*
Foreign Actor: Marcello Mastroianni *Yesterday, Today and Tomorrow*
British Actress: Audrey Hepburn *Charade*
Foreign Actress: Anne Bancroft *The Pumpkin Eater*

Left Pussy Galore: *'Do you want to play it the easy, or the hard way?'*

off to reveal a white dinner jacket, complete with carnation for the buttonhole. So Bond is off again. And, as with *From Russia With Love* (1963), a pre-credits sequence of breathless speed and impudence tips a colossal wink at the audience.

After these first five minutes of outrageous violence, callous fun and bland self-mockery, the tone is so firmly set that the film could get away with almost anything. Having hit on a gold-plated formula, the Broccoli–Saltzman team have had the wit to keep on developing it: their only worry now must be how far they can keep it up, in ensuring that each of Bond's adventures is more enjoyably extravagant (or extravagantly enjoyable) than the last one. Here, they have gone all out for sets and gadgetry. A laconic secret service man introduces Bond to the Aston Martin special, fitted out with radar, smoke-screen, flamethrowers, machine-gun headlamps and an ejector seat for unwanted passengers.

Later, all this equipment is of course put to good use. When Goldfinger wants to dispose of a recalcitrant ally, he has the man shot by Oddjob, who then drives the corpse to a yard in which cars are pulped for scrap metal. Into the works goes a gleaming Thunderbird; from it emerges a neat little cube of scrap. Sympathy, it goes without saying, is all for the car, with none to spare for the corpse. Ken Adam's sets, notably the operations room at the Kentucky ranch and the glittering vaults of Fort Knox, are masterpieces of technological fantasy. Only

characters as extreme as Gert Fröbe's bloated, tweedy Goldfinger, and Harold Sakata's entirely imperturbable Oddjob could live up to them, and even Honor Blackman's Pussy, in spite of the judo and the wardrobe, seems a trifle diminished. Characters, in *Goldfinger*, have to make an immediate impact: they will probably be dead before they get a second chance.

But the real trick of the formula – not, incidentally, Ian Fleming's formula at all, but the films' invention – is the way it uses humour. In all his adventures, sexual and lethal, Bond is a kind of joke superman, as preposterously resilient as one of those cartoon cats. It may be Paul Dehn's collaboration on the script which here gives a new finesse to the jokes; or it may simply be a growing confidence on the part of everyone concerned, and most notably of Sean Connery himself. *Goldfinger* really is a dazzling object lesson in the principle that nothing succeeds like excess.

WHAT THEY SAY NOW ...
As the balance between the frivolous and the suspenseful, maintained with such elegance in Ian Fleming's novels, began to tip starkly in favour of the former, so the Bond series lost much of the sizzling style for which it had been prized in the first place. (That was not to return until Pierce Brosnan slipped into the familiar tuxedo, and brought new sparkle to the old one-liners, in the 1995 *GoldenEye*.)

But all the successful elements are still in place, and in fine working order, in *Goldfinger*, from the stunning Shirley Bassey title song to the peerless Ken Adam production design, Sean Connery's debonair-as-hell Bond and the natty gadgets and runarounds (the gleaming Aston Martin should've been billed above the title). The years may have allowed certain details to curdle – Bond's diatribe against the Beatles, for instance, now makes him sound momentarily like a crotchety old grandfather rather than a supercool spy. But the jibes launched by a modern spoof such as *Austin Powers in Goldmember* (2002) scarcely leave a dent. You can't send up a picture in which the heroine is called Pussy Galore and the villain's henchman dispatches undesirables with a bowler hat – that's dotty and irreverent enough already.

CLASSIC QUOTE

Bond (about to be bisected by a laser): 'Do you expect me to talk?' Goldfinger: 'No, Mr Bond. I expect you to die.'

SCENE STEALER

Few passages in the whole cycle carry the dreadful menace of the moment when Bond finds Jill Masterson dead in his bed.

Nothing as humdrum as a shooting or strangulation – she is covered from top to toe in gold paint. It isn't only the visual shock of this glinting corpse, or the thought of her surreal suffering. It's the intrinsic mixture of sex and violence contained in this grimly glamorous image which really startles. The killing of Bond's wife in the later entry *On Her Majesty's Secret Service* (1969) may be more moving, but it is the perverse inventiveness of this murder that haunts the memory – and the entire Bond series.

HOLDING THE BATON

One of the most prolific and distinguished names in British (and international) cinema for his film music, John Barry (born John Barry Prendergast, in York) had early experience with a military band. A rock'n'roll trumpeter, he formed the John Barry Seven group in the late 1950s. His first film score was for *Beat Girl* (1960), and he found fame for his work on a dozen Bond adventures, beginning with *Dr No* (1962), and for his Oscar-winning song and score for *Born Free* (1965). He won further Oscars for *The Lion in Winter* (1968), *Out of Africa* (1985) and *Dances With Wolves* (1990), as well as garnering BAFTA and *Golden Globe* awards.

JAMES BOND 007
BACK IN ACTION!

ALBERT R. BROCCOLI & HARRY SALTZMAN PRESENT

SEAN CONNERY

IN IAN FLEMING'S

GOLDFINGER Ⓐ

HONOR BLACKMAN
AS PUSSY GALORE

GERT FROBE
AS GOLDFINGER

TECHNICOLOR ®

SCREEN PLAY BY RICHARD MAIBAUM & PAUL DEHN

28

Dir: George LUCAS / USA
Released in Britain: 1999
Running Time: 133 minutes
Colour: Technicolor
Estimated Attendance: 13.59 million

The world had waited 16 years for George Lucas to deliver the first *Star Wars* prequel. What we got from the movie was groundbreaking digital technology, irritating new characters and an overwhelming sense that George Lucas had lost touch with his talent.

STAR WARS EPISODE I: THE PHANTOM MENACE

Director **George Lucas**
Producer **Rick McCallum**
Screenplay **George Lucas**
Director of Photography **David Tattersall**
Editor **Paul Martin Smith, Ben Burtt**
Production Designer **Gavin Bocquet**
Music **John Williams**

Qui-Gon Jinn • Liam Neeson
Obi-Wan Kenobi • Ewan McGregor
Queen Amidala/Padmé • Natalie Portman
Anakin Skywalker • Jake Lloyd
Shmi Skywalker • Pernilla Östergran
Yoda • Frank Oz
Senator Palpatine • Ian McDiarmid
Sio Bibble • Oliver Ford Davies
Captain Panaka • Hugh Quarshie
Jar Jar Binks • Ahmed Best
C-3PO • Anthony Daniels
R2-D2 • Kenny Baker
Chancellor Valorum • Terence Stamp
Boss Nass • Brian Blessed
Watto • Andrew Secombe
Darth Maul • Ray Park
Sebulba • Lewis Macleod
Wald • Warwick Davis
Captain Tarpals • Steven Speirs
Nute Gunray • Silas Carson

THE STORY

Two Jedi knights, Qui-Gon Jinn and his apprentice Obi-Wan Kenobi, are sent to the distant planet of Naboo to negotiate a dispute between the planet's leaders and the nefarious heads of the Trade Federation. Qui-Gon and Obi-Wan are ambushed; the Federation's blockade is a cover for an invasion of Naboo, sponsored by a shadowy Sith master, or dark Jedi. Landing on the planet, Qui-Gon and Obi-Wan help Naboo's Queen Amidala escape. Meanwhile the Sith lord sends his apprentice Darth Maul after Amidala.

On Tatooine, Qui-Gon meets a slave boy named Anakin Skywalker whom he identifies immediately as a born Jedi. Qui-Gon wins the boy's freedom by betting against Anakin's master on a pod race which Anakin wins over his arch rival. As the group leaves Tatooine, Darth Maul appears and duels with Qui-Gon. Amidala learns the Galactic Senate will not help Naboo. The Jedi Council is disturbed to hear a new Sith is at large, but refuses to let Qui-Gon train Anakin as a Jedi knight. Yoda believes Anakin is potentially vulnerable to the Dark Side. Amidala decides to go back to Naboo to mount an insurrection against the Federation. Qui-Gon, Obi-Wan and Anakin go with her. On Naboo, she convinces the Gunga to mount an assault, drawing droid forces away from the city, while her band sneak into the palace to capture the Federation's viceroy. Just as the Gunga are losing the battle, Anakin pilots a ship that destroys the Federation's command vessel. Darth Maul kills Qui-Gon in a light-sabre duel, but is then killed by Obi-Wan, who takes Anakin as his apprentice after Naboo is liberated.

WHAT THEY SAY ...

In the late 1990s, film-makers reached the point of diminishing returns with computer-generated effects. It became possible for films to spend vast sums on effects and still look laughably cheap (see, for instance, *The Mummy*, 1999).

The Phantom Menace doesn't have that problem, but almost nothing in it is based on photographing actual human beings in their environments. Every shot is such a complex technical achievement, so full of droids, aliens, spacecraft or gargantuan structures, that the movie takes on the hazy, ugly look of software.

Some of the film's grand set pieces are impressive. The great battle between the benevolent, amphibious Gunga and the Federation's droids is marvellous to behold. But Lucas's imagery often seems rooted in nothing particular. Compared with the visual wit and imagination of such science-fiction epics as *The Matrix* (1999) and *Starship Troopers* (1997), *The Phantom Menace*'s aesthetic seems leaden and outdated.

In a laboured quest for some light relief, Lucas and his enormous team of collaborators have created many cartoonish new species. Jar Jar Binks, with his rubbery platypus face, joke-Caribbean accent and jive walk right out of a 1970s blaxploitation movie, may amuse small children, but many adults will find *The Phantom Menace*'s quasi-racial typing patronising at best.

The biggest problem with *The Phantom Menace* is that it lacks narrative coherence. Logically, this wants to be the story of Obi-Wan Kenobi's early relationship with Anakin Skywalker (soon to become Darth Vader), but the two scarcely exchange a word until the movie's final scenes. Qui-Gon Jinn is the central character, and yet his relationship with Obi-Wan adds up to little more than a lot of graceful tandem swordplay. As Obi-Wan, Ewan McGregor is one of several outstanding actors, including Natalie Portman, who are given virtually nothing to do.

Things certainly pick up in the final half-hour or so of the movie, with a three-way light-sabre duel that ranks among the best combat scenes in the entire series. But *The Phantom Menace* only suffers by comparison with the feckless energy and enthusiasm of the original *Star Wars* (1977). The whole saga has never felt more like a twelve-year-old's efforts to emulate Tolkien; this instalment feels less like an opening chapter than a stammering, parenthetical preface. Matters improved with the next two pictures. But not by much.

CLASSIC QUOTE

Yoda: 'Fear is the path to the dark side. Fear leads to anger. Anger leads to hate. Hate leads to suffering. I sense much fear in you.'

IN THE CHAIR

George Lucas's talents are open to dispute – his most admirable contribution to the Star Wars series was to let Irvin Kershner direct *The Empire Strikes Back* (1980). But he's one canny businessman. On *The Phantom Menace*, he cut the same deal to which he had consented on the first *Star Wars*, waiving his salary in exchange for owning the negative of the final cut as well as secondary rights to tie-ins and toys.

Above *Queen Amidala (Natalie Portman)*

OSCARS

3 nominations

Sound
Sound Effects Editing: Ben Burtt, Tom Bellfort
Visual Effects

WHAT WON THAT YEAR?
Best Picture: *American Beauty*
Directing: Sam Mendes *American Beauty*
Actor in a Leading Role: Kevin Spacey *American Beauty*
Actress in a Leading Role: Hilary Swank *Boys Don't Cry*

BAFTAS

2 nominations

Sound
Special Visual Effects

WHAT WON THAT YEAR?
Film/British Film: *American Beauty*/ *East is East*
Direction: Pedro Almodovar *All About My Mother*
Actor: Kevin Spacey *American Beauty*
Actress: Annette Bening *American Beauty*

29

Dir: Basil DEARDEN / UK
Released in Britain: 1950
Running Time: 84 minutes
Black and white
Estimated Attendance: 13.3 million

Two conflicting stereotypes – the warm-hearted bobby on the beat, and the cold-eyed, pistol-brandishing thug – clashed in this most famous of homegrown police movies. In the process, a stylish star (Dirk Bogarde) and a cherished television series (*Dixon of Dock Green*) were born …

THE BLUE LAMP

Director **Basil Dearden**
Producer **Michael Balcon**
Screenplay **T. E. B. Clarke**
Director of Photography **Gordon Dines**
Editor **Peter Tanner**
Production Designer **Gavin Bocquet**
Music **Ernest Irving**

PC George Dixon • Jack Warner
PC Andy Mitchell • Jimmy Hanley
Tom Riley • Dirk Bogarde
Sergeant Roberts • Robert Flemyng
Divisional Detective Inspector Cherry • Bernard Lee
Diana Lewis • Peggy Evans
Spud • Patric Doonan
PC Jock Campbell • Bruce Seton
PC Taff Hughes • Meredith Edwards
Sergeant Brooks • Clive Morton
Alf Lewis • Frederick Piper
Maisie • Dora Bryan
Mrs Dixon • Gladys Henson
Herself • Tessie O'Shea
Chief Inspector Hammond • William Mervyn
PC Tovey • Charles Saynor
Station Sergeant • Campbell Singer
Sergeant Grace Millard • Gwynne Whitby
PC Lock • Anthony Steel
Superintendent Harwood • Sidney Pointer

THE STORY

PC George Dixon and new recruit PC Andy Mitchell are sent to investigate the disappearance of Diana Lewis, girlfriend of young thug Tom Riley and his cohort Spud. George tries to persuade Ma Dixon to let Andy lodge with them, taking the room of their son, Bert, who was killed in the war. She is reluctant, but soon warms to Andy and relents. That night, Andy is on his beat when he hears a scream and rushes to investigate. A jeweller and his mistress have been robbed by two youths, who stole their shop keys. Tom and Spud rob the jeweller's shop, knocking out PC Taff Hughes before making their escape. The only evidence is a belt that Taff pulled from Tom's coat.

Opposite *Community policing: PC Andy Mitchell (Jimmy Hanley) with Queenie (Gene Neighbors)* **This page** *'Take that!' PC Taff Hughes (Meredith Evans) is felled by Tom Riley (Dirk Bogarde)*

OSCARS

WHAT WON THAT YEAR
Best Motion Picture: *All about Eve*
Directing: Joseph L. Mankiewicz *All about Eve*
Actor: José Ferrer *Cyrano de Bergerac*
Actress: Judy Holliday *Born Yesterday*

BAFTAS

1 nomination, **1 winner**

British Film

WHAT WON THAT YEAR?
Film: *All About Eve*

Next day, Tom meets Diana. She is spotted by Andy, who recognises her from her missing person's report and brings her in. Diana becomes hysterical, and is allowed to leave. As she goes, an officer spots her compact, which resembles one missing from the jewellers' job. Tom and Spud have obtained guns and, with Diana's inside information, begin planning to hold up the Coliseum cinema, where she works. That night, they go to the nearby music hall to establish an alibi, before heading for the Coliseum. But while they hold up the box office, they are disturbed by customers, who fetch the nearby Dixon. George tries to reason with Tom, but he panics and shoots George. Desperate, Tom and Spud make their getaway, but a passer-by gets their number-plate.

Ma and Andy visit George in hospital. Meanwhile the car has been found. Andy finds a group of children playing with a pistol and returns to the station with the young girl who found it, Queenie. He learns that George is dead; the investigation has become a murder case. A hunt turns up Tom's coat, which matches the belt. They trace the coat to Diana's father, who tells them Diana lent it to a boyfriend. Tom, increasingly desperate, learns that police are looking for Diana. He decides to go to the police to try to establish his innocence, but is caught unawares when questioned about the coat. After an identity parade, Tom is released, but tailed. He heads home to find Diana gone. He finds her at Spud's and, when she refuses to go with him, he tries to strangle her. Inspector Campbell arrives but is fought off by Tom and Spud, who steal a car and get away. A chase ensues, ending in a crash in which Spud dies. Tom flees into a dog stadium. The doors are locked, trapping him inside while police reinforcements are called. Tom is cornered near the exits. He points his gun, but is trapped by the departing crowd, and the officers disarm him.

WHAT THEY SAID THEN …

The latest production from Ealing Studios unavoidably courts comparison with Hollywood; it must be said that comparison on all major counts is unfavourable. The story is no more nor less conventional than that of *The Naked City* or *The Street With No Name* (both 1948). There is sterling location work: camera units cover various parts of London, including Ladbroke Grove, the Edgware Road, Cranbourne Street and White City. The routine of police investigation is carefully documented. Where *The Blue Lamp* attempts more than most current Hollywood thrillers is in its humanisation of the police force, its horde of minor characters.

But in the casting lies a fatal flaw. Jimmy Hanley and Jack Warner have been presenting allegedly authentic British types on the screen for at least five years; by now their personalities are wholly tabloid. Their dialogue – quips, quirks and Cockney bonhomie – is effectively prefabricated.

The representation of criminals is less conventional; the actors, Patric Doonan and Dirk Bogarde, have individuality and flair. Inevitably one of them inhabits an immaculately flyblown room right on top of the underground railway, and his girlfriend is a peculiar amalgam of Ealing and Hollywood – the inept Purley blonde, trying to masquerade under a Cockney accent, alternately kissed and slapped, and worked up by the director to a state of perpetual hysteria.

The film's American equivalents may only be two-dimensional, but at least they achieve a spontaneous and convincing representation of the orthodox. The attempt in *The Blue Lamp* to go beyond this, to put all kinds of Real British Life on the screen, results in the mixture of coyness, patronage and naive theatricality which has vitiated British films for the last ten years. This, it need hardly be added, is now a serious offence.

Opposite *A collection of press posters for the film* **Right** *'Stick 'em up!' Tom (Dirk Bogarde) holds up the Coliseum box office and a frightened cashier (Doris Yorke)*

WHAT THEY SAY NOW ...

Probably the most famous of all British police films, *The Blue Lamp* is a classic example of the Ealing Studios ethos of inclusiveness. The film was scripted by the ex-policeman T. E. B. Clarke (adapted from a story by Ted Willis and Jan Read), who was the writer who arguably did most to define the studio's post-war identity.

In a pseudo-documentary opening, the film offers itself as an examination of a new breed of young criminal, hardened by the war years, whose recklessness and violence contrasts with the discipline of the older criminal fraternity. Dirk Bogarde's edgy performance as loose cannon Tom Riley launched his career, but the centre of the film is Jack Warner's unimpeachable PC George Dixon – even though Dixon is shot by Riley around halfway through and dies shortly after. But spare your tears. Dixon made a remarkable recovery from his untimely death, becoming known to millions of TV viewers as *Dixon of Dock Green* in the BBC series of that name.

George Dixon is the kind of ordinary hero who had become a commonplace of Ealing films during the war period. He is an unassuming moral giant of a man, loved by all those around him and always ready with a reassuring song and a piece of simple wisdom. The scene in which Mrs Dixon (played by Gladys Henson) learns of her husband's death is a masterpiece of understated emotion, moving without falling into sentimentality.

As a British response to developments in the crime genre, however, the film is less successful. While there is a convincing fury to Bogarde's performance, the picture lacks the moral complexity of the Hollywood film noir of the 1940s. In place of the ambiguities of film noir – its blurring of the boundaries between hero and villain – *The Blue Lamp* offers a very English vision of honest, cheerful bobbies unwavering in their determination to root out crime.

SCENE STEALER

The most interesting part of *The Blue Lamp* is arguably the memorable climax, in which the fugitive Tom is finally captured at the greyhound stadium thanks to an impromptu alliance of police and criminals. It's a very Ealing conclusion: the community comes together, abandoning its internal divisions to defeat a common threat and restore the social order.

THE MAN WITH THE GUN

The violent sexuality that Dirk Bogarde brings to the role of Tom almost unbalances the film's sober intentions. Later, the astoundingly popular *Doctor in the House* (1954), which features at number 36 in the Ultimate Film list, initiated Bogarde's 'Idol of the Odeons' phase. But he grew heartily tired of his popular image and deliberately sought to change it. In 1961, he starred as the gay barrister in *Victim* (also directed by Basil Dearden), the first mainstream film to tackle the issue of homosexuality. Soon he acquired a sly, furrowed gravitas in *The Servant* (1963), which marked the emergence of the new Bogarde. He played the film's eponym with a riveting aura of opportunism, adducing weapons of sex and class hatred in a blackly comic tussle for power. He made three further films for that picture's director, Joseph Losey, and thereafter became, in his own words, 'a European actor', memorably associated with the likes of Luchino Visconti, Alain Resnais and Bertrand Tavernier.

30

Dir: William WYLER / USA
Released in Britain: 1960
Running Time: 217 minutes
Colour: Technicolor
Estimated Attendance: 13.2 million

In its day, *Ben-Hur* was a record-breaking phenomenon – the most expensive movie ever made, trailing behind it a chariot full of Academy Awards. Indeed, its Oscar tally remains equalled but still unbeaten. Has its epic lustre likewise endured?

BEN-HUR

Director **William Wyler**
Producer **Sam Zimbalist**
Screenplay **Karl Tunberg**, adapted from the novel
  by Lew Wallace
Director of Photography **Robert Surtees**
Editor **Ralph E. Winters**
Art Directors **William A. Horning, Edward C. Carfagno**
Music **Miklós Rózsa**

Judah Ben-Hur • Charlton Heston
Quintus Arrius • Jack Hawkins
Esther • Haya Harareet
Messala • Stephen Boyd
Sheik Ilderim • Hugh Griffith
Miriam • Martha Scott
Tirzah • Cathy O'Donnell
Simonides • Sam Jaffe
Balthazar • Finlay Currie
Pontius Pilate • Frank Thring
Drusus • Terence Longdon
Tiberius • George Relph
Sextus • André Morell
Quasteor • David Davies
Flavia • Marina Berti
Malluch • Adi Berber
Amrah • Stella Vitelleschi
Mary • José Greci
Joseph • Laurence Payne
Spintho • John Horsley

THE STORY

In the seventh year of the reign of Augustus Caesar, Prince Judah Ben-Hur is born into a wealthy Jewish family about the same time as Jesus Christ. Years later, he is reunited with his boyhood friend, Messala, who has taken over command of the Roman garrison in Jerusalem. When Ben Hur refuses to inform against other Jewish patriots, Messala condemns him to certain death as a galley slave and imprisons his mother, Miriam, and sister, Tirzah, in a dungeon.

For three years Ben-Hur suffers the brutalities of Roman war galleys, until he is freed, adopted, and brought to Rome by Quintus Arrius, the Roman Admiral whose life he saves in battle. Although lauded as an athlete, Ben-Hur insists upon returning to Jerusalem in the hope of tracing his family. On the way he encounters Sheik Ilderim, who plans to race his chariot against the Romans at the Jerusalem games. Having astonished the Sheik by his horsemanship, Ben-Hur arrives at his derelict home and immediately confronts Messala, who tells him that his mother and sister are dead.

Ben-Hur agrees to ride for Ilderim in the chariot race against Messala. He drives Messala to the ground and accepts the victor's laurel from the Governor, Pontius Pilate. But Messala has his revenge. With his dying breath he tells Ben-Hur that Miriam and Tirzah are alive but lepers. Heartbroken, Ben-Hur defies Pilate and sets out to raise a rebellion. But he is caught up in the procession to Calvary, sees Miriam and Tirzah miraculously healed, and is converted to Christianity. With Christ's death and Ben-Hur's rebirth a new era begins, and Ben-Hur looks forward to a future with Esther, a beautiful slave girl who has loved him secretly for years.

WHAT THEY SAID THEN ...

Ben-Hur is dignified and conventional, with an academic air reminiscent of some prestige productions of the 1930s. It progresses harmlessly from schoolroom scripture-book frescoes of the Byre and the carpenter's shed to the Sermon on the Mount. As the third Hollywood version of Major General Lew Wallace's novel (the first was made in 1907), it seems faithful to the period (1880) and moral tone in which it was written. Freudians may find little difficulty in categorising the relationship between Ben-Hur and Messala as it burgeons from slow handshakes to whippings and a blood-drenched death scene. But in fact the whole tear-bedaubed conception is a Victorian one, embracing as it does Frank Thring's portrayal of Pontius Pilate as an exquisite, Oscar Wildean figure, a wilting orgy reminiscent

Opposite *Thirsty work: Ben-Hur is offered water by Jack Hawkins as Quintus Arrius* **Above** *Where did you get that hat? William Wyler and Charlton Heston share a joke on set* **Below** *Muscle-bound Charlton Heston shows he's been working out as Roman galley slave Ben-Hur*

Above Ben-Hur (Charlton Heston) is whipped but unbowed *Below* The spectacular setting for the chariot race *Opposite above* Here's one for William Wyler's scrapbook *Opposite below* Stephen Boyd rides to his doom as Messala

of *Intolerance* (1916), and the sudden switch in Jack Hawkins's Quintus Arrius from a sort of 19th-century flogging headmaster to a Dickensian uncle-figure.

Despite moments of elegiac beauty, William Wyler's handling is for the most part laboured, falling into a series of cliché situations and tableaux, tediously static love scenes and violent crises, to all of which Charlton Heston's hero responds with the rigid propriety of a very tall boy scout.

Fortunately there are compensations – some unexpected (the compelling presence of Stephen Boyd's Messala, the artful comic relief of Hugh Griffith's Welsh-accented sheik), others of the kind one has a right to expect from the third longest and the most expensive ($15,000,000) movie to date. The galley scenes have a magisterial horror; the pageantry of the arena and the detail of the scenes behind the races display an impressive precision; the chariot race itself, staged by Andrew Marion and Yakima Canutt, is a tour de force.

WHAT THEY SAY NOW ...

Subtitled *A Tale of the Christ*, the self-important pseudo-religiosity of *Ben-Hur* is the excuse for its regular television airings at Easter and Christmas. But it is a genuinely entertaining spectacle, and one can even forgive Charlton Heston's joyless determination to embody dignity throughout. In contrast Stephen Boyd's pizzazz as Messala lifts all their scenes together. The sea battle and the chariot race (paid lavish homage in the pod race sequence in *Star Wars Episode I: The Phantom Menace*, 1999) shine as jewels in the crown of this handsome epic.

CLASSIC QUOTE

Quintus Arrius: 'Your eyes are full of hate, Forty-One. That's good. Hate keeps a man alive.'

SCENE STEALER

Constructed at Rome's Cinecittà Studios and in its day the largest outdoor set ever built, the circus arena packed with thousands of extras is the setting for what remains one of the most thrilling action sequences ever filmed: the chariot race,

a breakneck eleven minutes that took five weeks to shoot and gives the Semitic peoples rooting for Ben-Hur and his stellar white steeds a rare triumph over the hated Romans. But Judah's glory is brief as he learns from Messala that his mother and sister are in the Valley of the Lepers. 'It goes on,' gloats Messala. 'It goes on, Judah. The race, the race is not over.'

BEHIND THE SCENES

Heston fretted about his charioteering and horsemanship until the legendary stuntman Yakima Canutt, who staged the sequence (with his son Joe as Heston's stunt double), wearily pointed out: 'Chuck, trust me. You're going to win the race.' The notorious homoerotic frisson between Messala and Judah was the mischievous suggestion of uncredited screenwriter Gore Vidal. Wyler warmed to the subtext and worked it up with Boyd but cautioned, 'For God's sake, don't tell Chuck!' For proof that Heston really was oblivious, see the hilarious javelin-throwing scene.

IN THE CHAIR

William Wyler, a production assistant on the 1920s *Ben-Hur*, was the master of many genres and had already won two Oscars for direction (for *Mrs Miniver*, 1942, and *The Best Years of Our Lives*, 1946 – the latter arguably his masterpiece, and both also in the Ultimate Film list). Esteemed as a craftsman and a stylist (not to mention a perfectionist nicknamed '90-Take Wyler'), he was notable for eliciting career-best and Oscar-winning performances from a string of actors, and for employing techniques such as deep focus. Considering *Ben-Hur*'s commercial and artistic supremacy – a record eleven Oscars and America's biggest box-office take in a decade – it is sad and surprising to note Wyler's swift fall from fashion in the 1960s, when he made only five more films.

Since the release of

Dr No in 1962, James Bond has been one of the few enduring icons of British cinema. Representing sophistication, style, predatory sexuality and unerring poise even in the tightest of narrative corners, Bond has given British audiences a comforting fixed point in a world that has become increasingly unpredictable.

James Bond made his first appearance in Ian Fleming's novel *Casino Royale* in 1952. Fleming, a veteran of Naval Intelligence, created Bond in his own image and protected him jealously. This made bringing him to the screen a lengthy and delicate process. *Casino Royale* was produced for American television in 1954, and the rights were subsequently bought by American agent Charles K. Feldman. The rights to the other books were bought by Harry Saltzman, who teamed up with Albert R. Broccoli, another producer eager to bring Bond to the screen. Calling themselves Eon Productions, they found a sympathetic studio in United Artists, who offered a six-picture deal, beginning with *Dr No* in 1962.

Dr No was made for $1.1 million – a relatively small sum even in 1962 – and starred a little-known Scottish actor, Sean Connery, as Bond. Fleming was doubtful about the film, not least because he

had wanted either Noël Coward or Cary Grant to play Bond, but he was surprised by the quality of the finished product. So were critics and audiences, and *Dr No* eventually grossed nearly $60 million worldwide.

There have been 20 'official' Bond films released by Eon Productions. Yet despite the fact that the series has been in the rudest of health since Pierce Brosnan took over the part in 1995, only one post-1970s title makes the Ultimate Film

Opposite above George Lazenby is On Her Majesty's Secret Service *Opposite below* Sean Connery removes his wetsuit to reveal a white tuxedo, complete with red carnation, in Goldfinger **Left from top** Roger Moore dons the white tuxedo in A View to a Kill; Timothy Dalton gets the Licence to Kill; The World is not Enough for Pierce Brosnan

list – *Die Another Day*, which was a major box-office success in 2002. Five actors have appeared as Bond: Connery, George Lazenby, Roger Moore, Timothy Dalton and Brosnan. Two other Bond films have emerged since 1962: *Casino Royale*, an incoherent all-star comedy, and *Never Say Never Again*, with an older but still eminently charismatic Connery.

Each film uses a selection of narrative elements that can be juggled endlessly: the 'Bond Girls', invariably beautiful and receptive to Bond's attentions; the megalomaniac villains (keeping with the times, the menace in the 1997 *Tomorrow Never Dies* came from a Rupert Murdoch-style media baron); exotic locations in which Bond invariably causes havoc; the bizarre array of henchmen put up against the super-spy; the ingeniously enhanced cars; lengthy chases involving anything from speedboats to tanks.

Other elements have changed with time and taste. Q's gadgets, for example, began in low-key fashion and gradually escalated in importance before it was decided to return them to the background. The role of M was initially an avuncular guardian, then a bad tempered civil servant and finally a tough-talking, unsentimental woman; and the roles played by the Superpowers evolved as the Cold War thawed and the Communist bloc finally disintegrated. Most strikingly, Bond himself has altered. In *GoldenEye* (1995), he was rightly labelled a 'dinosaur' by the mocking M. By the time Bond smarted at his betrayal by a lover in *The World Is Not Enough* (1999), it could be argued that he had become virtually human.

Dir: Steven SPIELBERG / USA
Released in Britain: 1983
Running Time: 115 minutes
Colour: Deluxe
Estimated Attendance: 13.13 million

He is afraid. He is alone. He is three million light years from home. He is also a waddling, bug-eyed oddball with skin like chamois leather, who had the nation sobbing into its popcorn. *Jaws* (1975) and *Jurassic Park* (1993) may have been bigger hits, but *E.T. The Extra-Terrestrial* is the Spielberg movie that stole hearts.

E.T. THE EXTRA-TERRESTRIAL

Director **Steven Spielberg**
Producers **Steven Spielberg, Kathleen Kennedy**
Screenplay **Melissa Mathison**
Director of Photography **Allen Daviau**
Editor **Carol Littleton**
Production Designer **James D. Bissell**
Music John Williams

Mary • Dee Wallace
Elliott • Henry Thomas
'Keys' • Peter Coyote
Michael • Robert MacNaughton
Gertie • Drew Barrymore
Greg • K. C. Martel
Steve • Sean Frye
Tyler • C. Thomas Howell
Pretty Girl • Erika Eleniak
Schoolboy • David O'Dell
Science Teacher • Richard Swingler
Policeman • Frank Toth

THE STORY

An alien spacecraft has come to earth on the outskirts of a Los Angeles suburb. Its inhabitants are frightened back into the craft – and into space – by a group of men,who are apparently searching for them. One of the aliens is inadvertently left behind, and he takes shelter in the back garden of a house where 10-year-old Elliott lives with his mother, Mary, older brother, Michael, and younger sister, Gertie. After being initially wary of the creature, Elliott tries to make his guest at home, hiding him from Mary but introducing him to his brother and sister. 'E.T.' (who has already established an empathetic relationship with Elliott) eventually communicates that he would like to 'phone home'.

The children help him build the necessary device, while the searchers in radio vans close in. On Halloween the children smuggle E.T. out of the house, and Elliott spends the night with him in the hills as he tries to communicate with his own people. E.T. sickens, and Elliott, becoming ill himself, returns home, whereupon the searchers break into the house and set up equipment for reviving both the boy and the extra terrestrial. Eventually, the sympathetic bond between the two is broken and Elliott recovers while E.T. apparently dies. But a message from 'home' restores him, and Elliott persuades Michael and their school friends to help transport him back to the woods, where the spacecraft returns and Elliott bids E.T. a sad farewell.

WHAT THEY SAID THEN ...

E.T. The Extra-Terrestrial revives the child in all of us, but at the expense of any adult sense of wonder. It does this, in fact, with a literal amputation, since its most striking feature is that adult males are never shown above the midriff until nearly the end of the film. This truncating motif is a manifestation of Elliott's psychological state. The boy comes from a broken home, his father having recently left for Mexico with another woman. So the disappearance of his father becomes the graphic elimination of the male above a certain height – and drives Elliott to a secret companion, ageless and sexless, with whom he establishes such a deep sympathy that it threatens his life.

The film's complexities are eventually obliterated by the high-spirited-kids-and-indestructible-families ethic of Disney. Not so alien to Disney, either, are the religious trappings of this sweet optimism: a mother called Mary, the resurrection of E.T., and then his revelation, robed in white, to his disciples (the kids on their bikes). These trappings confirm a more general undertone to the upbeat ending of *Close Encounters of the Third Kind* (1977). It might be interesting to speculate how Spielberg, a nice Jewish boy, got from *The Ten Commandments* as inspiration in *Close Encounters* to this *New Testament* flimflam.

This is not to suggest that pessimism (say, Elliott having to give up E.T., the child-within-him, more completely than he does here) would inevitably be preferable to optimism. Just that there are puzzling, frustrating and finally

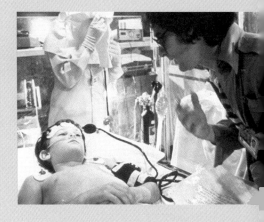

Above *Elliott (Henry Thomas, on bed) is coached though a difficult scene by director Steven Spielberg* **Left** *With E.T. The Extra Terrestrial, Spielberg created one iconic image (left) and hijacked another (for the poster,* **Below***)*

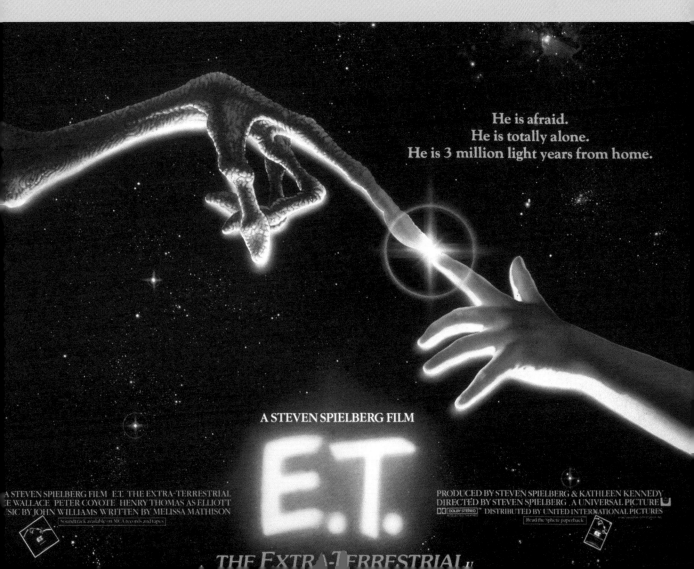

He is afraid.
He is totally alone.
He is 3 million light years from home.

A STEVEN SPIELBERG FILM

E.T.

A STEVEN SPIELBERG FILM E.T. THE EXTRA-TERRESTRIAL
E WALLACE PETER COYOTE HENRY THOMAS AS ELLIOTT
SIC BY JOHN WILLIAMS WRITTEN BY MELISSA MATHISON
Soundtrack available on MCA records and tapes

PRODUCED BY STEVEN SPIELBERG & KATHLEEN KENNEDY
DIRECTED BY STEVEN SPIELBERG . A UNIVERSAL PICTURE
DOLBY STEREO DISTRIBUTED BY UNITED INTERNATIONAL PICTURES
Read the sphere paperback

THE EXTRA-TERRESTRIAL

evasive leaps in the film's optimism. Spielberg is ready to sacrifice any logic of plot or character, and certainly of theme, for his celebratory climax, and so can turn the sinister search party hunting E.T. from an oppressively official presence into a benevolent one at the end, without ever indicating what their exact function is.

Spielberg's talent for fantasy is so complete that you want to call it something else, a graphic reinvention of the world. Here it amounts to what might be experienced by anthropomorphised cartoon characters – Tom and Jerry, perhaps – playing in a world occupied by headless, harrying people, who interfere with their (and Spielberg's) delight in knocking over the furniture.

WHAT THEY SAY NOW ...

E.T. is at once the most straightforward and most complex of Steven Spielberg's works. Its simple premise can be effectively summarized by screenwriter Melissa Mathison's original title *E.T. and Me*. But beneath this fairy-tale-like account of a young boy's friendship with an alien is a film of enormous richness that probes existing anxieties surrounding the breakdown of family life.

With a terrific feel for the rhythms of Elliot's suburban milieu, Spielberg encourages us to view the wise, benign E.T. as a surrogate for Elliot's estranged father. This theme made E.T. the object of countless analyses by Freudian-inclined critics, who were especially excited by the film's suggestive imagery – male authority figures shot only from the waist down, a house wrapped in womb-like transparent sheets, and so on. (The writer Andrew Sarris said that Freudians and children were the best kind of audiences for the movie.) One thing is clear: Spielberg – himself the child of a troubled marriage who claimed that E.T was about his parents' divorce – charges Elliot's relationship to E.T. with an intensity of feeling seldom seen elsewhere in his work.

Above E.T. and Elliott share a moment *Right* Gertie (Drew Barrymore) bids farewell to E.T. in the heart-wrenching final scene *Far right* E.T. gets into character as Spielberg calls 'Action!'

If there's a paternal resonance to the dynamic between Elliot and E.T., their partnership is also one of cinema's great love stories and its break-up at the end of the film is as potent a tear-jerker as the parting that closes *Brief Encounter* (1945). Spielberg is held responsible for a sugar-coated sentimentality that has infantilised American cinema. There may be a child-like sense of wonderment to the guileless innocence of E.T., but the film also recognises the fearful insecurities and vulnerabilities involved in being young. As with the best of Disney, it's not the huge, effects-driven set pieces that resonate but the quiet emotional grace notes. 'The equivalent of the mother ship landing in *Close Encounters*,' Spielberg said, 'is, in *E.T.*, perhaps a tear out of Henry Thomas's eye.'

CLASSIC QUOTE
E.T.: 'E.T. phone home.'

SCENE STEALER
Elliot has rescued E.T. from probing government scientists and is taking him on his bike to a rendezvous point the alien has arranged with his mother ship. He's accompanied by his friends, who are also cycling. The scientists take chase in their cars through the hilly suburban neighbourhood. They're on the point of catching up with the boy, when E.T. uses his powers to make the cyclists airborne. As night falls, their bikes are silhouetted gliding past a moon of chalky brightness.

BEHIND THE SCENES
Designed by Carlo Rambaldi, E.T. was based on a 'compilation drawing' Spielberg did using the features of Carl Sandburg, Ernest Hemingway and Albert Einstein. Its development cost nearly a tenth of what was, for Spielberg, a tight budget.

HOLDING THE BATON
John Williams's music for Steven Spielberg's 1974 theatrical debut *The Sugarland Express* marked the beginning of a collaboration that lasts to this day. The composer and director are well matched: with lushly orchestrated, insistently melodic themes that evoke the rousing classically influenced scores of studio films from the 1930s and 1940s, Williams's music is the tonal equivalent of Spielberg's grand, populist style. The composer's work has been described by some as bombastic, but this criticism neglects the skill with which his music enhances the dramatic import of existing footage: would *Jaws* be quite so terrifying, for instance, without his foreboding strings accompaniment? Williams also provided the score for *Star Wars* (1977), an achievement that, added to his music for Spielberg's movies, makes him the most successful composer ever. An accomplished jazz pianist, he is also adept at working in other musical registers, as demonstrated by his spare, jazzy score for *Catch Me If You Can* (2002).

32

Dir: Cecil B. DEMILLE / USA
Released in Britain: 1952
Running Time: 154 minutes
Colour: Technicolor
Estimated Attendance: 13 million

THE GREATEST SHOW ON EARTH

Director/Producer **Cecil B. DeMille**
Producers **Cecil B. DeMille, Fredric M. Frank**
Screenplay **Barré Lyndon, Theodore St John, Fredric M. Frank**, adapted from a story by Theodore St John and Frank Cavett
Director of Photography **George Barnes**
Editor **Anne Bauchens**
Art Directors **Hal Pereira, Walter Tyler**
Music **Victor Young**

Buttons • James Stewart
Holly • Betty Hutton
Sebastian • Cornel Wilde
Brad • Charlton Heston
Phyllis • Dorothy Lamour
Angel • Gloria Grahame
FBI Inspector Gregory • Henry Wilcoxon
Klaus • Lyle Bettger
Henderson • Lawrence Tierney
Himself • Emmett Kelly
Himself • Cucciola
Herself • Antoinette Concello
Himself • John Ringling North
Himself • Tuffy Genders
Harry • John Kellogg
Jack Steelman, Assistant Manager • John Ridgely
Circus Doctor • Frank Wilcox
Mr Loyal, The Ringmaster • Bob Carson
Buttons's Mother • Lillian Albertson
Violet • Julia Faye

Cecil B. DeMille was regarded as a master of showbiz spectacle – not least by himself – so it came as little surprise when he eventually made a film played out under the big top. But the result, while popular with audiences and the Academy, is one of his least fondly remembered works.

THE STORY

The Ringling Bros. and Barnum & Bailey Circus, 'The Greatest Show on Earth', is starting a long tour. Brad, the manager, has engaged a famous French aerialist, Sebastian, as a star attraction: Holly, a trapeze artist with whom Brad is in love, has to be displaced from the centre ring. She is bitterly disappointed. On the tour, other characters are introduced: Buttons, the Clown, always wearing his make-up in case the FBI should get him – a doctor years ago, he joined the circus to escape a murder charge; Angel, the elephant girl, and her jealous colleague, Klaus; Phyllis, the iron-jaw girl, an old flame of Sebastian; and Sebastian himself, a confident French charmer who immediately flirts with Holly.

Rivalry on the trapezes develops between Holly and Sebastian. The latter, attempting a spectacular trick, falls and paralyses one arm. Holly, out of pity, decides she loves him. Angel then makes play for Brad, and the jealous Klaus, after trying to kill her by making an elephant stand on her face, is fired by Brad. Klaus falls in with crooks, who plan an attack on the circus train at night. The attack goes wrong, and there is a train crash in which Klaus is killed. Brad is pinned under the wreckage, Sebastian gives his blood for a transfusion and Buttons operates, knowing that he will give himself away to the FBI by doing so.

The circus is badly damaged and it is impossible to put up the big top in the next town. Holly, however, stages a mammoth parade and brings the townspeople to see the show in the open. She and Brad are reunited and 'The Greatest Show on Earth' goes on.

WHAT THEY SAID THEN ...

It was perhaps inevitable that DeMille should be drawn to the oversized spectacle of the circus. More unexpected is his flat, tabloid approach. Perhaps it wouldn't have mattered if the other compensations had been there – a sign of real feeling for circus life, for instance, with its danger and tawdriness. But too many of the circus acts look faked, the backgrounds are one-dimensional, and DeMille himself intervenes from time to time with an insanely megalomaniac commentary, stressing nothing but size and expense. Over a quite ordinary series of shots of the big top being dismantled after a show, and the business of packing up going quietly on, he describes the scene as 'a mad chaos of man and beast'. Apart from one impressive shot of the big top itself

OSCARS

5 nominations, **2 winners**

Best Motion Picture
Directing: Cecil B. DeMille
Costume Design (Color): Edith Head, Dorothy Jeakins, Miles White
Film Editing: Anne Bauchens
Writing (Motion Picture Story): Frederic M. Frank, Theodore St. John, Frank Cavett

WHAT WON THAT YEAR?
Directing: John Ford *The Quiet Man*
Actor: Gary Cooper *High Noon*
Actress: Shirley Booth *Come Back, Little Sheba*

BAFTAS

WHAT WON THAT YEAR?
Film and British Film: *The Sound Barrier*
British Actor: Ralph Richardson *The Sound Barrier*
British Actress: Vivien Leigh *A Streetcar Named Desire*
Foreign Actor: Marlon Brando *Viva, Zapata!*
Foreign Actress: Simone Signoret *Casque d'Or*

Below *Fallen hero Sebastian (Cornel Wilde) is helped from the arena by Button the Clown (James Stewart) and Charlton Heston's Brad*

being erected, there is not a visually striking effect in the film. Dorothy Lamour, though billed as the iron-jaw girl, does nothing except croon numbers into a single microphone in the arena (she could never have been heard); Betty Hutton is energetic as Holly; James Stewart makes an unengaging clown; Charlton Heston has little to do as Brad.

With so much apparatus to play with, DeMille and the film can hardly fail to give an impression of vastness, activity and a certain picturesque atmosphere; but this cannot conceal an almost heroic lack of imagination throughout.

WHAT THEY SAY NOW ...

Cecil B. DeMille's extraordinary instinct for crowd-pleasing entertainment had led him to master the quasi-biblical spectacle, often spicing his ambitious religious epics with licentious orgy scenes to illustrate just how right the moralists were to condemn such excesses. In 1952 he made his modern-day circus epic, securing full co-operation from Ringling Brothers and Barnum & Bailey, even going so far as to use their slogan as his title. It is ponderously long, at 153 minutes; its best moments are those documentary-like scenes of life on the road, the parades through Middle-American towns, and the struggle to get the big top aloft.

But the interlocking stories are banal, with Charlton Heston especially bland as the harried boss coping with temperamental performers, sick animals and gangsters muscling in on the action. The climactic high point is a train wreck which, in spite of occasionally obvious miniatures, comes at the right moment to relieve the general tedium. DeMille's film was a box-office triumph and won the Oscar for Best Picture, in a year when the favourite was *High Noon*. All DeMille's other Academy Awards had been honorary.

33

Dir: David LEAN / UK, USA
Released in Britain: 1957
Running Time: 160 minutes
Colour: Technicolor
Estimated Attendance: 12.6 million

The impression we have today of David Lean was truly forged with the release of *The Bridge on the River Kwai*. Here, he fused the epic with the intimate to create the grand, sweeping style of cinema for which he would forever be known.

THE BRIDGE ON THE RIVER KWAI

Director **David Lean**
Producer **Sam Spiegel**
Screenplay **Michael Wilson and Carl Foreman (on restored version), Pierre Boulle (on original prints)**, adapted from the novel by Pierre Boulle
Director of Photography **Jack Hildyard**
Editor **Peter Taylor**
Art Director **Don Ashton**
Music **Malcolm Arnold**

Shears • William Holden
Major Warden • Jack Hawkins
Colonel Nicholson • Alec Guinness
Colonel Saito • Sessue Hayakawa
Major Clipton • James Donald
Colonel Green • André Morell
Captain Reeves • Peter Williams
Major Hughes • John Boxer
Grogan • Percy Herbert
Baker • Harold Goodwin
Nurse • Ann Sears
Captain Kanematsu • Henry Okawa
Lieutenant Miura • Keiichiro Katsumoto
Yai • M. R. B. Chakrabandhu
Siamese Girl • Vilaiwan Seeboonreaung
Siamese Girl • Ngamta Suphaphongs
Siamese Girl • Javanart Punynchoti
Siamese Girl • Kannikar Dowklee
Lieutenant Joyce • Geoffrey Horne

THE STORY

A battalion of British war prisoners, under the command of Colonel Nicholson, is employed by the Japanese on the 'death railway'. Specifically, their task is to build a bridge on the River Kwai, a vital link in Japanese military communications. When officers are ordered to work alongside the men, Nicholson cites the Geneva Convention. Refusing as a matter of principle, he is subjected by Colonel Saito, the Japanese commandant, to brutal imprisonment. Nicholson stands firm and wins a moral triumph. He then takes charge of the building operations, determined to restore his men's morale and to demonstrate to the Japanese the invincibility of the British soldier. The bridge, as he sees it, will be a symbol of British achievement; and in driving his men ruthlessly he wholly loses sight of the fact that he is now aiding the enemy.

Meanwhile, a small British commando force, led by Major Warden and joined by Shears, an American sailor who had previously escaped, is trekking through the jungle. Their mission is the destruction of the Kwai bridge. Nicholson, realising that a sabotage attempt is being made on his bridge, alerts the Japanese commandant. In the fight that follows, Shears, Saito and Nicholson are killed, but Warden manages to detonate the charges and the bridge is destroyed. The final comment comes from the British medical officer, a horrified onlooker: 'Madness, madness'.

WHAT THEY SAID THEN ...

The Bridge on the River Kwai tells, in effect, two interlocking stories. One is that of Colonel Nicholson, the soldier who lives and dies by the book of rules, brave, utterly confident and supremely wrong-headed. The other is that of the commando trek through the jungle and the manoeuvres leading up to the destruction of the bridge. The Nicholson section of the story is written with a fierce sense of dramatic irony and the script repeatedly develops its situations on two levels. Nicholson's stand against the Japanese is magnificent and idiotic; his obsession with the bridge has grandeur as well as absurdity; his relationship with Saito shows the opposition and points of contact between two men living largely by the same code. The script and Alec Guinness's playing make these points forcefully.

David Lean's direction, however, tends to work against the ironic effect by emphasising heroism at the expense of absurdity. The film, a highly assured piece of technical craftsmanship, is made rather too literally for the double-edged character of its central drama. On to this drama has been grafted the commando story, and the adventures of Shears during his escape from the camp. Here again there is some carrying over of the ironic overtones and some passing reflections on the nature of courage.

Much of this lengthy episode is straight war adventure, conventionally developed and made with a good deal of attention to production values. The climax, the actual destruction of the bridge, is a director's set piece. It is worth noting that the novel drives home the irony, and the conclusion that nobody wins, by ending on the failure to destroy the bridge. Altogether, this Anglo-American production has some sophisticated and telling comments to make on the conduct of men in war, but it jeopardises these by aspiring simultaneously to the status of war epic.

WHAT THEY SAY NOW ...

David Lean's plans to film Richard Mason's novel, *The Wind Cannot Read*, for Alexander Korda had come to nothing. However, his new project was also to have a jungle setting, and brought his first collaboration with legendary producer Sam Spiegel, who approached Lean with *The Bridge on the River Kwai* while he was still

Above *Colonel Nicholson (Alec Guinness) steps forward to face Colonel Saito (Sessue Hayakawa)*
Below *David Lean proving himself a hands-on director*

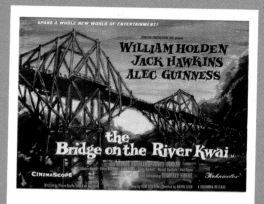

shooting *Summer Madness* (1955). Significantly, Lean was attracted by the story's epic quality, and saw a drama of Shakespearean dimensions in the tragic relationship between Saito and Nicholson. He wrote the script with Michael Wilson, although the screen credit went to the book's author, Pierre Boulle.

It is a film of two halves. The first story is replete with ironies. Nicholson, having endured terrible punishment for refusing to allow his officers to perform manual labour, actively encourages them to do so once he has decided that the bridge must be built as well as possible to demonstrate British superiority. He himself sees no irony in this, nor realises that he, the great upholder of the Geneva Convention, is collaborating with the enemy by becoming obsessed with the building of the bridge.

The second story comes as something of a shock. We seem to be watching a completely different film when the theme of the commando raid on the bridge is introduced. This segment is much more straightforwardly told, with plenty of action sequences and conventional heroics. Lean achieves some memorable images, especially the opening, a wonderful aerial shot of the jungle. A marvellous cut shows Shears's head filling the screen and appearing to come out of the sun. When the Japanese open fire on the commandos in the jungle, hundreds of birds rise up from the trees and fill the sky.

CLASSIC QUOTE
Colonel Nicholson: 'We can teach these barbarians a lesson in Western methods and efficiency that will put them to shame. We'll show them what the British soldier is capable of doing.'

SCENE STEALER
As the inaugural train approaches the bridge a suspicious Colonel Nicholson finds the wire connecting the hidden charges with its remote detonator, and raises the alarm, causing the raiding party to break cover and start firing. Mortally wounded, he falls on the plunger, blowing up his beloved bridge while the train is crossing it.

BEHIND THE SCENES
David Lean shot the film in Sri Lanka, or Ceylon as it was then known, and the bridge was specially constructed. Its destruction was a supreme test of nerve: would all the cameras fail as an expensive set piece was destroyed? In the event, the sequence was safe, although careful examination reveals continuity lapses, such as the disappearance of the locomotive amid the wreckage.

IN THE CHAIR
Sam Spiegel's production was the first test of David Lean's capability of directing an international epic, and it won him his first Oscar as well as setting him on the path he was to follow for the rest of his career. Never again would Lean direct a 'small' film.

Opposite That's blown it! A mortally wounded Colonel Nicholson (Guinness) collapses on top of the detonator **This page** Shears (William Holden) takes no prisoners

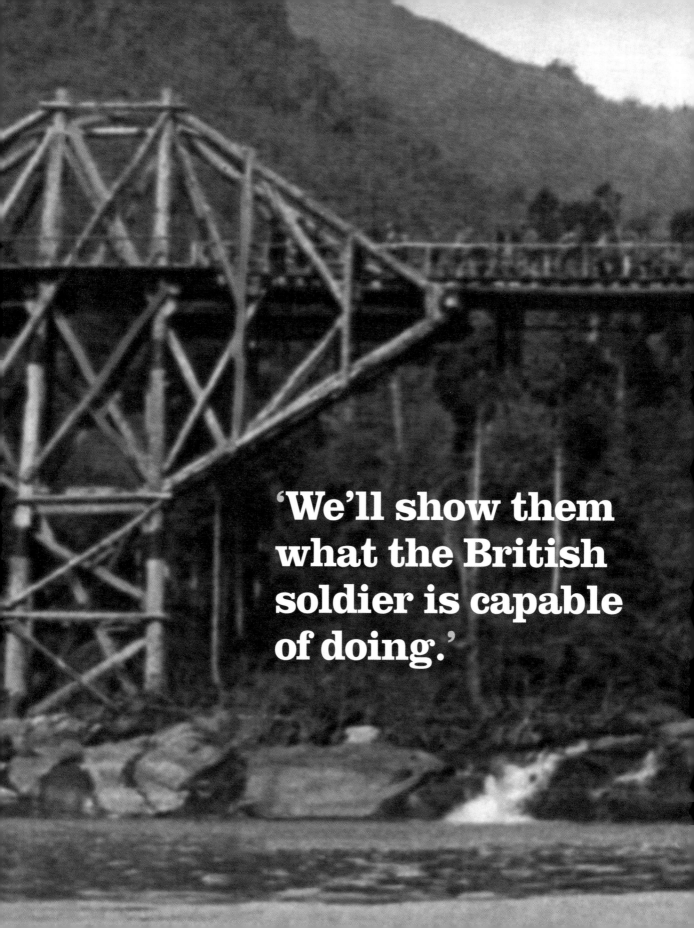

'We'll show them what the British soldier is capable of doing.'

34

Dir: Lewis GILBERT / UK
Released in Britain: 1977
Running Time: 125 minutes
Colour: Eastmancolor
Estimated Attendance: 12.46 million

Above right *The Lotus Esprit plumbs the depths*
Below right *Evil henchman Jaws (Richard Kiel, top) towers over Anya (Barbara Bach, below) and Bond (Roger Moore, right)*

For many audiences, Sean Connery will always be James Bond. But Roger Moore has an equal number of Bond outings in *The Ultimate Film* list, including *The Spy Who Loved Me*, his highest entry in the poll. It was 1977, Jubilee year, and Bond paid his own unique tribute to the Union Jack.

THE SPY WHO LOVED ME

Director **Lewis Gilbert**
Producer **Albert R. Broccoli**
Screenplay **Christopher Wood, Richard Maibaum,** based on the novel by Ian Fleming
Director of Photography **Claude Renoir**
Editor **John Glen**
Production Designer **Ken Adam**
Music **Marvin Hamlisch**

James Bond • Roger Moore
Major Anya Amasova • Barbara Bach
Stromberg • Curt Jürgens
Jaws • Richard Kiel
Naomi • Caroline Munro
General Gogol • Walter Gotell
Minister of Defence • Geoffrey Keen
M • Bernard Lee
Captain Benson • George Baker
Sergei • Michael Billington
Felicca • Olga Bisera
Q • Desmond Llewelyn
Sheikh Hosein • Edward De Souza
Max Kalba • Vernon Dobtcheff
Hotel Receptionist • Valerie Leon
Miss Moneypenny • Lois Maxwell
Liparus Captain • Sydney Tafler
Fekkesh • Nadim Sawalha
Log Cabin Girl • Sue Vanner
Rubelvitch • Eva Rueber-Staier

THE STORY

From his headquarters aboard the submarine *Atlantis*, off the coast of Sardinia, Stromberg, a shipping magnate who dreams of destroying the world and creating a new civilisation beneath the sea, has hired scientists – whom he later murders – to design a device to track nuclear submarines. Stromberg uses a giant tanker, the *Liparus*, to 'kidnap' a British and a Soviet submarine. When he discovers that a female assistant has passed microfilm of the tracking device to an Egyptian middleman, Fekkesh, for sale to the highest bidder, he has her killed, then sends strong-arm men to recover the film.

British agent James Bond and the Russian Anya Amasova are detailed by their governments to obtain the film. The pair meet in Egypt, where Stromberg'shenchman, Jaws, murders Fekkesh and another contact, Kalba, and then attempts to kill Bond and Anya. His ploy backfires, however, and they get the film. Instructed by their superiors to co-operate, the two agents trail Stromberg to Sardinia where they evade his elaborate attempts to kill them. The agents reconnoitre the *Liparus* in an American submarine which is then captured by Stromberg.

Bond subsequently overpowers his guards, releases the submarine's crew and takes control of the hangar housing the *Liparus* and Stromberg's equipment. At the last minute, Bond foils Stromberg's scheme to blow up Moscow and New York; he relays false information to the two submarines which instead blow up each other. Bond penetrates *Atlantis*, kills Stromberg and frees Anya, moments before the US Navy blows up the hideout.

WHAT THEY SAID THEN …

'Tell Bond to pull out,,' says M; cut to 007 in coitus with (anonymous) damsel in mountain chalet. Responding to the call of duty, Bond polishes off sundry (anonymous) attackers before soaring off a cliff on skis, a Union Jack parachute blossoming over his head. In the ensuing two hours, seaside-postcard smut and comic-strip feats of derring-do continue unabated, suggesting that the makers are

being driven to desperate extremes to keep the formula going.

Sometimes, however, it is difficult to determine how deliberate the absurdities are. The strip-cartoon aspect of the film extends beyond such running gags as the presence of a superhuman, steel-toothed heavy called 'Jaws', who emerges unscathed from one lethal hardship after another and drops huge boulders on his toes in careless moments, and permeates the structure itself. Narrative coherence has been disregarded in favour of a succession of self-contained set pieces.

This might not matter if these were more precisely organised or less derivative of earlier movies in the series – a train sequence out of *From Russia with Love* (1963), for instance, and a death-dealing car straight out of *Goldfinger* (1964). Indeed, where Ian Fleming's novel offered an attempt to ring some changes in terms of scale and viewpoint, the film seems to do nothing more than anthologise its forerunners. For all the expensive hardware and location shooting, it resembles a Saturday serial risen grandiloquently above its station. Still, Claude Renoir's visuals are often easy on the eye, even if Marvin Hamlisch's insistent score is never quite so kind to the ear.

WHAT THEY SAY NOW ...

History teaches us many things, not least of which is that the Bond series became increasingly bland and sluggish until Roger Moore was put out to pasture in the mid-1980s. *The Spy Who Loved Me* – which was only Moore's third outing as 007 after *Live and Let Die* (1973) and *The Man with the Golden Gun* (1974) – doesn't look so terrible to modern eyes. But then we know now that there would be worse to come – *Moonraker* (1979), *For Your Eyes Only* (1981), *Octopussy* (1983), *A View to a Kill* (1985) – before more stringent quality control measures were introduced.

As it is, the picture has a stirring title song (Carly Simon belting out 'Nobody Does It Better'), one iconic moment (the unveiling of the Union Jack parachute), an impressive car (the sleek white Lotus Esprit, which emerges dramatically from the sea to the amazement of stunned sunbathers) and one authentically menacing villain (the metal-dentured Jaws). Unfortunately, that character descends into toothless caricature by the end of the picture. Much the same can be said for Bond himself.

CLASSIC QUOTE

Log Cabin Girl: 'James, I need you!'
James Bond: 'So does England.'

BEHIND THE SCENES

Any car featured in a Bond film experiences a boost in popularity, but customers seeking a Lotus Esprit faced a three-year wait after the release of *The Spy Who Loved Me*.

35

Dir: Richard THORPE / USA
Released in Britain: 1951
Running Time: 109 minutes
Colour: Technicolor
Estimated Attendance: 12.4 million

Despite taking the tenor Enrico Caruso as its subject, *The Great Caruso* was less concerned with authenticity than with giving lovers of *The Jolson Story* (1946) more of the same: tears and tunes. In fact, its success outstripped that of the earlier film, bringing it to an impressive position in *The Ultimate Film* list.

THE GREAT CARUSO

Director **Richard Thorpe**
Producer **Joe Pasternak**
Screenplay **Sonya Levien, William Ludwig**, adapted
    from the biography by Dorothy Caruso
Director of Photography **Joseph Ruttenberg**
Editor **Gene Ruggiero**
Art Directors **Cedric Gibbons, Gabriel Scognamillo**
Musical Supervision **Johnny Green**

Enrico Caruso • Mario Lanza
Dorothy Benjamin • Ann Blyth
Louise Heggar • Dorothy Kirsten
Maria Selka • Jarmila Novotna
Carlo Santi • Richard Hageman
Park Benjamin • Carl Benton Reid
Giulio Gatti-Casazza • Eduard Franz
Alfredo Brazzi • Ludwig Donath
Jean de Reszke • Alan Napier

THE STORY

Enrico Caruso, possessor of a gigantic singing voice, fails to win his beloved Musetta because her father intervenes. With his talent acclaimed, he embarks from Naples to the Metropolitan Opera in New York where, among sophisticates, he is initially regarded as uncultured and uncouth. However, the magic of his larynx attracts wealthy patrons and endears him to Dorothy Benjamin, the socialite daughter of disapproving parents, who becomes his wife. Singing is his first love, and as the adulation escalates so does his drive to outdo his success and his health fails, leading to his early, much-mourned death.

WHAT THEY SAID THEN …

A Technicolor biography of the famous tenor, covering his birth in Naples, his early struggles as a singer, his arrival in America, his triumphs and failures, his marriage to the daughter of a wealthy Metropolitan Opera patron, and the final loss of his voice, and death. The film is laced throughout with the musical illustrations of this dazzling career, including brief extracts from *Pagliacci*, *Tosca*, *Aida*, *Rigoletto*, *La Soheme*, *Martha*, *Cavalleria Rusticana*, *La Gioconda*, *Lucia dr Lanunermoor*, as well as the inevitable 'Ave Maria', 'Because', and some Italian folk songs. It is a conventionally romanticised rather than a factual portrait, with a high-powered soundtrack; but Mario Lanza has an impressive voice and sings tirelessly, and the rest of the cast support him adequately.

WHAT THEY SAY NOW …

When MGM made *The Great Caruso* they must have had the extraordinary success of *The Jolson Story* in mind, because the film, far from being an accurate biography of the Neapolitan tenor's brief but chequered career as the most-celebrated opera singer (and womaniser) of the *belle époque*, is largely fictionalised. It is really an excuse to showcase lavish production numbers dressed only vaguely to resemble operatic staging of the actual era. The local-boy-makes-good story line expended little time on social examination, and employed clichéd signposts on which to hang the set pieces.

The star, Mario Lanza, had emerged from a Philadelphia Italian family as a singing prodigy, and had already achieved a two-million hit single with 'Be My Love' from his earlier film, *The Toast of New Orleans* (1950). His weight was always a handicap, and his muscular build frequently ballooned into corpulence, making it difficult for him to sustain romantic leads. His voice was strong and defined, and he attacked each song with exceptional power and clarity. Purists would undoubtedly have argued that he was not a Caruso impersonator, and wisely he performed the famous arias in his own style. The distinctive voice was a supreme asset, but sadly, like the great Caruso himself, Lanza also died young, burned out by high living at 38.

But the film was one of the most successful MGM musicals of all time, albeit from a very different department of the studio that produced *An American in Paris*, also released in 1951. In addition, it spawned one of the biggest-selling albums in recording history. Among the operatic stars who appeared alongside Lanza in the film was Dorothy Kirsten, whose pure soprano tones blended well with his magnificent voice. Highlights included the Quartet from *Rigoletto*, Lanza's heart-wrenching 'Celeste Aida' and his spiritual rendering of 'Ave Maria'. Grand opera was made popular as a consequence of the film, but in a way that reduced celebrated great moments to the banality of easily requested radio hits.

CLASSIC QUOTE
Dorothy: 'I loved you from the first moment you sang"

SCENE STEALER
An old, lilting waltz by the nineteenth-century Mexican composer Juventino Rosa, 'Sobra los Olas' was given lyrics by Paul Francis Webster and, as 'The Loveliest Night of the Year', became a number one hit worldwide. Even Ann Blyth manages to warble a chorus of the evocative melody.

IN THE CHAIR
Richard Thorpe's other great achievement in film musicals is *Jailhouse Rock* (1957). He was a typical journeyman of the old school who had churned out many Westerns and a few *Tarzan* films, and was regarded by MGM as a reliable director who could be trusted to deliver on time and on budget, without costly reshoots. His imagination, however – compared with that of Vincente Minnelli, for instance – was strictly limited.

OSCARS
3 nominations, **1 winner**

Costume Design (Color): Helen Rose, Gile Steele
Music (Scoring of a Musical Picture): Peter Herman Adler, Johnny Green
Sound Recording: Douglas Shearer

WHAT WON THAT YEAR?
Best Motion Picture: *An American in Paris*
Directing: George Stevens *A Place in the Sun*
Actor: Humphrey Bogart *The African Queen*
Actress: Vivien Leigh *A Streetcar Named Desire*

BAFTAS

WHAT WON THAT YEAR?
Film and British Film: *The Lavender Hill Mob* and *La Ronde*

Above right *Ship to shore: Caruso (Mario Lanza) in full voice* **Right** *Caruso and Dorothy (Ann Blyth) catch up on their fan mail*

36

Dir: Ralph THOMAS / UK
Released in Britain: 1954
Running Time: 91 minutes
Colour: Technicolor
Estimated Attendance: 12.2 million

Some years before the *Carry On* series seduced the nation, some of the same talents who would be associated with those ribald pictures delivered a slightly subtler species of knockabout comedy. Its innocent charms endure, and it has something else to recommend it – Dirk Bogarde actually appearing to enjoy himself on screen.

DOCTOR IN THE HOUSE

Director **Ralph Thomas**
Producer **Betty E. Box**
Screenplay **Nicholas Phipps**
Director of Photography **Ernest Steward**
Editor **Gerald Thomas**
Art Director **Carmen Dillon**
Music **Bruce Montgomery**

Simon Sparrow • Dirk Bogarde
Joy • Muriel Pavlow
Richard Grimsdyke • Kenneth More
Tony Benskin • Donald Sinden
Isobel • Kay Kendall
Sir Lancelot Spratt • James Robertson Justice
'Taffy' Evans • Donald Houston
Stella • Suzanne Cloutier
Briggs • George Coulouris
'Rigor Mortis' • Joan Sims
May • Gudrun Ure
Jessup • Harry Locke
Sister Virtue • Jean Taylor Smith
Doctor Parrish • Ernest Clark
Mrs Cooper • Maureen Pryor
Book Salesman • Richard Wattis
Magistrate • Nicholas Phipps
Dean • Geoffrey Keen
Demonstrator • Martin Boddey
Policeman • Cyril Chamberlain

THE STORY

Simon Sparrow, a serious young medical student, arrives at St Swithin's Hospital. He makes friends with Grimsdyke, who is reluctant to qualify since he has been left £1,000 a year for the duration of his training; Benskin, who is principally interested in girls; and Evans, who is only interested in football. Together, these four go through their medical education – examinations, encounters with nurses, irate sisters, patients, and with a distinguished surgeon who helps them out of a difficulty by blackmailing the dean. After his five years as a student, Simon falls in love with a nurse, qualifies and begins his career as a doctor; Benskin and Grimsdyke, not for the first time, fail to pass their examinations.

WHAT THEY SAID THEN ...

Doctor in the House, adapted from the book by Richard Gordon, works its way with determined high spirits through the repertoire of medical-student jokes. The jerky, hit-or-miss narrative style keeps the action moving at a fair pace and, although much of the humour is obvious, Kenneth More, as the resourceful Grimsdyke, has some very amusing moments. The other players – notably James Robertson Justice as the surgeon and Geoffrey Keen as the dean – mostly present familiar caricatures in an efficient manner.

WHAT THEY SAY NOW ...

So successful was the formula of *Doctor in the House*, the highest-grossing British film of 1954, that six more followed. None came anywhere near matching the exuberant *joie de vivre* of the original. Richard Gordon, author of the comic novels, and co-screenwriter with Nicholas Phipps, had embroidered some of his own adventures as a medical student and subsequent career as a young doctor, striking a vein of humour that proved to be immensely popular with the post-war reading public. The film found the same success among cinemagoers.

In hindsight, the quartet of clownish students – Dirk Bogarde as Simon Sparrow, the author's alter ego; Donald Sinden as the bibulous ladies' man,

Benskin; Donald Houston as Taffy, the Welsh rugby fanatic; Kenneth More as Grimsdyke, the constant exam flunky – all seem far too old to be undergraduates, even allowing for the fact that in the 1950s young people often tended to dress like their parents. Only Grimsdyke has an excuse to look so mature, since his legacy seems to depend on his perpetual studenthood, and passing would spell disaster.

What innocent times these were, when boozing in the local hostelry, college japes (pinching a rival's mascot and engaging in flour battles) and tender yearnings for pretty nurses while evading matron's eagle eye were the main preoccupations of the doctors-in-training at St Swithin's. The sole hint of menace emanates from the gruff and terrifying surgeon Sir Lancelot Spratt (James Robertson Justice in his most beloved role). Even he eventually turns out to be a softy at heart, having engaged in the same antics himself in his own college days, and protects them all from the ire of the narrow-minded dean (Geoffrey Keen).

CLASSIC QUOTE
Among the most famous comic lines in British cinema is the one uttered by Dirk Bogarde as Sparrow. His mind is elsewhere as he stands with his group of fellow white-coated students around the bedside of a patient in the teaching hospital during Sir Lancelot's rounds. The great man breaks off his lecture on blood flow during surgery to demand of Sparrow:

'You. What's the bleeding time?'

'Er … ten past ten.'

SCENE STEALER
Medical students often own skeletons to further their knowledge. The one that Dirk Bogarde acquires is inadequately wrapped in paper, and it spills out while he is riding on a bus, just as a newspaper headline about a serial murderer at large has caught the attention of some elderly, frightened passengers.

IN THE CHAIR
Ralph Thomas was the older brother of Gerald Thomas, the director of the *Carry On* films who also worked as editor on *Doctor in the House*. Its producer, Betty E. Box, was the wife of Peter Rogers, who was to produce all the *Carry Ons*. In comparison with this later long-running series, the *Doctor* films are positively subtle in their humour, especially compared to the various *Carry Ons* that exploited hospital backgrounds.

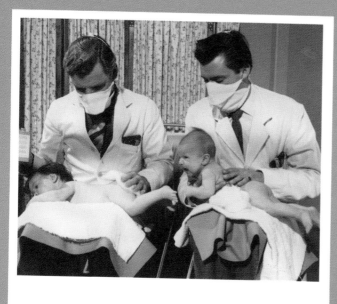

OSCARS

WHAT WON THAT YEAR?
Best Motion Picture: *On the Waterfront*
Directing: Elia Kazan *On the Waterfront*
Actor: Marlon Brando *On the Waterfront*
Actress: Grace Kelly *The Country Girl*

BAFTAS
3 nominations, **1 winner**

Film and British Film
British Actor: Kenneth More
British Screenplay: Nicholas Phipps

WHAT WON THAT YEAR?
Film and British Film: *Hobson's Choice* and *Le Salaire de la Peur*
British Actress: Yvonne Mitchell *The Divided Heart*
Foreign Actor: Marlon Brando *On the Waterfront*
Foreign Actress: Cornell Borchers *The Divided Heart*

Left *Double vision: perpetual student Grymsdyke (Kenneth More, left) and Simon Sparrow (Dirk Bogarde) gingerly handle two babies*

37

Dir: John LASSETER / USA
Released in Britain: 2000
Running Time: 95 minutes
Colour: Technicolor
Estimated Attendance: 12.18 million

Sequels that surpass the original film are rare. But then the second *Toy Story* movie is something special. The highest-ranking computer animation on the Ultimate Film list put technology to the service of good old-fashioned storytelling and disproved the adage that they don't make 'em like that anymore. They do – just differently.

TOY STORY 2

Director **John Lasseter**
Producers **Helene Plotkin, Karen Robert Jackson**
Screenplay **Andrew Stanton, Rita Hsiao, Doug Chamberlin, Chris Webb**, adapted from a story by John Lasseter, Pete Docter, Ash Brannon, Andrew Stanton
Director of Photography **Sharon Calahan**
Editors **Edie Bleiman, David Ian Salter, Lee Unkrich**
Production Designer **William Cone, Jim Pearson**
Music **Randy Newman**

Voice of Woody • Tom Hanks
Voice of Buzz Lightyear • Tim Allen
Voice of Jessie • Joan Cusack
Voice of Stinky Pete the Prospector • Kelsey Grammer
Voice of Mr Potato Head • Don Rickles
Voice of Slinky Dog • Jim Varney
Voice of Rex • Wallace Shawn
Voice of Hamm • John Ratzenberger
Voice of Bo Peep • Annie Potts
Voice of Al McWhiggin • Wayne Knight
Voice of Andy • John Morris
Voice of Andy's Mom • Laurie Metcalf
Voice of Mrs Potato Head • Estelle Harris
Voice of Sarge • R. Lee Ermey
Voice of Barbie • Jodi Benson
Voice of The Cleaner • Jonathan Harris
Voice of Wheezy • Joe Ranft
Voice of Emperor Zurg • Andrew Stanton
Voice of Aliens • Jeff Pidgeon
Additional Voice • Jack Angel

THE STORY

When his shoulder is injured, the cowboy toy Woody is left behind while his young owner Andy goes off to cowboy camp. While rescuing Wheezy the Penguin from a yard sale, Woody is spotted and stolen by Al, a toy-store manager. Woody is actually a merchandising tie-in for *Woody's Roundup*, a television puppet show from the 1950s. He will complete a set along with Jessie the cowgirl, Bullseye the horse and the still-boxed Stinky Pete the Prospector, all of whom Al wants to sell for a fortune to a Japanese toy museum.

Buzz Lightyear, another of Andy's toys, organises a rescue party that tracks Al to his store. There, Buzz is boxed up and replaced by a new Buzz Lightyear model. Woody is persuaded by Jessie to stay with the collection. But when the first Buzz and his rescuers find him, they convince Woody to return to Andy. Stinky Pete, however, is determined to go to the museum and sabotages the rescue. The toys follow Al to the airport and spring the others during baggage handling. Stinky Pete is tucked into the rucksack of a little girl, while Woody saves Jessie from the plane's cargo hold with Buzz and Bullseye's help. Andy returns and Jessie and Bullseye are adopted into his toy family.

WHAT THEY SAY ...

Although a triumph of cutting-edge technology, demonstrating fully the possibilities of computer animation, *Toy Story* has become such a popular film because of its profound, almost old-fashioned humanity. Woody, Buzz and the toy gang are alive in the way all great cartoon creatures are alive (in no small part thanks to canny voice casting). Like this sequel, the first film has an extremely sophisticated, surprisingly melancholy understanding of the importance, resonance and tragically brief shelf life of the average plaything.

The follow-up may be inevitably less fresh and misses the freakish presence of Sid's mutant toys (the three-eyed grab-machine aliens from the first film,

however, have a nice cameo), but it makes a few minor, effective upgrades. Randy Newman's musical numbers, for example, are integrated so as to serve the plot points. *Toy Story 2* focuses even more tightly than the first film on the plight of creatures who are only 'alive' as long as they can retain the attention of their quixotic owners. Their in-built obsolescence is ultimately as poignant as the tiny life spans of the *Blade Runner* replicants.

So while the plot sets up Woody's rescue from the loathsome Al, affording the opportunity for all manner of extravagant action scenes – including a splendid, protracted peril ride through the airport at the finale – the script takes care to show the downside of toy life. Jessie, for instance, sings about the loss of her teenage owner's love, signified by the junking of cowgirl ephemera in favour of make-up and pop records. The toy villain, one of those sad but valuable items who remains pristine in his original 1950s box, yearns for a life in a museum, but Woody and the film finally recognise that toys have no real value, no life, unless they are played with.

Of course, any film with this message that comes (albeit at one remove) from Walt Disney with an attendant merchandising blitz, has to cope with an ironic bite. Those in the know, especially exasperated parents, will love the cynical gags about the toy business: Rex the dinosaur discovers that a Buzz Lightyear video game can't be won without the purchase of a tie-in manual; in the store Tour Guide Barbie explains an aisle-load of Buzz figures by noting that 'in 1995, short-sighted retailers understocked'. Barbie's licensees refused to allow her to appear in the original, which means she comes in for some hilarious joshing here and is presented as an airhead next to the spunkier Bo Peep and Jessie.

Al, the discount-toy entrepreneur, is a target for criticism, but the film takes advantage of his obsessions to fill in the backgrounds of its own inventions. Video games and the *Star Wars* franchise are parodied as the film delves into the relationship between Buzz and Zurg, while it also perfectly evokes the ramshackle charm – represented by *Howdy Doody* in the US and *Muffin the Mule* in the UK – of vintage 1950s puppet television, with an attendant panoply of lunch-boxes, toy gramophones, cereal promotions (Cowboy Crunchies) and

Above *A threadbare Woody is left behind*
Below *Intergalactic action figure Buzz Lightyear (right) leads his fellow toys to safety*

snake-in-the-boot jack-in-the-boxes. The film revisits the 1950s for much of its inspiration, rediscovering in the era the dawn of marketing. But a full measure of *Toy Story 2*'s success can be gauged by its undeniable appeal for children who have never seen a Western television show or played with a cowboy toy.

CLASSIC QUOTE

Jessie: 'You never forget kids like Emily or Andy, but they forget you.'

SCENE STEALER

Several sequences stand out as master filmmaking – Woody's makeover at the hands of the elderly cleaner; Buzz and the other toys crossing a busy highway under cover of traffic cones. But for evidence of the warped, inspired minds at work here, see the truly disturbing nightmare that Woody has after his arm is torn, in which he is dropped into a dustbin full of writhing, clawing, dismembered limbs.

BEHIND THE SCENES

Incredibly, Disney had lined up *Toy Story 2* as a straight-to-video release. But early test screenings of some sequences provoked such a positive response that the company spared the film this terrible fate. And rightly so – it's one of the finest pictures with which that studio has been associated.

AT THE MICROPHONE

Tom Hanks won two Best Actor Oscars in a row for *Forrest Gump* (1994) and *Philadelphia* (1993), but *Toy Story 2* – for which he provides the voice for Woody, as he did in the first picture – marks his only showing in the Ultimate Film list. It's one of his most inventive performances – funny, subtle, bewitching. Indeed, *Toy Story* started the trend for using A-list performers on animated features, continued in other Pixar features (including *Finding Nemo* (2003), *The Incredibles* (2004) and *Cars* (2006)) as well as DreamWorks' *Shrek* series (2001 and 2004) and *Shark Tale* (2004).

OSCARS

1 nomination

Music (Original Song): "When She Loved Me" Randy Newman

WHAT WON THAT YEAR?
Best Picture: *American Beauty*
Directing: Sam Mendes *American Beauty*
Actor in a Leading Role: Kevin Spacey *American Beauty*
Actress in a Leading Role: Hilary Swank *Boys Don't Cry*

BAFTAS

WHAT WON THAT YEAR?
Film/British Film: *Gladiator*/ *Billy Elliot*
Direction: Ang Lee *Crouching Tiger, Hidden Dragon*
Actor: Jamie Bell *Billy Elliot*
Actress: Julia Roberts *Erin Brockovich*

38

Dir: Mervyn LEROY / USA
Released in Britain: 1943
Running Time: 124 minutes
Black and white
Estimated Attendance: 12 million

Left *Dazed and confused: Major Charles Rainier
(Ronald Colman) wonders where the movies would
be without amnesia*

Greer Garson appears twice in *The Ultimate Film* list.
But it was this melodrama that had UK cinemagoers
weeping in the aisles as they watched to see whether
her new husband, whose amnesia had cleared to return
him to his life before he met her, would see sense and
sweep her off her feet (again). Pass the handkerchief …

RANDOM HARVEST

Director **Mervyn LeRoy**
Producers **Sidney A. Franklin, Claudine West**
Screenplay **George Froeschel, Arthur Wimperis**,
    adapted from the novel by James Hilton
Director of Photography **Joseph Ruttenberg**
Editor **Harold F. Kress**
Art Director **Cedric Gibbons**
Music **Herbert Stothart**

Charles Rainier • Ronald Colman
Paula Ridgeway • Greer Garson
Dr Jonathan Benet • Fritz van Dongen
Kitty • Susan Peters
Dr Sims • Henry Travers
'Biffer' • Reginald Owen
Harrison • Bramwell Fletcher
Sam • Rhys Williams
Sheldon • Aubrey Mather
Mrs Deventer • Margaret Wycherly
Chetwynd • Arthur Margetson
George • Melville Cooper
Julian • Alan Napier
Lydia, Chet's Wife • Jill Esmond
Jill, Kitty's Mother • Marta Linden
Bridget • Ann Richards
Julia • Norma Varden
Henry Chilcet • David Cavendish
Tobacconist • Una O'Connor
The Vicar • Ivan Simpson

THE STORY

On Armistice Day, 1918, Major Charles Rainier escapes from the asylum where, under the name of John Smith ('Smithy'), he is being cared for, having lost his memory and his speech after being blown up at the front. He meets Paula, who is a member of a theatrical troupe. She devotes herself to him and, although he does not regain his memory, he becomes a normal member of society again and they marry. One day he goes to Liverpool on business, is knocked down and regains his memory but forgets the immediate past. He returns to his real home and devotes himself to business, becoming a leader of industry. Paula comes to him as his secretary, but he does not recognise her. Charles goes into Parliament after a brief romance with another woman, Kitty, whom he marries. This marriage of convenience continues for some years until, through a series of coincidences, he regains his memory and recognises his wife as Paula.

WHAT THEY SAID THEN …

This is a most affecting film, thanks to the acting abilities of Greer Garson and Ronald Colman. Although Hollywood has tried to take every precaution to reproduce the English scene, some small error of detail or behaviour frequently fractures the illusion. A word of praise must be said for Susan Peters's sincere performance as Kitty, the young girl with whom Rainier has a brief and rather tragic romance before marrying Paula for the second time.

WHAT THEY SAY NOW …

Where would the movies be without amnesia? The same year Greer Garson won her Oscar for Mrs Miniver she scored hugely again in this emotionally turbulent tale of memory loss, gracefully adapted from James Hilton's novel. Colman, a touchingly convincing shell-shock victim of the Great War, wanders in a literal and metaphoric fog from an asylum in provincial England. From there he falls into the arms of Garson's saintly but vivacious flame-haired entertainer Paula.

OSCARS
7 nominations

Outstanding Motion Picture
Directing: Mervyn LeRoy
Actor: Ronald Colman
Actress in a Supporting Role: Susan Peters
Interior Decoration/Art Direction (Black and White)
Music (Music Scoring of a Dramatic or Comedy Picture): Herbert Stothart
Writing (Screenplay): Claudine West, George Froeschel, Arthur Wimperis

WHAT WON THAT YEAR?
Outstanding Motion Picture: *Mrs Miniver*
Directing: William Wyler *Mrs Miniver*
Actor: James Cagney *Yankee Doodle Dandy*
Actress: Greer Carson *Mrs Miniver*

BAFTAS
Not awarded until 1947

Left *Greer Garson as Paula Ridgeway displays her legs and exuberance in the music hall sequence* **Below** *Mervyn LeRoy (left) in conversation with Ronald Colman*

(It's a rare treat to see the ethereal Garson displaying her legs and exuberance in the music hall sequence, belting out a crowd-pleaser in a Highland showgirl costume.) Long-suffering is too inadequate a description for the tragically bereft Paula, who endures a series of hanky-wringing blows with dignity and devotion. This is fabulous poppycock, elevated by superb performances, and by its tasteful insistence on the superiority of a simple life with love over a privileged life without passion.

CLASSIC QUOTE
'Smithy': 'My life began with you.'

SCENE STEALER
Rich and powerful Charles Rainier is in his office, some years after he forgot his life with Paula. He calls in his remarkable, efficient secretary Margaret. The door opens and Margaret enters. That's when the viewer realises what Charles doesn't – Margaret is Paula.

BEHIND THE SCENES
Colman, who had previously starred in Frank Capra's adaptation of Hilton's *Lost Horizon* (1937) and was at the zenith of his romantic hero heyday, actually had fought on the French front in the First World War. He had been invalided out, giving him a particular affinity with 'Smithy'. Greer Garson's personal favourite of her films, this is also, legend has it, the movie (although disguised with different plot details) that Holden Caulfield is so withering about whilst recounting his trip to Radio City Music Hall in J. D. Salinger's *The Catcher In The Rye*: 'It was so putrid I couldn't take my eyes off it'. The title *Random*

Harvest comes from a line in the novel about bombs dropped at random, but in the film refers to Rainier's ancestral home.

IN THE CHAIR
Having made his name directing social realist dramas in Warner Brothers's gangster cycle, including *Little Caesar* (1931) and *I Am A Fugitive From A Chain Gang* (1932), Mervyn LeRoy's versatility is still somewhat surprising. But the bounce he brought to lighter fare such as *Gold Diggers of 1933* (1933) might be traced to his childhood career as 'The Singing Newsboy'. After moving to MGM he happily put his energies into romantic melodrama (*Waterloo Bridge*, 1940) and notched up impressive credits as a producer (*The Wizard Of Oz*, 1939). Unlike so many of his generation his reputation survived into the 1960s (with *Gypsy*, 1962, a late highlight) when he retired.

Dir: Andrew **ADAMSON**, Kelly
ASBURY, Conrad **VERNON** / USA
Released in Britain: 2004
Running Time: 92 minutes
Colour: Technicolor
Estimated Attendance: 11.78 million

Walt Disney is behind the top three animated features at the UK box office, but in fourth place is DreamWorks, for whom animation studio PDI made *Shrek 2*. And with a vicious Fairy Godmother, a preening Prince Charming and a cross-dressing Pinocchio, this sure is a long way from Disney.

SHREK 2

Directors **Andrew Adamson, Kelly Asbury, Conrad Vernon**
Producers **Aron Warner, David Lipman, John H. Williams**
Screenplay **Andrew Adamson, Joe Stillman, J. David Stem, David N. Weiss**, story by **Andrew Adamson**, based on the book by William Steig
Editors **Michael Andrews, Sim Evan-Jones**
Production Designer **Guillaume Aretos**
Music **Harry Gregson-Williams**

Voice of Shrek • Mike Myers
Voice of Donkey • Eddie Murphy
Voice of Princess Fiona • Cameron Diaz
Voice of Queen Lillian • Julie Andrews
Voice of Puss in Boots • Antonio Banderas
Voice of King Harold • John Cleese
Voice of Prince Charming • Rupert Everett
Voice of Fairy Godmother • Jennifer Saunders
Voice of Wolf • Aron Warner
Voice of Page/Elf/Nobleman/Nobleman's Son • Kelly Asbury
Voice of Pinocchio/Three Pigs • Cody Cameron
Voice of Gingerbread Man/Cedric/Announcer/Muffin Man/Mongo • Conrad Vernon

THE STORY

Returning home from their honeymoon, newlywed ogres Shrek and Princess Fiona receive an invitation to a royal ball hosted by Fiona's parents, the king and queen of Far, Far Away. Accompanied by Donkey, the couple travel to the kingdom, where their physical appearance shocks Queen Lillian and King Harold (who previously locked their 'cursed' daughter in a castle from which she was saved by Shrek). Following a disastrous family dinner, Fiona's tears summon the Fairy Godmother, who's unimpressed that her son Prince Charming was denied the chance to rescue and wed the princess. Threatening to renege on a deal they once made, the Fairy Godmother orders Harold to redress the situation.

Harold hires feline assassin Puss In Boots to eliminate Shrek. When his ambush is foiled, Puss swears loyalty to Shrek and tells him of Harold's plot. Shrek, Puss and Donkey infiltrate the Fairy Godmother's factory, stealing a Happily Ever After potion that transforms Shrek and (working from afar) Fiona into attractive humans. Donkey becomes a white stallion. However, the effect will only become permanent if Shrek kisses his bride before midnight.

Prince Charming dupes Fiona into thinking he's the human Shrek. Shrek discovers Harold and the fairy Godmother's alliance but is captured by knights. Harold is given a love potion for Fiona that will make her fall for the first man she kisses. Shrek escapes and storms the castle where a ball is being held for Charming and Fiona. Charming's kiss has no effect, since Harold chose not to give her the potion. A wand blast aimed at Shrek is blocked by Harold and reflected back at the Fairy Godmother. She disappears, while Harold reverts to his frog state and gives his blessing to Shrek and Fiona. After midnight passes, the couple kiss and become ogres again.

WHAT THEY SAY ...

One of the distinguishing features of the original computer-animated *Shrek* (2001), was its irreverence towards fairy tales – a stock source for many mainstream cartoons – and towards Walt Disney, an arguably cheekier move in

Hollywood where inter-studio rivalry is usually kept in the boardroom, well away from the multiplex screens. Here the anti-Mouse agenda has been toned down, but much of the humour remains gleefully satirical.

The film opens with a montage that parodies *From Here to Eternity*, *The Lord of the Rings* and *Spiderman* in quick succession, while the key setting is Far, Far Away, a storybook-kingdom inversion of Los Angeles. Though the set-up pivots on a *Guess Who's Coming to Dinner*/*Meet the Parents* antagonism between newlywed ogre Shrek and his royal in-laws, the chief baddie is the Fairy Godmother, a bullying power freak whose narcissistic son, Prince Charming, is equally hateful.

As lively as these characterisations are, the most appealing addition to the Shrek cast list is Antonio Banderas's Puss In Boots. His smouldering feline assassin is a send-up of his swashbuckling role in *The Mask of Zorro* (1998), and he delivers many of *Shrek 2*'s funniest moments – coughing up a hairball in an ambush, or duetting with Eddie Murphy's motor-mouth Donkey on 'Livin' La Vida Loca'.

This is a slick, entertaining follow-up, albeit one whose hip knowingness precludes the emotional engagement of Pixar's best work. On a technical front, too, PDI is a notch below its formerly Disney-backed rival, particularly in the area of draughtsmanship: some of the character rendering has the lumpy texture of claymation. Yet it would be churlish to deny *Shrek 2*'s visually sumptuous elements: there's a memorable moment when Shrek and Donkey eye their rippling reflections in a lake, while the 'beauty's only skin-deep' message is well served by the fact that there's more life and expressiveness in Princess Fiona's face when she's an ogre than when she's in more conventionally attractive human form.

CLASSIC QUOTE
Donkey to Puss In Boots: 'The position of annoying talking animal has been filled.'

BEHIND THE SCENES
Animated features released in non-English-speaking countries are always dubbed by different actors, but *Shrek 2* was the first time that different voices were used for the UK and US versions, to ensure maximum relevance to the respective audiences. The Ugly Stepsister is played by Jonathan Ross in the UK print, and Larry King in the US one; likewise, Joan Rivers is replaced in Britain by Kate Thornton in the role of Red Carpet Correspondent.

Top Princess Fiona and Shrek meet the parents
Middle Cool cat: the undisputed star of Shrek 2 *is*
Puss in Boots *Bottom* The Fairy Godmother (right)
has a stern word with her son, Prince Charming

40

Dir: John GUILLERMIN / USA
Released in Britain: 1975
Running Time: 165 minutes
Colour: Deluxe
Estimated Attendance: 11.78 million

Before Spielberg and Lucas claimed 1970s audiences as their own, the disaster movie was the main attraction. Producer Irwin Allen was its ringmaster, manufacturing stories of mayhem and carnage in which the bets were on to see which celebrities would perish, and in what order.

THE TOWERING INFERNO

Director **John Guillermin**
Producer **Irwin Allen**
Screenplay **Stirling Silliphant**, adapted from the novels
   The Tower by Richard Martin Stern and The Glass
   Inferno by Thomas M. Scortia and Frank M. Robinson
Director of Photography **Fred J. Koenekamp**
Editors **Harold F. Kress, Carl Kress**
Production Designer **William J. Creber**
Music **John Williams**

Michael O'Hallorhan • Steve McQueen
Doug Roberts • Paul Newman
James 'Jim' Duncan • William Holden
Susan Franklin • Faye Dunaway
Harlee Claiborne • Fred Astaire
Patty Simmons • Susan Blakely
Roger Simmons • Richard Chamberlain
Lisolette Mueller • Jennifer Jones
Security Chief Jernigan • O. J. Simpson
Senator Gary Parker • Robert Vaughn
Dan Bigelow • Robert Wagner
Lorrie • Susan Flannery
Paula Ramsay • Sheila Mathews
Will Giddings • Normann Burton
Mayor Ramsay • Jack Collins
Kappy • Don Gordon
Scott • Felton Perry
Carlos • Gregory Sierra
Mark Powers • Ernie Orsatti
Deputy Firechief No. 1 • Dabney Coleman

THE STORY

Doug Roberts, designer and architect of the Glass Tower, the world's tallest building at 138 stories, flies in to San Francisco for the inauguration ceremony. After talking with James Duncan, the Glass Tower's builder, he learns that the ceremony is to be held before all the safety checks have been installed and that Simmons, Duncan's son-in-law, has installed inferior wiring in an effort, sanctioned by his father, to trim costs.

Meanwhile Jernigan, the security chief, has noticed a failure in the video equipment followed by an unusually high rise in temperature in one part of the building. Roberts and Jernigan discover a fire, but Duncan, tied up with Mayor Ramsay, Senator Parker and various other illustrious guests, refuses to move the party out for what he calls a 'store room fire', until fire chief O'Hallorhan orders him to do so. By this time only one lift works and the guests form a queue; Roberts's editor girlfriend Susan helps prevent panic. Guests are discovered in parts of the building hitherto thought empty: publicist Dan Bigelow finds himself trapped in an apartment with his secretary Lorrie, and they both perish. Jernigan manages to rescue gallery owner Lisolette's cat but Lisolette herself dies in the fire. A deaf woman and her two children are rescued by Roberts, who breaks in to their flat on a floor already in flames and leads them to safety down a shattered stairwell.

An attempt to land a helicopter on the roof fails when it explodes. Guests are selected by lots to go down the scenic elevator but another explosion causes it to seize up. O'Hallorhan orders a helicopter to lift the whole elevator off the building to safety. Meanwhile guests leave the banquet suite via a ski lift attached to a nearby high-rise building. After the women and children have been saved, O'Hallorhan and Roberts extinguish the fire by blowing up the water storage tanks: Simmons panics before the final blast and dies in the attempt to escape. The survivors are rescued. O'Hallorhan finds Robins and tells him that fires like this will continue until architects ask men like himself how to build safely.

Above *Paul Newman and Steve McQueen (**Opposite above**) were engaged in a war over who had the most dialogue, and who got top billing* **Right** *Flaming hell: an inferno created to order on set* **Below** *Firefly: a helicopter comes to the rescue* **Opposite below** *Escaping The Towering Inferno*

WHAT THEY SAID THEN ...

The latest entrant into the disaster movie stakes carries all the comfortable and familiar earmarks of workmanlike low-budget science fiction. This is reinforced by the film's tall building complex, complete with ingenuous model shots and the ever-so-privileged view we are allowed of the interior of 'the world's tallest building', with its gliding visions of futuristic décor and deep-pile carpet. In fact, the setting up of the disaster is in every way more interesting than what follows, as we observe the slow progress of the fire – unperceived by the banks of sophisticated computer and video equipment in the Tower's security room – and its rapid escalation to danger level as the guests collect for the inauguration ceremony. (The film's only true villain is unmasked in the person of Richard Chamberlain as the builder's wastrel son-in-law, given to shaving the specifications on the quiet.)

Nothing later in the film can really match the sequences in which doors are flung open to reveal walls of flame, a lift arrives and ejects a man ablaze who lurches out into the grotesquely soignée surroundings, or the collapse of a rococo suite as the fire gains hold. John Guillermin drives his film on with a kind of efficiency that sidesteps the exploration of any implicit ambiguities, finally flattening the whole thing until only some bizarre disasters and ever wilder rescue attempts are left to maintain interest. Statutory thrills are provided in the shape of hazardous journeys (more than faintly unconvincing) down shattered stairwells, and the film's final set piece, the plucking of the scenic elevator and the twelve occupants (chosen by lots) from the side of the building by a helicopter.

Predictably, the big star syndrome, indulged as excessively here as in *The Poseidon Adventure* (1972), tends to operate finally to deadly effect as several generations of blue-eyed charmers act their roles as if each were under a separate bell jar. Representing the combined efforts of 20th-Century Fox and Warner Brothers and deriving from no less than two skyscraper novels, *The Towering Inferno* is everything the film industry understands by the term 'movie magic' – a piece of harmless, resolutely overblown and occasionally effective hokum.

WHAT THEY SAY NOW ...

In 1972 *Inferno*'s producer, Irwin Allen, had kick-started the modern-day disaster movie cycle with *The Poseidon Adventure*, a smash hit with the public despite critical disdain. *Inferno* reprised the trick, reaping yet more brickbats (Pauline Kael nominated it for her 'Dumb Whore Award of 1974') and an even heftier bonanza at the box office. The cycle duly proceeded on its merry, lucrative way with ever bigger and better bangs, shrugging off the merciless spoofing of Jim Abrahams and the Zucker brothers in *Airplane* (1980) and its sequels. In 1997 Jim Cameron proved the genre still had mileage to spare with *Titanic*, which is essentially *Inferno* tipped on its side and launched into the water.

CLASSIC QUOTE

O'Hallorhan (about to set the charges for the water tanks): 'So, how do I get down?' (Long pause) 'Oh ... shit.'

BEHIND THE SCENES

Steve McQueen originally signed for the role of Doug Roberts, the architect. But when he read the script, he realised that the plum role was Fire Chief O'Hallorhan. He swapped over, and Paul Newman was brought in to play Roberts. McQueen, fiercely ambitious, had long envied and resented Newman. As soon as the casting was announced McQueen started furiously counting lines in the script, and discovered he had 12 fewer than Newman. 'Goddamn it, he's always twisting my melon,' he raged. Screenwriter Stirling Silliphant was hastily called in to provide 12 more lines for McQueen's character. Then McQueen got started on the billing. Whose name would come first? Agents haggled, but neither side would give way. Finally a compromise was painfully hammered out. McQueen's name would appear on the left of the title frame and publicity material – Newman's on the right but higher up. Technically it was equal billing. But a gloating McQueen knew people would read left to right.

OSCARS

8 nominations, **3 winners**

Best Picture
Actor in a Supporting Role: Fred Astaire
Art Direction/Set Decoration: William Creber, Ward Preston, Raphael Bretton
Cinematography: Fred Koenekamp, Joseph Biroc
Film Editing: Harold F. Kress, Carl Kress
Music (Original Dramatic Score): John Williams
Music (Song): "We May Never love Like This Again" Al Kasha, Joel Hirschhorn
Sound: Theodore Soderberg, Herman Lewis

WHAT WON THAT YEAR?
Best Picture: *The Godfather Part II*
Directing: Francis Ford Coppola *The Godfather Part II*
Actor: Art Carney *Harry and Tonto*
Actress: Ellen Burstyn *Alice Doesn't Live Here Anymore*

BAFTAS

3 nominations, **2 winners**

Art Direction: William Creeber
Supporting Actor: Fred Astaire
Anthony Asquith Award for Original Film Music: John Williams (also for *Jaws*)

WHAT WON THAT YEAR?
Film: *Alice Doesn't Live Here Anymore*
Direction: Stanley Kubrick *Barry Lyndon*
Actor: Al Pacino *The Godfather Part II/Dog Day Afternoon*
Actress: Ellen Burstyn *Alice Doesn't Live Here Anymore*

No other form of entertainment in

Britain could compete with cinema during World War II.
Despite a freeze on new cinema buildings, the exigencies
of the blackout and the reduced number of imported
Hollywood films, weekly cinema attendance actually
went up during the war, from 19 million in 1939 to 30
million in 1945. And although British film producers
faced many difficulties, including a loss of production
facilities when some studios were requisitioned for

storage space, the industry
entered a golden age. After the
financial slump of the 1930s
film-makers found a renewed
sense of vigour and relevancy,
and produced films that were
both critically acclaimed and
popular with audiences.

Few would have foreseen
such a robust future for British film at the outbreak of war. In
September 1939 the government closed all cinemas for fear of
heavy air-raid casualties. But politicians were quick to realize
the role film could play in rallying audiences behind the war
effort, and the cinema doors were open again a few months later.

It wasn't long before film's usefulness in advancing the allied
cause was granted official recognition, with the establishment of
the Film Division within the Ministry of Information. Responsible
for the flow of public information about the war effort, the MOI

supervised content for the newsreels
that accompanied features. The MOI
sponsored Michael Powell and Emeric
Pressburger's *49th Parallel*, whose
huge success puts it at number 65
on the Ultimate Film list. But its main
feature-film activities were largely
restricted to approving scripts. And
while Powell and Pressburger's
The Life and Death of Colonel Blimp

(1943), an affectionate send-up of military pomposity, provoked the displeasure of Churchill, few films were banned.

The MOI's most direct involvement in production was the establishment of the Crown Film Unit, a division (formerly part of the Post Office) dedicated to producing documentaries. It was run by John Grierson, who had long argued that film was an invaluable tool for informing and educating the public; his progressive agenda is evident in much of the CFU documentaries. The Unit's output included information pictures about such humdrum topics as rationing. But it also produced films of great artistry, notably the poetic, formally daring work of Humphrey Jennings. In his rousing *Listen to*

Opposite above A scene from the Blitz in London Can Take It! *Opposite below Women take to the factories in* Millions Like Us *Above Roger Livesey in* The Life and Death of Colonel Blimp *Below A scene from Humphrey Jennings's rousing* Listen to Britain *Bottom Clifford Evans in* The Foreman Went to France

Britain, iconic images of British life are edited to a soundtrack of popular and classical music. The image it provides of the country pulling together is both a piece of reportage and an idealistic vision of social cohesion that anticipates the post-war liberal consensus.

The documentary ethos seeped into fiction films, whose portrayal of 'ordinary' folk reflected the experiences of their audiences. Often made by CFU veterans, films such as *Millions Like Us* (1943) and *The Foreman Went to France* (1942) – both about working class characters' experience of the war – satisfied the MOI's preference for 'realism'. But while this approach dominated – and continues to haunt modern British film and television – there was escapism, too. *The Wicked Lady* (1945) was a typical example of the ripe melodramas that the Gainsborough studio made to encourage audiences to forget present troubles. It hit a nerve: *The Wicked Lady* is the second highest British entry in *The Ultimate Film* list.

41

Dir: Anthony ASQUITH / UK
Released in Britain: 1944
Running Time: 108 minutes
Black and white
Estimated Attendance: 11.7 million

Romance, sex and class tensions collide in Anthony Asquith's surprisingly murky Gainsborough melodrama, with Phyllis Calvert as the maid meant for a better life, and a sneering James Mason in his usual role as the villain audiences loved to hate.

FANNY BY GASLIGHT

Director **Anthony Asquith**
Producer **Edward Black**
Screenplay **Doreen Montgomery**, adapted from the novel by Michael Sadlier
Director of Photography **Arthur Crabtree**
Editor **R. E. Dearing**
Art Director **John Bryan**
Music **Cedric Mallabey**

Fanny • Phyllis Calvert
Lord Manderstoke • James Mason
Chunks (Joe Boggs) • Wilfred Lawson
Harry Somerford • Stewart Granger
Lucy Beckett • Jean Kent
Alicia • Margaretta Scott
Fanny as a Child • Ann Stephens
Lucy as a Child • Gloria Sydney
Mrs Hopwood • Nora Swinburne
Kate Somerford • Cathleen Nesbitt
Mrs Somerford • Helen Haye
William Hopwood • John Laurie
Clive Seymore • Stuart Lindsell
Mrs Heaviside • Amy Viness
Carver • Ann Wilton
Dr Lowenthal • Guy LeFeuvre

THE STORY

London, 1870. Young Fanny and Lucy are playing with a ball in the street when it falls into a cellar. Going to retrieve it, Fanny discovers a wine bar-cum-brothel called 'The Hopwood Shades' in the basement of the house owned by her father, William Hopwood. This discovery causes her parents to send her away to boarding school, shortly after she receives a mysterious birthday present from one Clive Seymore.

Ten years later, Fanny returns home, but the happy atmosphere is shattered by an incident in which Lord Manderstoke forces his way into The Hopwood Shades and, when evicted, starts a brawl that ends with Hopwood fatally falling under the wheels of a horse-drawn carriage. At the inquest, Manderstoke is exonerated and The Hopwood Shades is closed.

Close to death, Mrs Hopwood sends Fanny to stay with the mysterious Clive Seymore, who turns out to be a Cabinet minister – and Fanny's real father. But since this revelation would lead to scandal, she has to take a lowly position as a maid. While working for Seymore, she meets his secretary Harry Somerford. A mutual attraction develops, although he is under the impression that she is Seymour's mistress – an understandable mistake given that they seem rather closer than master and servant would normally be. Seymore's wife Alicia is under the same impression, and decides to use this as leverage to secure a divorce from Seymore, as she is conducting a torrid affair with Lord Manderstoke. Under pressure, Seymore is forced to reveal his true relationship with Fanny, whereupon Alicia threatens to expose him for fathering an illegitimate child – a revelation that would end his political career. Caught in a vicious circle, Seymore kills himself and Fanny flees, taking a job in a rough working-class pub.

She is tracked down by Harry and the two fall in love, despite the objections of Harry's female relatives, who believe that there is an insurmountable class division between the two and that she will damage his social standing. He is prepared to ignore all this for love of Fanny, but Fanny decides that his career is more important than her, and she flees again. Teaming up with her childhood friend Lucy and visiting a deceptively upmarket but in reality somewhat

Above Pistols at dawn: Harry (Stewart Granger, left) prepares to face Lord Manderstroke (James Mason) *Below* Outside The Hopwood Shades

insalubrious dance establishment, Fanny encounters Lord Manderstoke again, but she is rescued by Harry before things turn nasty. They realise that they were meant for each other.

Fanny and Harry go to Paris, where by chance they spot Lucy performing as a dancer. Visiting her backstage, they encounter Lord Manderstoke, who is Lucy's lover. After Harry dashes a glass of champagne in his face (twice, to get the message across) he is challenged to a duel. Harry and Manderstoke duel with pistols at dawn. Manderstoke is killed, but Harry is seriously wounded. At Harry's bedside, Fanny confronts his sister, who eventually comes to realise that only his love for Fanny can give him the strength he needs to recover.

WHAT THEY SAID THEN ...

This is a polite version by Doreen Montgomery of the Michael Sadlier novel. The production departments should pride themselves on their meticulous attention to detail. Asquith's directing is clean-cut, sure and sensitively evocative of his period atmosphere. There is unusually fine work, too, from practically every member of a well-chosen cast. Phyllis Calvert, as Fanny, is gentle but capable of determined action in the interests of her love. James Mason strives mightily and mostly successfully with the difficult melodramatics of the Manderstoke role. Margaretta Scott's portrait of the cabinet minister's wife is outstanding in its hard, brittle clarity.

OSCARS

WHAT WON THAT YEAR?
Best Motion Picture: *Going My Way*
Directing: Leo McCarey *Going My Way*
Actor: Bing Crosby *Going My Way*
Actress: Ingrid Bergman *Gaslight*

BAFTAS
Not awarded until 1947

WHAT THEY SAY NOW …

Fanny by Gaslight was made to cash in on the success of *The Man in Grey* (1943), and used many of the same ingredients: lead actors Phyllis Calvert, James Mason and Stewart Granger; a nineteenth-century setting that provided plenty of opportunities for lavish costume display; a similar mix of archetypal 'good' and 'bad' male and female characters; and a surprisingly racy and distinctly un-British attitude towards sexuality.

Anthony Asquith was the biggest 'name' director to work on a Gainsborough melodrama, and his experience helped wring rather more impressive production values than the budget might otherwise have allowed. There are also some strikingly imaginative touches, such as the face of Clive Seymore (Stuart Lindsell) literally fragmenting in the mirror prior to his suicide, paralleling his mental breakdown as he realises he's run out of options.

Where *Fanny by Gaslight* is a clear advance on *The Man in Grey* is that it has a much more sophisticated understanding of the social context underlining both the drama itself and the demands of the 1944 audience. Harry's speech about how class divisions would be abolished within 100 years, allowing him to marry whoever he pleases, was clearly aimed at a largely female audience that had itself set aside social differences as a result of the war. The film underscores this by placing all the working-class characters in an overwhelmingly positive light.

The attitude displayed here towards sexuality is rather more complex and intriguing. From the opening scenes of Fanny's discovery of The Hopwood Shades (the word is never used, but it is clearly a brothel) and the fact that her mother was less than faithful, through to James Mason's portrait of Lord Manderstoke as a man blending absolute moral corruption with devastating sensuality, *Fanny by Gaslight* both shies away from and celebrates the liberating power of living dangerously in an environment where the slightest transgression could bring about social catastrophe.

IN THE CHAIR

In a career lasting around 40 years, Anthony Asquith worked with most major British stars, including Leslie Howard, Laurence Olivier, Dirk Bogarde and Richard Burton. He made films in a variety of popular genres as well as quality pictures based upon key works of British drama. Among the latter are notable adaptations from George Bernard Shaw (*Pygmalion*, 1938) and Oscar Wilde (*The Importance of Being Earnest*, 1952), and a number of movies based on the work of Terence Rattigan, with whom Asquith had a long collaborative relationship beginning in the 1930s and lasting until his final film in 1964.

Above left James Mason's Lord Manderstroke, a blend of absolute moral corruption with devastating sensuality, toys with Lucy (Jean Kent) and Fanny (Phyllis Calvert) *Above* Director Anthony Asquith on the set of his later film, The Importance of Being Earnest

Dir: Alfred E. GREEN / USA
Released in Britain: 1947
Running Time: 128 minutes
Colour: Technicolor
Estimated Attendance: 11.6 million

Al Jolson's catchphrase was 'You ain't heard nothin' yet', which usually presaged hours of non-stop performing; you can hear those words in this film of the entertainer's life, but everything else in the movie should be taken with a fistful of salt.

THE JOLSON STORY

Director **Alfred E. Green**
Producer **Sidney Skolsky**
Screenplay **Stephen Longstreet, adapted by Harry Chandlee and Andrew Solt**
Director of Photography **Joseph Walker**
Editor **William A. Lyon**
Art Directors **Stephen Goosson, Walter Holscher**
Music Director **Morris W. Stoloff**

Al Jolson • Larry Parks
Julie Benson • Evelyn Keyes
Steve Martin • William Demarest
Tom Baron • Bill Goodwin
Cantor Yoelson • Ludwig Donath
Al as a Boy • Scotty Beckett
Mrs Yoelson • Tamara Shayne
Ann Murray • Jo Carroll Dennison
Lew Dockstader • John Alexander
Father McGee • Ernest Cossart
Dick Glenn • William Forrest
Ann as a Girl • Ann E. Todd
Oscar Hammerstein • Edwin Maxwell
Jonsey • Emmett Vogan
Florez Ziegfeld • Eddie Kane
Roy Anderson • Jimmy Lloyd

THE STORY

Little Asa Yoleson, the cantor's son, distresses his father by hanging out at the vaudeville theatre when he should be in temple singing Kol Nidre. Eventually he runs away from his orthodox parents in Washington DC to go on the road, first in a musical act and then as a minstrel singer. Years pass, and he is headlining, and on the path that will make Al Jolson 'the world's greatest entertainer'. New Orleans introduces him to jazz rhythms and a sympathy for black music. His blackface routine entrances New York and leads him on to Hollywood where he makes a worldwide hit in *The Jazz Singer*, often regarded as the first talkie. A compulsive entertainer, he allows his love of applause and the spotlight to mess up his private life, and constantly seeks 'the bluebird' which he hopes will bring him personal happiness. His marriage to a fellow performer Julie Benson ends when, unable to resist the call to do a number when they visit a night club, he launches in to a set that will last into the small hours, continuing long after she has walked out of his life for ever.

WHAT THEY SAID THEN ...

This is the story of the singer Al Jolson, though perhaps it should be called the 'fairy story', since the programme states that 'characters and incidents portrayed and names used are fictitious'. Larry Parks gives an excellent imitation of Jolson, apart from the singing, which is done by Jolson himself. Evelyn Keyes is charming as Julie, and William Demarest gives a good performance as the vaudeville performer who first launched Jolson on his career and afterwards became his manager. Those who enjoy Jolson's overpowering sentimentality should revel in this two hours and nine minutes of fictitious biography; and even those who find it embarrassing will probably admit that this is a well-directed and acted Technicolor musical.

WHAT THEY SAY NOW ...

Al Jolson had indeed been a monumental star, but at the time *The Jolson Story* went into production his day was done, his vigorous delivery eclipsed by the more relaxed vocal style of Bing Crosby, Frank Sinatra and Perry Como. Columbia's film followed a formulaic pattern, and was little more than a framework on which to hang a succession of Jolson's greatest hits. He himself recorded them all anew, but was too old to play himself convincingly on screen as a young man. The task fell to the comparatively unknown actor Larry Parks, who painstakingly learned at first hand the mannerisms, postures and stage tricks of the great man. Parks's mime act is one of the most convincing in screen history and manages to convey the dynamic intensity of an astonishing performer.

The story, however, was heavily sanitised and elided much of Jolson's life, especially when it came to his wives. The fictitious Julie Benson, played as a gentile by Evelyn Keyes, was a substitute for Ruby Keeler who refused co-operation, and who had in fact been his third wife, the first two being omitted for the sake of plot simplicity. It mattered little. The film achieved a domestic gross of $7.6 million, which in 1946 was astronomical, and Jolson was suddenly reinstated as 'the world's greatest entertainer'.

In a strange aftermath, the popularity of the film brought a sequel, *Jolson Sings Again* (1949), which began at the exact point the first one ended and went on to show how the filming of *The Jolson Story* resurrected the career and fortunes of Al Jolson. It even had a surreal sequence in which Parks as Jolson advises Parks as Parks how to be Jolson. Both films played fast and loose with the real story, and although the songs are most certainly Jolson's, they are often presented out of context and sequence, and even assigned to the wrong shows and films. Jolson himself would have loved to have been back on screen and not merely on the soundtrack, and he achieved it during the 'Swanee' number in *The Jolson Story*. It is he, and not Larry Parks, who is seen in long shot.

CLASSIC QUOTE

Jolson: 'You ain't heard nothin' yet.'

BEHIND THE SCENES

Parks's career collapsed in ruins after *Jolson Sings Again* when the House Un-American Committee fingered him for having earlier been a card-carrying communist. He became the only actor among many writers and directors to be blacklisted, barred from ever working again in Hollywood.

Top left *'My dear old Swanee.' Larry Parkes is Al Jolson, the original black and white minstrel*
Left *Julie Benson (Evelyn Keyes) brushes off Al Jolson and walks out of his life forever*

OSCARS

6 nominations, **2 winners**

Actor: Larry Parks
Actor in a Supporting Role: William Demarest
Cinematography (Color): Joseph Walker
Film Editing: William Lyon
Music (Scoring of a Musical Picture): Morris Stoloff
Sound Recording: John Livadary

WHAT WON THAT YEAR?
Best Motion Picture: *The Best Years of our Lives*
Directing: William Wyler *The Best Years of our Lives*
Actor: Fredric March *The Best Years of our Lives*
Actress: Olivia de Havilland *To Each His Own*

BAFTAS

WHAT WON THAT YEAR?
Film: *The Best Years of our Lives*
British Film: *Odd Man Out*

43

Dir: Herbert WILCOX / UK
Released in Britain: 1946
Running Time: 102 minutes
Black and white
Estimated Attendance: 11.5 million

PICCADILLY INCIDENT

Director/Producer **Herbert Wilcox**
Screenplay **Nicholas Phipps**, adapted from a story by
  Florence Tranter
Director of Photography **Max Greene**
Editor **Flora Newton**
Art Director **William C. Andrews**
Music **Anthony Collins**

Diana Fraser • Anna Neagle
Captain Alan Pearson • Michael Wilding
Joan Draper • Frances Mercer
Virginia Pearson • Coral Browne
Sir Charles Pearson • A. E. Matthews
Judd • Edward Rigby
Sally Benton • Brenda Bruce
Sam • Leslie Dwyer
Mrs Millgan • Maire O'Neill
Bill Weston • Michael Laurence
radio operator • Michael Medwin

For the next film in his London series after *I Live in Grosvenor Square* (1945), the director Herbert Wilcox failed to secure the same leading man, Rex Harrison. No matter – with Anna Neagle as the star, and the beginning of her successful on-screen pairing with Michael Wilding, this tear-jerker was soon packing them in.

THE STORY

In a London air raid two people meet: Alan's a marine captain and Diana's in the Wrens, the women's branch of the navy. They quickly marry before she leaves for Singapore, shortly before its fall to the Japanese. Her ship is torpedoed and she is posted missing, presumably drowned.

After much unhappiness Alan remarries, this time to an American Wave, the equivalent of the British Wrens. In fact, his wife is still alive, having been cast ashore onto a remote island along with other survivors who have to eke out an existence for three years before being rescued. When Diana is eventually repatriated to Britain she endures the agony of finding that a new wife is in her stead and that there is also a small son. Nobly she pretends that she no longer loves her husband and she must have a divorce. Another air raid intervenes and she is killed, easing the awkward dilemma, except that of the child who will be forever considered as having been born out of wedlock.

WHAT THEY SAID THEN …

The serious intention of the film is confined to the prologue and epilogue, in which a weighty legal view is ponderously delivered of the injustice suffered by illegitimate children. In between, it is a normal human drama, with a beginning that is unquestionably more convincing than the end. The opening scenes that take place in the London Blitz are authentic, and the characterisations by Michael Wilding and Anna Neagle unusually true to life. Until the depressing early-morning parting at Waterloo Station, all goes quietly but well. But with Diana's departure for Singapore the story becomes more fanciful. Scenes at home remain credible, but the desert island existence of Diana and her colleagues, though done with a commendable lack of glamour, is a little harder to believe.

On her return to England both Diana and Alan cease to behave like real people at all, and the happy coincidence by which the falling wall kills her rather than him is altogether too much like a trick ending. It remains quite an entertaining film, and the social problem involved will probably interest people without scaring them, but it certainly seems a pity that so promising a beginning should have tailed off to such an unsatisfactory ending.

OSCARS

WHAT WON THAT YEAR?
Best Motion Picture: *The Best Years of Our Lives*
Directing: William Wyler *The Best Years of Our Lives*
Actor: Fredric March *The Best Years of Our Lives*
Actress: Olivia de Havilland *To Each His Own*

BAFTAS

Not awarded until 1947

WHAT THEY SAY NOW...

The unjustness of the effect of illegitimacy on the innocent initially suggested the possibility of a serious social comment. But instead, *Piccadilly Incident* swelled into a somewhat overwrought weepie, a three-handkerchief emotional drama that was so successful at the box office that queues snaked along several streets wherever it was showing. In fact, *Piccadilly Incident* was the third most popular film at the UK box office in 1946 (and the second biggest British film of that year), following behind *The Wicked Lady* and *The Bells of St Mary's*.

Herbert Wilcox had initially hoped that Rex Harrison would have been able to reunite with Anna Neagle after *I Live in Grosvenor Square*, but he had gone to Hollywood. Next on Wilcox's list was John Mills, but he, too, was unavailable. As it transpired, Michael Wilding was hired instead, and the film attracted over a million more cinemagoers than the earlier Harrison-led picture. Wilding's appearance here began a dazzling partnership repeated in several other films, notably the 'London' series, of which this was the second entrant.

BEHIND THE SCENES

In the 1940s, 27 years before his James Bond debut, Roger Moore made early and uncredited appearances in seven films, including *Piccadilly Incident*. (He was finally billed in the likes of *Honeymoon Deferred* and *The Last Time I Saw Paris* in the early 1950s.) The movie also provided the first screen outing, again uncredited, for Michael Medwin, a British actor whose subsequent career (*Hindle Wakes*, 1952; *Night Must Fall*, 1964; and *O Lucky Man!*, 1973) was more distinguished, if less starry, than Moore's.

Top *Young and in love, Diana (Anna Neagle) and Alan (Michael Wilding) after their hurried wedding* (**above**) **Right** *American Wave Joan Draper (Frances Mercer) and Alan with their unfortunate baby boy*

44

Dir: J Lee THOMPSON / UK, USA
Released in Britain: 1961
Running Time: 157 minutes
Colour: Technicolor
Estimated Attendance: 11.4 million

Uncomplicated action, American machismo, British pluck and yet more action were the order of the day in this adaptation of the Alistair MacLean thriller. But while audiences flocked to see Gregory Peck and David Niven storm the island of Kheros, critics were less enamoured of the MacLean formula.

THE GUNS OF NAVARONE

Director **J. Lee Thompson**
Producer **Carl Foreman**
Screenplay **Carl Foreman**, adapted from the novel by
  Alistair MacLean
Director of Photography **Oswald Morris**
Editor **Alan Osbiston**
Production Designer **Geoffrey Drake**
Music **Dimitri Tiomkin**

Captain Keith Mallory • Gregory Peck
Corporal Miller • David Niven
Colonel Andrea Stavros • Anthony Quinn
CPO Butcher Brown • Stanley Baker
Major Roy Franklin • Anthony Quayle
Private Spyros Pappadimos • James Darren
Maria Pappadimos • Irene Papas
Anna • Gia Scala
Commander Jensen • James Robertson Justice
Squadron Leader Barnsby • Richard Harris
Commandant • Albert Lieven
Cohn • Bryan Forbes
Major Baker • Allan Cuthbertson
Oberst Muesel • Walter Gotell
Group Captain • Norman Wooland
Major Weaver • Michael Trubshawe
Sergeant Grogan • Percy Herbert
Sessler • George Mikell
Nicolai • Tutte Lemkow
Bride • Cleo Scouloudi

THE STORY

In 1943 a British force is pinned down on Kheros, an island off Turkey, under threat of German bombardment. The only escape is by sea, but the route is dominated by the giant guns of Navarone, which are set into the cliff and are impregnable against air attack. As a desperate measure, a sabotage team is sent to Navarone: Major Franklin; Mallory, an expert mountaineer; Miller, an explosives expert; Andrea, a Greek officer; and Brown and Pappadimos, trained killers.

Their boat goes down in a storm, but they land safely with their equipment and scale the almost sheer cliff face that is the only unguarded approach to the island. Franklin falls, however, breaking his leg, and Mallory takes over command. After crossing the island they make contact with the local Resistance, in the form of Maria, a sturdy partisan, and Anna, a girl who has been literally struck dumb after Gestapo torture. But the Germans are alerted to their presence and the entire group is rounded up. Through a trick, Andrea overcomes the guards and they manage to escape in German uniform, leaving Franklin behind primed with false information which he believes to be true.

Just before the raid on the guns. Miller discovers that Anna is a traitor and tries to goad Mallory into shooting her, but the bullet is finally fired by Maria. Together, Mallory and Miller sabotage the guns, while the others stage diversionary actions. As the British destroyers approach the straits, a gigantic explosion shatters the cliff. The survivors watch it from the sea.

WHAT THEY SAID THEN ...

Carl Foreman, as writer and producer, puts so much into the films he works on that they belong at least as much to him as to their directors. *The Guns of Navarone* takes up themes that have concerned him before: questions of courage, responsibility, men's responses to the actions they have to take to survive in war – issues which probably mean more to Foreman than the adventure story context in which they are set. But he has not managed to integrate these points. The moral arguments cut into the action without

THE GREATEST HIGH ADVENTURE EVER FILMED!

COLUMBIA PICTURES presents

GREGORY PECK · DAVID NIVEN · ANTHONY QUINN
STANLEY BAKER · ANTHONY QUAYLE · JAMES DARREN

in CARL FOREMAN'S

THE GUNS OF NAVARONE

IRENE PAPAS · GIA SCALA and Guest Stars JAMES ROBERTSON JUSTICE · RICHARD HARRIS

Screenplay by CARL FOREMAN · Based on the novel by ALISTAIR MACLEAN · Produced by CECIL F. FORD · Music Composed and Conducted by DIMITRI TIOMKIN · J. LEE THOMPSON · Directed by CARL FOREMAN · CINEMASCOPE & TECHNICOLOR

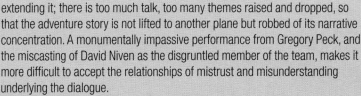

'GREAT GUNS!'..
A THRILLING MIGHTY AND MASTERLY PRODUCTION
Daily Mirror

Above Captain Keith Mallory (Gregory Peck) and Corporal Miller (David Niven) show off their matching duffle coats **Opposite top** The story mapped out, showing why the guns have got to go **Opposite below** An early poster design **Below** Carl Foreman enjoying the sunshine on location

extending it; there is too much talk, too many themes raised and dropped, so that the adventure story is not lifted to another plane but robbed of its narrative concentration. A monumentally impassive performance from Gregory Peck, and the miscasting of David Niven as the disgruntled member of the team, makes it more difficult to accept the relationships of mistrust and misunderstanding underlying the dialogue.

The failure extends beyond the script. J. Lee Thompson has not the ability of the Hollywood veterans to hold a long picture together. Individual scenes – the first approach to the fortress, across a quiet square with a song coming over a radio; the surreal moment when the guns are fired and the crews in their protective clothing line up behind them, hands to their ears – are dramatically staged. But the sense of topography and timing, of where on the island we are at any given moment, is confused, and the action moves in a series of jerks.

The Guns of Navarone sets its sights high: the introduction defines the epic scale of the undertaking, and the investment of time, money, effort and sheer talent has been enormous. However, the gap between intention and achievement is as wide as it is regrettable.

WHAT THEY SAY NOW ...

With the Second World War receding into the past, the time had come when uncritical flag-waving treatments of the conflict no longer sufficed. Films were starting to explore the moral ambiguities behind the heroics. Carl Foreman, screenwriter on *The Bridge on the River Kwai* (albeit pseudonymously, as he was then still subject to the Hollywood blacklist) and *High Noon*, saw Alastair MacLean's wartime adventure as perfect material for his preferred style of 'thinking man's action movie'.

The plot follows MacLean's favourite pattern – a diverse group of individuals are pulled together to carry out a near-impossible mission. Despite tensions, mishaps, internal bickering and – a regular MacLean ploy – a traitor in their midst, they finally succeed, although a few of them die in the attempt. The same 'Mission Impossible' formula would go on to be exploited in a whole string of Second World War adventure movies, including *The Heroes of Telemark* (1965), *Where Eagles*

OSCARS
7 nominations, **1 winner**

Best Motion Picture
Directing: J. Lee Thompson
Film Editing: Alan Osbiston
Music: Dmitri Tiomkin
Sound: John Cox
Special Effects: Bill Warrington, Vivian C. Greenham
Writing (Screenplay based on Material from Another Medium):
  Carl Foreman

WHAT WON THAT YEAR?
Best Motion Picture: *West Side Story*
Directing: Robert Wise, Jerome Robbins *West Side Story*
Actor: Maximilian Schell *Judgment at Nuremberg*
Actress: Sophia Loren *Two Women*

BAFTAS
1 nomination

British Screenplay: Carl Foreman

WHAT WON THAT YEAR?
Film: *The Hustler/Ballad of a Soldier*
British Film *A Taste of Honey*
British Actor: Peter Finch *No Love for Johnnie*
British Actress: Dora Bryan *A Taste of Honey*
Foreign Actor: Paul Newman *The Hustler*
Foreign Actress: Sophia Loren *The Women*

Dare (1968, from another MacLean novel) and, given an effectively cynical slant, Robert Aldrich's *The Dirty Dozen* (1967). In 1978 Foreman made a belated attempt to cash in on the success of the original with *Force 10 from Navarone* (from yet another MacLean novel), which fell woefully flat.

CLASSIC QUOTE

Miller: 'Sir, I've inspected this boat, and I think you ought to know that I can't swim.'

BEHIND THE SCENES

Navarone was originally assigned to Alexander Mackendrick, director of *The Ladykillers* (1955) and *Sweet Smell of Success* 1957), but he was taken off the picture after a few days. According to Mackendrick, it was because the mythic elements he was trying to introduce into the story didn't enthuse Carl Foreman. But cinematographer Ossie Morris ascribes the rift to Mackendrick's famed perfectionism. 'Sandy's a deep-thinking, intellectual director, and he just wanted everything to be right … He was working very hard. But we didn't actually turn much film in the camera … In the end, I don't think that went down too well with the powers that be in California.' Mackendrick was ousted, and the more pliable J. Lee Thompson took over.

Another early casualty was the actor Kenneth More. Hugely popular in Britain, More had never made much impact internationally. *Navarone*, in which he was offered the role of Sergeant Miller, looked like his breakthrough. But More was under contract to the Rank Organisation, who were loaning him out to Columbia for the movie. At the Rank Christmas dinner More got drunk and heckled a dull speech by the all-powerful Rank boss, John Davis. In response, Davis blocked More's loan-out. The role went to David Niven, and More's film career never recovered.

Dir: Alfonso CUARÓN / UK, USA
Released in Britain: 2004
Running Time: 141 minutes
Colour: Technicolor
Estimated Attendance: 11.29 million

For a series of films that had delighted the public but not always the critics, it was third time lucky for Harry Potter. A new director, some daring casting and Harry's most gripping adventure yet made all the difference; finally the cinematic Harry had come of age.

HARRY POTTER AND THE PRISONER OF AZKABAN

Director **Alfonso Cuarón**
Producers **David Heyman, Chris Columbus, Mark Radcliffe**
Screenplay **Steve Kloves**, based on the novel by J. K. Rowling
Director of Photography **Michael Seresin**
Editor **Steven Weisberg**
Production Designer **Stuart Craig**
Music **John Williams**

Harry Potter • Daniel Radcliffe
Ron Weasley • Rupert Grint
Hermione Granger • Emma Watson
Madame Rosmerta • Julie Christie
Rubeus Hagrid • Robbie Coltrane
Albus Dumbledore • Michael Gambon
Uncle Vernon • Richard Griffiths
Sirius Black • Gary Oldman
Professor Lupin • David Thewlis
Professor Severus Snape • Alan Rickman
Aunt Petunia • Fiona Shaw
Professor Minerva McGonagall • Maggie Smith
Peter Pettigrew • Timothy Spall
Professor Sibyll Trelawney • Emma Thompson
Mrs Molly Weasley • Julie Walters
Mr Arthur Weasley • Mark Williams
Aunt Marge • Pam Ferris
Dudley Dursley • Harry Melling
James Potter • Adrian Rawlins
Lily Potter • Geraldine Somerville

THE STORY

When adolescent wizard Harry Potter runs away from his uncle's house, he discovers that Sirius Black, allegedly a follower of the evil Lord Voldemort, has escaped from Azkaban prison and is out to kill him. When the train back to Hogwarts is searched by Dementors, the prison guards who suck happiness from those they encounter, Harry faints. In class, Buckbeak (a hippogriff) attacks pupil Draco Malfoy after Malfoy insults him. When Harry is forbidden to join an outing to Hogsmeade village, he's given a map that shows the movements of everyone in school, and reveals a secret passage which Harry follows under an invisibility cloak. At Hogsmeade he eavesdrops on a conversation and learns that Black is his godfather and that he betrayed Harry's dead parents to Voldemort.

New teacher Professor Lupin shows Harry how to focus on a happy memory to ward off the Dementors. Harry's friend Ron Weasley's pet rat Scabbers is apparently eaten by their classmate Hermione Granger's cat. Buckbeak is sentenced to death for attacking Malfoy. Harry sees Peter Pettigrew, the wizard Black is accused of killing, walking past him on the magic map, but cannot see him in person.

Harry, Ron and Hermione find Scabbers just before Buckbeak's execution. The rat escapes again and Ron chases him into the roots of the dangerous Whomping Willow tree; a dog (in fact Black in animal form) grabs Ron and pulls him under the roots. Hermione and Harry follow into a tunnel. Lupin arrives; he and Black explain that it's Pettigrew, who has been living as Scabbers, who betrayed Harry's parents. Lupin – a werewolf – transforms in the moonlight. Black reverts to dog form to fight Lupin and prevent him from harming the children. The werewolf flees at the sound of a howl; Harry and the injured Black are attacked by Dementors.

Above A new broom? Instead Harry (Daniel Radcliffe) flies Buckbeak the hippogriff **Below** Michael Gambon dons the late Richard Harris's beard to play Professor Dumbledore

Harry wakes in the school infirmary where he learns of Black's recapture. Since the authorities won't believe in Black's innocence, headmaster Albus Dumbledore tells Hermione to turn back time by three hours; she and Harry untie Buckbeak and fly him to free Black from the school tower.

WHAT THEY SAY ...

Alfonso Cuarón's film is much more accomplished visually than either of its predecessors directed by Chris Columbus.. The magic, here, works not just on the level of weird and wonderful ghosts and monsters but through a series of haunting images that draw attention to key themes, and a breadth of imagination that goes far beyond anything described in J. K. Rowling's original book. Moments of telling imagery, such as the slow frosting of the train window as the Dementors approach and its unfreezing to reveal a fragile child's hand pressed against the glass, convey more than any amount of literary faithfulness.

In such sequences – and in particular the moonlight transformation of a character into a werewolf which remains all the more unsettling for retaining its human dimensions – *Harry Potter and the Prisoner of Azkaban* introduces a darker terror appropriate to its disturbing back-story of an innocent man locked up and subjected to mental torture. In a lighter vein, there are also enjoyable scenes of adolescent playfulness; even the studious Hermione has time to ask, 'Is that really what my hair looks like from the back?' as she watches her earlier self putting back the clocks.

One of Rowling's faults as a novelist is a tendency to deliver exposition through unwieldy chunks of dialogue that interrupt the action, a fault repeated by Columbus.

OSCARS
2 nominations

Music (Original Score): John Williams
Visual Effects

WHAT WON THAT YEAR?
Best Picture: *Million Dollar Baby*
Directing: Clint Eastwood *Million Dollar Baby*
Actor in a Leading Role: Jamie Foxx *Ray*
Actress in a Leading Role: Hilary Swank *Million Dollar Baby*

BAFTAS
5 nominations, **1 winner**

Alexander Korda Award for Outstanding British Film
Production Design: Stuart Craig
Achievement in Special Visual Effects
Make-Up & Hair: Amanda Knight, Eithné Fennell, Nick Dudman
Orange Film of the Year

WHAT WON THAT YEAR?
Film: *The Aviator*
Alexander Korda Award for Outstanding British Film: *My Summer of Love*
David Lean Award for Achievement in Direction: Mike Leigh *Vera Drake*
Actor in a Leading Role: Jamie Foxx *Ray*
Actress in a Leading Role: Imelda Staunton *Vera Drake*

Cuarón handles such scenes much better, for instance by filming Harry overhearing the supposed history of his relationship with Black from under his invisibility cloak in a fast-moving exchange that works much better than the novel's laboured original. But the omission of key speeches in the final scenes, to identify the makers of the magic Marauder's Map and explain their relationships, leaves the plot seeming nonsensical and deprives the film of its potential emotional complexity.

Still, there are enough pleasant surprises among the cast to go some way toward compensating. Michael Gambon makes a very human headmaster as Dumbledore, while Gary Oldman, as the haunted prisoner Sirius Black, and David Thewlis as the hard-done-by Professor Lupin are more than a fair substitute for Kenneth Branagh's irritating Lockhart in the second film. Both Hermione and Harry also come into their own, demonstrating feelings that render them more than the ciphers of the previous outings.

CLASSIC QUOTE
Hermione: 'If you're going to kill Harry, you have to kill us too.'
Sirius: 'Only one will die tonight.'

BEHIND THE SCENES
Richard Harris, who played Professor Dumbledore in the first two *Harry Potter* films, died in October 2002, shortly before the release of the second movie. Rumours abounded that he would be replaced by Ian McKellen, who was at that point nearing the end of his tenure as another wise mentor in a fantasy series – Gandalf in *The Lord of the Rings*. The part finally went to Michael Gambon.

IN THE CHAIR
A transfusion of fresh blood was just what the *Harry Potter* series needed at this stage, and the remarkable Alfonso Cuarón was an inspired choice. It might seem a strange leap for this Mexican auteur to go straight from his politically charged sex comedy of 2001, *Y Tu Mama Tambien* (*And Your Mother Too*), in which two libidinous young friends compete for the attentions of an older woman, to the helm of one of the biggest franchises in modern cinema. But Cuarón has a track record in mainstream fantasy – it is said he won the *Harry Potter* job on the strength of his tender film version of *A Little Princess* (1995). In addition, his modern-day *Great Expectations* (1998), starring Ethan Hawke, Gwyneth Paltrow and Robert De Niro, had already showed him to be an audacious film stylist.

Left top Draco Malfoy (Tom Felton) provokes an attack from Buckbeak the hippogriff **Left above** Director Alfonso Cuarón (left) works his magic with Daniel Radcliffe and Gary Oldman

46

Dir: David LEAN / USA
Released in Britain: 1967
Running Time: 193 minutes
Colour: Metrocolor
Estimated Attendance: 11.2 million

Top Doctor at work: Yuri Zhivago (Omar Sharif)

Doctor Zhivago was David Lean's costliest but also his most profitable film. Yet it attracted so many negative comments from critics that Lean's confidence was sapped, and it was some years before his next film, *Ryan's Daughter* (1970), went into production. The public, on the other hand, adored it.

DOCTOR ZHIVAGO

Director **David Lean**
Producer **Carlo Ponti**
Screenplay by **Robert Bolt**, adapted from the novel by
  Boris Pasternak
Director of Photography **Freddie Young**
Editor **Norman Savage**
Production Designer **John Box**
Music **Maurice Jarre**

Yuri Zhivago • Omar Sharif
Lara • Julie Christie
Pasha Antipov/'Strelnikoff' • Tom Courtenay
Yevgraf Zhivago • Alec Guiness
Anna Gromeko • Siobhan McKenna
Alexander Gromeko • Ralph Richardson
Komarovsky • Rod Steiger
Tonya Gromeko • Geraldine Chaplin
Tonya Komarova, the Girl • Rita Tushingham
Amelia • Adrienne Corri
The Bolshevik • Bernard Kay
Kurt, Medical Professor • Geoffrey Keen
Kostoyed • Klaus Kinski
Sasha • Jeffrey Rockland
Liberius • Gérard Tichy
Razin • Noel Willman
Yuri, Aged 8 Years • Tarek Sharif
Petya • Jack MacGowran
David, Young Engineer at Dam • Mark Eden

THE STORY

Yuri Zhivago, orphaned as a boy, is brought up in the family of Alexander Gromeko, whose daughter Tonya he later marries after qualifying as a doctor. During his years in Moscow as a student, Yuri several times comes across Lara, the beautiful daughter of a dressmaker, Amelia. The most dramatic encounter is at a Christmas party where Lara shoots her mother's protector Komarovsky, a political opportunist who has seduced her. Lara is led away from the party by Pasha, a revolutionary idealist whom she later marries.

Moscow is caught up in the Great War; Yuri works as a doctor at the front where he again comes across Lara, now a nurse. Returning to Moscow, Yuri finds the city transformed by the revolution, his family's house requisitioned, and himself under suspicion for the poetry he has published. Yevgraf, his half-brother and a Bolshevik police commissar, urges Yuri to take his family away from Moscow to their country estate at Yuryatin in the Urals.

Discovering that Lara is living in a nearby town, Yuri visits her, but is captured by the Red Army partisans and forced into service as a doctor. Yuri deserts the unit and struggles back across the snow-bound Steppes until he reaches Lara's house. Meanwhile Yuri's family have been deported to France. Komarovsky reappears to persuade Yuri to flee Russia, but Yuri refuses and is separated from Lara. Years later, still searching for Lara, Yuri dies on a Moscow street. Lara disappears into a labour camp, but their daughter lives on to be found by Yevgraf.

WHAT THEY SAID THEN ...

The best one can say of *Doctor Zhivago* is that it is an honest failure. Boris Pasternak's sprawling novel is held together by its unity of style, by the driving force of its narrative, by the passionate voice of a poet who weaves a mass of diverse characters into a single tapestry. And this is precisely what is absent from David Lean's film. Somewhere in the two years of the film's making the spirit of the novel has been lost.

OSCARS
10 nominations, **5 winners**

Best Picture
Directing: David Lean
Actor in a Supporting Role: Tom Courtenay
Art Direction (Color): John Box, Terry Marsh, Dario Simoni
Cinematography (Color): Freddie Young
Costume Design (Color): Phyllis Dalton
Film Editing: Norman Savage
Music (Music Score – Substantially Original): Maurice Jarre
Sound: A.W. Watkins, Franklin E. Milton
**Writing (Screenplay – Based on Material from Another
   Medium): Robert Bolt**

WHAT WON THAT YEAR?
Best Picture: *The Sound of Music*
Directing: Robert Wise *The Sound of Music*
Actor: Lee Marvin *Cat Ballou*
Actress: Julie Christie *Darling*

BAFTAS
3 nominations

Film
British Actor: Ralph Richardson (also for *The Wrong Box/Khartoum*)
British Actress: Julie Christie (also for *Farenheit 451*)

WHAT WON THAT YEAR?
Film: *Who's Afraid of Virginia Woolf?*
British Film: *The Spy Who Came in from the Cold*
British Actor: Richard Burton *The Spy Who Came in from the Cold*
British Actress: Elizabeth Taylor *Who's Afraid of Virginia Woolf?*
Foreign Actor: Rod Steiger *The Pawnbroker*
Foreign Actress: Jeanne Moreau *The Sleeping Car Murders*

Above Lara (Julie Christie) takes aim **Right** The
deserted dacha **Overleaf** Star-crossed lovers
Lara and Doctor Yuri Zhivago (Omar Sharif)

Tsarist Moscow is brilliantly re-created in visual terms, but handled in a way that suggests that Pasternak's massive characters are little more than anaemic old maids and angry young men who should know better. And this charade-like interpretation of the rumblings of a new age is echoed in the film's treatment of the revolution, which appears as merely a series of irritating interruptions of daily life ('Oh Lord, not another purge,' mutters Ralph Richardson wearily, as though commenting on the weather).

The film fares better when it gets out into the country: the endless sweep of plains on the long train journey to the Urals, the partisan brigade shooting down a band of white-smocked boys in a field of golden corn, the charge across the ice. But even here Freddie Young's photography stays in the mind only as a book of picture postcards. The impression of ephemeral prettiness is underlined by Maurice Jarre's jangling music score.

Nor is the film redeemed by its acting, which is undistinguished, though this is hardly the fault of the actors, since for the most part all they are required to do is to register the appropriate expression. Omar Sharif comes across as a full-blown romantic without ever suggesting that there is any depth to Zhivago; Julie Christie struggles conscientiously as Lara, but the part is too big for her or anyone else.

WHAT THEY SAY NOW ...
Italian producer Carlo Ponti had initially thought of *Doctor Zhivago* as a vehicle for his wife, Sophia Loren. When MGM brought in David Lean, the director chose Julie Christie instead. After a series

METRO · GOLDWYN · MAYER
PRESENTS
A CARLO PONTI PRODUCTION
DAVID LEAN'S FILM
OF BORIS PASTERNAK'S

DOCTOR ZHIVAGO

STARRING
GERALDINE CHAPLIN · JULIE CHRISTIE · TOM COURTENAY · ALEC GUINNESS · SIOBHAN McKENNA · RALPH RICHARDSO
OMAR SHARIF (AS ZHIVAGO) · ROD STEIGER · RITA TUSHINGHAM · Screen Play by ROBERT BOLT · Directed by DAVID LEAN · PANAVISION and METROCOLOR

of financial failures, MGM was desperately looking for a hit, and so gave Lean carte blanche. He turned to many of the cast and crew from his previous film, *Lawrence of Arabia* (1962), including, belatedly, cinematographer Freddie Young. Initially Lean had hired Nicolas Roeg, who had shot second unit on *Lawrence*, but they didn't get along and after a few weeks he was replaced.

Lean even begins the film as he did *Lawrence*, with a long prologue leading into the main bulk of the narrative, which is told in flashback. He had previously used such a structure for *In Which We Serve* (1942) and *Brief Encounter* (1945). Unlike *Lawrence*, however, the flashback bookends the narrative to provide some sense of closure, providing a more upbeat end to the film. Initially, it also serves to make it clear that Zhivago and Lara will eventually become lovers – they don't actually speak to each other until 80 minutes into the film.

As Komarovsky, Rod Steiger (a late replacement for James Mason) steals every scene that he is in, clearly revelling in playing such a morally varied and ambiguous character. Just as good is Tom Courtenay who, as his change from the idealistic young Pasha to the weary and embittered Strelnikov indicates, is given a substantial character arc. In this respect, Sharif, Christie

and Geraldine Chaplin in the main roles are saddled with rather static and passive characters, giving them less scope to shine.

CLASSIC QUOTE
Pasha: 'They rode them down, Lara. Women and children, begging for bread. There will be no more 'peaceful' demonstrations.'

SCENE STEALER
It has to be the revelation of the 'Ice Palace' rising out of the frozen Steppes, the deserted dacha with its interior as chilly and icicle-laden as the eaves and gables outside. The construction of the set was as much a challenge for the production designer John Box as it was for the director of photography Freddie Young, and both won Oscars for their work on *Doctor Zhivago*.

BEHIND THE SCENES
Night filming in Madrid, where scenes of the Russian revolution were restaged, were interrupted by the police who had been tipped off by disturbed residents that a real uprising was taking place, and an attempt was being made to depose General Franco.

47

Dir: George Roy HILL / USA
Released in Britain: 1974
Running Time: 129 minutes
Colour: Technicolor
Estimated Attendance: 11.08 million

THE STING

Director **George Roy Hill**
Producers **Tony Bill, Michael Phillips, Julia Phillips**
Screenplay **David S. Ward**
Director of Photography **Robert Surtees**
Editor **William H. Reynolds**
Art Director **Henry Bumstead**
Music **Scott Joplin**

Henry Gondorff • Paul Newman
Johnny Hooker • Robert Redford
Doyle Lonnegan • Robert Shaw
Lt William Snyder • Charles Durning
J. J. Singleton • Ray Walston
Billie • Eileen Brennan
Kid Twist • Harold Gould
Eddie Niles • John Heffernan
FBI Agent Polk • Dana Elcar
Erie Kid • Jack Kehoe
Loretta • Dimitra Arliss
Luther Coleman • Robert Earl Jones
Mottola • James Sloyan
Floyd • Charles Dierkop
2nd Bodyguard • Lee Paul
Crystal • Sally Kirkland
Benny Garfield • Avon Long
Combs • Arch Johnson
Granger • Ed Bakey
Cole • Brad Sullivan

American cinema was on fire in the mid-1970s, full of anger and energy and innovation. But it was a movie that harked back to gentler times which acted as a magnet to mass audiences, and a balm to Academy voters, helped no end by Scott Joplin's bestselling soundtrack.

THE STORY

After working a lucrative confidence trick – inadvertently at the expense of influential racketeer Doyle Lonnegan – Luther Coleman is killed by Lonnegan's thugs. His younger partner, Johnny Hooker, seeks out Luther's former buddy in Chicago, Henry Gondorff, to learn the Big Time and hopefully to enlist his help in avenging Luther. Gondorff agrees to 'take' Lonnegan because of the money involved. Knowing that Lonnegan has a weakness for horses and poker, they construct a phoney betting club in Chicago, and work a poker trick on a New York to Chicago train journey which results in Lonnegan losing a large sum of money to Gondorff. Pretending to be working against his partner Gondorff, Hooker then persuades Lonnegan that he can beat Gondorff's betting operation by getting results early with the aid of a friend in the telegraph office. Lonnegan, although interested, subjects the proposition to various tests; but thanks to the con men assembled by Gondorff, the betting club has a complete air of authenticity.

Hooker, meanwhile, is being followed by the FBI; by Snyder, a crooked cop; and by the two men who killed Luther, as well as (unknown to him) by a man sent by Gondorff in case he falls into any traps. The big day arrives when Lonnegan is to place his huge bet and clean up at Gondorff's expense; and an elaborate charade takes place during which Lonnegan thinks he sees Hooker and Gondorff killed during a raid by the FBI. But this, too, is a Gondorff ploy, and after the mystified Lonnegan has abandoned his money and been hustled away by the anxious Snyder, Gondorff and Hooker celebrate the biggest con they have ever worked.

OSCARS

10 nominations, **7 winners**

Best Picture
Directing: George Roy Hill
Actor: Robert Redford
Art Direction/Set Decoration: Henry Bumstead, James Payne
Cinematography: Robert Surtees
Costume Design: Edith Head
Film Editing: William Reynolds
Music (Adaptation Score): Marvin Hamlisch
Sound: Ronald K. Pierce, Robert Bertrand
Writing (based on Factual material or Material Not Previously Published or Produced): David S. Ward

WHAT WON THAT YEAR?
Actor: Jack Lemmon *Save the Tiger*
Actress: Glenda Jackson: *A Touch of Class*

BAFTAS

WHAT WON THAT YEAR?
Film: *Lacombe Lucien*
Direction: Roman Polanski *Chinatown*
Actor: Jack Nicholson *The Last Detail/Chinatown*
Actress: Joanne Woodward *Summer Wishes, Winter Dreams*

Left Henry Gondorff (Paul Newman, with cigar) deals a blinder *Opposite below* Johnny Hooker (Robert Redford, centre) isn't the one being taken for a ride

WHAT THEY SAID THEN …

This is the most elaborate 'heist' film to date, piling red herrings on top of each other in thick profusion and working up to an outrageously jokey and calculated finale. The tone, with the chummy relationship between Newman and Redford, is naturally reminiscent of *Butch Cassidy and the Sundance Kid* (1969). It is a thoroughly old-fashioned, professional piece of entertainment, a little overlong but sufficiently well written and played to carry an audience along in the best Hollywood sense.

Robert Shaw is the odd man out, making rather heavy weather of an admittedly ungrateful part. But the film's real pleasures are to be found in its sheer physical beauty: employing an ace team of veterans – cameraman Robert Surtees, designer Henry Bumstead, editor William Reynolds, costume designer Edith Head – Hill has produced the richest re-creation of a 1930s milieu to date. Surtees's lighting and movement give almost every shot a central point of interest. The sleazy little back streets, the stuffy hotel rooms and cafés are contrasted with the steely, grid-like outlines of the city towering above. The set decorations give a splendidly lived-in quality to the betting rooms and apartments, and the merging of settings and real locations is uncommonly smooth. If nothing else, the film marks a return to the kind of solid, peculiarly American type of filmmaking that seems to be the prerogative of the generation of technicians employed here.

WHAT THEY SAY NOW …

The oddest thing about *The Sting* is that it won seven Oscars – beating *The Exorcist* and *Cries and Whispers* in the year between *The Godfather* and *The Godfather Part II*. The movie, in other words, was a conspicuous throwback in the middle of the richest experimental period American cinema had seen in decades – a straightforward light entertainment bulked out to prestige-picture dimensions with its marquee cast, baggy screenplay and expensively crafted re-creation of 1930s Chicago. Commercially foolproof, there's no doubt that it got the Academy fogey vote, as *Rocky* would three years later – both indications of the countervailing populist mentality in Hollywood that made it difficult for the mavericks to survive for long.

Nowadays it's tempting to see *The Sting*'s fetish for its period as part and parcel of an industry nostalgia for genre, but as pure entertainment it's too gilded and overstuffed – too Oscar-hungry – to prance along as pleasurably as it wants to. Clever plot mechanics were always the aces up its sleeve, not the onerous characterisation and hand-me-down Butch-and-Sundance star banter. Those maddeningly catchy Scott Joplin rags help to sustain its most transparent illusion: one of being light on its feet.

CLASSIC QUOTE

Gondorff to Hooker: 'Glad to meet you, kid, you're a real horse's ass.'

Dir: Francis Ford COPPOLA / USA
Released in Britain: 1972
Running Time: 172 minutes
Colour: Technicolor
Estimated Attendance: 11 million

Family life was never going to be the same after Francis Ford Coppola's breakthrough movie, a vast but impeccably detailed portrait of a close-knit Mafia clan. Practically every moment here offers a master class in filmmaking, from the opening party sequence to the chilling closing massacre. See it and weep.

THE GODFATHER

Director **Francis Ford Coppola**
Producer **Albert S. Ruddy**
Screenplay **Mario Puzo, Francis Ford Coppola**, adapted from the novel by Mario Puzo
Director of Photography **Gordon Willis**
Editors **William H. Reynolds, Peter Zinner**
Production Designer **Dean Tavoularis**
Music **Nino Rota**

Don Vito Corleone • Marlon Brando
Michael Corleone • Al Pacino
Sonny Corleone • James Caan
Kay Adams • Diane Keaton
Tom Hagen • Robert Duvall
Connie Rizzi • Talia Shire
Fredo Corleone • John Cazale
Clemenza • Richard Castellano
Captain McCluskey • Sterling Hayden
Jack Woltz • John Marley
Barzini • Richard Conte
Sollozzo • Al Lettieri
Tessio • Abe Vigoda
Carlo Rizzi • Gianni Russo
Cuneo • Rudy Bond
Johnny Fontane • Al Martino
Mama Corleone • Morgana King
Luca Brasi • Lenny Montana
Paulie Gatto • John Martino
Bonasera • Salvatore Corsitto

THE STORY

In August 1945 Don Vito Corleone, known as 'Godfather' to the many Italian immigrants in New York dependent upon his help and protection, presides over his daughter Connie's wedding to the young bookmaker Carlo Rizzi. The lavish ceremony at his Long Beach home is attended by crowds of relatives and friends, among them Tom Hagen, the Don's right-hand man and legal adviser. Hagen attends a meeting that has been requested with the Don by Virgil Sollozzo, a leading member of the Tattaglia Family, closest rivals to the Corleones. Sollozzo proposes that the Don participate in a drug-running operation, and although the Don turns the offer down, Sollozzo notices that Sonny, the eldest Corleone son, is interested.

A few weeks later, the Godfather is shot down in the street, clearly so that the way will be open for the Tattaglias to do a deal with Sonny. The old man survives, however, and while he slowly recovers, the Corleones take their revenge. Michael, the youngest son, shoots both Sollozzo and McClusky, the corrupt police chief who has been helping him, and is then rushed to Sicily to be out of harm's way during the ensuing warfare. He marries a Sicilian girl, Apollonia, and for two years lives happily in an obscure mountain village until the news reaches him that Sonny has been killed and that the Don has resumed command of the Corleones. Shortly afterwards, Apollonia is killed in an explosion intended for Michael and set off by Fabrizio, one of his own bodyguards.

Michael returns to New York to find that the Don has made peace with all the rival families and that an uneasy truce exists. He marries an American girl, Kay, and sets about taking over the reins from the Godfather, who is now keen to retire. When Don Vito dies suddenly, the Godfather's long-range planning finds an efficient champion in Michael. With a series of ruthless murders he settles old scores, disposes of the weak members of his own ranks and restores the Corleones to full supremacy.

Opposite Michael Corleone (Al Pacino) broods and (**above**) opens fire as he follows reluctantly in his father's footsteps **Below** Luca Brasi (Lenny Montana), soon to be 'sleeping with the fishes'

WHAT THEY SAID THEN ...

With a sequel already on the way, *The Godfather* is perhaps more of a social phenomenon than a movie, a curious compendium of legend, fantasy, rumour and thinly disguised fact. That the size of its audience has broken all records indicates the same kind of response as was given to the gangster films of the 1930s (the truth looks so much better in make-up).

Yet breaking the rules, *The Godfather* deals not with the wages of sin but with such upright human virtues as honour, loyalty, justice and the exercise of power. Its personalities, far from being social outcasts, are hard-working members of the community, pursuing the decent living conditions that are the right of every United States immigrant. The Godfather himself, while he may have been capable of a slight indiscretion in his youth, is now undoubtedly a man of the highest integrity. And in this sense, despite the hangovers from the old gangster movie tradition – the careful period reconstructions, the vintage cars, the lush furnishings – *The Godfather* is a modern tale about contemporary private enterprise.

The really remarkable aspect of the film is that in terms of style it is so self-effacing – one might unkindly call it the *Love Story* of gangster cinema. Coppola has played completely safe and, apart from tinkering a little with the death scenes (the Godfather's, for example, takes rather longer) has mostly filmed Puzo's narrative just as it comes. One result is that the film is far too long.

OSCARS
10 nominations, **3 winners**

Best Picture
Directing: Francis Ford Coppola
Actor: Marlon Brando (note: award refused)
Actor in a Supporting Role: James Caan
Actor in a Supporting Role: Robert Duvall
Actor in a Supporting Role: Al Pacino
Costume Design: Anna Hill Johnstone
Film Editing: William Reynolds, Peter Zinner
Sound: Bud Grenzbach, Richard Portman, Christopher Newman
Writing (Screenplay Based on Material from Another Medium):
    Mario Puzo, Francis Ford Coppola

WHAT WON THAT YEAR?
Directing: Bob Fosse *Cabaret*
Actress: Liza Minnelli *Cabaret*

BAFTAS
5 nominations, **1 winner**

Actor: Marlon Brando (also for The Nightcomers)
Costume Design: Anna Hill Johnstone
Supporting Actor: Robert Duvall
Most Promising Newcomer to Leading Film Roles: Al Pacino
The Anthony Asquith Momorial Award: Nino Rota

WHAT WON THAT YEAR?
Film: *Cabaret*
Direction: Bob Fosse *Cabaret*
Actor: Gene Hackman *The French Connection/The Poseidon Adventure*
Actress: Liza Minelli *Cabaret*

Another, inevitably, is confusion; lesser characters arrive and abruptly depart without it being certain whether we should regret their passing. The holocaust at the end, rather too glibly intercut with a new Corleone baptism, needs particularly careful attention if one is keeping score.

With due allowance given to the obvious charm of the wedding reception and the seductive landscapes of the Sicilian sequences, *The Godfather* is primarily borne along by its battery of excellent performances, two of them by Coppola's 'regulars' Robert Duvall and James Caan, who already proved their worth so impressively in *The Rain People* (1969). The film's big discovery is Al Pacino, whose transition from gauche outsider to hardened and inevitable successor to the Godfather is portrayed with finely calculated intensity. Almost, but not quite, he steals the film from Brando who, sinking with a sinister calm into the network of folds on his face, nevertheless gives an effortless authoritative impersonation of the Don. Despite some curiously unmemorable qualities, *The Godfather* would be unimaginable without Brando's hypnotic presence – the elegant gestures, the murmuring comments, the unbending poise.

WHAT THEY SAY NOW ...

It was the event film of the 1970s, with dialogue, characters and imagery instantly entering the popular consciousness. It made stars of Pacino and Caan, and gave Brando a triumphant comeback. Not since Warner Brothers' crime cycle of the 1930s had the underworld so captured the public imagination. But in adapting Mario Puzo's bestseller Coppola turned pulp into opera. Plainly put, *The Godfather* is fully deserving of its reputation as one of the greatest American films ever made.

The reasons are numerous: Coppola's authoritative grip on an ordered, fastidiously constructed narrative, Dean Tavoularis's richly detailed design, the weight given to a fabulous supporting ensemble, Gordon Willis's striking cinematography, Nino Rota's melodic score. Take your pick.

The Godfather has long been criticised for glorifying the Mafia. But time and two more pictures have drawn out the

Opposite *The formidable Don Corleone (Marlon Brando)* **Above** *Francis Ford Coppola gets comfortable on the bed where,* **Above right***, studio boss Jack Woltz (John Marley) gets a head start from his prize thoroughbred*

despair and nihilism in the material. *The Godfather Part II* of 1974 is even more compelling in its study of power shading into moral decay. The flawed *Part III* of 1990 sees Michael Corleone get his just desserts with Shakespearean finality. *The Godfather* continues to entrance, however, for its mythic exploration of family, albeit one cursed in blood and ambition.

CLASSIC QUOTE

Don Corleone: 'I'm gonna make him an offer he can't refuse.'

SCENE STEALER

The producer who refuses to cast Don Vito's godson Johnny Fontane in his film awakens, panicked to find his bed and silk pyjamas sticky with blood. Fearfully he pulls the sheet away and, shrieking, discovers the severed head of his magnificent thoroughbred stallion at his feet.

BEHIND THE SCENES

So numerous are the anecdotes (Brando did *not* stuff his cheeks with cotton, but had resin blobs clipped to his back teeth; Sinatra, universally believed to be the model for crooner Johnny Fontane, *did* attack Puzo in a restaurant, calling him a 'stool-pigeon'; the baby being baptised during the climax is Coppola's infant daughter Sofia) that there are volumes of *Godfather* lore and trivia.

IN THE CHAIR

Shortly after its premiere *Variety* reported, '*The Godfather* is an historic smash of unprecedented proportions.' At the time, Francis Ford Coppola was holed up in a hotel writing the screenplay for *The Great Gatsby* (1974) to relieve his financial problems because he believed *The Godfather* was going to be a disaster. Suddenly he was the most important filmmaker around. His subsequent career has been marked by an ambitious range of enterprises (the American Zoetrope studio, publishing, winemaking), dramatic reversals, the famously fraught production of *Apocalypse Now* (1979) and lavish style exercises like *The Cotton Club* (1984) and *Bram Stoker's Dracula* (1992).

49

Dir: Roland **EMMERICH** / USA
Released in Britain: 1996
Running Time: 145 minutes
Colour: Deluxe
Estimated Attendance: 10.79 million

Independence Day remains the highest-placed science fiction movie in the Ultimate Film list, after the work of Spielberg and Lucas. With nasty aliens, eye-blistering special effects, the end of the world as we know it *and* Will Smith on the menu, how could it have failed?

INDEPENDENCE DAY

Director **Roland Emmerich**
Producer **Dean Devlin**
Screenplay **Dean Devlin, Roland Emmerich**
Director of Photography **Walter Lindenlaub**
Editor **David Brenner**
Production Designers **Oliver Scholl, Patrick Tatopoulos**
Music **David Arnold**

Captain Steven Hiller • Will Smith
President Thomas J. Whitmore • Bill Pullman
David Levinson • Jeff Goldblum
Marilyn Whitmore • Mary McDonnell
Julius Levinson • Judd Hirsch
Constance Spano • Margaret Colin
Russell Casse • Randy Quaid
General William Grey • Robert Loggia
Albert Nimziki • James Rebhorn
Marty Gilbert • Harvey Fierstein
Major Mitchell • Adam Baldwin
Dr Brakish Okun • Brent Spiner
Miguel • James Duval
Jasmine Dubrow • Vivica A. Fox
Alicia • Lisa Jakub
Dylan • Ross Bagley
Patricia Whitmore • Mae Whitman
Captain Watson • Bill Smitrovich
Tiffany • Kiersten Warren
Captain Jimmy Wilder • Harry Connick Jr

THE STORY

July 2. Radio signals buzzing across monitors in the USA prove to be emanating from a massive spaceship. As government agencies try to communicate with the ship, and a half dozen smaller vessels that have taken up positions across the world, a New York cable executive, David Levinson, discovers that the signal is actually a countdown. David and his father, Julius, drive to Washington DC to pass the information to David's former wife, Constance, who gave up on her marriage for a job with the President. Meanwhile, a fighter pilot, Captain Hiller, takes leave of his fiancée and her son in order to 'kick E.T.'s butt,' while Russell Casse, a former Vietnam pilot turned alcoholic crop-duster with three kids, explains to anyone who will listen how he was once abducted by aliens.

July 3. The smaller alien ships begin to attack the earth. The President and most of his staff, along with David and his father, escape the White House just before it is blown up. They travel to Roswell, New Mexico – Area 51 – where, since the 1950s, government scientists have been studying a spaceship identical to those in the invading force. The President launches an unsuccessful nuclear attack. David discovers a way to disarm the invaders' defence system with a computer virus. He and Steven, who has gunned down one of the aliens in a dogfight, navigate the older spacecraft to the mother ship in order to plant the virus. A convoy of survivors arrive in Roswell, including the pilot's girlfriend, her son and the wounded First Lady, who then dies.

July 4. Steven and David hack in to the alien computer system, disarming its defence shields. The US launches a successful air strike on the extra-terrestrials. They spread the word via Morse code to the rest of the world's armies, all of whom are then able to assist in defeating the enemy.

Opposite *David Levinson (Jeff Goldblum) ponders the end of the world as we know it* **This page** *Captains Steven Hiller (Will Smith) and Jimmy Wilder (Harry Connick Jr) prepare to 'whup E.T.'s ass* **Overleaf** *The Washington Monument no longer dominates the skyline*

OSCARS
2 nominations, **1 winner**

Sound
Visual Effects

WHAT WON THAT YEAR?
Best Picture: *The English Patient*
Directing: Anthony Minghella *The English Patient*
Actor in a Leading Role: Geoffrey Rush *Shine*
Actress in a Leading Role: Frances McDormand *Fargo*

BAFTAS
2 nominations

Sound
Achievement in Special Visual Effects

WHAT WON THAT YEAR?
Film: *The English Patient*
David Lean Award for Achievement in Direction:
   Joel Coen *Fargo*
Actor in a Leading Role: Geoffrey Rush *Shine*
Actress in a Leading Role: Brenda Blethyn *Secrets & Lies*

WHAT THEY SAY ...

The good news is that Hollywood can still make good, solid, goose-bump movies where neat effects keep time with story, characters and loads of good cheer. Doomsday aside, *Independence Day* is weirdly upbeat in mood, a gloss on the same vibrations that end *Dr Strangelove* (1964), but without the venom. The director Roland Emmerich doesn't have Kubrick's wit, style or intellectual reach, but he does have a feel for epic moviemaking. The picture works best when the odds are laughably impossible, as when half a dozen spaceships hang over the world's major cities, and all that stands between life and death are three impeccably fit American men with good hair.

Less like new science fiction than old-fashioned hokum, *Independence Day* is an SF disaster film lent a whiff of *X Files*-era paranoia. It was hugely popular, but not universally liked: its rather gung-ho attitude prompted Tim Burton to make the savage *Mars Attacks!* in response. (Tellingly, that pricklier picture flopped.)

Independence Day may be goofy, but it's not dumb, barely cheating at story level. Still, there are nagging deficiencies. Unlike the directors of so many blockbusters, Emmerich knows that what makes a movie are its people; unlike Spielberg he doesn't spend time shading them in. The problem is partly logistical, the headaches of effects and extras, and partly inspirational; the film never shakes the B-movie tag.

In the end, this may be the key to the film's success. Firmly located between art and trash, *Independence Day*'s success is in being bigger but never better than its audience. Its mediocrity is its greatest triumph. This may be the most cheerful movie about the apocalypse ever. Faced with the end, there's barely one character in the film who sheds a tear. Most simply swallow fear and turn towards danger. Like the audience, they know that it will all be over soon.

CLASSIC QUOTE

President Whitmore: 'I saw its thoughts. I saw what they're planning to do. They're like locusts. They're moving from planet to planet ... their whole civilization. After they've consumed every natural resource they move on. And we're next. Nuke 'em. Let's nuke the bastards.'

IN THE CHAIR

German-born Roland Emmerich had already directed some likeable science fiction adventures, including *Stargate* (1994). But after *Independence Day*, his work became defined by its bombast: *Godzilla* (1998) and *The Patriot* (2000) were turgid and unpopular; *The Day After Tomorrow* (2004) was an apocalypse fantasy unable to successfully integrate its environmental concerns.

50

Dir: Gerald THOMAS / UK
Released in Britain: 1959
Running Time: 85 minutes
Black and white
Estimated Attendance: 10.4 million

The *Carry On* film – naughty but nice, raucous but politically conservative – was a staple part of the British cinemagoer's diet throughout the 1960s. But it is one of the first in the series, from 1959, that enjoys the distinction of being the only *Carry On* title in *The Ultimate Film* list.

CARRY ON NURSE

Director **Gerald Thomas**
Producer **Peter Rogers**
Screenplay **Norman Hudis**, based on an idea by Patrick Cargill and Jack Beale
Director of Photography **Reginald Wyer**
Editor **John Shirley**
Art Director **Alex Vetchinsky**
Music **Bruce Montgomery**

Bernie Bishop • Kenneth Connor
Nurse Dorothy Denton • Shirley Eaton
Hinton • Charles Hawtrey
Matron • Hattie Jacques
Ted York • Terence Longdon
Percy Hickson • Bill Owen
Jack Bell • Leslie Phillips
Nurse Stella Dawson • Joan Sims
Nurse Georgie Axwell • Susan Stephen
Oliver Reckitt • Kenneth Williams
Colonel • Wilfrid Hyde White
Nurse Frances James • Susan Beaumont
Nurse Helen Lloyd • Ann Firbank
Sister • Joan Hickson
Bert Able • Cyril Chamberlain
Mick • Harry Locke
Norm • Norman Rossington
Henry Bray • Brian Oulton
Mrs Janie Bishop • Susan Shaw
Jill Thompson • Jill Ireland

Above *Back in the NHS: Hinton (Charles Hawtrey) gets huffy* **Opposite** *Cruel to be kind: Matron (Hattie Jacques) dishes out the medicine*

THE STORY

A reporter, finding himself in hospital for an appendectomy, starts to chronicle life in the ward after observing his oddball fellow patients, who are a mixed bag of eccentrics, malingerers and social misfits. He is handicapped in his task by becoming romantically involved with a pretty nurse. The fierce matron exerts a rule by terror, inflicting a stern regime on patients and nurses alike, and eventually generates feelings of anarchy which culminate in a freelance attempt by the ward inmates to remove a bunion so that its sufferer can go off on holiday with his latest conquest.

WHAT THEY SAID THEN …

A somewhat stale farce, mixing slapstick, caricature and crudely anatomical humour, puts life in a public hospital ward into the same cheerlessly rollicking category as the barrack room. Predictably, the main butt is Matron, and at least one sequence implies a strongly intended criticism of the type of matron who makes a fetish of details that have no real bearing on the patients' wellbeing whatever.

WHAT THEY SAY NOW …

The success of the National Service army farce *Carry On Sergeant* (1958) led to this sequel which featured several of the same cast, among them Terence Longdon, Shirley Eaton, Kenneth Connor, Bill Owen, Charles Hawtrey, Kenneth Williams and Hattie Jacques, who played the memorable matron. The formula, a co-mingling of abundant *double entendres* together with jokes about nurses' underwear, bedpans and body parts, tickled the public and helped to establish the *Carry On*s as the longest-running comedy series in British film history. The hospital setting was so effective that it was reprised in later entrants in the series, including *Carry On Doctor* (1967), *Carry On Again Doctor* (1969) and *Carry On Matron* (1972). *Twice Round the Daffodils* (1962) emerged from the same stable. Joan Sims made her *Carry On* debut in *Carry On Nurse* and was to appear in 23 more.

For all their apparent risqué vulgarity, the *Carry On*s were as socially subversive as a Donald McGill saucy postcard, and in retrospect seem astonishingly innocent. The films were made quickly and cheaply, often utilising parts of Pinewood Studios themselves for locations. Even when the subjects called for exotic locations, such as for *Carry On Jack* (1963), it was Frensham Ponds, near Guildford, that stood in for the coast of Spain.

A repertory company of performers appeared in film after film, apparently content to stay before the public, even though the salaries would never make them rich. The camaraderie was essential to the spirit of the films and accounts for much of the popularity. The production team of Peter Rogers, producer, and Gerald Thomas, director, was always consistent, and they became a permanent presence at Pinewood. Everyone concerned seemed reluctant to let the series come to a natural end and there were numerous attempts, mostly aborted, to hitch the *Carry On* formula to some passing bandwagon.

One unfortunate idea that came to fruition was *Carry On Emmanuelle* in 1978, a disastrous attempt to exploit some refracted naughtiness merely by referencing the popular soft-core pornography heroine in the title. There was even talk in the 1980s that a *Carry On Dallas* was in the offing, to capitalise on the success of the US soap opera *Dallas*. Mercifully it never happened. The last *Carry On* was *Carry On Columbus* in 1992, a late and less happy entrant, and although there has been an attempt at a latter-day revival it is perhaps better that it should not happen, enabling the old films to stay firmly within their period as a reminder of a gentler, departed time.

CLASSIC QUOTE

Nurse [after a patient has reluctantly lowered his pyjama bottoms]: 'What a fuss about such a little thing.'

SCENE STEALER

Wilfrid Hyde-White is found having his rectal temperature taken with a daffodil instead of a thermometer.

IN THE CHAIR

Gerald Thomas, who directed all the *Carry On*s, died in 1993, not long after *Carry On Columbus* was released. His friend and colleague Peter Rogers, producer of them all, announced that *Carry On London* would go into production in 2005.

OSCARS

WHAT WON THAT YEAR?
Best Motion Picture: *Ben-Hur*
Directing: William Wyler *Ben-Hur*
Actor: Charlton Heston *Ben-Hur*
Actress: Simone Signoret *Room at the Top*

BAFTAS

WHAT WON THAT YEAR?
Film: *Ben Hur*
British Film: *Sapphire*
British Actor: Peter Sellers *I'm All Right Jack*
British Actress: Audrey Hepburn *The Nun's Story*
Foreign Actor: Jack Lemmon *Some Like It Hot*
Foreign Actress: Shirley MacLaine *Ask Any Girl*

Roll your eyes down

the list and you will find just about every specimen of masculinity. The strapping Clark Gable sits atop the list, thanks to his role as Rhett Butler in *Gone with the Wind*. Scowling, saturnine James Mason, an actor

who freely admitted that he despised many of his roles in British films of the 1940s, has two films in the top 10: *The Wicked Lady* and *The Seventh Veil*. 'He was one of the few people who could really frighten me, and yet at the same time he was the most gentle and courteous of men,' his co-star Ann Todd observed, summing up his appeal in a nutshell.

James Dean, Marlon Brando and Montgomery Clift, the 'Method boys', aren't much in evidence. Brando pops up under layers of make-up in *The Godfather* (number 48), but if it's youthful, leather-clad swagger and rebellion you're after, only John Travolta makes the top 20 (with his comb-twirling turn in *Grease*). If you're looking for rip-roaring character acting as a film's main selling point, you have to scroll down to 61 and Jack Nicholson's bravura turn in *One Flew Over The Cuckoo's Nest*.

Far left *'Method boy' Montgomery Clift in* A Place in the Sun **Left** *Cary Grant stars in* The Philadelphia Story, *but only its remake* High Society *makes* The Ultimate Film *chart* **Above** *Everyone's favourite* Rebel without a Cause, *James Dean* **Opposite above** *1930s box-office favourite George Formby, armed with a toothy smile and his ever-present ukulele* **Opposite below** *Norman Wisdom didn't laugh his way into the list*

Just as with the leading ladies, the list is as notable for its omissions as its inclusions. Cary Grant doesn't make the cut. James Stewart barely registers. There is more space than might have been imagined for English gentleman types. Leslie Howard (second fiddle to Gable in *Gone with the Wind*) registers with *49th Parallel*, in which he played a pipe-smoking idealist. Ronald Colman, too, is well represented, with *Lost Horizon* and *Random Harvest*, and Hugh Grant gets a look-in.

Comedians are in short supply. Charlie Chaplin crawls under the wire with *The Great Dictator*, but you'll search in vain for films from Norman Wisdom (hugely popular in the 1950s) and George Formby (a box-office favourite of the 1930s and early 1940s). Inevitably, the list is top-heavy with blockbusters and event movies in which the leading men were just cogs in big wheels. Sean Connery, Roger Moore and Pierce Brosnan have Bond titles on the list, while Charlton Heston flexes his muscles in *Ben-Hur*. Alec Guinness can be found (although not really as a leading man) in both *Star Wars* and *The Bridge on the River Kwai*. Paul Newman and Robert Redford feature for *The Sting* but not for *Butch Cassidy and the Sundance Kid*, which most critics thought their best movie together. Kenneth More and Dirk Bogarde make it with the whimsical *Doctor in the House*, but there's no sign of Laurence Olivier in his Shakespeare adaptations. Orson Welles waxing lyrical about cuckoo clocks in his cameo as Harry Lime clearly helped push *The Third Man* up the list.

In among the dinosaurs, spaceships, ocean liners and sharks, little space is left for character actors. That's why it's such a surprise (and relief) to discover Ealing's modest drama *The Blue Lamp* (with Jack Warner as the lovable policeman slain by Dirk Bogarde's delinquent) holding its own in the top 30.

51

Dir: Herbert WILCOX / UK
Released in Britain: 1945
Running Time: 114 minutes
Black and white
Estimated Attendance: 10.3 million

The success in *The Ultimate Film* list of films directed by Herbert Wilcox and starring his wife Anna Neagle is given another boost by the ranking at number 51 of *I Live in Grosvenor Square*. War, love, honour, tragedy and a well-appointed London address in the title – this film had it all.

I LIVE IN GROSVENOR SQUARE

Director/Producer **Herbert Wilcox**
Screenplay **Nicholas Phipps, William D. Bayles**,
    adapted from a story by Maurice Cowan
Directors of Photography **Max Greene, Otto Heller**
Art Director **William C. Andrews**
Music **Anthony Collins**

Lady Patricia Fairfax • Anna Neagle
Major David Bruce • Rex Harrison
Sgt John Patterson • Dean Jagger
Duke Of Exmoor • Robert Morley
John's Mother • Jane Darwell
Mrs Wilson • Nancy Price
Mrs Catchpole • Irene Vanbrugh
Innkeeper • Edward Rigby
Vicar • Walter Hudd
Sgt Benji Greenbrugh • Elliott Arluck
Bates • Aubrey Mallalieu
Lt Lutyens • Michael Shepley
Taxi Driver • Charles Victor
Paratrooper • Ronald Shiner
Merridew • Percy Walsh
1st Girl in Guard's Van • Brenda Bruce
Paratrooper • John Slater
Trewhewy • Cecil Ramage
Parker • H. R. Hignett
2nd Girl in Guard's Van • Shelagh Fraser

THE STORY

Sergeant John Patterson of the US Air Force, billeted in the Grosvenor Square house of the Duke of Exmoor, is invited to the Duke's castle. After a cool beginning, he comes to know and love the Duke's granddaughter, Lady Patricia Fairfax, now a WAAF corporal. Patricia returns his love, but is already engaged to an Englishman, Major David Bruce. The latter gives her up under protest. But John feels that he is in the wrong and ceases to see Patricia, who makes it up with David. Subsequently the Englishman, realising that she is really in love with John, does the noble thing in his turn and relinquishes her to the American, who, however, is killed in an air crash shortly after. David and his paratroopers set out for the Continent.

WHAT THEY SAID THEN ...

This production has been made with an eye on each side of the Atlantic. It makes rather obvious fun of the differences between our customs, and includes such striking contrasts as a ducal ball and jitterbugging at the Rainbow Club. Although it is pleasing to see the real (rather than a Hollywood) London and rural England, it is a pity that the middle-class sergeant from Arizona had to fall in love with an aristocrat whose home and background are almost as unlike those of most English people's as the average American's. Anna Neagle is an attractive Patricia; Dean Jagger and Rex Harrison are good as the opposing lovers; Robert Morley makes a nice old man of the Duke, and there is a strong supporting cast. Direction is good, but the film is too long, and interest flags at times.

WHAT THEY SAY NOW ...

A slew of films in the mid-1940s were based on the wartime 'hands-across-the-Atlantic' concept of Britain and America united by ancient roots and a common purpose, in particular Powell and Pressburger's *A Canterbury Tale* (1944) and *A Matter of Life and Death* (1946), and Asquith's *The Way to the Stars* (1945). All are better than Herbert Wilcox's contribution, which emphasises the new mateyness of the toffs. In war the aristocracy must make

Above *Love triangle: Lady Patricia (Anna Neagle) is caught in the middle between Sgt John Patterson (Dean Jagger, left) and Major David Bruce (Rex Harrison)* **Above right** *True love? Lady Patricia and David reignite their on–off affair* **Below** *Comedy of manners: American Sgt Patterson takes tea with the Duke of Exmoor (Robert Morley)*

OSCARS

WHAT WON THAT YEAR?
Best Motion Picture: *The Lost Weekend*
Directing: Billy Wilder *The Lost Weekend*
Actor: Ray Milland *The Lost Weekend*
Actress: Joan Crawford *Mildred Pierce*

BAFTAS

Not awarded until 1947

sacrifices just as much as the common folk, but they still seem to exert some feudal influence, especially in the country village that, presciently in view of the forthcoming 1945 general election, narrowly elects a Labour MP.

Dean Jagger is pleasant and well mannered as the American sergeant, a middle-class engineer who in civvy street helped build the Hoover Dam, and Anna Neagle delivers one of her standard patrician performances with her usual delicacy. Rex Harrison is the third arm of the triangle, and Robert Morley plays the whimsical duke, much beset by the government, which first requisitions his London home, then his ancestral castle. The usual jokes about two nations divided by a common language are reeled out. Jagger's buddy, an NCO from Brooklyn, is frequently seen quoting from the little booklet issued to all US servicemen stationed in Britain explaining local customs – and the helpful advice that if they say they feel like a bum the British will think they look like their own backsides.

Anna Neagle, who became Herbert Wilcox's wife, renowned for portraying royalty and assorted great British women, was in reality an ex-chorus girl, born in Forest Gate in East London and a lifelong West Ham supporter, and she never made any secret of her humble origins. Nevertheless, this was the first of a series of hugely successful films with Mayfair settings in which she was always a blueblood, with Michael Wilding as her partner, after Rex Harrison had made himself unavailable by decamping to Hollywood.

Although the post-war Mayfair films made mountains of money it did not stop Wilcox from lapsing later into bankruptcy. Dame Anna, as she had become, returned to work to rescue their fortunes, and found her popularity with public had remained intact.

CLASSIC QUOTE

Sergeant Patterson [on realising that his opponent in love, Major Bruce, has graciously stepped aside]: 'Well, that's the kind of a guy he is.'

SCENE STEALER

Anna Neagle, with her American friend, visits Rainbow Corner, the official GI hangout just off Piccadilly Circus. When invited to dance, she tentatively begins to jitterbug, eventually allowing herself to be swung off her feet in all directions.

52

Dir: William WYLER / USA
Released in Britain: 1942
Running Time: 134 minutes
Black and white
Estimated Attendance: 10.2 million

Britain's wartime pluck got a cinematic salute from across the Atlantic in the shape of *Mrs Miniver*. This portrait of ordinary English folk was low on authenticity but high on good will. Greer Garson exuded elegance, dignity and impeccable glamour – even as all around her the bombs fall.

MRS MINIVER

Director **William Wyler**
Producer **Sidney A. Franklin**
Screenplay **Arthur Wimperis, George Froeschel, James Hilton, Claudine West**, adapted from the novel by Jan Struther
Director of Photography **Joseph Ruttenberg**
Editor **Harold F. Kress**
Art Director **Cedric Gibbons**
Music **Herbert Stothart**

Kay Miniver • Greer Garson
Clem Miniver • Walter Pidgeon
Carol Beldon • Teresa Wright
Lady Beldon • Dame May Whitty
Foley • Reginald Owen
James Ballard • Henry Travers
Vin Miniver • Richard Ney
Vicar • Henry Wilcoxon
Toby Miniver • Christopher Severn
Gladys • Brenda Forbes
Judy Miniver • Clare Sandars
Ada • Marie De Becker
German Flyer • Helmut Dantine
Fred, The Porter • John Abbott
Simpson • Connie Leon
Horace • Rhys Williams
Miss Spriggins • Mary Field
Nobby • Paul Scardon
Ginger • Ben Webster
George, The Innkeeper • Aubrey Mather

THE STORY

A village in Kent, 1939. Mr and Mrs Miniver, a prosperous middle-class couple, welcome home their eldest son Vincent, presently studying in Oxford. Carol Beldon, daughter of Lady Beldon, pays them a visit. She has heard that Mr Ballard, the local railway porter, is to enter the rose that he has named after Mrs Miniver in the upcoming village flower fete. Knowing that her grandmother prefers to be the only entrant in that contest, she asks Mrs Miniver to persuade Mr Ballard to withdraw, but this polite request angers the fiery Vincent. At the annual yachting society dance, Vincent apologises to Carol; the two fall head over heels in love with one another, although Carol leaves the following morning for Scotland.

Britain declares war against Germany. The Minivers' maid Gladys is upset because her husband Horace is called up. Vincent subsequently decides to join the Royal Air Force; welcoming Carol on her return from Scotland, he kisses her for the first time.

Eight months pass. Now a qualified pilot, Vincent proposes to Carol, who accepts. As Mr Miniver assists in his motor boat with the evacuation of British troops from Dunkirk, Vincent is called up for duty. An injured German airman, parachuted into her garden, holds Mrs Miniver at gunpoint; when he collapses from his wound, she hands him over to the police. Mr Miniver returns, and Vincent flies back safely.

After Mrs Miniver assuages the reservations of Lady Beldon, Vincent and Carol marry. Returning from their honeymoon in Scotland, the young couple discover that the Miniver house has been bombed.

At the annual flower show, Lady Beldon decides to award Mr Ballard first prize for his 'Miniver' rose. When news of an incoming German aerial attack is announced, Mrs Miniver and Carol drive Vincent back to his air base. As he is defending the skies, Carol is killed during a bombardment. At the service to honour the dead of the village, the vicar urges his parish to carry on the fight for freedom.

WHAT THEY SAID THEN ...

This is a most moving film, directed with great insight and sympathy by William Wyler. The acting of Greer Garson as Mrs Miniver is superb and that of Walter Pidgeon as her husband quite impeccable. The film is as gracious a tribute as could be paid to Britain's real life in time of stress and agony. The 'little boats of Dunkirk' have been portrayed as realistically and dramatically as could be wished. The illusion of England is excellent, and in so good a film any slight defects may be forgiven.

WHAT THEY SAY NOW ...

Filmed on the MGM back lot in Hollywood with a large cast of Americans (although Greer Garson in the title role was British), *Mrs Miniver* presents an image of rural England at war so quaint as to be unrecognisable to contemporary audiences. Far from being the 'average middle-class English family' introduced in the credits, the Minivers enjoy a level of abundant consumption that would have seemed unthinkable for 'ordinary' British cinemagoers, even before rationing – in the opening reel Mr and Mrs Miniver's shopping spree includes a new convertible car and a *haute couture* hat. –Elsewhere, there are walk-on parts for pistol-wielding village bobbies, and the exteriors are dappled in suspiciously Californian-looking sunlight.

But while some British critics slated the film , its many incongruities were happily ignored by local audiences, who flocked to it in large numbers. One reason for this popularity is the film's stirring support for the British cause during the war. It was conceived before America entered the war by producer Sidney Franklin as his 'salute to England', and the film's rousing image of British resolve under fire had incalculable propaganda potency – recognised at the time by Winston Churchill. Another factor in the film's success in Britain may be its Americanised take on the class system. Equally at ease with the maid as the lady of the manor, the Minivers' breezy and relaxed style was arguably more Californian in conduct than Home Counties – a refreshing change, perhaps, from British cinema's own depiction of the home front, naturally more sensitive to the nuances of class.

SCENE STEALER

Leading a service of remembrance for those in the village killed by a recent air raid, the vicar gives a passionate rallying cry to carry on the war. Delivered from a makeshift pulpit in the bombed-out shell of the ancient church, the speech ('This is the people's war ... We are the fighters') proved such an effective piece of propaganda that President Roosevelt had it broadcast on the *Voice of America* and printed on leaflets that were distributed throughout Europe.

Top right What's in a name? James Ballard (Henry Travers) presents Mrs Miniver (Greer Garson) with the sweet-smelling rose named after her **Above right** *Having parachuted into her garden, German Flyer Helmut Dantine holds Mrs Miniver at gunpoint*

OSCARS

12 nominations, **6 winners**

Outstanding Motion Picture
Directing: William Wyler
Actor: Walter Pidgeon
Actor in a Supporting Role: Henry Travers
Actress: Greer Garson
Actress in a Supporting Role: Dame May Whitty
Actress in a Supporting Role: Teresa Wright
Cinematography (Black and White): Joseph Ruttenberg
Film Editing: Harold F. Kress
Sound Recording: Douglas Shearer
Special Effects: A. Arnold Gillespie, Warren Newcombe, Douglas Shearer
Writing (Screenplay)

WHAT WON THAT YEAR?
Actor: James Cagney *Yankee Doodle Dandy*

BAFTAS

Not awarded until 1947

53

Dir: Richard DONNER / USA
Released in Britain: 1979
Running Time: 143 minutes
Colour: Technicolor
Estimated Attendance: 10.19 million

In the wake of *Jaws* (1975) and *Star Wars* (1977),
every studio sought its own blockbuster hit.
Superman was one of the best, with a cast as fine as
the special effects, genuine drama and a hero who
almost made it seem cool to wear underwear outside
your trousers.

SUPERMAN

Director **Richard Donner**
Producer **Pierre Spengler**
Screenplay **Mario Puzo, David Newman, Leslie Newman, Robert Benton**, from a story by Mario Puzo
Director of Photography **Geoffrey Unsworth**
Editor **Michael Ellis**
Production Designer **John Barry**
Music **John Williams**

Jor-El • Marlon Brando
Lex Luthor • Gene Hackman
Superman/Clark Kent • Christopher Reeve
Lois Lane • Margot Kidder
Otis • Ned Beatty
Perry White • Jackie Cooper
Pa Kent • Glenn Ford
Elder 1, Krypton • Trevor Howard
General Zod, Krypton • Terence Stamp
Non, Krypton • Jack O'Halloran
Eve Teschmacher • Valerie Perrine
Vond-Ah, Krypton • Maria Schell
Ma Kent • Phyllis Thaxter
Lara, Krypton • Susannah York
Young Clark Kent • Jeff East
Jimmy Olsen • Marc McClure
Ursa, Krypton • Sarah Douglas
Elder 2, Krypton • Harry Andrews
Elder 3, Krypton • Vass Anderson
Elder 4, Krypton • John Hollis

Opposite Flying tonight: Lois Lane (Margot Kidder) enjoys a spectacular first date with Superman (Christopher Reeve)

THE STORY

Just before the destruction of their planet Krypton, Jor-El and his wife Lara launch their son to Earth, where his dense molecular structure will lend him superhuman powers. The boy is found in the American Midwest by childless Jonathan Kent and his wife Martha, and grows to a dawning awareness of his special abilities. At age thirty he arrives, as shy, bumbling Clark Kent, to work as a reporter on the *Daily Planet* newspaper in Metropolis; he is smitten by the briskly ambitious Lois Lane, and first unveils his secret identity as Superman when Lois is involved in a helicopter accident. Superman's crime-fighting exploits are soon the talk of the town. He takes Lois on a flight around the city, and her resulting story attracts the interest of master criminal Lex Luthor, who is planning a fiendish coup (to blow all of California west of the San Andreas Fault into the sea, so converting the worthless land he has bought up east of the Fault into the new West Coast). Luthor acquires a radioactive fragment of Kryptonite, which came from Superman's destroyed home and which Luthor deduces will be lethal to the Man of Steel.

Superman is saved, however, by Luthor's mistress, Eve Teschmacher, and manages to stop one of the two army missiles Luthor has secretly programmed to carry out his plan. The other strikes the Fault, almost splitting California in two. Lois dies in a rock fall, but Superman circles the globe, reversing its motion until time is turned back and Lois resurrected. Finally, he delivers Luthor to jail.

WHAT THEY SAID THEN …

On dramatic grounds, *Superman* is rather weak, both because Lex Luthor's late-developing scheme to found a new West Coast, for all its ingenuity, is confusingly plotted. It is also undercut by the writers' decision to reserve most of their parody for Luthor – which reduces his villainy to the smirking camp of the *Batman* TV serial. The film also intersects here with the most barren genre imaginable, the straightforward disaster movie.

Apart from the *Daily Planet* sequences, however, which are sprightly paced and sprinkled with *Front Page* cross-talk, the most successful section is that of

Superman growing up in the idyllic Midwest. Here, the painterly treatment of figures in a landscape achieves the kind of directness and simplicity that can contain the Nietzschean/evolutionary overtones which inevitably cling to our hero. That the film fails to maintain this tone is also inevitable once it submits to the need to fulfil its pyrotechnic promise and return to comic-strip adventure. Finally, we can never be convinced by Superman – as we are by the Common Man turned Visionary Artist of *Close Encounters* (1977) – so that we too can participate in the filmmaker/hero's visions.

WHAT THEY SAY NOW ...

Superheroes had not been taken seriously by a mainstream audience, or treated seriously by filmmakers, until *Superman* swept into cinemas. Its poster bore a classic promise: 'You'll believe a man can fly.' That was the essence of its success: the audience's faith and wonderment. It did plenty to earn our trust, boasting excellent special effects and flying sequences (which inevitably look slightly careworn to our eyes, spoilt as they are by the blemishless beauty of computer-generated imagery), awe-inspiring sets and a likeably upright hero in the shape of new star Christopher Reeve.

The picture – though not its increasingly jokey sequels – can take some credit for the gravitas later brought to films like the 1989 *Batman* and the two *X-Men* films (2000 and 2003). What's striking now is its patience, and the patience it demands from us: it's almost an hour before we are treated to our first glimpse of the Superman costume.

CLASSIC QUOTE

Lex Luthor: 'We all have our little faults. Mine's in California.'

BEHIND THE SCENES

Of the three subsequent sequels, only *Superman II* (1980) – directed by Richard Lester, who did uncredited work on the first film – meets (and, in places, surpasses) the standard of the original. An attempt in the 1990s to revive the series, with a screenplay by comic-book-nut Kevin Smith (director of *Clerks* and *Chasing Amy*) and Nicolas Cage in the lead, came to nothing. At the time of writing, Warner Brothers is preparing a new *Superman* project, after an encouraging response to its other superhero makeover, *Batman Begins* (2005); a young-Superman TV series, *Smallville*, has run for some years to much acclaim.

OSCARS
4 nominations, **1 winner**

Film Editing: Stuart Baird
Music (Original Score): John Williams
Sound
Special Achievement Award (Visual Effects)

WHAT WON THAT YEAR?
Best Picture: *The Deer Hunter*
Directing: Michael Cimino *The Deer Hunter*
Actor in a Leading Role: Jon Voight *Coming Home*
Actress in a Leading Role: Jane Fonda *Coming Home*

BAFTAS
5 nominations, **1 winner**

Cinematography: Geoffrey Unsworth
Production Design: John Barry
Sound Track
Supporting Actor: Gene Hackman
**Most Promising Newcomer to Leading Film Roles:
   Christopher Reeve**

WHAT WON THAT YEAR?
Film: *Julia*
Direction: Alan Parker *Midnight Express*
Actor: Richard Dreyfuss *The Goodbye Girl*
Actress: Jane Fonda *Julia*

Dir: Sharon MAGUIRE / USA, France, UK
Released in Britain: 2001
Running Time: 92 minutes
Colour: Technicolor
Estimated Attendance: 10.15 million

Bridget Jones's Diary **had no trouble transforming its literary success into box-office takings. With Working Title and Richard Curtis behind the scenes, and Hugh Grant in the cast, this tale of a singleton's search for love had a comforting Englishness from which Miramax's backing and an American lead actress could not detract.**

BRIDGET JONES'S DIARY

Director **Sharon Maguire**
Producers **Tim Bevan, Eric Fellner, Jonathan Cavendish**
Screenplay **Helen Fielding, Andrew Davies, Richard Curtis**, adapted from the novel by Helen Fielding
Director of Photography **Stuart Dryburgh**
Editor **Martin Walsh**
Production Designer **Gemma Jackson**
Music **Patrick Doyle**

Bridget Jones • Renée Zellweger
Mark Darcy • Colin Firth
Daniel Cleaver • Hugh Grant
Bridget's Dad • Jim Broadbent
Bridget's Mum • Gemma Jones
Shazza • Sally Phillips
Jude • Shirley Henderson
Tom • James Callis
Natasha • Embeth Davidtz
Una Alconbury • Celia Imrie
Penny Husbands-Bosworth • Honor Blackman
Uncle Geoffrey • James Faulkner
Mrs Darcy • Charmian May
Mr Fitzherbert • Paul Brooke
Perpetua • Felicity Montagu
Handsome Stranger • Charlie Caine
Simon in Marketing • Gareth Marks
Elderly Man • John Clegg
Himself • Salman Rushdie
Kafka Author • Matthew Bates

THE STORY

Thirty-something Bridget Jones works for a London publisher and spends her free time despairing at her nonexistent love life. While visiting her parents, Pam and Colin, she is introduced to the human-rights lawyer Mark Darcy, but takes against him when she overhears him disparage her. At work, Bridget begins an e-mail flirtation and then an affair with her boss, Daniel Cleaver. Bridget runs into Mark at a number of social occasions and perseveres in disliking him, a fact she reveals in her diary in which she records her daily weight, and her cigarette and alcohol consumption.

When Bridget discovers a naked woman in Daniel's flat, she dumps him and gets a job as a reporter on a current-affairs show. Meanwhile, her mother, Pam, leaves Colin for a shopping-channel presenter. [run on]Bridget presents an item about a political refugee's trial, and scores a scoop when Mark, the refugee's lawyer, grants her an exclusive interview. She grows ever more attracted to Mark, especially when he helps her prepare for a dinner party. The evening is spoiled by the arrival of Daniel and the two men fight in the street. By Christmas Bridget is on the verge of revealing her feelings for Mark when it is announced that he is getting engaged to Natasha, another lawyer. Pam is reconciled with Colin. Just before Bridget is about to embark on a mini-break to Paris with her friends, Mark shows up to confess his love to her, but leaves when he accidentally reads the negative diary entries about him. Bridget runs after him in her underwear and they kiss in the snow.

WHAT THEY SAY ...

Bridget Jones's Diary has been lumped in with the late-twentieth-century crop of chick-lit, chick-flicks and female-oriented sitcoms. Its most obvious coevals, in terms of popularity, are the television series *Ally McBeal* and *Sex And The City*, the latter based on a newspaper column written by Candace Bushnell, just as Bridget

OSCARS
1 nomination

Actress in a Leading Role: Renée Zellweger

WHAT WON THAT YEAR?
Best Picture: *A Beautiful Mind*
Directing: Ron Howard *A Beautiful Mind*
Actor in a Leading Role: Denzel Washington *Training Day*
Actress in a Leading Role: Halle Berry *Monster's Ball*

BAFTAS
4 nominations

Alexander Korda Award for Outstanding British Film of the Year
Actress in a Leading Role: Renée Zellweger
Actor in a Supporting Role: Colin Firth
Screenplay (Adapted): Helen Fielding, Andrew Davies, Richard Curtis

WHAT WON THAT YEAR?
Film: *The Lord of the Rings: The Fellowship of the Ring*
Alexander Korda Award for Outstanding British Film of the Year: *Gosford Park*
David Lean Award for Direction: Peter Jackson *The Lord of the Rings: The Fellowship of the Ring*
Actor in a Leading Role: Russell Crowe *A Beautiful Mind*
Actress in a Leading Role: Judi Dench *Iris*

Opposite Working girl: Bridget gets busy
Top right Turning over a new leaf: Mark Darcy (Colin Firth) presents Bridget (Renee Zellwegger) with a brand new diary **Right** Mark and Daniel Cleaver (Hugh Grant) fight for Bridget's affections

was based on a column that author Helen Fielding penned for *The Independent*. All concern successful career girls fretting over the unattainable goal of 'having it all'. But it makes all the difference that Bridget is British and a single discrete story, while the two others are American and ongoing series. Given that the film was partly backed by a US distributor (Miramax), it's a welcome surprise that so much of the novel's cultural specificity has survived. Bridget still weighs herself in stones and what little psychobabble she espouses is treated with audible irony.

Home-grown commentators might point to *Bridget Jones* as an example of how the British accept, even celebrate, failure – as in *Notting Hill* (1999), another Brit 'RomCom' written by *Bridget Jones's* co-screenwriter Richard Curtis – but the happy ending negates such a reading. In the end, Bridget gets her man, in contrast with the US programmes whose open-endedness ensures the girls rarely end up with what they want.

A mild puncturing of the fictional illusion is essayed with the casting of Colin Firth as Darcy. Firth played Jane Austen's haughty hero Mr Darcy in the BBC adaptation of *Pride and Prejudice*, a show the book's Bridget watches compulsively and which was written by Andrew Davies, a co-author of the

Bridget Jones screenplay. As in the book, the real and the imaginary are covertly blurred here. Hugh Grant, whose real-life dalliance with a Hollywood prostitute is snickered over in the book, plays the false-start love interest Cleaver and is given the shockingly self-immolating line, 'I'm a terrible disaster with a posh voice and a bad character.' Salman Rushdie and Jeffrey Archer appear as themselves. Richard Curtis is Helen Fielding's ex-boyfriend. Sharon Maguire, the model for one of Bridget's best friends, is the film's director.

It would be easy to write off *Bridget Jones* as an exercise in preening nepotistic narcissism. Except that it's really rather good – funny, engaging and winning in its self-deprecating modesty, albeit in a big-budget sort of way. It's hard not to like a film where the characters pause during a hilariously clumsy fight in a restaurant to join in singing 'Happy Birthday' to another customer, or mime drunkenly to 'All by Myself' using a bread stick as a mike.

CLASSIC QUOTE
Bridget [answering phone]: 'Bridget Jones, wanton sex goddess, with a very bad man between her thighs ... Mum! ... Hi.'

55

Dir: Pete DOCTER / USA
Released in Britain: 2002
Running Time: 95 minutes
Colour: Monaco colour
Estimated Attendance: 9.93 million

A universe inhabited exclusively by monsters – big, small, slimy, furry, one-eyed or multi-limbed – gave Pixar its first venture into all-out fantasy after the 'real' worlds of the *Toy Story* films (1995 and 1999) and *A Bug's Life* (1998). But could the company retain its magic touch in these garish pastures new?

MONSTERS, INC.

Director **Pete Docter**
Producer **Darla Anderson**
Screenplay **Andrew Stanton, Daniel Gerson**, based on
  an original story by Pete Docter, Jill Culton,
  Jeff Pidgeon, Ralph Eggleston
Editor **James Austin Stewart**
Production Designers **Harley Jessup, Bob Pauley**
Music **Randy Newman**

Voice of James P. 'Sulley' Sullivan • John Goodman
Voice of Mike Wazowski • Billy Crystal
Voice of Boo • Mary Gibbs
Voice of Randall Boggs • Steve Buscemi
Voice of Henry J. Waternoose • James Coburn
Voice of Celia • Jennifer Tilly
Voice of Roz/'Number 1' • Bob Peterson
Voice of Yeti • John Ratzenberger
Voice of Fungus • Frank Oz
Voice of Needleman/Smitty • Daniel Gerson
Voice of Floor Manager • Steve Susskind
Voice of Flint • Bonnie Hunt
Voice of Mr Bile, 'Phlegm' • Jeff Pidgeon

THE STORY

The town of Monstropolis is powered by the screams of human children. These screams are collected by the elite scarers of Monsters, Incorporated, who enter children's rooms at night via their closet doors. The town is facing an energy crisis because of the increasing difficulty of scaring modern children. The top scarer at Monsters, Inc. is James P. 'Sulley' Sullivan, who lives with his best friend and scare assistant Mike Wazowski. One night, returning to the factory for some paperwork, Sulley inadvertently allows a human girl to enter Monstropolis, where children are forbidden. Discovering that, contrary to popular belief, children are not toxic, Sulley forms a bond with the girl, whom he names Boo.

Attempting to find Boo's closet door and return her home, Sulley and Mike discover that rival scarer Randall Boggs has created a machine that forcibly extracts screams from children. It emerges that Randall is being sponsored by the company's CEO, Henry J. Waternoose, who banishes Sulley and Mike to the Himalayas. Returning to the factory, the duo rescue Boo from Randall and expose Waternoose. Waternoose is arrested by the Child Detection Agency, whose director, Roz, has been working undercover at Monsters, Inc. Roz orders Boo's door to be shredded after the girl returns home. The energy crisis is resolved by the discovery that children's laughter produces more power. Mike rebuilds Boo's door. Sulley enters and is greeted by Boo.

WHAT THEY SAY ...

Monsters, Inc. is the fourth wholly computer-generated animated feature from production outlet Pixar (as usual, backed by Disney), and represents the studio's most sophisticated use of CGI technology. Two and half million rendermarks (a measure of computing power) were required to produce the movie (this compares with 1.1 million for *Toy Story 2*, 2000). One significant breakthrough is the convincing depiction of hair/fur, primarily that of the eight-foot monster Sulley. In perhaps the movie's most impressive shot, the huge number of individual hairs of Sulley's blue and purple coat are subjected to the twin rigours of wind and snow.

But it is the film's careful attention to narrative and characterisation that pulls us in, not the beautifully rendered visuals.

In contrast to the bawdy iconoclasm of *Shrek* (produced in 2001 by Disney/Pixar's big rivals DreamWorks/PDI), *Monsters, Inc.* favours a more gentle approach to subversion. One of the best gags in the movie is the idea that monsters are as fearful of 'toxic' human children as the kids are of them. What slightly undercuts the conceit is that the movie's pastel-coloured menagerie is so uniformly cuddly, lacking any of the repugnance of *Shrek*'s eponymous ogre. Endowed with John Goodman's emollient vocal delivery, the ursine Sulley wouldn't look out of place on *Sesame Street*. His sidekick Mike (voiced by a wisecracking Billy Crystal), a limbed pea-green sphere dominated by a giant single eye (which yields a terrific sight gag – a salad-bowl-sized contact lens) is too pitiably squat to be intimidating. Even the story's villain, Steve Buscemi's lizard-like Boggs, looks like a pliable plastic toy.

The first Pixar feature not to be directed by John Lasseter, *Monsters, Inc.* departs from its forerunners in taking a fantasy locale for its central setting (the worlds depicted in the *Toy Story* films and *A Bug's Life* were based in recognisable earthly environments). The alternative universe it portrays has an insularity that gives the movie much of its escapist charm. There are, however, several external resonances. The need for a new energy source as Monstropolis's traditional resources dwindle ties in neatly with the crisis of complacency that drives the plot – the notion that 'kids don't get scared like they used to'. It is only by a hair that the movie avoids suggesting that the entertainment industry might have played a role in desensitising children.

CLASSIC QUOTE

Mike: 'Oh, that's great, blame it on the little guy. How original. He must've read the schedule wrong with his one eye.'

BEHIND THE SCENES

George Lucas so admired the work of Pixar that he selected *Monsters, Inc.* to be the film before which the first trailers for *Star Wars Episode II: Attack of the Clones* (2002) would be shown in US cinemas. Which, depending on your opinion of *Attack of the Clones*, is either a glowing compliment or a grave insult.

OSCARS
4 nominations, **1 winner**

Animated Feature Film
Music (Original Score): Randy Newman
Music (Original Song): 'If I Didn't Have You' Randy Newman
Sound Editing: Gary Rydstrom, Michael Silvers

WHAT WON THAT YEAR?
Best Picture: *A Beautiful Mind*
Directing: Ron Howard *A Beautiful Mind*
Actor in a Leading Role: Denzel Washington *Training Day*
Actress in a Leading Role: Halle Berry *Monster's Ball*

BAFTAS

WHAT WON THAT YEAR?
Film: *The Pianist*
Alexander Korda Award for Outstanding British Film: *The Warrior*
David Lean Award for Achievement in Direction: Roman Polanski *The Pianist*
Performance by an Actor in a Leading Role: Daniel Day-Lewis *Gangs of New York*
Performance by an Actress in a Leading Role: Nicole Kidman *The Hours*

Opposite top Sulley (voiced by John Goodman) reads the schedule with two eyes **Above left** Boo! It's more afraid of you than you are of it? The child (voiced by Mary Gibbs) scares the monster Sulley **Left** Eye, eye: Mike (centre, left voiced by Billy Crystal) and Sully enjoy another day at the office

56

Dir: Stanley KUBRICK / UK
Released in Britain: 1972
Running Time: 136 minutes
Colour: Warnercolor
Estimated Attendance: 9.9 million

Only one of Stanley Kubrick's pictures made it onto *The Ultimate Film* list. But it's easy to see why it was *A Clockwork Orange*. Released during the early-1970s' outcry over sex and violence in movies, it was set to pour petrol on the fire. And its withdrawal by Kubrick only fanned the flames of its notoriety.

A CLOCKWORK ORANGE

Director/Producer **Stanley Kubrick**
Screenplay **Stanley Kubrick**, based on the novel by
  Anthony Burgess
Director of Photography **John Alcott**
Editor **Bill Butler**
Production Designer **John Barry**
Music **Wendy Carlos**

Alex DeLarge • Malcolm McDowell
Frank Alexander • Patrick Magee
Dim • Warren Clarke
Mrs Alexander • Adrienne Corri
Dolin, Conspirator • John Savident
Minister of the Interior • Anthony Sharp
Cat Lady • Miriam Karlin
Pee, Dad • Philip Stone
Em, Mum • Sheila Raynor
Dr Brodsky • Carl Duering
Georgie • James Marcus
Stage Actor • John Clive
Chief Guard • Michael Bates
Tramp • Paul Farrell
Joe, the Lodger • Clive Francis
Prison Governor • Michael Gover
Deltoid, PR • Aubrey Morris
Prison Chaplain • Godfrey Quigley
Dr Branom • Madge Ryan
Psychiatrist • Pauline Taylor

THE STORY

In England in the near future, Alex DeLarge and his three teenage 'droogs', Dim, Pete and Georgie, have a typically enjoyable evening during which they break into an isolated homestead, attack the owner, Mr Alexander, and rape his wife. Next day Alex heads a plundering expedition to a luxurious health farm, the suspicious owner of which, the Cat Lady, alerts the police seconds before Alex breaks in and kills her. Abandoned by his gang, Alex is arrested and sentenced to fourteen years in prison. After two years, he makes a bid for freedom by volunteering to undergo the experimental shock treatment advocated by the Minister of the Interior.

Alex is duly brainwashed; after two weeks he is released into society, incapable of countenancing sex and violence or of listening to his beloved Beethoven's Ninth without being assailed by nausea. His nervous parents greet him with the news that their new lodger has taken his place, and a homeless Alex wanders along the Embankment, where he is recognised by a former victim and set upon by a gang of tramps. He is rescued by two policemen – Dim and Georgie, who have found their place in society. They beat him and abandon him in the countryside. Alex staggers to the nearest house; its owner, Mr Alexander, paralysed since Alex's assault and crazed by the subsequent death of his wife, combines personal revenge with a scheme to discredit the Government, and drives Alex to attempt suicide by his repeated playing of Beethoven's Ninth.

Slowly recovering in hospital, Alex accepts a lucrative offer from the Minister, anxious to demonstrate to the press and public that he has done the boy no lasting harm. Alex lies contentedly in his hospital bed, dreaming of rape to the stirring strains of Beethoven.

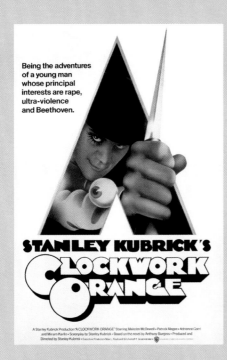

Being the adventures of a young man whose principal interests are rape, ultra-violence and Beethoven.

STANLEY KUBRICK'S
CLOCKWORK ORANGE

A Stanley Kubrick Production "A CLOCKWORK ORANGE" Starring Malcolm McDowell · Patrick Magee · Adrienne Corri and Miriam Karlin · Screenplay by Stanley Kubrick · Based on the novel by Anthony Burgess · Produced and Directed by Stanley Kubrick · Executive Producers Max L. Raab and Si Litvinoff ·

Below left *Stanley Kubrick (second right) films the assault on Mrs Alexander (Adrienne Corri, second left) by Dim (Warren Clarke, left) and Alex (Malcolm McDowell, centre)* **Below right** *Faces and phalluses: Alex looms large*

WHAT THEY SAID THEN ...

If *A Clockwork Orange* emerges as Stanley Kubrick's most cynical and disturbing film to date, this is less because – as was already the case in *Dr Strangelove* (1964) – its nightmare future represents a recognisable extension of the present day, than because it so comprehensively reduces its audience to the level of its characters, all of them perfectly adapted to the cynical system which contains them.

The opening shot of Alex with his false eyelashes, bowler hat and inflated codpiece seemingly establishes him as an alien and antipathetic being. Yet as he moves around the inexorable treadmill of his destiny, our sympathies imperceptibly shift, and the comic-strip caricatures through which Kubrick moves him transform Alex from thug to victim to the vicarious agent of our own carefully induced anarchy. If we are shocked by Alex's violations, it is only on an intellectual level, since Kubrick carefully distances his effects, postponing our physical discomfort for the moment when the 'therapists' screw their clamps on to Alex's eyes. By the time Alex regains consciousness in his hospital bed, Kubrick has us rooting for him to resume his thuggery – the only way of renouncing this dehumanised society.

Kubrick controls his audience with the same calculated precision that he imposes on his material, obliging us to shed our humanity so that Alex may acquire it. He achieves this complicity, not merely through Alex's confidential monologues with their conspiratorial initiations into his secret language, but through an impeccable balancing of the fantastic and the real that flatters every paranoiac nightmare. He moves his gaudily painted cardboard characters through real locations, and choreographs their vicious acts to a finely chiselled score of popular classics that gives them the inevitability and even the grace of a familiar ballet. The film's dynamic movement is punctuated by arresting tableaux which seem only a short nightmare away from reality, like that of the

Cat Lady fighting off her assailant with a bust of Beethoven as he smashes at her with a giant china phallus. As Malcolm McDowell's superlative Alex observes, 'It's funny how the colours of the real world only seem real when you viddy them on a film.' In Kubrick's film, they seem even more real than in Anthony Burgess's novel, since so many of the things that Burgess prophesied (the thugs enlisting in the police force) have already come to pass.

WHAT THEY SAY NOW …

A Clockwork Orange is the most controversial of Stanley Kubrick's work. Its depiction of sex and violence earned the film an X certificate in the UK and US and provoked a storm of fury in the press. Even today the film makes for unsettling viewing. Kubrick never flinches from showing the consequences of Alex's behaviour – the rape of the writer's wife is especially gruelling – but he orchestrates these moments with such exhilarating panache we can't help be drawn into the droogs' world.

Kubrick used Wendy Carlos's electronic versions of Rossini and Beethoven to give some of the violent scenes a dreamy unreality. His excessive stylisation creates a film of troubling ambivalence that denies its audience the comfort of moral certainty. It is perhaps the fullest expression of the director's pessimistic outlook: 'Everyone is fascinated by violence,' he said of the film. 'Our interest … reflects the fact that on the subconscious level we are very little different from our primitive ancestors.'

Made some ten years after Kubrick had settled in Britain, *A Clockwork Orange* is also the director's most English film. Filmed on location in and around London, it perfectly captures the grey brutalist architecture of the period and plastic, pop-art-influenced interior design. With a cast of British stalwarts (Patrick Magee, Steven Berkoff and, in dazzling form, Malcolm McDowell), the film's portrait of Alex's crime spree had especial resonance given longstanding British anxieties over youth delinquency, from the press scares about Teddy Boys in the 1950s to punk, for whom *A Clockwork Orange* would be a signature film. It was ironic, then, that Kubrick should have withdrawn his movie from UK distribution following reports of alleged copy-cat crimes, a ban that was only revoked after his death in 1999.

CLASSIC QUOTE
Alex: 'I like to viddy the old pictures now and then.'

SCENE STEALER
Imprisoned for murder, Alex submits to the 'Ludovico' therapy, said to purge offenders of their violent urges. Strapped to a chair, he is made to watch a succession of extreme images on a cinema screen, his eyelids prised open by spidery clamps.

Opposite top Brainwashed and broken, Alex is tended to by the Minister of the Interior (Anthony Sharp) *Opposite below* The Moloko Bar kid: Alex raises a glass **Above** Stanley Kubrick and Malcolm McDowell take a break from the gruelling aversion therapy sequence

BEHIND THE SCENES

Before Kubrick acquired the rights, the Rolling Stones had expressed interest in starring in a film adaptation of the novel. Mick Jagger was to have played Alex, the rest of the band his droogs.

IN THE CHAIR

For his 1951 debut film, a short documentary about a prize fighter, the 21-year-old Stanley Kubrick served as cinematographer, sound recordist, co-screenwriter as well as director. Although he would delegate some of these roles during his long Hollywood career, he rarely relinquished his tight control. Given unprecedented freedom by his studio financiers following the success of *Dr Strangelove* and *2001: A Space Odyssey* (1968), Kubrick supervised every detail of production during often notoriously long shoots. The result are films of impeccable formal precision that often push available technologies to their limit: the effects shots in *2001*, for instance, paved the way for *Star Wars* (1977) and *Close Encounters* (1977). Some detractors have detected a chilly and over-calculated perfectionism in his work. But whether it's the grim comedy of *Dr Strangelove*, the piercing tragedy of *Barry Lyndon* (1975) or the unsettling horror of *The Shining* (1980), Kubrick's films rarely leave the viewer unmoved.

Dir: Peter FAIMAN / Australia, USA
Released in Britain: 1987
Running Time: 102 minutes
Estimated Attendance: 9.8 million

A simple culture-clash comedy became the surprise hit of 1987 thanks to bright-eyed comedian Paul Hogan, whose success had been previously restricted to television. He provided a charming counterbalance to the aggressive go-getting heroes found in other late-1980s hits like *Top Gun* (1986) and *Wall Street* (1987).

'CROCODILE' DUNDEE

Director **Peter Faiman**
Producer **John Cornell**
Screenplay **Paul Hogan, Ken Shadie, John Cornell**, adapted from an original story by Paul Hogan
Director of Photography **Russell Boyd**
Editor **David Stiven**
Production Designer **Graham Walker**
Music **Peter Best**

Michael J. 'Crocodile' Dundee • Paul Hogan
Sue Charlton • Linda Kozlowski
Walter Reilly • John Meillon
Neville Bell • David Gulpilil
Con • Ritchie Singer
Ida • Maggie Blinco
Donk • Steve Rackman
Nugget • Gerry Skilton
Duffy • Terry Gill
Trevor • Peter Turnbull
Rosita • Christine Totos
Angelo • Graham Walker
Burt, Roo Shooter • David Bracks
Peter, Roo Shooter • Brett Hogan
Richard Mason • Mark Blum
Sam Charlton • Michael Lombard
Doorman • Irving Metzman
Gus • Reginald VelJohnson
Danny • Rik Colitti
Pimp • John Snyder

THE STORY

On assignment in Australia, New York reporter Sue Charlton follows up a story about a legendary figure called Michael J. 'Crocodile' Dundee. Flying out to the remote outback town of Walkabout Creek, Sue is met by Dundee's friend and business associate Walter Reilly, owner of Never Never Tours. Dundee arrives and offers to show Sue the remote spot where he was attacked by a giant crocodile. Sue and Dundee trek into the bush, where they encounter drunken kangaroo hunters, deadly snakes, and a crocodile from which Sue is saved by Dundee. Sue persuades Dundee to return with her to New York. Invited to a 'Welcome Home' dinner at Sue's father's house, Dundee is devastated when her fiancé Richard publicly announces his official engagement to Sue. Leaving the party alone, the drunken Dundee is dropped on Broadway by chauffeur Gus. The next day, Dundee goes walkabout, heading for Grand Central Station subway. Sue arrives at the hotel, chases after Dundee and, on a crowded platform, tells him that she loves him.

WHAT THEY SAID THEN ...

While the decision to set the first half of *'Crocodile' Dundee* in Australia and the second half in the US makes sound commercial sense (as the film's success at the American box-office testifies), it also emphasises a split in the film's overall conception. In the early scenes Mick Dundee's self-mocking tone and wry humour tend to suggest that he is a fraud, with the story about his struggle with the killer crocodile growing more exaggerated with every telling. Similarly, there is an incident in which Dundee looks first at his partner Walter's watch, then at the sun, before announcing the time and suggesting that he and Sue should make a move. All of which serves to undercut Dundee's image as an Indiana Jones-style hero, especially when seen in the context of his commercial involvement in the Never Never Tours company.

However, once the action moves to New York, any residual doubts about his authenticity are instantly effaced, as if the contrast between his ingenuous charm and the New Yorker's sophisticated cynicism were enough to establish his heroic status. An Aussie innocent abroad, Dundee now casts an oblique light on the absurdities of Manhattan cocaine snorting, pretentiousness and materialism. This is a none too original idea, and the targets are equally predictable, but Dundee's disarming naivety does yield some choice comic moments, and one or two quite touching ones.

Asked what he thinks of New York, Dundee replies that it's 'A real lunatic asylum. That's why I like it. I fit right in.' This telling phrase is the key to the film's main strength, and to its major weakness. Dundee is never developed beyond the level of a mythical cypher, and for all his shrewd observations on urban lifestyles he fits in a little too comfortably. This makes his commentary a rather muffled one, and allows for the ridiculous ending in which he gets the girl. The film's humour is clearly derived from the sketch format of the star's TV series, *The Paul Hogan Show*, with each episode looking as if it has been set up to facilitate the one-liner which caps it. First-time film director Peter Faiman also displays a distinctly televisual style, especially in the studio sequences that punctuate the location shots of the outback.

WHAT THEY SAY NOW ...

Whatever charm *'Crocodile' Dundee* had on its 1987 release has long since dissipated. Part of the problem is its star, Paul Hogan, whose initially interesting mixture of macho cool and little-boy-lost innocence now looks like a relic of a bygone age. That's no problem in itself – there is no modern equivalent either for, say, Henry Fonda in *The Lady Eve* (1941). But the difference is that 1980s upper-middle-class New York is not a place that has too much allure for the modern viewer, at least not unless it's Jay McInerney or Bret Easton Ellis capturing its seedy essence. The gags in *'Crocodile' Dundee* have now been worn thin; its fish-out-of-water story, old when it was used in 1987, endlessly recycled; any uniqueness eradicated by two cash-in sequels; and the viewer's fondness for Hogan eclipsed by his blatantly self-regarding *Almost An Angel* (1990).

CLASSIC QUOTE

New York mugger: 'I've got a knife.'
Dundee: 'That's not a knife.' He produces his massive bowie blade. '*That's* a knife.'

OSCARS
1 nomination

Writing (Screenplay Written Directly for the Screen): Paul Hogan, Ken Shadie, John Cornell

WHAT WON THAT YEAR?
Best Picture: *Platoon*
Directing: Oliver Stone *Platoon*
Actor in a Leading Role: Paul Newman *The Color of Money*
Actress in a Leading Role: Marlee Matlin *Children of a Lesser God*

BAFTAS
2 nominations

Actor in a leading Role: Paul Hogan
Original Screenplay: Paul Hogan, Ken Shadie, John Cornell

WHAT WON THAT YEAR?
Film: *A Room with a View*
Achievement in Direction: Woody Allen *Hannah and Her Sisters*
Actor in a Leading Role: Bob Hoskins *Mona Lisa*
Actress in a Leading Role: Maggie Smith *A Room with a View*

Right *'That's a knife'*

58

Dir: Andrew STANTON / USA
Released in Britain: 2003
Running Time: 104 minutes
Colour: Technicolor
Estimated Attendance: 9.79 million

Computer animation reached new heights with the fifth feature from Pixar, where an entire underwater world was realised with shimmering beauty and perfection. As PDI/DreamWorks battled to become the new animation kingpins, *Finding Nemo* showed that in 2003 Pixar were still ahead – by a fin.

FINDING NEMO

Director **Andrew Stanton**
Producer **Graham Walters**
Screenplay **Andrew Stanton, Bob Peterson, David Reynolds**, from an original story by Andrew Stanton
Directors of Photography **Sharon Calahan, Jeremy Lasky**
Editor **David Ian Salter**
Production Designer **Ralph Eggleston**
Music **Thomas Newman**

Voice of Marlin • Albert Brooks
Voice of Dory • Ellen DeGeneres
Voice of Nemo • Alexander Gould
Voice of Gill • Willem Dafoe
Voice of Bloat • Brad Garrett
Voice of Peach • Allison Janney
Voice of Gurgle • Austin Pendleton
Voice of Bubbles • Stephen Root
Voice of Deb (& Flo) • Vicki Lewis
Voice of Jacques • Joe Ranft
Voice of Nigel • Geoffrey Rush
Voice of Crush • Andrew Stanton
Voice of Coral • Elizabeth Stanton
Voice of Squirt • Nicholas Bird
Voice of Mr Ray • Bob Peterson
Voice of Bruce • Barry Humphries
Voice of Anchor • Eric Bana
Voice of Chum • Bruce Spence
Voice of Dr P. Sherman, Dentist • Bill Hunter
Voice of Darla • LuLu Ebeling

THE STORY

The Great Barrier Reef. Clownfish Marlin becomes overprotective of his only son Nemo, whose 399 siblings were eaten by a barracuda. Stung by his father's observation that he's not a strong swimmer, Nemo sets out for a boat on a dare and is captured by a diver, a Sydney-based dentist named Sherman, who relocates him to his office aquarium. Marlin sets off to look for Nemo, joined by Dory, a regal blue tang. They have a run-in with some sharks, stray into a school of jellyfish and are rescued by turtles. After being swallowed by a whale, Marlin and Dory escape up his spout to find themselves in Sydney Harbour.

Meanwhile, Nemo has befriended the other denizens of the tank, led by Gill. When they learn that Sherman plans to give Nemo to his fish-killing niece Daria, Gill and the others plot Nemo's escape, which involves getting near the window where he can make a bolt for the harbour. A pelican, Nigel, will help him. Eventually Nigel meets Marlin and Dory during his travels and acts as a go-between. Although the escape doesn't go to plan, Nemo breaks out through the sewage system into the harbour where he meets Dory. Marlin has become entangled in a net, but Dory and Nemo save him. Reunited, father and son return to the Great Barrier Reef.

WHAT THEY SAY ...

Technically *Finding Nemo* offers the requisite benchmark advances in computer animation on the previous features from Pixar Studios. It has become expected that with each new movie the company shows off its mastery of a new challenge. In *Toy Story* (1995) it was its rendering of, among other things, computer-modelled movement, in *A Bug's Life* (1998) it was light, in *Monsters, Inc.* (2001) it was fur. Here it is water, a high-tide mark of animation skill handled with extraordinary precision in all its aspects, from choppy surfaces to the inkiest murk.

The underwater universe where most of the film is set is a ravishing panorama of iridescent colours and shifting shapes, pierced by shafts of limpid sunlight. Employing a degree of detail that will go unnoticed by most viewers,

OSCARS
4 nominations, **1 winner**

Animated Feature Film
Music (Original Score): Thomas Newman
Sound Editing: Gary Rydstrom, Michael Silvers
Writing (Original Screenplay): Andrew Stanton, Bob Peterson, David Reynolds

WHAT WON THAT YEAR?
Best Picture: *The Lord of the Rings: The Return of the King*
Directing: Peter Jackson *The Lord of the Rings: The Return of the King*
Actor in a Leading Role: Sean Penn *Mystic River*
Actress in a Leading Role: Charlize Theron *Monster*

BAFTAS
1 nominations

Screenplay (Original): Andrew Stanton, Bob Peterson, David Reynolds

WHAT WON THAT YEAR?
Film: *The Lord of the Rings: The Return of the King*
Alexander Korda Award for the Outstanding British Film: *Touching the Void*
David Lean Award for Achievement in Direction: Peter Weir *Master and Commander: The Far Side of the World*
Actor in a Leading Role: Bill Murray *Lost in Translation*
Actress in a Leading Role: Scarlett Johansson *Lost in Translation*

Above left Like father, like son: Nemo (left) and Marlin *Left* Nemo and Dory face the fangs of Bruce, the shark whose pledge to vegetarianism is about to lapse

the animation department even dapples in briny flecks of micro particles, while the aquatic characters move exactly as they ought, pushing through the variously coloured waters. One could pay it no greater compliment than to say that, when it comes to the backgrounds, you often forget you're watching an animated movie.

However, the narrative is fractionally less rich than Pixar's previous efforts, despite the fact that the film is directed by one of the company's top scriptwriters, Andrew Stanton (who also co-directed *A Bug's Life*). More conventional in its quest theme and more didactic in delivering its lessons about letting children discover their own limits, *Finding Nemo* lacks the subtlety of, say, *Toy Story* and *Toy Story 2* (1999). Those films have more of the sublime about them, even though Nemo more directly confronts the issue of loss with the *Bambi*-like death of the mother in the first reel. Still, Nemo creates an awe-inducing sense of the infinite in its watery vistas. But the dangers that lurk at every turn tend towards the abstract, and the film lacks a villain to compare with the nefarious grasshopper Hopper in *A Bug's Life*. *Finding Nemo* is so polished a film that you almost take its show of skill for

granted. Certainly it is better than US studios' recent traditionally animated efforts, including DreamWorks's leaden *Sinbad* (2003) or Disney's back-catalogue cash-in *The Jungle Book 2* (2003). And yet, partly spurred by Pixar's success, feature animation has experienced a renewed vigour, with such recent masterworks as Hayao Miyazaki's *Spirited Away* (2001) and Sylvain Chomet's *Belleville Rendezvous* (2003), both made mostly with traditional 2D animation. These are the work of animators who are pushing upstream towards innovation. *Finding Nemo*, for all its qualities, seems to be coasting in safer waters.

SCENE STEALER
Marlin and Dory's encounter with a trio of Australian sharks, voiced by Barry Humphries (aka Dame Edna Everage), Eric Bana (later to play the lead in Ang Lee's *The Hulk*, 2003) and Bruce Spence (an Australian character actor known internationally from *Mad Max 2*, 1981). The sharks are in an AA-style recovery group, having sworn off fish. (Their mantra: 'Fish are friends not food.') But a whiff of Dory's blood soon changes their minds and a terrifying chase ensues.

59

Dir: Barry SONNENFELD / USA
Released in Britain: 1997
Running Time: 98 minutes
Colour: Technicolor
Estimated Attendance: 9.73 million

The deserved success of *Men in Black* – yet another summer blockbuster overflowing with aliens, special effects and gunplay – proved that you can have all the technology in the world at your disposal, but that's nothing without warmth and wit (a lesson learned, perhaps, from the film's executive producer, Steven Spielberg).

MEN IN BLACK

Director **Barry Sonnenfeld**
Producers **Walter F. Parkes, Laurie MacDonald**
Screenplay **Ed Solomon**, based on the Malibu Comic
   by Lowell Cunningham
Director of Photography **Don Peterman**
Editor **Jim Miller**
Production Designer **Bo Welch**
Music **Danny Elfman**

Agent K/'Kay' • Tommy Lee Jones
James Darrel Edwards III/Agent J/'Jay' • Will Smith
Laurel • Linda Fiorentino
Edgar • Vincent D'Onofrio
Zed • Rip Torn
Jeebs • Tony Shalhoub
Beatrice • Siobhan Fallon
Gentle Rosenberg • Mike Nussbaum
Van Driver • Jonathan Gries
Jose • Sergio Calderon
Arquillian • Carel Struycken
INS Agent Janus • Fredric Lane
D • Richard Hamilton
1st Lieutenant Jake Jensen • Kent Faulcon
Mikey • John Alexander
Perp • Keith Campbell
Orkin Man • Ken Thorley
Mr Redgick • Patrick Breen
Mrs Redgick • Becky Ann Baker
Passport Officer • Sean Whalen

THE STORY

One night, while busting a truck-load of illegal Mexican immigrants, US state troopers are overruled in their arrest by two mysterious government agents, who swiftly identify a disguised extra-terrestrial named 'Mikey' among the foreign party. Startled, Mikey attacks and is shot dead by agent K, whose ageing partner D realises that he has finally grown too slow for his job. Using a high-tech memory eraser, K blanks the troopers' memories of the encounter, and then erases his former partner's memory of his entire career.

In New York, athletic cop James Edwards has an alien encounter. At Police headquarters, Edwards's report provokes derision from all except morgue technician Laurel, but K arrives and wipes all their memories except Edwards's. K enlists Edwards's help to identify the alien's weapon, then wipes Edwards's memory. Impressed, K has Edwards recruited by the MiB, a top-secret agency policing alien activity on earth. Edwards becomes K's new partner, and is given the name J. When two friendly aliens attempt to leave New York in a hurry, K's fears are aroused.

In their investigation, K and J discover that an interstellar force is poised to destroy Earth if a tiny galaxy in a pendant hanging from the collar of a pet cat is not returned safely. K and J race against the clock to retrieve the galaxy and prevent Earth's destruction. Having destroyed the bug and retrieved the galaxy, K asks J to wipe his entire career memory.

WHAT THEY SAY ...

Far and away the most consistently impressive of the late-1990s blockbusters, *Men in Black* is a hugely enjoyable romp which demonstrates that spectacular special effects and whiz-bang visuals need not preclude witty, intelligent screenwriting or engaging characterisation. Barry Sonnenfeld is clearly relaxed and confident enough to be able to orchestrate the on-screen pyrotechnics

OSCARS

3 nominations, **1 winner**

Art Direction/Set Decoration: Bo Welch, Cheryl Carasik
Makeup: Rick Baker, David LeRoy Anderson
Music (Original Score or Comedy Score): Danny Elfman

WHAT WON THAT YEAR?
Best Picture: *Titanic*
Directing: James Cameron *Titanic*
Actor in a Leading Role: Jack Nicholson *As Good As It Gets*
Actress in a Leading Role: Helen Hunt *As Good As It Gets*

BAFTAS

1 nomination

Achievement in Special Visual Effects

WHAT WON THAT YEAR?
Film: *The Full Monty*
Alexander Korda Award for Outstanding British Film: *Nil By Mouth*
David Lean Award for Achievement in Direction: Baz Luhrmann
  William Shakespeare's Romeo + Juliet
Actor in a Leading Role: Robert Carlyle *The Full Monty*
Actress in a Leading Role: Judi Dench *Mrs Brown*

Above right J (Will Smith) cradles a bouncing
baby alien *Right* Barry Sonnenfeld (left) directs
Tommy Lee Jones (centre) as K, and Will Smith

efficiently, without letting them dominate or overshadow the drama. It is a tribute to his even-handed direction that the script retains such prominence, lashing together elements of sci-fi comic-book satire and 1960s spy-television chic with enthusiasm and ease.

The picture benefits, too, from tapping into an unlikely chemistry between Will Smith and Tommy Lee Jones, both of whom riff merrily on the abrasively affectionate odd-couple dialogue with cocky charm. Smith, in particular, continues to impress as a rising star whose experience in the areas of television and music video have expanded, rather than diluted, his ample screen talents. While *Independence Day* (1996) established him as a quirky ensemble player who could hold his own amidst lavish special effects, *Men in Black* sees him blossoming into a fully fledged leading man, blessed with genuine star quality, oodles of charm and a smart sense of comic timing which perfectly complements his obvious physical assets.

Jones, meanwhile, has one of the few faces whose granite-like features can allow him to deliver lines like, 'Put up your hands, and all of your flippers,' without cracking so much as a smirk, but which still retains enough mobile sensitivity to suggest genuine pathos when remembering his lost childhood love. Only the imposing Linda Fiorentino gets somewhat lost in the heady mix – we could well have tolerated more of her spikily incisive and spike-heeled mortician.

In a marketplace increasingly dominated by empty spectacle, the promise of the franchise continuing, and spicing up subsequent summers, must have seemed enticing in 1997. But when it finally arrived in 2002 *Men in Black II* proved a woeful disappointment.

CLASSIC QUOTE

Kay: 'Fifteen hundred years ago, everybody 'knew' that the earth was the centre of the universe. Fife hundred years ago, everybody 'knew' that the earth was flat. And fifteen minutes ago, you 'knew' that humans were alone on this planet. Imagine what you'll 'know' tomorrow.'

IN THE CHAIR

Barry Sonnenfeld made his name as director of photography on the first three Coen Brothers films (*Blood Simple*, 1984; *Raising Arizona*, 1987; and *Miller's Crossing*,1990). He also shot *Big* (1988) and *When Harry Met Sally* (1989); his last film before turning to directing with *The Addams Family* (1991) was Rob Reiner's Stephen King adaptation *Misery* (1990). His career as a director has been commercial but fun, taking in *Get Shorty* (1995) and a witty *Addams Family* sequel (1993), though it was hardly encouraging to see him treading water with *Wild Wild West* (1999) or *Men in Black II* (2002).

Dir: Sam WOOD / USA
Released in Britain: 1944
Running Time: 125 minutes
Colour: Technicolor
Estimated Attendance: 9.7 million

It said 'Ernest Hemingway' on the credits, but admirers of that novelist could smell a fake from a mile away. Hollywood had removed the politics, and the heart, from *For Whom The Bell Tolls*. But that didn't stop it becoming the second-biggest film of 1944 for UK audiences.

FOR WHOM THE BELL TOLLS

Director/Producer **Sam Wood**
Screenplay **Dudley Nichols**, based on the novel by Ernest Hemingway
Director of Photography **Ray Rennahan**
Production Designer **William Cameron Menzies**
Editors **John F. Link, Sherman Todd**
Music **Victor Young**

Robert Jordan • Gary Cooper
Maria • Ingrid Bergman
Pablo • Akim Tamiroff
Agustín • Arturo de Córdova
Anselmo • Vladimir Sokoloff
Rafael • Mikhail Rasumny
Fernando • Fortunio Bonanova
Andrés • Eric Feldary
Primitivo • Victor Varconi
Pilar • Katina Paxinou

THE STORY

Robert Jordan, an American schoolteacher and expert dynamiter, volunteers to fight for the Republicans in Spain. Having blown up an enemy train, he flees across country with Kashkin, a wounded Russian volunteer. At Kashkin's request, Jordan shoots him. In Madrid Jordan reports to General Golz, who sends him to join a guerrilla band in the mountains led by Pablo, a surly individual with a weakness for drink. Also in the band are Pilar, Pablo's tough, resourceful common-law wife, a kindly old peasant called Anselmo, the proud, fiery Agustin, and Maria, a beautiful young woman who was tortured and gang-raped by the Fascists. She and Jordan are immediately drawn to each other, arousing Pablo's jealousy.

Pablo also resents the American's intrusion, and opposes his plan to blow up a nearby bridge to prevent a counterattack against a forthcoming Republican offensive, objecting that it will bring down the wrath of the enemy. Pilar rallies the rest of the guerrillas against Pablo, who drunkenly insults them all and is punched by Agustin. Pablo storms off, but later returns and agrees to the assault on the bridge. Jordan enlists another guerrilla group, led by El Sordo, to help in the mission, but soon afterwards El Sordo's group is annihilated by enemy aircraft. Deducing that the enemy have intelligence of the planned offensive, Jordan sends word to Golz to call it off. While awaiting developments, he and Maria become lovers.

The next morning the Republican offensive begins, and Jordan realises the bridge must be blown. The band attack the bridge and Jordan succeeds in blowing it up just as a column of enemy tanks approach, but most of the guerrillas are killed and he is mortally wounded. Telling Pablo and Pilar to take Maria to safety, he remains behind with a machine-gun to cover their escape. As the enemy cavalry attack his position, smoke from his gun fills the screen and a bell tolls.

WHAT THEY SAID THEN ...

This film version of Hemingway's novel has none of the original's depth, intensity or passion, except for one or two brief moments. Those moments are when Ingrid Bergman rises above the beauty-parlour make-up, the unearthly spotless cleanliness, to convey an emotional upwelling with memorable mastery; or when Katina Paxinou, as the guerilla leader Pilar, suggests a richness of experience worthy of Hemingway's original. There is some competent acting from supporting players, but the film remains essentially melodrama, magnificent but shallow.

WHAT THEY SAY NOW ...

During World War II, Hollywood, rather to its bemusement, found itself having to produce quite a number of movies that supported left-wing and even openly Communist causes in the name of 'allied solidarity'. Many of these films, such as the enthusiastically pro-Soviet *The North Star* (1943) and the outspokenly Stalinist *Mission to Moscow* (1943), caused grave embarrassment to the studio heads when, a few years later, they were asked to explain themselves before the House Un-American Activities Committee. Most of them hastened to disown such films, pleading that they had been heavily lent on by the rabid socialists of the Roosevelt administration.

Paramount never found itself having to apologise for *For Whom the Bell Tolls*, having made the pre-emptive strike of sucking all the politics out of it first. Franco is never mentioned, nor the Falangists; references to fascism are few and muted. 'You may get the impression', noted James Agee sardonically, 'that Gary Cooper is simply fighting for the Republican Party in a place where the New Deal has got particularly out of hand.' Challenged about this, Paramount studio head Adolph Zukor responded, 'It's a great picture, without political significance. We are not for or against anybody,' – a fairly remarkable statement for 1943. Even so, when the movie was re-issued in the 1950s, the studio excised about 40 minutes of the original's 170-minute running time.

BEHIND THE SCENES

The role of Maria was originally offered to the Norwegian-born actress Vera Zorina, who duly cut her hair short and spent three weeks of pre-production set-ups with Gary Cooper in the Sierra Nevada where the movie was to be shot. But Hemingway insisted on Ingrid Bergman, whom he had recently met and been enchanted by. Paramount was reluctant, but Hemingway refused to sign the deal until they agreed. Zorina threatened to sue the studio, which settled out of court.

OSCARS
9 nominations, **1 winner**

Outstanding Motion Picture
Actor: Gary Cooper
Actor in a Supporting Role: Akim Tamiroff
Actress: Ingrid Bergman
Actress in a Supporting Role: Katina Paxinou
Interior Decoration (Color): Hans Dreier, Haldane Douglas, Bertram Granger
Cinematography (Color): Ray Rennahan
Film Editing: Sherman Todd, John Link
Music (Music Score of a Dramatic or Comedy Picture): Victor Young

WHAT WON THAT YEAR?
Outstanding Motion Picture: *Casablanca*
Directing: Michael Curtiz *Casablanca*
Actor: Paul Lukas *Watch on the Rhine*
Actress: Jennifer Jones *The Song of Bernadette*

BAFTAS
Not awarded until 1947

Opposite top The bell tolls for Jordan (Gary Cooper) and Maria (Ingrid Bergman)
Left A bridge too far: Jordan succeeds in blowing the bridge, but is mortally wounded

The possibility of being

able to record television off-air and watch pre-recorded videos at home became a talking point at the end of the 1960s. By that time video recorders were being used widely in broadcasting studios, but the reel-to-reel equipment was bulky, expensive and impractical for home use. Electronic manufacturers vied to find a simpler format, and for a while the leaders in the race were Sony and Philips. The latter launched a domestic

cassette recorder in 1972, the first of several ingenious inventions, and Sony announced their Betamax system in 1975. Both, however, eventually lost out to VHS, the system devised by JVC, which cornered the market after a lengthy format war. Experts claimed Betamax to be superior in quality, but VHS proved to be simpler and cheaper, and by the beginning of the 1980s home ownership of video cassette recorders had become widespread.

Initially videotape, both blank and pre-recorded, was costly, and rental exchanges sprang up to allow consumers to hire tapes for short periods. The ability to watch relatively new cinema films in home comfort was now within easy reach, and distributors ensured that a plentiful flow of product was available. Almost every hit single on audio was matched by a music video; Michael Jackson's *Thriller* of 1982 achieved 45 million sales. Fitness videos, such as Jane Fonda's workout series from 1984 onwards, were immensely popular. A boom in cheap, explicit horror movies led to the 'Video Nasties' controversy in the early 1980s, when shops were subject to police raids. It was all good publicity for the video revolution.

For two decades home video ruled. The price of pre-recorded tapes dropped from earlier exorbitant prices, making it possible for anyone to create their own private film library. Off-air recordings could be made on blank tape.

Left An early Betamax video recorder
Above New developments: a double-sided High Definition DVD and (*Below*) a machine on which to play it

Yet the effect on cinema attendances was negligible. Audience decline was arrested in the mid-1980s by the advent of multiplex cinemas, and the subsequent building boom ensured that year-on-year audience figures increased. Many complexes even had video shops on their premises. In fact, if the figures for home viewing were added to cinema attendance, more people were watching films than ever before.

However, VHS had drawbacks. A more stable and easily-accessed system was sought. Attempts were made to find alternatives using disks, either laser-based or optical, or a mixture of both. Winning out against the others, without another deadly format war that had marred the introduction of VCRs, was the disk-based DVD. Its advantages over VHS were powerful. The units were smaller, more compact, and less prone to damage. Any point on a disk could be quickly accessed without the need for lengthy rewinding. There was room for extras, deleted scenes, 'making of' documentaries, add-on commentaries, to say nothing of sub-titles

in different languages. The image quality was stable and clean, and it was possible for films to be seen in their intended ratios, ending the undesirable 'pan-and-scan' techniques that marred so many widescreen films on video.

By 2005 the VHS was virtually dead, a casualty of DVD. And DVD, too, was facing its own obsolescence as even better home-viewing systems loomed on the horizon.

61

Dir: Milos FORMAN / USA
Released in Britain: 1976
Running Time: 134 minutes
Colour: Deluxe
Estimated Attendance: 9.65 million

Ken Kesey's revolutionary
1960s novel depicting society as
a mental institution was a gift
to the rebel-friendly climate of
1970s American cinema. And
who better to play its fierce,
iconoclastic hero than Jack
Nicholson, mascot of misfits
and outsiders everywhere?

ONE FLEW OVER THE CUCKOO'S NEST

Director **Milos Forman**
Producers **Saul Zaentz, Michael Douglas**
Screenplay **Lawrence Hauben, Bo Goldman**, based on
the novel by Ken Kesey
Director of Photography **Haskell Wexler**
Editors **Lynzee Klingman, Sheldon Kahn**
Production Designer **Paul Sylbert**
Music **Jack Nitzsche**

R. P. McMurphy • Jack Nicholson
Nurse Ratched • Louise Fletcher
Harding • William Redfield
Chief Bromden • Will Sampson
Billy Bibbit • Brad Dourif
Cheswick • Sydney Lassick
Taber • Christopher Lloyd
Martini • Danny DeVito
Scanlon • Delos V. Smith Jr
Candy • Marya Small
Rose • Louisa Moritz
Dr Spivey • Dean R. Brooks
Turkle • Scatman Crothers
Sefelt • William Duell
Ellis • Michael Berryman
Colonel Matterson • Peter Brocco
Miller • Alonzo Brown
Warren • Mwako Cumbaka
Bancini • Josip Elic
Nurse Itsu • Lan Fendors

THE STORY

Randle P. McMurphy, charged with assault and statutory rape, arrives at the
State Mental Hospital. Irrepressibly cheerful, he soon clashes with Nurse
Ratched, who sees her efforts to soothe disturbed minds upset by his war on
apathy, which includes organising a truant excursion for an afternoon of deep-
sea fishing which is enjoyed by all. After a disturbance in the ward, provoked
partly by McMurphy's discovery that, unlike the voluntary patients, he is not free
to leave, McMurphy is given shock treatment along with two other patients, one
being the morose and supposedly deaf mute Chief Bromden. Chief now tells
McMurphy that he is using the asylum as a refuge from the world that destroyed
his father, but says that he is not ready when McMurphy invites him to escape.

McMurphy invites two girls, Candy and Rose, to the ward one night. At his
farewell party, McMurphy postpones his departure so that a repressed boy, Billy
Bibbit, can be entertained by Candy. Next morning, Billy is discovered by Nurse
Ratched in Candy's arms, and harried back into his sexual trauma. He commits
suicide. Attempting to strangle Nurse Ratched, McMurphy is removed for a
lobotomy that leaves him catatonic. Chief smothers him with a pillow and fulfils
his escape plan.

WHAT THEY SAID THEN ...

When Jack Nicholson's shaggily uncouth McMurphy first erupts into the State
Mental Hospital with a burst of raucous laughter, he plants a kiss on the startled
warder accompanying him. The area of conflict is clearly outlined: 'make love not
war' is the message. About midway through the film, the material is transformed
from a facile tract about the repressive society into an honest polemic. After
McMurphy's subjection to shock treatment, Forman gradually begins to build a
cold steady anger, not so much because McMurphy's rough-and-ready methods
are the answer to the problem but because they demonstrate that the apathy of
the patients is outweighed by that of the staff. In other words, that it is policy to
preserve any sort of status quo rather than risk upsetting any apple carts.

As one might expect, given the way Forman's characters are almost invariably presented as isolated units, uncertain whether to laugh or cry, whether they will be welcomed or bitten as they peer myopically out of their solitude, *One Flew Over the Cuckoo's Nest* has no problems enacting madness. Forman has articulated his approach by saying, 'I can only define "mental illness" as an incapacity to adjust within normal measure to ever-changing, unspoken rules. If you are incapable of making these constant changes, you are called by your environment crazy.' His uniformly brilliant cast are therefore presented, basically, as entirely normal.

Their difference lies purely in that inability to adjust to rules which makes their behaviour both exquisitely funny and infinitely touching. And once, at least, the film takes us right through the looking-glass into a world where fact is ruled by fantasy: the scene where Nicholson treats the cheering patients to a baseball commentary in front of a dead TV set whose blank screen, dimly reflecting the excited audience, seems to come alive with the spectacle.

WHAT THEY SAY NOW ...

Milos Forman made his name in the 1960s as one of the leading directors of the Czech New Wave. Strongly humanist, his work celebrated the awkward individual who finds him/herself at odds with the prevailing system. After the crushing of the Prague Spring in 1968 his satire *The Fireman's Ball* was banned and he quit Czechoslovakia for good, suspecting that his ironic, tragicomic vision would scarcely appeal to the new dispensation.

One Flew Over the Cuckoo's Nest was his second film in America, and provided an ideal vehicle for his social and political preoccupations. Kesey, like Forman, started out on his creative career in the 1960s, and *Cuckoo's Nest* comes as a late entry into the cycle of anti-establishment, anti-conformist American movies (often starring Jack Nicholson) that included *Easy Rider*, *M*A*S*H*, *The Graduate*, *Alice's Restaurant*, *Five Easy Pieces*, *Bad Company* and *The Last Detail*. Also redolent of the 1960s is its hint of misogyny — women are either ball-breaking bitches or easy-going whores.

Above Rivals: Nurse Ratched (Louise Fletcher) and McMurphy (Jack Nicholson) fight for the hearts and minds of the patients **Below** The film crew takes over the asylum

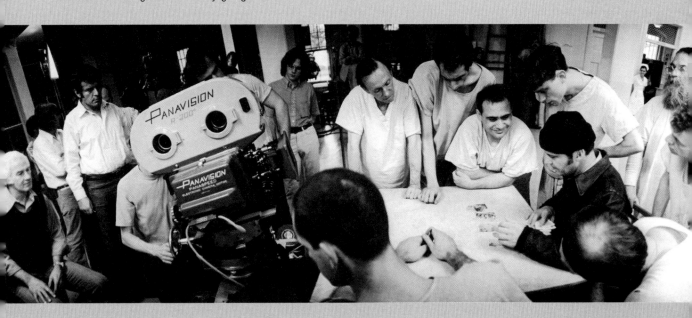

OSCARS
9 nominations, **5 winners**

Best Picture
Directing: Milos Forman
Actor: Jack Nicholson
Actress: Louise Fletcher
Actor in a Supporting Role: Brad Dourif
Cinematography: Haskell Wexler, Bill Butler
Film Editing: Richard Chew, Lynzee Klingman, Sheldon Kahn
Music (Original Score): Jack Nitzsche
Writing (Screenplay Adapted from Other Material):
   Lawrence Hauben, Bo Goldman

BAFTAS
10 nominations, **6 winners**

Film
Direction: Milos Forman
Actor: Jack Nicholson
Actress: Louise Fletcher
Anthony Asquith Memorial Award: Jack Nitzsche
Cinematography: Haskell Wexler, Bill Butler, William A. Fraker
Film Editing: Richard Chew, Lynzee Klingman, Sheldon Kahn
Screenplay: Lawrence Hauben, Bo Goldman
Sound Track
Supporting Actor: Brad Dourif

CLASSIC QUOTE
McMurphy (about Nurse Ratched): 'In one week I can put a bug so far up her ass, she don't know whether to shit or wind her wristwatch.'

SCENE STEALER
Refused permission by Nurse Ratched to disturb the sacred 'routine' and let the patients watch the World Series on television, McMurphy sits down in front of the blank TV screen and begins to improvise a commentary as if he could see the game. The other patients gather round and are soon yelling and punching the air with excitement. The scene isn't just gripping and exhilarating in itself, it also encapsulates the film's key themes of mass-suggestion and the liberating power of imagination. At the same time, Nurse Ratched watches frostily from behind the glass of her office. It's a crucial turning point: for the first time she realises that McMurphy isn't just a nuisance. He's a rival to her power, a dangerously disruptive force that must be stopped by whatever means necessary.

BEHIND THE SCENES
Ken Kesey's novel was published in 1962, and subsequently turned into a stage play by Dale Wasserman. Kirk Douglas triumphed on Broadway in the role of McMurphy and bought the rights, but by the time the film came to be made he decided that he was too old for the part. He handed the project over to his son Michael, who was just starting out as a producer. Douglas offered the lead to Nicholson after James Caan had turned it down. The role of Nurse Ratched was successively turned down by Anne Bancroft, Angela Lansbury and Ellen Burstyn. Most of the filming took place in a real mental institution, the Oregon State Hospital in Salem, and the hospital's director, Dean R. Brooks, made his screen debut as Dr Spivey. Extras were played by the hospital's inmates. Milos Forman noted that 'one of the criteria of casting was that we couldn't afford to have a prick in the company.'

This page Nonconformist: McMurphy is one of many roles that see Nicholson fenced off from mainstream society *Opposite top* Chief (Will Sampson) holds the lobotomised McMurphy *Opposite* Gone fishing: McMurphy takes the patients on an excursion

62

Dir: Charles WALTERS / USA
Released in Britain: 1956
Running Time: 106 minutes
Colour: Technicolor
Estimated Attendance: 9.6 million

Well, did you evah? In *High Society*, an old story is wheeled out again in new threads, set to a soundtrack of chirpy Cole Porter numbers, populated with a trio of solid-gold stars (Crosby, Kelly, Sinatra) and – hey presto – you have a hit on your hands.

HIGH SOCIETY

Director **Charles Walters**
Producer **Sol C. Siegel**
Screenplay **John Patrick**, adapted from the play
  The Philadelphia Story by Philip Barry
Director of Photography **Paul C. Vogel**
Editor **Ralph E. Winters**
Art Directors **Cedric Gibbons, Hans Peters**
Songs **Cole Porter**

C. K. Dexter-Haven • Bing Crosby
Tracy Samantha Lord • Grace Kelly
Mike Connor • Frank Sinatra
Liz Imbrie • Celeste Holm
George Kittredge • John Lund
Uncle Willie • Louis Calhern
Seth Lord • Sidney Blackmer
himself • Louis Armstrong
Mrs Seth Lord • Margalo Gillmore
Caroline Lord • Lydia Reed
Dexter-Haven's Butler • Gordon Richards
Edward, the Lords' Butler • Richard Garrick

Above *She's a diamond: Grace Kelly flaunts her engagement ring before retiring to marry Prince Rainier* **Opposite** *Louis Armstrong trumpets his arrival* **Overleaf** *Bing and Blue Eyes sing Cole Porter*

THE STORY

Tracy Lord, a Rhode Island heiress, is on the eve of her second marriage when her ex-husband, an unemployed millionaire named C. K. Dexter-Haven, returns to his house in Newport. His purpose is to win Tracy back, and he has several allies in the Lord family. At the same time, Tracy is blackmailed into allowing two magazine reporters, Mike Connor and Liz Imbrie, to cover her wedding to George Kittredge, a staid and ambitious businessman. During the day or two before the wedding, Tracy is forced into making some discoveries about her own character when both Dexter and her father accuse her of being arrogant and unforgiving. Overcoming his prejudices against the idle rich, Mike finds himself increasingly attracted to Tracy. On the night before the wedding, they are involved together in a drunken escapade. Shocked by his fiancée's behaviour, Kittredge breaks off the engagement. But Tracy now realises that it is Dexter whom she really loves, and Mike returns to the faithful Liz Imbrie.

WHAT THEY SAID THEN ...

The Philadelphia Story, made by George Cukor in 1941 with Katharine Hepburn, Cary Grant and James Stewart, was an exceptionally enjoyable comedy of manners. Anyone unacquainted with the original would scarcely deduce this from *High Society*, which adds colour, VistaVision, a surprisingly weary Cole Porter score and Louis Armstrong's band, shifts the locale from Philadelphia to Rhode Island, and quite misses the earlier film's sophisticated charm.

A good deal of the original script has in fact been retained, but the dialogue demands a more precise delivery than the present team can manage. Grace Kelly gives a slightly strained performance, with some unsuccessful ventures into the Hepburn territory; Bing Crosby is characteristically casual and Frank Sinatra characteristically brash. Among the supporting players, only Celeste Holm and Louis Calhern really gauge the tone of the material.

Where the dialogue has been altered, it appears to have been with the deliberate aim of reducing its sophistication and broadening its appeal – and in this case popularisation has meant vulgarisation. The plot manoeuvres look slightly shabby in their new context, and the introduction of Louis Armstrong to provide a sort of musical running commentary on the action merely overloads the film. The best of the numbers, sung at a party by Crosby and Sinatra, is 'Well, Did You Evah?' Nothing in the score specially written by Cole Porter for the film has the lift of this pre-war number.

WHAT THEY SAY NOW …

High Society is oh-so-1950s fluff for a dull day. Katharine Hepburn's earlier, wittier and more sophisticated prancing between Cary Grant and Jimmy Stewart is a better example of snappy screwball. However, this remake of *The Philadelphia Story* with a gloss of Cole Porter songs is still a 'swellegant' party. Hollywood princess Grace Kelly, in her last screen role, flirts more coolly between her yachtsman ex-husband Crosby (who looks more like her father than her true love but is pleasantly laconic for all that) and tabloid reporter Sinatra, amid preparations for her wedding to square John Lund. The graceful hi-jinks were transported from Philadelphia to Rhode Island to account for Louis Armstrong arriving with his combo en route to the Newport Jazz Festival as a fun chorus to the moneyed folks' antics. But the highlight of the high life remains, now as it was then, Crosby and Sinatra's ring-a-ding party piece.

CLASSIC QUOTE

Uncle Willy: 'My dear boy, this is the sort of day history tells us is better spent in bed.'

BEHIND THE SCENES

About to retire, to marry Prince Rainier of Monaco (with the attendant media frenzy boosting the film's hype), Kelly sports her own engagement ring. Production was underway before anyone realised that Porter's original score didn't have a suitable Crosby–Sinatra duet – partly the point of the exercise – so 'Well, Did You Evah?' was dusted off from an earlier Porter show.

IN THE CHAIR

Charles Walters's background as an actor-dancer-stage director brought him into MGM to choreograph lavish musicals like *Meet Me In St Louis* (1944) and *Ziegfeld Follies* (1946). As a director he was third banana after Vincente Minnelli and Stanley Donen, but his ability to deal with volatile stars (Judy Garland in *Easter Parade* (1948) and *Summer Stock* (1950)) made him a sound choice to marshal *High Society*'s three Oscar winners. He went on to direct Doris Day and Debbie Reynolds in the 1960s; Cary Grant's final film, *Walk, Don't Run* (1966), was also Walters's last.

OSCARS
2 nominations

Music (Scoring of a Motion Picture): Johnny Green, Saul Chaplin
Music (Song): 'True Love' Cole Porter

WHAT WON THAT YEAR?
Best Motion Picture: *Around the World in 80 Days*
Directing: George Stevens *Giant*
Actor: Yul Brynner *The King and I*
Actress: Ingrid Bergman *Anastasia*

BAFTAS

WHAT WON THAT YEAR?
Film: *Gervaise*
British Film: *Reach for the Sky*
British Actor: Peter Finch *A Town Like Alice*
British Actress: Virginia McKenna *A Town Like Alice*
Foreign Actor: François Perier *Gervaise*
Foreign Actress: Anna Magnani *The Rose Tattoo*

It was 1979, and James Bond – or rather Roger Moore – was showing his age. Would an adventure set partly in space be enough to convince the world that a Bond movie could be as thrilling as *Star Wars* – and that 007 was really just Luke Skywalker in a tuxedo?

MOONRAKER

Dir: Lewis GILBERT / UK, France
Released in Britain: 1979
Running Time: 126 minutes
Colour: Technicolor
Estimated Attendance: 9.41 million

Director **Lewis Gilbert**
Producer **Albert R. Broccoli**
Screenplay **Christopher Wood**, based on the novel
  by Ian Fleming
Director of Photography **Jean Tournier**
Editor **John Glen**
Production Designer **Ken Adam**
Music **John Barry**

James Bond • Roger Moore
Holly Goodhead • Lois Chiles
Hugo Drax • Michel Lonsdale
'Jaws' • Richard Kiel
Corinne Dufour • Corinne Clery
Manuela • Emily Bolton
Frederick Gray • Geoffrey Keen
Chang • Toshiro Suga
Miss Moneypenny • Lois Maxwell
Blonde Beauty • Irka Bochenko
Drax's Boy • Nicholas Arbez
M • Bernard Lee
Q • Desmond Llewelyn
Dolly • Blanche Ravalec
Museum Guide • Anne Lonnberg
Colonel Scott • Michael Marshall
Pilot, Private Jet • Jean-Pierre Castaldi
Hostess, Private Jet • Leila Shenna
General Gogol • Walter Gotell
Mission Control Director • Douglas Lambert

Opposite left Hugo Drax (Michel Lonsdale)
Opposite right Bond (Roger Moore) and Holly
Goodhead (Lois Chiles) in fetching his-'n'-hers
jumpsuits

THE STORY

British agent James Bond is assigned by his chief, M, to investigate the disappearance of a US-British 'Moonraker' space shuttle during a test flight. Billionaire Hugo Drax, ostensibly a philanthropic backer of space research but actually – it transpires – a megalomaniac bound on world domination, attempts unsuccessfully to dispose of Bond, but later sadistically kills Corinne (who has helped Bond). An address in Drax's California laboratory leads Bond to Venice, where he re-encounters Drax's assistant. Holly Goodhead, who is in fact a CIA agent; he survives the lethal attentions of Drax's minion Chang, and is then pursued to Rio, on the track of a further clue, by hit man 'Jaws'. The latter fails to kill Bond and Holly (who has arrived independently in Rio) on board a cable car, and Bond is then sent by M to the upper Amazon, where he is captured by Drax's female troops.

Drax then discloses his scheme to wipe out life on earth with space bombs containing a deadly poison, and to re-colonise the world with a 'pure' race which he will breed aboard his space station. Bond and Holly escape and stow away on a flight to the space station, where they succeed – with the help of Jaws, who has been converted to the side of virtue after falling in love – in foiling Drax and saving mankind.

WHAT THEY SAID THEN ...

If the preceding Bond opus, *The Spy Who Loved Me* (1977), rather resembled a conglomerate remake of the series to date, the latest instalment looks like nothing so much as a remake of *The Spy Who Loved Me*. In fact, the kind of double vision that has increasingly fogged the Bond pictures, as they have sought to parody an already parodic model, here becomes virtually complete. The notion of Bond as indestructible cartoon-man is overtly stated in a pre-credit sequence in which he is pushed out of an aircraft and steals another man's parachute after a mid-air struggle. Appropriately enough, this episode bears no relation to the ensuing plot, just as the gamut of tried-and-tested situations that follow are no more logically connected than the movie's picture-postcard itinerary from California to Venice and from Rio to Outer Space.

OSCARS
1 nomination

Visual Effects: Derek Meddings, Paul Wilson, John Evans

WHAT WON THAT YEAR?
Best Picture: *Kramer vs. Kramer*
Directing: Robert Benton *Kramer vs. Kramer*
Actor in a Leading Role: Dustin Hoffman *Kramer vs. Kramer*
Actress in a Leading Role: Sally Field *Norma Rae*

BAFTAS

WHAT WON THAT YEAR?
Film: *Manhattan*
Direction: Francis Ford Coppola *Apocalypse Now*
Actor: Jack Lemmon *The China Syndrome*
Actress: Jane Fonda *The China Syndrome*

The set pieces themselves, however, are scarcely inventive enough to extend the formula: the Venetian canal chase in which Bond converts his gondola into a hovercraft simply re-emphasises his invulnerability, and the Rio cable-car episode underlines the arbitrariness of the plot. If it is unsporting to ask why the villains should try to liquidate Bond in such a definitively public fashion, or why he would make himself such an obvious target, literal-minded objections about how Drax can have constructed a space-launch headquarters in the depths of the Amazon jungle must occur to even the most benevolent spectator (especially since the shift to the Brazilian interior produces nothing more surprising in the way of spectacle than a second waterborne chase).

WHAT THEY SAY NOW ...

Despite impressive sets by the ever-dependable Ken Adam, and a gently menacing villain played by the brilliant Michel Lonsdale, *Moonraker* represents the point at which the once devilishly inventive Bond series really reached a low ebb. One of the most disheartening changes is that the series had gone from setting trends, in films like *Goldfinger* (1964) and *Thunderball* (1965), to following them. It's obvious to the point of embarrassment that the picture is attempting to exploit the new-found obsession of the period with all things related to space travel. Things have come to a pretty pass when Bond is imitating *Star Wars* – and badly at that. The film has no logic, suspense or coherence. Worse, Moore is showing his age. It used to be that you feared for Bond's safety, for his very life. In *Moonraker*, you wonder if he will put his back out, or pull a hamstring.

CLASSIC QUOTE
Hugo Drax: 'Mr Bond, you persist in defying my efforts to provide an amusing death for you.'

BEHIND THE SCENES
Shirley Bassey delivered her third Bond theme, after 'Goldfinger' and 'Diamonds Are Forever'. Bernard Lee turned in his eleventh and final performance as M; he died in 1981. Judi Dench assumed the role, which had by then switched gender, beginning in 1995 with *GoldenEye*.

64

Dir: John BOULTING / UK
Released in Britain: 1959
Running Time: 105 minutes
Black and white
Estimated Attendance: 9.4 million

I'M ALL RIGHT JACK

Director **John Boulting**
Producer **Roy Boulting**
Screenplay **Frank Harvey, John Boulting,
   Alan Hackney**, based on the novel *Private Life*
   by Alan Hackney
Director of Photography **Max Greene**
Editor **Anthony Harvey**
Art Director **Bill Andrews**
Music **Ken Hare**

Stanley Windrush • Ian Carmichael
Major Hitchcock • Terry-Thomas
Fred Kite • Peter Sellers
Sidney De Vere Cox • Richard Attenborough
Bertram Tracepurcel • Dennis Price
Aunt Dolly • Margaret Rutherford
Mrs Kite • Irene Handl
Cynthia Kite • Liz Fraser
Windrush Sr • Miles Malleson
Mr Mohammed • Marne Maitland
Waters • John Le Mesurier
Magistrate • Raymond Huntley
Knowles • Victor Maddern
Dai • Kenneth Griffith
Charlie • Fred Griffiths
Perce Carter • Donal Donnelly

Opposite *Everybody out! Fred Kite (Peter Sellers)
protests from behind the factory gates*

The Boulting Brothers were responsible for some scathing and incisive portraits of modern British life, from *Brighton Rock* (1947) to *Private's Progress* (1956). Their biggest box-office success, though, was this shopfloor comedy that gave Peter Sellers one of his best-loved parts.

THE STORY

Innocent and ill equipped for the struggles of life, Stanley Windrush aspires vaguely to a career in industry. After some preliminary fiascos, he is given a job by his uncle, Bertram Tracepurcel, who is head of an arms factory. Bertram has a contract with an Arab buyer and is planning a strike as an excuse to pass the order on to his shady partner, Cox, at an increased cost to be split three ways with the buyer's agent. With the unsuspecting help of personnel manager Hitchcock, Bertram puts his plan into action. Stanley, ignorant of the facts of industrial life, finds himself up against the unions, led by shop steward Fred Kite, an expert agitator, and finally precipitates a crisis by demonstrating his potential working speed to an undercover time-and-motion observer hired by his uncle.

The plot, at first successful, gets out of hand when Cox's factory employees come out in sympathy with Stanley's co-workers, and when the press turn Stanley into a national hero. Asked to appear on a TV discussion panel with Kite and the three conspirators, Stanley reveals how he was duped, and shows the audience the case full of notes with which Cox had that very evening tried to bribe him. As usual, however, Stanley finds himself the scapegoat; he decides to seek refuge with his father in the untroubled world of a nudist colony.

WHAT THEY SAID THEN …

The Boulting Brothers have long been developing their popular line of ambivalent satire, latching on to the fashionable mood in films about innocents at large in a world of organised chaos. With *I'm All Right Jack* the cycle reaches its overconfident, irresponsible climax, extracting feverishly bright humour from strikes and trade unions, TV discussion panels and nudist films, advertising and the press, personnel management and class hostility, many of them targets still worth the hitting, all of them given ominously equal weight.

It seems, from the outset, to be the treatment of this swiftly paced material that is so lamentable; the writing is facetious, the acting often self-conscious, and the direction so laborious as to be totally without spontaneity or wit. Eventually, however, one traces the fundamental wrongness of the entertainment to its tone. It manages to offend every level of society. The workshy, gormless employees are ridiculed from a superior, bourgeois point of view. To balance the ugliness of the caricature, the employers are shown as double-dealing. Successful comedy is based on love of life, successful satire on indignation: the Boultings succeed in

OSCARS

WHAT WON THAT YEAR?
Best Motion Picture: *Ben-Hur*
Directing: William Wyler *Ben-Hur*
Actor: Charlton Heston *Ben-Hur*
Actress: Simone Signoret *Room at the Top*

BAFTAS

3 nominations, **2 winners**

British Actor: Peter Sellers
British Screenplay: Frank Harvey, John Boulting, Alan Hackney
Most Promising Newcomer to Film: Liz Fraser

WHAT WON THAT YEAR?
Film: *Ben-Hur*
British Film: *Sapphire*
British Actress: Audrey Hepburn *The Nun's Story*
Foreign Actor: Jack Lemmon *Some Like It Hot*
Foreign Actress: Shirley MacLaine *Ask Any Girl*

revealing neither, and their equivocal air of detachment can only produce the impression of a supercilious disinclination to come out into the open.

WHAT THEY SAY NOW …

For the first time here, the Boulting Brothers took comic swipes at all and sundry in a highly recognisable and everyday setting, creating a swingeing satire which upset many at the time, and is still capable of causing critical and political controversy. Taking the central characters from the Boultings' earlier *Private's Progress* and exploring their post-war careers in industry, *I'm All Right Jack* sets out to lampoon workers and management equally – not to mention the government, advertising and the media, and just about everybody else. As the title suggests, self-interest is the overriding principle.

Yet the film has often been interpreted solely as an attack on trade unions. To be sure, at the time of its release there was some concern about the escalating number of strikes and the increased power of union leaders. But maybe it was, above all, the performance of Peter Sellers as shop steward Fred Kite that skewed perceptions of the film.

The representatives of management and the upper classes are mainly well-loved actors going, brilliantly, through familiar paces. The characterisations are all familiar, even if, in some cases, only from *Private's Progress*. Sellers's meticulous portrayal, unlike anything he or anyone else had previously attempted, seems by contrast to come out of nowhere, so it is hardly surprising if it carries more satirical weight. With his officious jargon and idealistic dreams of Russia ('all them cornfields and ballet in the evenings'), Kite is a genuinely rounded creation, and is arguably treated more sympathetically than most of the other characters.

CLASSIC QUOTE

'Wherever you look it's a case of blow you, Jack, I'm all right.'

BEHIND THE SCENES

Peter Sellers, who won a BAFTA for his performance as Fred Kite, attempted to reprise the role 20 years after starring in *I'm All Right Jack*. In the early 1970s there was talk of doing a sequel, but the film stalled in development. In the late 1970s he performed a duet between 'Sir' Fred Kite and Margaret Thatcher (impersonated by June Whitfield) for a comedy record, although the track never made it onto the LP, *Sellers Market*.

IN THE CHAIR

Founding their company Charter Productions in 1938, the twin brother director-producer team of John and Roy Boulting established a reputation engaging with pressing, socially divisive subject matter, from the portrait of gangland violence in *Brighton Rock* to the examination of the workings of class at a prestigious public school in *The Guinea Pig* (1948). Their work in the 1950s describes a steady disillusionment with political institutions on both the left and the right: from the army in *Private's Progress* through the government in *Carlton-Browne of the FO* (1959) to the trade unions in *I'm All Right Jack*. This irreverent impatience with post-war British stuffiness chimes with the work of contemporary Angry Young Men, like Kingsley Amis, whose novel *Lucky Jim* they adapted. But while their unabashed, socially engaged treatment of contemporary issues anticipated the kitchen-sink realism of Free Cinema (represented by film-makers such as Tony Richardson and Lindsay Anderson), the Boultings' broad, comic style – which some have identified as the link between the polite good cheer of Ealing and the bawdy fun of Carry On – was never quite as fashionable as this acclaimed art-cinema genre.

Dir: Michael POWELL / UK
Released in Britain: 1941
Running Time: 124 minutes
Black and white
Estimated Attendance: 9.3 million

Despite being two of the most prolific and inspired talents in the history of British cinema, Michael Powell and Emeric Pressburger – or 'The Archers' as they were known – feature just once in the Ultimate Film list, with this wartime thriller that daringly adopts a German perspective.

49TH PARALLEL

Director **Michael Powell**
Producers **Michael Powell, Emeric Pressburger**
Screenplay **Emeric Pressburger**, from a scenario
   by Rodney Ackland, Emeric Pressburger
Director of Photography **Freddie Young**
Editor **David Lean**
Art Director **David Rawnsley**
Music **Ralph Vaughan Williams**

Kommandant Bernsdorff • Richard George
Lieutenant Ernst Hirth • Eric Portman
Lieutenant Kuhnecke • Raymond Lovell
Vogel • Niall MacGinnis
Kranz • Peter Moore
Lohrmann • John Chandos
Fahner • Basil Appleby
Johnnie Barras • Laurence Olivier
Albert, The Factor • Finlay Currie
Nick • On Ley
Peter • Anton Walbrook
Anna • Glynis Johns
Andreas • Charles Victor
David • Frederick Piper
Philip Armstrong Scott • Leslie Howard
George, The Indian • Tawera Moana
Art • Eric Clavering
Bob • Charles Rolfe
Andy Brock • Raymond Massey
US Customs Officer • Theodore Salt

THE STORY

1941. When a German U-boat is sunk in Hudson Bay off the coast of Canada, six members of the crew are stranded on land. Coming upon a remote outpost, the Nazis kill the Inuit chef and take the other two inhabitants, Johnny and Mac, captive. Johnny manages to alert help by radio, but is shot and injured. Responding to the alert call a plane is sent to their aide, but the Nazis overpower the crew, losing one man in the process. The five remaining Germans escape in the plane, but when they run out of fuel they are forced into a crash landing, killing the pilot. Wandering, the survivors come across a religious settlement, comprised mostly of ex-national Germans, where they claim to be itinerant labourers and are offered hospitality. The Nazi leader, Lt Hirth, believes he can convert these German settlers to Nazism, but his speech draws a bitter response from the community leader, Peter, who has already identified them from reports of their escape from Hudson Bay. Vogel, a reluctant Nazi, is invited to stay, but his intention to do so is discovered by the others, and he is summarily executed for treachery.

Now reduced to three, the Nazis resolve to head for Vancouver, where they plan to meet a Japanese ship. They board a train, but when it stops for an Indian pageant, one of them is captured, while the other two, Hirth and Lohrmann, are forced to flee. Trekking across the wilderness, they encounter an English explorer, Philip Armstrong Scott, who infuriates them by comparing them to the Blackfoot Indians he is researching. When Scott's crew turn in for the night, Hirth and Lohrmann imprison Scott and make their escape with his guns but, with Scott and his men in pursuit, Lohrmann rebels against his commanding officer, knocking him out and fleeing alone. However, he is cornered in a cave and Scott succeeds in overpowering him.

Recovering, Hirth continues alone, eventually stowing away on a goods train heading for the US border. There he meets Brock, a Canadian soldier gone AWOL. Subduing Brock, Hirth anticipates arriving on US soil where he can take advantage of American neutrality and demand deliverance to a German

embassy. But when the train is stopped and inspected by US customs officers, Brock convinces the officers to treat the two stowaways as unitemised freight and send them back to Canada. With the train returning to Hirth's inevitable capture in Canada, the triumphant Brock strikes him down.

WHAT THEY SAID THEN ...

Michael Powell is to be congratulated on his persistence with this at first apparently ill-starred film. It is an admirable piece of work from every point of view and credit should be given to everyone connected with the finished product. The story is excellent propaganda and most sincerely and dramatically unfolded, and the camera work is excellent. The acting throughout is admirable. Even so there is a temptation to say the honours go to Eric Portman as the leader of the Nazis. His performance puts him in the star class of film actors.

WHAT THEY SAY NOW ...

In the early months of 1940 Michael Powell met with Kenneth Clark (director of the National Gallery and recently appointed head of the Ministry of Information's new Films Division) and found himself invited to make a film for the war effort with MOI backing. He turned down the proposal of 'a film about mine-sweeping', and countered with the suggestion that he be sent to make a film in

Above *Stowaways: Lieutenant Huth (Eric Portman) holds Canadian deserter Brock (Raymond Massey) at gunpoint while attempting to cross the 49th parallel* **Below** *Michael Powell (centre, right) leans forward to take a closer look at the action*

Canada: 'The reason was that I'd read a feature article a few weeks before It was about the fact that Canada had come into the war in spite of French-Canadian resistance, and how eventually the influence of Canada would bring America into the war.' Clark was persuaded that the project was worth researching and came up with the funds to permit Powell, his film-making partner Emeric Pressburger and three associates to visit Canada, devise a storyline and plan the production.

Pressburger formulated the basic story idea during the Atlantic crossing; Powell elaborated on it for the Canadian authorities, who proved enthusiastically cooperative; the project was 'sold' to Duff Cooper (Minister of Information), over financial objections from the Treasury; and there was then a race to complete the script and the location filming before the onset of winter in the Arctic Circle.

The film violates rule one of all propaganda codes by taking The Enemy for its leading characters, and then proceeding to humanise them as a military group in terms familiar to all readers of military adventure: the inexperienced commanding officer, blustering his way through difficulties, using inflexibility to camouflage his insecurities; the all-but-insubordinate deputy, secure in his technical skills and scornful of the fact that his superior joined the Party only in 1936, whereas he has been a member since its inception; and the four ordinary rating-drones, one of whom turns out to have barely closeted humane impulses.

The situations into which Pressburger pushes this group are, naturally, designed to lay bare the ideological sinews behind the clicked heels and Hitler salutes. But the film conspicuously avoids any implication that German Nazis should be seen as a monolithic threat. Indeed, Pressburger's insistence on differentiating between the members of the Nazi group, coupled with the plot device of casting them as vastly outnumbered underdogs ('Two brave Nazis against 11 million Canadians', as a German headline has it in one of the climactic montages), produces some quite disturbing moral ambiguities – most remarkably in the Hitchcockian crowd scene at the Indian Day celebrations at Banff, where the suspense element is neatly double-edged: will the Nazis be clever enough to conceal their identities, or will one of them crack? The other side of this coin is the fact that the film's representatives of the Allied fighting spirit are, at best, a motley crew: the elderly and ineffectual Factor, a daffily disengaged English academic and a deserting Canadian soldier.

CLASSIC QUOTE

'Nazis! That explains everything! Your arrogance, your stupidity, your bad manners!'

IN THE CHAIR

The partnership of English director Michael Powell and Hungarian-born writer Emeric Pressburger was one of the

OSCARS

WHAT WON THAT YEAR?
Outstanding Motion Picture: *How Green Was My Valley*
Directing: John Ford *How Green Was My Valley*
Actor: Gary Cooper *Sergeant York*
Actress: Joan Fontaine *Suspicion*

BAFTAS

Not awarded until 1947

Left Michael Powell (centre) films the Nazi U-boat crew arriving in Canada **Opposite above** Johnnie Barras (Laurence Olivier) grabs the microphone **Opposite** Great Scott! The English explorer (Leslie Howard, centre) is captured by Nazis Huth (Eric Portman) and Lohrmann (John Chandos)

most inspired in the history of British cinema, producing a body of films notable for their passion and fantasy and quite unlike anything produced in a national cinema traditionally dominated by 'realism'.

The pair quickly distinguished themselves in the early 1940s with their well-executed propaganda films, including *49th Parallel* and *…One of Our Aircraft is Missing* (1942), but the spectacular Arabian Nights fantasy *Thief of Bagdad* (1940), co-directed by Powell without Pressburger, was an early taste of the fantasy that would increasingly inform their films.

In 1943 they established their own production company, Archers Film Productions, and began their most distinctive and personal phase, producing a run of vivid, passionate and beautiful films, including *The Life and Death of Colonel Blimp* (1943), *A Canterbury Tale* (1944), *A Matter of Life and Death* (1946), *Black Narcissus* (1947) and *The Red Shoes* (1948). The partners separated in 1957 and Powell went on to make the intense psychological horror *Peeping Tom* (1960), the critical backlash against which all but finished his career. Fortunately, the pair lived long enough to see their work gain new fans in the late 1970s and 1980s.

66

Dir: Frank CAPRA / USA
Released in Britain: 1937
Running Time: 132 minutes
Black and white
Estimated Attendance: 9.2 million

Frank Capra is best known for cherished favourites like *It Happened One Night* (1934) and *It's a Wonderful Life* (1946). But neither of those are on *The Ultimate Film* list. No, the Capra movies that really drew the crowds are *Mr Deeds Goes to Town* (1936, at number 90) and this moving drama about the search for inner peace.

LOST HORIZON

Director/Producer **Frank Capra**
Screenplay **Robert Riskin**, adapted from the novel by James Hilton
Director of Photography **Joseph Walker**
Editors **Gene Havlick, Gene Milford**
Art Director **Stephen Goosson**
Music **Dimitri Tiomkin**

Robert Conway • Ronald Colman
Sondra Bizet • Jane Wyatt
George Conway • John Howard
Maria • Margo
Henry Barnard • Thomas Mitchell
Alexander P. Lovett • Edward Everett Horton
Gloria Stone • Isabel Jewell
Chang • H. B. Warner
High Lama • Sam Jaffe
Prime Minister • David Torrence
Lord Gainsford • Hugh Buckler
Talu • Val Duran
Fenner • Milton Owen
Shanghai Airport Official • Richard Loo
Bandit Leader • Willie Fung
Bandit Leader • Victor Wong
Wynant • John Burton
Carstairs • John Miltern
Meeker • John T. Murray
Aviator • Dennis D'Auburn

THE STORY

Robert Conway, a British diplomat, is evacuating the small White population from a revolution at Baskul. On the last plane to leave, Conway travels with his brother George; Barnard, an absconding company promoter; Lovett, a fossil-hunter; and Gloria Stone, a consumptive girl. Kidnapped by the Tibetan pilot, they are taken miles beyond civilisation to Shangri-la, a kind of secular monastery, situated on a high plateau above the secluded and fertile Blue Valley, where Chang, the intellectual administrator of Shangri-la, welcomes them. The little kingdom is an Erewhon – a combination of a millionaire's playground, an economist's paradise and Nirvana. Absence of causes for worry makes men and women in their sixties appear in their twenties.

Gradually Conway and his friends, but not his brother, find contentment and a new non-commercial outlet for their talents. The High Lama, 200 years old, the founder and spiritual leader of Shangri-la, announces his approaching death to Conway. Dying, he bestows his mantle on him. But persuaded by his brother, Conway leaves for home with George and with Maria, an apparently young girl from Shangri-la. The perilous journey ends in tragedy: Maria turns old before their eyes and George commits suicide. Conway is discovered by missionaries and sent back to England; but en route the urge to return to Shangri-la is too strong and he leaves the ship at Singapore. Years afterwards, we are given to understand, he at last rediscovers Shangri-la.

WHAT THEY SAID THEN …

The story is Utopian fantasy on a grand scale. But inordinate length has disadvantages. The fundamental difficulty is that once Shangri-la is achieved the long passages of philosophical dialogue are not equal to the stupendous excitement of the kidnapping. The contrast between the Tibetan storm at 20,000 ft. and the sunny peace of Shangri-la is perfectly achieved, and the sound effects are excellently blended to suggest atmosphere. The acting is good: Ronald Colman and E. E. Horton are admirable, and H. B. Warner as Chang achieves natural sincerity and an outstanding performance; Thomas Mitchell is excellent as the company promoter; Isabel Jewell is equally convincing. Capra is not so happy with this vast canvas: there is little opportunity for the subtle humour which has marked his previous films. But the skill of the opening and the final sequences is unforgettable, and the film is an outstanding essay in the epic class.

WHAT THEY SAY NOW …

Although it has a naivety and innocence that show its age, and the sojourn in Shangri-la is talkative and languid, there are sequences in this epic adaptation of James Hilton's 1933 bestseller that are still thrilling (the China hijacking sequence that brings the Conway brothers, the con man, the palaeontologist and the dying floozy to the hidden paradise in Tibet) and haunting (the sequence of desperate events after leaving the enchanted valley). Its delicate beauty and atmosphere justify its seven Academy Award nominations, and its restored reputation as a gem of Hollywood's golden age.

CLASSIC QUOTE

Lord Gainsford: 'Gentlemen, I give you a toast. Here's my hope that Robert Conway will find his Shangri-la. Here's my hope that we all find our Shangri-la.'

SCENE STEALER

Despite her denial of the life-prolonging properties of Shangri-la, Maria begins to age rapidly as soon as she and the Conway brothers have left its boundaries. Before the eyes of the hysterical, desperate George, she withers into unnatural old age and dies.

BEHIND THE SCENES

Columbia's cheapskate philistine Harry Cohn so hated Sam Jaffe's style of performance that he insisted on an expensive re-shoot, on a new set, with Walter Connolly (Claudette Colbert's father in *It Happened One Night*). He hated that even more, so Jaffe was brought back for another re-shoot. Capra's original print ran six hours, cut to 132 minutes for release. The current restored version runs four minutes shorter, coming in at 128 minutes, with lost footage being replaced with stills over the soundtrack.

IN THE CHAIR

Frank Capra is celebrated as the purveyor of idealised small town American values in comedy fables about ordinary Joes, such as *It's a Wonderful Life*. But his two extraordinary classics, 1933's sensuous *The Bitter Tea of General Yen* (arguably his masterpiece of mood) and *Lost Horizon*, are complex works to which the adjective 'Capraesque' is not applicable.

OSCARS
7 nominations, **2 winners**

Outstanding Production
Actor in a Supporting Role: H. B. Warner
Interior Decoration: Stephen Goosson
Assistant Director: C. C. Coleman, Jr.
Film Editing: Gene Havlick, Gene Milford
Music (Scoring) Morris Stoloff, Dimitri Tiomkin
Sound Recording: John Livadary

WHAT WON THAT YEAR?
Outstanding Production: *The Life of Emile Zola*
Directing: Leo McCarey *The Awful Truth*
Actor: Spencer Tracy *Captains Courageous*
Actress: Luise Rainer *The Good Earth*

BAFTAS
Not awarded until 1947

Right The scent of paradise: George Conway
(John Howard) breathes in Maria (Margo)
in Shangri-la

Dir: George LUCAS / USA
Released in Britain: 2002
Running Time: 143 minutes
Colour: Deluxe
Estimated Attendance: 9.16 million

After the leaden disappointment of the first *Star Wars* prequel, the only way was up. And *Attack of the Clones* did offer slivers of excitement among the otherworldly costumes and even more otherworldly dialogue. Of course, the multiplexes were full, but was George Lucas still out-of-touch with his own material?

STAR WARS EPISODE II: ATTACK OF THE CLONES

Director **George Lucas**
Producer **Rick McCallum**
Screenplay **George Lucas, Jonathan Hales**,
   from a story by George Lucas
Director of Photography **David Tattersall**
Editor **Ben Burtt**
Production Designer **Gavin Bocquet**
Music **John Williams**

Obi-Wan Kenobi • Ewan McGregor
Senator Padmé Amidala • Natalie Portman
Anakin Skywalker • Hayden Christensen
Yoda • Frank Oz
Supreme Chancellor Palpatine • Ian McDiarmid
Shmi Skywalker • Pernilla Östergran
Jar Jar Binks • Ahmed Best
Sio Bibble • Oliver Ford Davies
Jango Fett • Temuera Morrison
C-3PO • Anthony Daniels
Ki-Adi Mundi/Nute Gunray • Silas Carson
R2-D2 • Kenny Baker
Jedi Knight Mace Windu • Samuel L. Jackson
Count Dooku/Darth Tyranus • Christopher Lee
Senator Bail Organa • Jimmy Smits
Cliegg Lars • Jack Thompson
Zam Wesell • Leeanna Walsman
Dormé • Rose Byrne
Dexter Jettster, 'Dex' • Ronald Falk

THE STORY

Padmé Amidala, former queen of the planet Naboo, comes to Coruscant to take her seat in the senate of the Republic. She becomes the target of an assassination attempt, and the Jedi knight Obi-Wan Kenobi and his apprentice Anakin Skywalker are assigned to protect her. They track the assassination attempt back to bounty-hunter Jango Fett, and through him to an alliance of commercial interests – perhaps under the control of 'the Dark Side' – who are seeking to secede from the Republic. Anakin accompanies Padmé back to Naboo where they begin to reveal their feelings for each other. Obi-Wan traces Jango to an ocean planet called Kamino, where an alien race has been building an army of clone warriors, and then to the barren world Geonosis, where Jango reports to Count Dooku, a powerful Jedi who leads the secession movement.

Chancellor Palpatine decides to use the clone army of Kamino to fight for the Republic. Anakin and Padmé travel to Tatooine, Anakin's home planet, where he finds that his mother has been kidnapped by bandits. He arrives too late to rescue her and massacres her kidnappers indiscriminately. The droid R2-D2 arrives on Tatooine, carrying a distress call from Obi-Wan. Anakin and Padmé follow him to Geonosis, where they are captured along with Obi-Wan and must battle monstrous beasts in a gladiatorial arena. They are rescued by a band of elite Jedi. Led by Yoda, the clone army arrives to defeat Dooku's army of droids in a massive battle. Obi-Wan and Anakin are injured fighting with Dooku. Yoda drives away Dooku, who escapes to Coruscant and reports to his master, an evil Sith Lord who is well pleased by events. Akanin and Padmé are married.

WHAT THEY SAY ...

This second prequel to the first *Star Wars* is a crisply managed entertainment that moves deftly from one dazzling digital setting to another and lards its story judiciously with well-executed action sequences. Yet even sympathetic observers can detect a disturbance in the Force. A quarter of a century after the first release of *Star Wars*, Lucas has become like Darth Vader, a prisoner of his own inflated mythopoetics. As the nomenclature of his universe becomes ever more ludicrous and his grand storyline grows in complexity and gaseousness, it increasingly seems that Lucas is a bored god who no longer cares about his creation one way or the other.

In any Lucas film (at least until now) the director eventually has to deal with actors, and the results in *Episode II* are no more encouraging than usual. It is easy to ridicule Lucas for his inability to depict the complexity of adult emotions, but his attempt here to capture the melodrama of teen romance – between Anakin (Hayden Christensen) and Padmé (Natalie Portman) – would seem chaste and dull by the standards of US network television.

This forbidden love is clearly meant to be the emotional core of the entire *Star Wars* prequel trilogy. But during the love scenes the pell-mell pace screeches to a halt while Portman and Christensen mumble their way dolefully through Lucas's abysmal dialogue against a variety of lovely artificial settings. Christensen tries throughout the movie to convey Anakin's inner torment with a sort of brooding Brando impersonation, but mainly comes off as a sulky vacuity. When Padmé points out, after his mother's death, that he isn't all powerful, he pouts: 'Well, I should be! Someday I will be!'

In this same scene, Padmé finally admits to Anakin that she loves him, just after he has confessed to her that he has massacred an entire village. Lucas gives no indication that he sees this contrast as grotesque or inappropriate; indeed, throughout the first two thirds of this trilogy he seems profoundly uncomfortable with the task of making the cute kid of *The Phantom Menace* and the dreamboat teen of this film grow into the monstrous tyrant in the impressive black headgear.

CLASSIC QUOTE

Mace Windu: 'Our intelligence points to disgruntled spice miners on the moons of Naboo.'

SCENE STEALER

The movie's best moments are oddly derivative. The exciting chase sequence through the vertiginous spaces of the city-planet Coruscant, in which Obi-Wan Kenobi (Ewan McGregor) and Anakin pursue the would-be assassin of Padmé Amidala, emulates the most memorable scene in *The Fifth Element* (1997). Later, when Obi-Wan, Anakin and Padmé fight phantasmagoric monsters in a desert amphitheatre, the touchstone seems to be *Gladiator* (2000).

OSCARS

1 nomination

Visual Effects

WHAT WON THAT YEAR?
Best Picture: *Chicago*
Directing: Roman Polanski *The Pianist*
Actor in a Leading Role: Adrian Brody *The Pianist*
Actress In a Leading Role: Nicole Kidman *The Hours*

BAFTAS

WHAT WON THAT YEAR?
Film: *The Pianist*
Alexander Korda Award for Outstanding British Film: *The Warrior*
David Lean Award for Achievement in Direction: Roman Polanski *The Pianist*
Performance by an Actor in a Leading Role: Daniel Day-Lewis *Gangs of New York*
Performance by an Actress in a Leading Role: Nicole Kidman *The Hours*

Above right 'Fully digitised am I!' In Attack of the Clones, for the first time Yoda (voiced by Frank Oz) was created entirely using computer graphics *Below right* Director George Lucas points the way for C-3PO (Anthony Daniels) in the Tunisian desert

68

Dirs: Wolfgang REITHERMAN, Hamilton
LUSKE, Clyde GERONIMI / USA
Released in Britain: 1961
Running Time: 79 minutes
Colour: Technicolor
Estimated Attendance: 9.1 million

More than a tenth of the titles in *The Ultimate Film* list are animated, nearly half of those using computer technology, but *One Hundred and One Dalmatians* is truly old school. There's nothing too slick here, just a good song, cute puppies and an eminently hissable villain.

ONE HUNDRED AND ONE DALMATIANS

Directors **Wolfgang Reitherman, Hamilton Luske, Clyde Geronimi**
Producer **Walt Disney**
Screenplay **Bill Peet**, based on the novel by Dodie Smith
Editors **Donald Halliday, Roy M. Brewer Jr**
Art director **Ken Anderson**
Music **George Bruns**

Voice of Pongo • Rod Taylor
Voice of Colonel/Jasper Badun • J. Pat O'Malley
Voice of Cruella De Vil • Betty Lou Gerson
Voice of Nanny/Queenie/Lucy • Martha Wentworth
Voice of Roger Radcliff • Ben Wright
Voice of Perdita • Cate Bauer
Voice • Dave Frankham
Voice • Frederic Worlock
Voice • Lisa Davis
Voice • Tom Conway

THE STORY

Pongo, a handsome Dalmatian owned by Roger, an artist, introduces his master to a charming young lady called Anita, who owns an equally charming lady Dalmatian, Perdita. Roger and Anita marry, and soon Perdita and Pongo are the proud parents of 15 Dalmatian puppies. But Anita's chic and unscrupulous friend Cruella De Vil hires two thugs, Jasper and Horace, to kidnap the puppies and hide them in a remote country house. Here, she already holds 84 puppies captive, intending to have a coat made from their skins.

Finding their human friends baffled by the crime, Pongo and Perdita appeal to the dogs of London. Signals sent out by the 'Twilight Bark' are heard in Suffolk by a shaggy retired sheepdog, the Colonel, who, with the help of Sergeant Tibbs, locates the puppies and guides Pongo and Perdita to the spot. Soon all 101 Dalmatians are making their way back to London, closely pursued by Cruella and her minions. The dogs, disguised as Labradors, stow away on a lorry, and finally outdistance their enemies who end up foiled and furious. Roger and Anita decide to set up a home for all the Dalmatians.

WHAT THEY SAID THEN ...

The Disney cartoon team's danger has always lain in lapses of taste, so it is especially pleasant to find a theme of infinite sentimental possibilities treated here with so much discretion. Once the slightly awkward opening passages of canine matchmaking are out of the way, the plot takes hold, and from the kidnapping onwards the tone of the film remains firm – even when frantic – and genuinely engaging. Equally improved, the backgrounds are lovingly done in soft, restrained colour that contrasts effectively with the strong and simple lines of the drawn figures. The animation of the humans is successful where they are caricatures like Cruella, but remains stiff and insipid in the case of the two young people.

The dogs, however, are distinct and undeniable personalities, from the pets who resemble their owners out for a stroll to the Great Dane of Hampstead, and the tiny yapping terrier who all but falls off a stone gatepost in her excitement. Otherwise, the gentle (and curiously dated) satire on British drawing-room comedy types comes over quite well, and is greatly helped by some well-chosen voices. But it is a pity that the puppies speak with the nasal whine of transatlantic moppets – a throwback to Disney's earlier, comic-sentimental style. Nevertheless, such reservations are tiny things to set against the delight and the fun of the film as a whole.

WHAT THEY SAY NOW …

There is no denying the inconsequentiality of *One Hundred and One Dalmatians*, but paradoxically this is one of its most winning qualities: how much more refreshing its scratchy, raucous lines and kinetic backgrounds feel next to the self-aggrandising pomposity of a *Lion King* (1994) or a *Pocahontas* (1995). And how much more affecting it is to witness the 'death' of a single puppy, later magically rubbed back to life, than it is to be bullied into feeling moved at anything in those later films.

The movie is short but not too sweet, soured as it is by the acidic presence of one of Disney's most memorably menacing villains, Cruella De Vil. Anyone who has seen the film can close their eyes now and conjure her sneering lips, her freakish purple-lidded eyes, the talon-like fingers brandishing a cigarette holder. Next to her, the characterisations are either twee (the dog owners who meet over their pooches) or knockabout (Cruella's bumbling goons), but that only increases the sense of danger – we know that no human being will be able to thwart her, and that the dogs' only hope lies with themselves, and the rest of the animal kingdom.

Whatever the film's shortcomings, it stands as a 24-carat classic alongside the dubious live-action spin-offs – the 1996 remake *101 Dalmatians* and its own sequel, *102 Dalmatians* (2000), both with Glenn Close camping it up as Cruella De Vil. In the Disney way of milking every possible asset down to the last drop, there was also a straight-to-video animated follow-up to the original picture, titled *101 Dalmatians II: Patch's London Adventure* (2003).

CLASSIC QUOTE

Cruella De Vil: 'I live for furs. I worship furs! After all, is there a woman in all this wretched world who doesn't?'

Above left *Spot the new coat: Cruella De Vil (voiced by Betty Lou Gerson) finds inspiration at her feet in the canine caper* **Left** *They call it puppy love: Pongo (voiced by Rod Taylor) with a couple of young dalmatians*

Dir: Irvin KERSHNER / USA
Released in Britain: 1980
Running Time: 124 minutes
Colour: Deluxe
Estimated Attendance: 9.09 million

Few fans would disagree that *The Empire Strikes Back* is the pinnacle of the *Star Wars* series. Thrilling, witty, lovingly crafted and ripe with tragedy and suspense: so this is what happens when George Lucas lets other people write and direct a *Star Wars* movie.

THE EMPIRE STRIKES BACK

Director **Irvin Kershner**
Producer **Gary Kurtz**
Screenplay **Leigh Brackett, Lawrence Kasdan**, from a story by George Lucas
Director of Photography **Peter Suschitzky**
Editor **Paul Hirsch**
Production Designer **Norman Reynolds**
Music **John Williams**

Luke Skywalker • Mark Hamill
Han Solo • Harrison Ford
Princess Leia Organa • Carrie Fisher
Lando Calrissian • Billy Dee Williams
C-3PO 'See-Threepio' • Anthony Daniels
Lord Darth Vader • David Prowse
Voice of Lord Darth Vader • James Earl Jones
Chewbacca • Peter Mayhew
R2-D2 'Artoo-Detoo' • Kenny Baker
Yoda • Frank Oz
Ben [Obi-Wan] Kenobi • Alec Guinness
Boba Fett • Jeremy Bulloch
Lando's Aide • John Hollis
Chief Ugnaught • Jack Purvis
Snow Creature • Des Webb
Yoda [Performing Assistant] • Kathryn Mullen
Voice of Emperor • Clive Revill
Admiral Piett (Imperial Forces) • Kenneth Colley
General Veers (Imperial Forces) • Julian Glover
Admiral Ozzel (Imperial Forces) • Michael Sheard

THE STORY

In flight again from the forces of the galactic Empire led by Lord Darth Vader, the Rebel Alliance has taken shelter on a frozen planet in the Hoth System. While on patrol, young Luke Skywalker is attacked by a snow creature, and in his delirium he hears his old mentor, Ben Obi-Wan Kenobi, instructing him to go to the Dagobah System for further instruction in the use of the 'Force'. When Hoth is overrun by Vader's stormtroopers, Luke heads for Dagobah with R2-D2, while his friend, Han Solo, barely escapes with his companion Chewbacca, Princess Leia Organa, and C-3PO.

Luke begins instruction under wizened old master Yoda, while Han heads for the Bespin System, where his old rival Lando Calrissian operates a mining colony. Darth Vader has preceded him, however; the group is captured and Han is tortured (Vader intends to lure Luke from Dagobah and press him into the service of the Empire).

Sensing his friends' danger, Luke abandons his training (despite warnings from Yoda and Ben Kenobi that he is still too inexperienced to resist Vader's dark influence). Luke confronts Vader in a light-sabre duel, during which the latter reveals that he is in fact Luke's long-lost father. Rejecting his enemy's blandishments, however, Luke is nearly ejected into space, before being rescued by Lando, Leia, Chewbacca and C-3PO, who have fought their way free from imperial stormtroopers. But Han has been put into a carbon-frozen state and taken away by a bounty hunter. The reunited friends gird themselves for his rescue and further battle with the Empire.

Above Princess Leia (Carrie Fisher), Han Solo (Harrison Ford), Luke Skywalker (Mark Hamill) and Chewbacca (Peter Mayhew) take arms against the evil Empire **Opposite** Lando (Billy Dee Williams) looks amazed to find himself in a Star Wars film

WHAT THEY SAID THEN ...

The *Star Wars* series, now in unpromising infancy, asks us to imagine and believe nothing – its technological sophistication does away with the need for the former, and its camp melding of myths in storyline and characters acknowledges the impossibility of the latter. With the revelation that Lucas has such a series in mind, even the genuinely 'fun' elements of the first film – its comic-strip eclecticism, its movie-serial dash and narrative tropes – are pedantically filled out and institutionalised, much as the galactic landscape is by effects technology. *Star Wars* will actually become an episode in a movie serial – to be subtitled *Episode IV: A New Hope*, with episodes I to III and VI to IX still to come – though to judge by *The Empire Strikes Back*, its continuing logic will simply be more of the same.

Empire begins, in fact, as if *Star Wars* had never been, with the Republicans still in flight from the Empire's totalitarian forces. That story counts for less than gimmicks, and characters less than both, might be judged from the lack of resonance in the one narrative revelation, concerning Darth Vader and Luke Skywalker. The choice of Irvin Kershner as director, presumably to help bring out the human elements over the comic-strip streamlining of Lucas's own direction, proves in the event ill advised: the human elements are cutely second hand and soon overplayed at the expense of comic-strip drive.

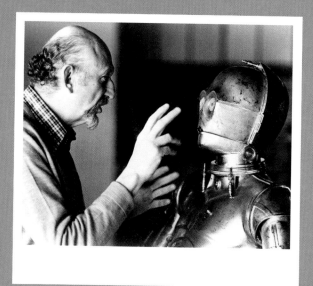

Above 'How many fingers?' Director Irvin Kershner
with C-3PO (Anthony Daniels)

OSCARS
3 nominations, **2 winners**

Art Direction/Set Decoration
Music (Original Score): John Williams
Sound
Special Achievement Award (Visual Effects)

WHAT WON THAT YEAR?
Best Picture: *Ordinary People*
Directing: Robert Redford *Ordinary People*
Actor in a Leading Role: Robert De Niro *Raging Bull*
Actress in a Leading Role: Sissy Spacek *Coal Miner's Daughter*

BAFTAS
3 nominations, **1 winner**

Original Film Music: John Williams
Production Design: Norman Reynolds
Sound: Peter Sutton, Ben Burtt, Bill Varney

WHAT WON THAT YEAR?
Film: *The Elephant Man*
Direction: Akira Kurosawa *Kagemusha*
Actor: John Hurt *The Elephant Man*
Actress: Judy Davis *My Brilliant Career*

The defence that this is all good clean fantasy, closer to sword and sorcery than science fiction, is also scuttled by the imaginative shortcomings of the Yoda episode, where Muppetry meets *The Lord of the Rings*. What the series so far appeals to is the audience's cynicism rather than its wonder: this is *Buck Rogers* on a super-colossal budget, inviting us to lose ourselves in the gloss not the story.

WHAT THEY SAY NOW ...

'It is a dark time for the Rebellion ...' Darth Vader hunts callow hero Luke Skywalker, roguish Han Solo has bounty hunter Boba Fett snapping at his heels and the evil Empire has a new array of techno terrors with which to plague the beleaguered freedom fighters.

Time has confirmed this as the best picture in George Lucas's touchstone franchise of modern cinema, a knockout sequel with more dazzling, Oscar-winning special effects, more personality and romance blossoming in the lead trio, and engaging new characters (like Billy Dee Williams's dashing scoundrel Lando Calrissian), all proficiently handled by studio workhorse Irvin Kershner. Action ranges from the spectacular ice planet where Luke has a hypothermic misadventure and the Rebels their first epic land battle, to the literally cliffhanging climax when Solo's past catches up with him and arch fiend Vader imparts the shocking revelation at the heart of the *Star Wars* myth.

Empire evokes the hectic thrills of 1930s serials and is all the more likeable for it. The cracking screenplay by Leigh Brackett (noted for her collaborations with Howard Hawks) and Lawrence Kasdan hurtles along with a spirited sense of romantic fun, boasting one-liners that became catchphrases, and ever weirder alien creatures. Restored by Lucas in 1997 with digitally enhanced effects and an additional three minutes, this rollicking popcorn adventure is arguably as entertaining as ever. If only he had learned his lesson from *Empire* and let a writer and director other than himself preside over Episodes I to III.

CLASSIC QUOTE

Darth Vader: 'I am your father.'

BEHIND THE SCENES

Mark Hamill, who plays Luke Skywalker, was in a car accident before filming started. Although he denied that his injuries were disfiguring, dialogue in the wampa scene refers to his altered appearance.

IN THE CHAIR

Irvin Kershner was one of the first directors to get his break (*Stakeout on Dope Street*, 1958) from B-movie king Roger Corman, who later took Francis Ford Coppola and Martin Scorsese under his wing. Kershner, a former documentary-maker, crafted fine dramas that are all but forgotten (*The Hoodlum Priest*, 1961, *Loving*, 1970) before commercialism beckoned. His accomplished *The Return of a Man Called Horse* (1976) was, like *The Empire Strikes Back*, another sequel superior to the original film. After *Empire* it was mostly downhill, although he did direct a Bond film (*Never Say Never Again*, 1983).

Dir: John BADHAM / USA
Released in Britain: 1978
Running Time: 119 minutes
Colour: Movielabcolor
Estimated Attendance: 9.02 million

From the moment John Travolta strode through a Brooklyn neighbourhood at the start of *Saturday Night Fever* to the sound of the Bee Gees' 'Stayin' Alive', it was clear that the disco revolution had found a charismatic figurehead. So how well has the movie, not to mention the moves, stood the test of time?

SATURDAY NIGHT FEVER

Director **John Badham**
Producer **Robert Stigwood**
Screenplay **Norman Wexler**, adapted from a story
   by Nik Cohn
Director of Photography **Ralf D. Bode**
Editor **David Rawlins**
Production Designer **Charles Bailey**
Music **Barry Gibb, Robin Gibb, Maurice Gibb**

Tony Manero • John Travolta
Stephanie • Karen Lynn Gorney
Bobby C. • Barry Miller
Joey • Joseph Cali
Double J. • Paul Pape
Annette • Donna Pescow
Gus • Bruce Ornstein
Flo • Julie Bovasso
Frank Manero Jr • Martin Shakar
Frank Manero Sr • Val Bisoglio
DJ • Monti Rock III
Fusco • Sam Coppola
grandmother • Nina Hansen
Linda • Lisa Peluso
Doreen • Denny Dillon
Pete • Bert Michaels
Paint Store Customer • Robert Costanza
Becker • Robert Weil
Girl in Disco • Shelly Batt
Connie • Fran Drescher

THE STORY

Nineteen-year-old Tony Manero, from an Italian-American neighbourhood of Brooklyn, lives for the Saturday nights he spends with his gang at the disco, where he is the acknowledged king. He also dates Stephanie, who boasts of her show business PR job and her intention to leave Brooklyn for Manhattan. She agrees, however, to partner him in an upcoming dance contest, and Tony drops his regular partner Annette. One of his friends, Gus, is meanwhile beaten up by rival Puerto Ricans, and another, Bobby, is anguished about a girl he has made pregnant and the pressure he is under to marry her.

To avenge Gus, Tony and his friends raid a Puerto Rican gang, the Barracudas, who turn out not to be the culprits. On the night of the contest, angrily rejecting what he sees as the hypocrisy of his environment, Tony turns over the first prize presented to him and Stephanie to a Puerto Rican couple. Stephanie flees when he makes advances to her, and he drives off with his friends, who gang-rape the drunk but inexperienced Annette, while the desperate Bobby skylarks on a bridge and falls to his death. Arriving contrite at Stephanie's new apartment, Tony announces that he is also leaving Brooklyn and they agree to be friends.

WHAT THEY SAID THEN ...

John Badham's frenetic, relentlessly exaggerated direction does its best to make instant iconography of the film's dance sequences and its star, John Travolta. The disco sequences are effectively self-contained and claustrophobic, with an overwhelming, pounding rhythm that the film artificially tries to carry over into its sociological scene-setting outside. But a barrage of optical effects and tricked-up camerawork too often reduces even the dances to the kind of gaudy display that might be considered 'eye catching' on a *Top of the Pops* show.

Travolta fares even worse, since the film is prepared to leave him alone and show his paces only on the dance floor, but otherwise buttresses his moody if scarcely intense presence with some slavish camera angles. Norman Wexler's script, in fact, seems almost deliberately to undermine the vigour and novelty of the disco element with its creaking fiction of a confined but perceptive boy from an ethnic ghetto who finally sees the limitations of his background and sets about transcending them. Some of the comedy works reasonably well, such as the ritual of exchanged slaps and insults at the Manero dinner table.

However, most details of character and setting are ultimately reduced to simplistic icons, mingling with such overused bric-a-brac as posters of Farrah Fawcett-Majors, *Rocky* and Al Pacino. The latter inspires one complete little scene in which Tony wakes blearily from a night at the disco, remembers the girl who complimented him by comparing him to Pacino, and startles his grandmother by stalking nearly naked to the bathroom repeating the 'Attica!' chant from *Dog Day Afternoon*.

WHAT THEY SAY NOW ...

For all the corniness evident in the scenes of Tony's home life, *Saturday Night Fever* remains intermittently powerful, thanks largely to the film's surprisingly grimy worm's-eye view of Brooklyn, and the sharp contrast provided by its cheerfully sincere dance routines (and the jubilant soundtrack, including a generous helping of classic Bee Gees numbers.) Travolta's dirty-sweet charisma is given full rein, as

Above *Jive Talkin': Tony Manero (John Travolta) throws some moves* **Below** *Tony points out his medallions and hairy chest with Stephanie (Karen Lynn Gorney) behind him* **Opposite** *'Would ya just watch the hair!' Tony poses with cigarette* **Opposite far right** *Together under the mirrorball*

it had been once before in *Carrie* (1976), and would be only a few more times, in *Blow Out* (1981), *Pulp Fiction* (1994) and *Get Shorty* (1995). You can see the boy was going to be a star. It's just a pity he didn't have much clue where to go next.

But in 1978 he was the personification of cool. So popular was *Saturday Night Fever* that the year after its release a cleaned-up version opened to allow younger viewers to enjoy it without being sullied by the bad language and scenes of sexual violence.

CLASSIC QUOTE:

Stephanie: 'Nice move. Did you make that up?'
Tony: 'Yeah, well I saw it on TV first, then I made it up.'

BEHIND THE SCENES

John Badham replaced the film's original director, John G. Avildsen, at the last moment. Avildsen had made *Rocky*, which is idolised by Tony Manero in *Saturday Night Fever*; Sylvester Stallone, writer-star of *Rocky*, would later direct the unintentionally hilarious *Saturday Night Fever* sequel, *Stayin' Alive*, in 1983.

OSCARS

1 nomination

Actor in a Leading Role: John Travolta

WHAT WON THAT YEAR?
Best Picture: *Annie Hall*
Directing: Woody Allen *Annie Hall*
Actor in a Leading Role: Richard Dreyfuss *The Goodbye Girl*
Actress in a Leading Role: Diane Keaton *Annie Hall*

BAFTAS

2 nominations

Anthony Asquith Award for Original Film Music: The Bee Gees
Sound Track

WHAT WON THAT YEAR?
Film: *Julia*
Direction: Alan Parker *Midnight Express*
Actor: Richard Dreyfuss *The Goodbye Girl*
Actress: Jane Fonda *Julia*

Given that the sole

criterion for the Ultimate Film list is box-office totals – or, more crudely, bums on seats – it is hardly surprising that a fair number of now quite obscure titles make the grade. Tastes change, after all. And back in 1948 the brittle sentimentality of *Spring in Park Lane* clearly struck a chord with the still war-weary British public. What's far more unexpected is how many well-remembered and perennially popular movies *don't* feature in the UK box-office top 100.

Sometimes, of course, it's because their success wasn't achieved at the box office. The classic example is surely *It's a Wonderful Life* (1946), a woeful flop on its initial release in Britain and in America. Only with its repeated showings on television over the past quarter-century, usually at Christmas time, did Frank Capra's dark-tinged comedy work its way into people's hearts.

Citizen Kane (1941), now regularly ranked top of most critics' list of all-time great films, also did poorly when it opened – not so much because of audience indifference, but thanks to a sustained campaign of sabotage by the Hearst press. Others, while not box-office disasters, built their reputation more slowly. *Casablanca* (1942), that mine of

bittersweet romance and quotable lines ('Round up the usual suspects!' 'Of all the gin-joints in the world …'), was regarded as just another passable wartime thriller when it first appeared.

But other absences are harder to explain. Apart from the atypically stately *Rebecca* (1940), no Hitchcock movies figure on the list; no *Psycho* (1960), *Rear Window* (1954), *Vertigo* (1958) or *Strangers on a Train* (1951). Not a single Clint Eastwood film, whether cop movie or Western, makes the cut. In fact,

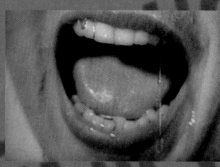

Westerns in general make an unimpressive showing, their sole representative being the ponderous *The Big Country* (1958). Whatever happened to *High Noon* (1952), *Shane* (1953), *The Magnificent Seven* (1960), *The Wild Bunch* (1969) and *Rio Bravo* (1959)?

Crime movies pull in the crowds, surely? Apparently not: *The Godfather* (1972) makes it, but look in vain for *The Maltese Falcon* (1941), *The Big Sleep* (1946), *White Heat* (1949), *The Italian Job* (1969) and *Chinatown* (1974). Horror just scrapes in with *The Exorcist* (1973), but Frankenstein, Dracula and their cohorts are left outside with the undead. Classic comedy fares scarcely better; Chaplin qualifies with *The Great Dictator* (1940), but no such luck for Laurel and Hardy or the Marx Brothers. Nor does a single one of the great Ealing comedies slip through the door – not *Passport to Pimlico* (1949), *Whisky Galore!* (1949), *The Lavender Hill Mob* (1951) or *The Ladykillers* (1955). Even the much-loved *Genevieve* (1953) fails to get a look in.

How about those stars whose mere presence can guarantee box-office success? Alas, no sign of a Cary Grant movie here. Ditto James Cagney, Marilyn Monroe and John Wayne. Even Arnold

Schwarzenegger, it seems, won't be back.

Box-office success and lasting fame, it would appear, have only a tenuous connection. Who can recall a single frame of the 1960 *The Swiss Family Robinson*? Whereas who can't conjure up treasured moments from *Bonnie and Clyde* (1967), *The Graduate* (1967), *Sunset Boulevard* (1950), *Taxi Driver* (1976), *To Kill a Mockingbird* (1962) or *Brief Encounter* (1945)?

Still, there are always consolations: *Top Gun* (1986) didn't make it either.

Dir: Guy HAMILTON / UK
Released in Britain: 1973
Running Time: 121 minutes
Colour: Eastmancolor
Estimated Attendance: 9 million

When Sean Connery hung up his tuxedo and Walther PPK after 1971's *Diamonds Are Forever*, Roger Moore stepped into the breach, and was derided almost immediately by critics. (Is that what made him arch his eyebrows?) But audiences were enthusiastic enough to ensure that Moore's first outing as 007 became the fifth most popular Bond movie of all time.

LIVE AND LET DIE

Director **Guy Hamilton**
Producers **Harry Saltzman, Albert R. Broccoli**
Screenplay **Tom Manciewicz**, based on the novel by
  Ian Fleming
Director of Photography **Ted Moore**
Editors **Bert Bates, Raymond Poulton, John Shirley**
Art Director **Stephen Hendrickson**
Music **George Martin**

James Bond • Roger Moore
Doctor 'Mr Big' Kananga • Yaphet Kotto
Solitaire • Jane Seymour
Sheriff J. W. Pepper • Clifton James
Tee Hee • Julius Harris
Baron Samedi • Geoffrey Holder
Felix Leiter • David Hedison
Rosie Carver • Gloria Hendry
M • Bernard Lee
Miss Moneypenny • Lois Maxwell
Adam • Tommy Lane
Whisper • Earl Jolly Brown
Quarrel • Roy Stewart
Harry Strutter • Lon Satton
First Cab Driver • Arnold Williams
Mrs Bell • Ruth Kempf
Charlie • Joie Chitwood
Beautiful Girl • Madeleine Smith
Dambala • Michael Ebbin
Salesgirl • Kubi Chaza

THE STORY

When three secret agents are killed on the same day, James Bond is packed off on the trail of Mr Big, master criminal of the New York underworld. Encouraged by meeting the fortune teller Solitaire, but discouraged by two thugs ordered to kill him, Bond transfers his investigation to the Caribbean island of San Monique, where he meets the local CIA agent Rosie Carver who shows her eagerness to co-operate. She arranges to show Bond the way to the castle of Dr Kananga, known to be linked with Mr Big; but when Bond realises that she is a double agent luring him into a trap, she is shot. Bond makes his own way to Kananga's lair and finds Solitaire in residence; next morning the pair make their escape from the island.

They are eventually recaptured in New Orleans by Mr Big, who removes his face to reveal the features of Kananga. He sentences Solitaire to be sacrificed at a voodoo snake ceremony in San Monique and Bond to be fed to the crocodiles. Bond escapes by powerboat to San Monique, arriving in time to cut Solitaire loose from the voodoo ceremony but also to fall once again into Kananga's hands. As the criminal prepares to dump them both into a shark pool, Bond blows Kananga to pieces and, together with Solitaire, leaves to catch a train.

WHAT THEY SAID THEN ...

The eighth Bond film is packed with cheap melodramatic perils of the kind that were being evaded by Pearl White and Helen Holmes over 50 years ago: snakes in the bathroom, voodoo scarecrows in the bushes, poisoned darts, the crocodile compound and, that old favourite, the shark pool. In this atmosphere, the mechanical miracles that we have come to expect from 007 seem irrelevant. The emphasis is far more on the equally time-honoured attraction of the chase, here given a whole series of variations which serve to ginger up what would otherwise be a tediously inactive narrative. The double-decker bus and the low

OSCARS

1 nomination

Music (Song): 'Live and Let Die' Paul McCartney, Linda McCartney

WHAT WON THAT YEAR?
Best Picture: *The Sting*
Directing: George Roy Hill *The Sting*
Actor: Jack Lemmon *Save the Tiger*
Actress: Glenda Jackson *A Touch of Class*

BAFTAS

WHAT WON THAT YEAR?
Film: *Day for Night*
Direction: François Truffaut *Day for Night*
Actor: Walter Matthau *Pete n'Tillie/Charley Varrick*
Actress: Stephane Audran: *The Discreet Charm of the Bourgeoisie/
   Just Before Nightfall*

Opposite 'Lord knows I'm a Voodoo Chile':
Baron Samedi (Geoffrey Holder) **Left above**
'One of them new car boats' **Left** Bond
(Roger Moore, in his first outing in the part) pulls
a fast one on double agent Rosie Carver
(Gloria Hendry)

bridge; the airport pursuit in which cars and planes are tangled into expensive ruin; the headlong powerboat chase through the Louisiana bayous in which Bond speeds his machine not just across water but through gardens and over cars as well.

Roger Moore makes a very British 007, somewhere between Patrick MacNee and Fleming's original concept, but the style only works occasionally, as with his 'Same time tomorrow, Mrs Bell?' to the speechless flying pupil in the private plane he has just reduced to matchwood. Otherwise he develops his role charmlessly, from a clownish fall guy in the first half to a caddish automaton in the second.

Somewhere at the back of the script is an ingenious idea about fates and furies, while the curious encounters with Baron Samedi suggest a chunk of plot that nobody finally cared to face up to. But while we don't expect the 007 formula to be complex or realistic, it's sad to find that the flavour has been so expensively diluted. Like the musical score for the film (honourably excepting the Paul McCartney title song), the same old notes are still being struck, but new hands seem to have mangled the life out of them.

WHAT THEY SAY NOW ...

Live and Let Die was Roger Moore's first outing as James Bond, although he had been considered for the role way back in the early 1960s. The film is an intriguing mishmash: a British spy thriller with incongruous blaxploitation elements. The filmmakers borrowed ideas and characters from such films as *Shaft* (1971) and *Superfly* (1972), in the process laying themselves open to accusations of racism.

The intention was to make Bond more 'hip'. With the suave but rather formal Moore as 007, that was always going to be an uphill struggle. Still, this was a lively enough affair to exorcise memories of Sean Connery (whom many had said was irreplaceable as Bond, an impression reinforced by George Lazenby's stuttering efforts in *On Her Majesty's Secret Service* (1969). Moore may have lacked Connery's mean streak, but he had a nice line in eyebrow-raising, self-deprecating humour. And Hamilton staged some memorable set pieces, including a spectacular boat chase, while filling the film with flamboyant character turns from the likes of Yaphet Kotto as Kananga and Clifton James as the hick sheriff, J. W. Pepper.

Dir: Charles CHAPLIN / USA
Released in Britain: 1941
Running Time: 126 minutes
Black and white
Estimated Attendance: 9 million

It's just a comedy, right? Wrong. *The Great Dictator* not only showcases some of Charlie Chaplin's most inspired routines, but deploys them in a compassionate argument against tyranny and fascism. Few films can both raise a smile and pack a punch. This is one.

THE GREAT DICTATOR

Director/Producer/Screenplay/Music **Charles Chaplin**
Directors of Photography **Karl Struss, Roland Totheroh**
Editor **Willard Nico**
Art Director **J. Russell Spencer**

Adenoid Hynkel, Dictator of Tomania • Charles Chaplin
Benzini Napaloni, Dictator of Bacteria • Jack Oakie
Schultz • Reginald Gardiner
Garbitsch • Henry Daniell
Herring • Billy Gilbert
Madame Napaloni • Grace Hayle
Bacterian Ambassador • Carter De Haven
People of the Ghetto, a Jewish Barber • Charles Chaplin
Hannah • Paulette Goddard
Mr Jaeckel • Maurice Moscovich
Mrs Jaeckel • Emma Dunn
Mr Mann • Bernard Gorcey
Mr Agar • Paul Wiegel
Client at the Barber's • Chester Conklin
Woman in the Ghetto • Esther Michelson
SS Man's Assistant • Hank Mann
Woman in the Ghetto • Florence Wright
SS Man • Eddie Gribbon
Man in the Ghetto • Robert O. Davis

THE STORY

A barber serving as a private in a defeated army in November 1918 is involved in an aeroplane crash which leaves him robbed of his memory. He returns not to the little barber's shop which he owned before the war, but to an asylum. In the outside world there emerges the dictatorship of Hynkel, who bears a remarkable facial resemblance to the barber. One day the barber escapes from the asylum and returns to his empty shop. He starts to wipe the scrawled word 'Jew' from his window and at once falls foul of a gang of Hynkel's followers.

Meanwhile Hynkel is planning the invasion of 'Osterlich' and, requiring funds for munitions, decides to approach a rich Jewish banker for a loan. For a short time the Jews enjoy a respite. The banker firmly refuses to lend money for such an object and Hynkel, in fury, orders intensified persecution; the barber is sent to a concentration camp. Complications arise through the action of Napaloni, dictator of a neighbouring State. He, too, is planning to invade Osterlich, and Hynkel, in high displeasure, summons him to a private conference. Publicly their meeting is a gala, privately a brawl. Hynkel's troops invade Osterlich and the barber, who has broken out from the prison camp, is mistaken for the dictator and rides in state through the land, eventually finding himself led onto a lofty platform from which Hynkel is expected to address the assembled troops. But instead of continuing his impersonation of Hynkel, the barber launches forth into a passionate denunciation of tyranny and greed. At first the crowd listen in puzzled silence. Then, as the truth of his message sinks into their hearts, they start to cheer him thunderously.

WHAT THEY SAID THEN ...

The many subsidiary episodes – each a pure gem of imaginative creation – which have been grouped around the central theme tend to obscure the general outline of the film. But in spite of its shortcomings as a work of art, *The Great Dictator* raises the cinema to a new level as a force in world affairs. The tide of Chaplin's genius carries all before it in alternate waves of humour and pathos. As always, Chaplin has excelled in the selection and direction of his cast, so that it is not easy to pick on any individual performance as outstanding where the general level is so high.

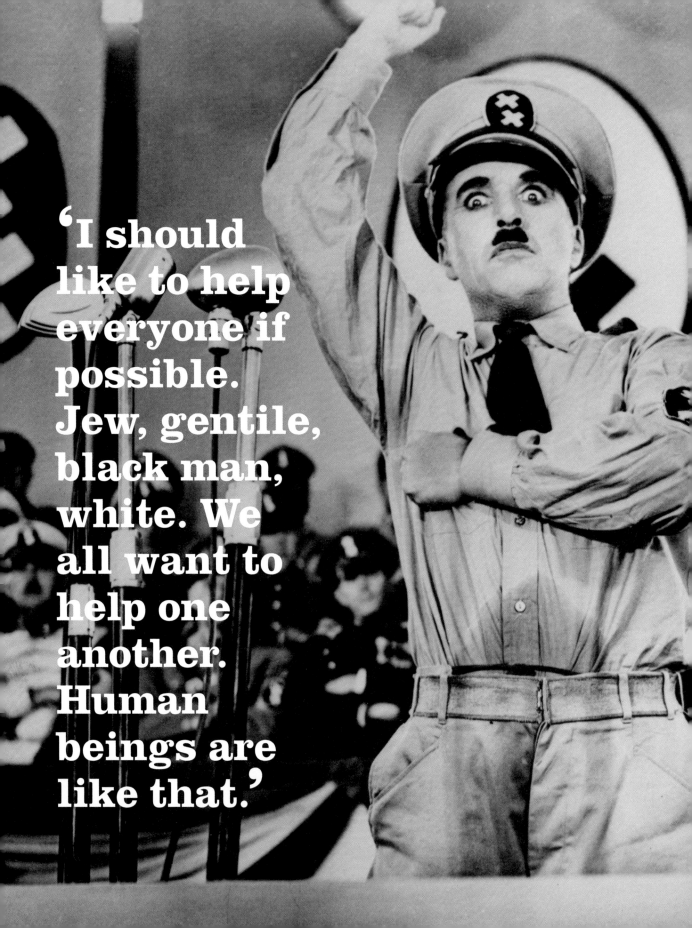

'I should like to help everyone if possible. Jew, gentile, black man, white. We all want to help one another. Human beings are like that.'

This page Love at first sight, Hynkel (Chaplin) declares himself Emperor of the World and plucks the globe from its stand **Opposite** Election time? Another politician kisses a baby

OSCARS
5 nominations

Outstanding Production
Actor: Charles Chaplin
Actor in a Supporting Role: Jack Oakie
Music (Original Score): Meredith Willson
Writing (Original Screenplay): Charles Chaplin

WHAT WON THAT YEAR?
Outstanding Production: *Rebecca*
Directing: John Ford *The Grapes of Wrath*
Actor: James Stewart *The Philadelphia Story*
Actress: Ginger Rogers *Kitty Foyle*

BAFTAS NOT AWARDED UNTIL 1947

Paulette Goddard, as the working-class Jewish girl in love with the barber, contributes a charming and spirited performance, and Jack Oakie, as Napaloni, acts with delightful spontaneity.

WHAT THEY SAY NOW ...
The years go by and Chaplin falls in and out of fashion. One generation finds him repulsive; another is invigorated by his ability to capture human misfortune and knockabout gags in the same frame. *The Great Dictator* is a battleground for fans and detractors. Its comic style is sublime but archaic. The scene in which the Jewish barber shaves a client to the tune of Brahms's Hungarian Dance Number Five; Hynkel's dance with the inflatable globe; the moment on the platform in which the Tomanian top brass perform a slapstick routine with a gaggle of folding chairs – all might happily have featured in a film made 20 years previously. And the picture is sentimental: the final speech – in which the Jewish barber impersonates the tyrant Adenoid Hynkel, but clearly speaks for Chaplin himself – is a confusion of ideas, some of which sound like platitudes.

But Chaplin stares straight through the lens into your eyes with a directness and sincerity that is unmistakable. America was not yet in the war when *The Great Dictator* opened in its cinemas – who could have sat easily in their seat as Chaplin described a world in which greed and hate had 'goose-stepped us into misery and bloodshed'? No political comedy ever had such impact, before or since.

CLASSIC QUOTE
The Barber (addressing a crowd that believes him to be Adenoid Hynkel): 'I'm sorry, but I don't want to be an emperor. That's not my business. I don't want to rule or conquer anyone. I should like to help everyone if possible. Jew, gentile, black man, white. We all want to help one another. Human beings are like that.'

SCENE STEALER
One of the iconic moments of Chaplin's career: Hynkel, his face bright with simpering megalomania, declares himself the emperor of the world, and – to prove the point – plucks a globe from its stand. He spins it on his finger with a dry chuckle, propels it delicately towards the ceiling, rolls it along his arms, lies face down on his massive mahogany desk and pats it back into the air with his bottom. Finally, he climbs down from the desk and attempts to embrace the entire planet – which bursts in his face, leaving him with a forlorn hank of rubber in his hand.

BEHIND THE SCENES
The Great Dictator began its journey to the screen when the British film-maker Ivor Montagu sent Chaplin a book of Nazi propaganda entitled *The Jews Are Looking at You*, in which he found himself described as a 'disgusting Jewish acrobat'. Chaplin was not Jewish, though he was often assumed to be so: 'I do not have that honour' was his standard reply when he was asked the question directly. *The Great Dictator* was one of the few films of the period that dared to address the issue of German anti-Semitism. Many of Chaplin's friends and collaborators attempted to dissuade him from this course – some feared that it might inspire reprisals against Jews living in Nazi-occupied territory. But he stuck to his guns, and was instrumental in shifting American public opinion towards involvement in the war against Hitler.

BEHIND THE CAMERA
Charlie's brother Sydney was present on set, taking colour home movies of his sibling at work. Thus we know that the Tomanian soldiers wore a slatternly shade of scarlet. And thanks to this footage, we also have proof of an alternative ending in which Hynkel's armies lay down their weapons and dance.

73

Dir: William WYLER / USA
Released in Britain: 1958
Running Time: 166 minutes
Colour: Technicolor
Estimated Attendance: 9 million

THE BIG COUNTRY

Director **William Wyler**
Producers **William Wyler, Gregory Peck**
Screenplay **James R. Webb, Sy Bartlett, Robert Wilder**, based on the novel by Donald Hamilton
Director of Photography **Franz Planer**
Editors **Robert Belcher, John Faure**
Art Director **Frank Hotaling**
Music **Jerome Moross**

James McKay • Gregory Peck
Julie Maragon • Jean Simmons
Patricia Terrill • Carroll Baker
Steve Leech • Charlton Heston
Rufus Hannassey • Burl Ives
Major Henry Terrill • Charles Bickford
Ramon • Alfonso Bedoya
Buck Hannassey • Chuck Connors
Rafe Hannassey • Chuck Hayward
Dude Hannassey • Buff Brady
Cracker Blackie Hannassey • Jim Burk
Hannassey Woman • Dorothy Adams
Terrill Cowboy • Chuck Roberson
Terrill Cowboy • Bob Morgan
Terrill Cowboy • John McKee
Terrill Cowboy • Slim Talbot

Opposite top *One lump or two? Julie Maragon (Jean Simmons) taking time out with her horse*
Opposite centre *Hats off from Steve Leech (Charlton Heston) to James McKay (Gregory Peck)*
Opposite bottom *Charlton Heston as the Terrills' aggressive foreman, Steve Leech*

Westerns have gone in and out of favour for almost 100 years. But only one made a significant enough impression at the UK box office to be included here. And perhaps it's no coincidence that it is directed by William Wyler, who, with three other films on the list, could truly be said to have possessed the popular touch.

THE STORY

James McKay retires from the sea and travels to the southwestern village of San Rafael to claim the hand of Pat Terrill, the spoilt daughter of Major Henry Terrill, the richest man in the district. Set upon by a drunken gang of Hannassey boys, whose father Rufus has long feuded with the Major over water rights, McKay disappoints Pat by refusing to fight back, and by trying to prevent her father's brutal reprisals. The Hannasseys make the next move by kidnapping Julie Maragon, owner of the Big Muddy stretch which lies between the rivals' grazing grounds, and promising her freedom when she sells them the disputed land. But McKay, who has left Pat and fallen in love with Julie, has already bought Big Muddy in a last attempt to end the feud by offering both sides equal access to water. He now rides into the Hannasseys' retreat to rescue Julie, and eventually accomplishes his mission – but only after the two old men have killed each other in a final encounter.

WHAT THEY SAID THEN …

Though its basic story – the feud over water – is familiar and its physical action slight, *The Big Country* has been blown up into a long, ambitious Western in the style of *Giant* (1956). In an attempt to support its size, it fumbles tentatively with the pacifist implications of Wyler's previous film, *Friendly Persuasion* (1956), and devotes considerable attention to the dramatic values of contrast and choice: between the modest courage of McKay and the inflamed self-assertion of the foreman, Leech; between the thoughtless selfishness of Pat and the simple integrity of Julie; between the aristocracy of the Terrills and the squalor of the Hannasseys. For the most part the approach is superficial and pedestrian, and descends to its most embarrassingly explicit *Boy's Own* level in the beautifully shot love-hate fight between McKay and Leech by the light of the moon.

Relationships never crystallise; attempts to explore the manners and appearances of the period are defeated by visual clichés and the almost hygienic beauty of the pictorial compositions; the kidnapping episode is weakly contrived; and the pivotal character of McKay, played on a monotonously self-righteous note by Gregory Peck, never comes alive. It is mainly due to the power of the climactic canyon battle, and Burl Ives's interesting playing as

OSCARS
2 nominations, **1 winner**

Actor in a Supporting Role: Burl Ives
Music (Musical Score of a Dramatic or Comedy Picture):
  Jerome Moross

WHAT WON THAT YEAR?
Best Motion Picture: *Gigi*
Directing: Vincente Minnelli *Gigi*
Actor: David Niven *Separate Tables*
Actress: Susan Hayward *I Want To Live!*

BAFTAS
1 nomination

Film

WHAT WON THAT YEAR?
Film: *Ben-Hur*
British Film: *Sapphire*
British Actor: Peter Sellers *I'm All Right Jack*
British Actress: Audrey Hepburn *The Nun's Story*
Foreign Actor: Jack Lemmon *Some Like it Hot*
Foreign Actress: Shirley MacLaine *Ask Any Girl*

Rufus, that this remains a sympathetic film, augmented by Jean Simmons and a spirited Carroll Baker.

WHAT THEY SAY NOW ...

William Wyler started his directorial career churning out two-reel silent Westerns for Universal – one per week for an average budget of $2,000 – and even if *The Big Country* is cast on a rather more ambitious scale, its plot could well have come straight out of one of those primitive efforts. Where *The Big Country* differs from the norm is that the two sides are morally equivalent. The Terrills may have polished patrician manners and eat off fine linen, while the Hannasseys live in squalor, but when it comes down to it both families are motivated by blind intransigence and greed.

It is tempting to see this film as Wyler's sardonic comment on the Cold War, with the Terrills standing in for the USA, the Hannasseys for the Soviets, and Gregory Peck's soft-spoken easterner the voice of reason. Many critics have dismissed it as overblown, and the pacing is certainly on the stately side. But Wyler's use of the landscape is deliberately grandiose, showing his characters attempting to match their impressive surroundings with equally outsize gestures, and deriding the futility of their efforts.

CLASSIC QUOTE

Rufus Hannassey (to his son Buck, who's planning to woo Julie Maragon): 'Treat her right. Take a bath sometime.'

SCENE STEALER

The long-anticipated fight between McKay and the Terrills' foreman Steve Leech. Seeing no need to make a public display of his courage, McKay insists they settle their differences at night, far out on the prairie. Wyler uses the scene to underline his pacifist message. As the two men swing wildly at each other, his camera pulls back to an extreme long shot, reducing them to a pair of squabbling insects lost in the vast moonlit silence of the plain.

74

Dirs: David HAND, Perce PEARCE / USA
Released in Britain: 1942
Running Time: 70 minutes
Colour: Technicolor
Estimated Attendance: 9 million

One of Disney's masterpieces, *Bambi* was seen by nine million people at UK cinemas. That's nine million gasps at the revolutionary animation techniques and nine million handkerchiefs sodden with tears after the death of Bambi's mother. Not to mention the incalculable millions of children asking their parents to explain the word 'twitterpated' …

BAMBI

Directors **David Hand, Perce Pearce**
Producer **Walt Disney**
Screenplay **Larry Morey**, based on the novel by
   Felix Salten
Director of Photography **Chuck Wheeler**
Art Directors **Robert Cormack, David Hilberman, John**
   Hubley, Tom Codrick, Al Zinnen, McLaren Stewart,
   Lloyd Harting, Dick Kelsey
Music **Edward Plumb, Frank Churchill**

Voice of Bambi • Hardie Albright, John Sutherland,
Donnie Dunagan, Bobby Stewart
Voice of Bambi's Mother • Paula Winslowe
Voice of Thumper • Peter Behn

THE STORY

In the forest a fawn, Bambi, is born; the animals flock to admire him. As Bambi grows up, he is taught the lore of the forest by his mother. He frolics in the spring and summer, watches the fading autumn tints and suffers through the cold winter. Then Man comes, and Bambi's mother is killed. Bambi grows up. He falls in love with Faline and, after a forest fire, becomes Prince of the Forest in the place of his father. Faline gives birth to twin fawns, and once again animals come to worship a new-born princeling.

WHAT THEY SAID THEN …

This is an enchanting film. The fight in the dark between the stags, the hound chase and the fire are very frightening, and children may howl with misery when Bambi's mother is shot. The trees, the foliage, the changing seasons, the light and shade are perfect, while Thumper the rabbit deserves to remain one of the entrancing animal characters of fairyland. Disney knows how to make his effects, he chooses his music to suit every mood, he is just right with baby animals. And as for humans – they ought never to be seen.

WHAT THEY SAY NOW …

In terms of animated technique, *Bambi* comes at the culmination of the Golden Age of Disney, the last of the run of five feature-length films that set a standard of drawn-cel animation that has yet to be surpassed. The multiplane technique, developed by Ub Werks and first used in Disney's Oscar-winning 1937 short *The Old Mill*, comes into its own in the very first shot of *Bambi*, where the camera tracks slowly through a shadowy forest for 90 seconds before anything happens. Reviewers at the time grumbled at the slowness of the story and at the meticulous pursuit of pictorial realism. But it's these elements, tracing the passage of the seasons, that now look so impressive, while the cutesy antics of Thumper and friends become wearisome.

Several of Disney's pet obsessions reach their apotheosis in *Bambi*, not least the theme of the absent or dead mother, also evident in *Snow White* (1937), *Pinocchio* (1940) and *Dumbo* (1941). And Disney's often-remarked misanthropy is at its strongest in this film. Man never appears, but his unseen presence is malignant, manifested in the shooting of Bambi's mother (and later of Bambi himself), the pack of savage hounds that hunt Faline, and the forest fire sparked off by a hunter's neglected campfire.

SCENE STEALER

The death of Bambi's mother is one of the greatest weepy moments in all cinema. After the privations of winter, the two deer are happily cropping the first growth of the new spring grass. In long shot we see them outlined starkly against the snowfield, out in the open and exposed. The music turns ominous, the camera tracks slowly in like a stalker, Bambi's mother raises her head, eyes wide with alarm. 'Run, Bambi! Run for the thicket!' A shot rings out as the two bound across the snow, Bambi in the lead. 'Faster, Bambi! Don't look back!' Another shot is heard as Bambi gains the shelter of the woods. 'We made it, Mother! Mother? Mother, where are you?' The huge shape of the great stag, the Prince of the Forest, looms up. 'Your mother can't be with you any more.' A single tear forms in Bambi's eye. 'Come, my son.' Together they walk away into the falling snow.

BEHIND THE SCENES

Work on *Bambi* started in 1937; it was planned as Disney's second animated feature after *Snow White*. But the boss's demand for perfection delayed the project until after the release of *Pinocchio*, *Fantasia* (1940) and *Dumbo*. In the forest backgrounds Disney insisted on a degree of naturalism unprecedented in animation, and for the fight between Bambi and his rival for the affections of Faline he encouraged his animators to go for the supposed impossible – black on black.

The film was based on the novel *Bambi – A Life in the Woods* by the Austrian writer Felix Salten, first published in 1926. The book was brought to Disney's attention by one of his animators, Maurice Day. By way of thanks Disney planned to hold the world premiere in Day's home town of Damariscotta, Maine. But the Maine authorities objected, fearing the movie would offend the local hunting fraternity.

OSCARS
3 nominations

Music (Scoring of a Dramatic or Comedy Picture):
    Frank Churchill, Edward Plumb
Music (Song): 'Love Is a Song' Music by Frank Churchill,
    Lyrics by Larry Morey
Sound Recording: Sam Slyfield

WHAT WON THAT YEAR?
Outstanding Motion Picture: *Mrs. Miniver*
Directing: William Wyler *Mrs. Miniver*
Actor: James Cagney *Yankee Doodle Dandy*
Actress: Greer Garson *Mrs. Miniver*

BAFTAS NOT AWARDED UNTIL 1947

Opposite Bambi and Faline flee the forest fire
Left above Aromatic attraction: two skunks
get together in the forest **Left** Bambi and
Thumper

75

Dir: Alfred **HITCHCOCK** / USA
Released in Britain: **1940**
Running Time: **131 minutes**
Black and white
Estimated Attendance: **8.9 million**

The only Hitchcock movie on the Ultimate Film list is one of the master's most bizarrely funny, and most haunting, works. Joan Fontaine plays a woman competing with the memory of her new husband's late wife. And if you think her character has to go through hell, Fontaine had it just as bad.

REBECCA

Director **Alfred Hitchcock**
Producer **David O. Selznick**
Screenplay **Robert E. Sherwood, Joan Harrison**, based on the novel by Daphne du Maurier
Director of Photography **George Barnes**
Editor **Hal C. Kern**
Art Direction **Lyle Wheeler**
Music **Franz Waxman**

Maxim de Winter • Laurence Olivier
Mrs de Winter • Joan Fontaine
Jack Favell • George Sanders
Mrs Danvers • Judith Anderson
Beatrice Lacey • Gladys Cooper
Major Giles Lacey • Nigel Bruce
Frank Crawley • Reginald Denny
Colonel Julyan • C. Aubrey Smith
Coroner • Melville Cooper
Edythe Van Hopper • Florence Bates
Ben • Leonard Carey
Dr Baker • Leo G. Carroll
Frith • Edward Fielding
Tabbs • Lumsden Hare
Chalcroft • Forrester Harvey
Robert • Philip Winter

THE STORY

Maxim de Winter has gone to the South of France to forget the death of his beautiful wife Rebecca. He meets a timid, bullied, badly dressed companion-secretary who falls in love with him. He asks her to marry him, and she accepts, though horrified at the thought of becoming mistress of Manderley. The dead Rebecca pervades the whole house, while a jealous and sinister-looking housekeeper, Mrs Danvers, makes life intolerable for the frightened girl. Rebecca is supposed to have been drowned while sailing in a storm. After another storm a diver discovers her boat with a body in it, and the boat has been scuttled. Maxim confesses to his wife that he had hated Rebecca, who was heartless, cruel and unfaithful. He struck her and killed her, and sank the boat to make it seem like an accident. Last-minute evidence shows that Rebecca had just heard she had cancer. This results in a verdict of accidental death. Maxim returns to his wife to find Manderley in flames, and they are thus enabled to start life afresh.

WHAT THEY SAID THEN ...

Admittedly, this story belongs to an artificial world more akin to Victorian melodrama than to the present day, but it is none the less compelling, with suspense, dramatic situations and an unexpected and effective climax. There are few characteristically Hitchcockian touches in the direction. He has been content to unfold the plot clearly and straightforwardly, successfully creating an eerie atmosphere. The acting of a practically all-star cast is admirable. Laurence Olivier is excellent as the sardonic Maxim, making the character credible and sympathetic. Joan Fontaine gives a brilliant performance. She is shy and pathetically helpless, but shows when roused that she has courage to fight for the man she loves. It would be invidious to single out individuals in so competent a supporting company who all give of their best.

WHAT THEY SAY NOW ...

Hitchcock's first American picture is more visually conservative than most of his British work – *Rebecca* has no trick shots with glass ceilings or reel-long takes –

Above *Something wicked this way comes: Mrs Danvers (Judith Anderson) confronts the new Mrs de Winter (Joan Fontaine)* **Below** *Man of shadows: Maxim de Winter (Laurence Olivier)*

but the director's trademark fascination with the pathology of domestic life is present more vividly than ever. This is dark, dirty fun for armchair Freudians, and even the subsidiary relationships have a flavour of the perverse. Joan Fontaine's nameless heroine is employed as 'paid companion' to Florence Bates's Mrs Van Hopper – a monster of pomaded femininity who stubs out her fags in a pot of cold cream and treats her employee as a salaried gimp. Judith Anderson's Mrs Danvers, the glacial housekeeper of Manderley, nurses a necrophiliac desire for her late mistress that seems more powerful than the passion between the central couple.

At the centre of the story is the strange marriage between Fontaine's character and Olivier's brooding Maxim de Winter. It's an alliance between a gawky virgin and a widowed sadist; a woman whose past is so blank and unfingermarked that she does not even seem to possess a name, and a man whose past is so sinister and burdensome that it has driven him to contemplate suicide. There's something of Humbert and Lolita about this coupling: he taps her forehead with a patronising finger, chides her for biting her nails, asks her to promise never to grow up. (To emphasise the inequality of their ages, Olivier's

Top *The second Mrs de Winter experiences a wardrobe malfunction* **Above** *The future bride pours tea for her bullying boss, Mrs Van Hopper (Florence Bates)*

hair is sloshed with grey make-up that, in conjunction with his fussy moustache, now give him the look of Chaplin's Monsieur Verdoux.) Fontaine, though, is the screen natural: notice how often Olivier blinks during takes, while Fontaine's eyes remain clear and open. A hint, perhaps, of the inner strength that will emerge as she uncovers the mystery of her predecessor.

CLASSIC QUOTE

Maxim de Winter: 'This isn't at all your idea of a proposal, is it? It should be in a conservatory. You in a white frock with a red rose in your hair and a violin playing in the distance. And I should be making violent love to you behind a palm tree.'

SCENE STEALER

Stern memos from the Hays Office forbade Hitchcock from suggesting a lesbian relationship between Mrs Danvers and Rebecca. The scene in which the housekeeper shows the second Mrs de Winter around Rebecca's bedroom escaped their notice. Judith Anderson, as Mrs Danvers, rubs her face in Rebecca's furs, inviting her new mistress to do the same. She opens the lingerie drawer and enthuses about the nuns who sewed Rebecca's smalls. She invites Fontaine's character to sit at the dressing table and mimes the repeated sweeps of the brush through Rebecca's hair; Hitchcock shoots these movements as long, stately strokes – like the jabs of the knife in *Psycho* (1960).

BEHIND THE SCENES

Spite and paranoia characterised the atmosphere on the set of *Rebecca*. Its source was Laurence Olivier's contempt for his co-star Joan Fontaine. Resentful that his lover, Vivien Leigh, had failed to win the leading role, he went out of his way to undermine Fontaine's confidence. (When she informed him of her recent marriage to the actor Brian Aherne, he spat back, 'Couldn't you do better than that?') But it was Alfred Hitchcock who took that sentiment and nurtured it until it was visible on the screen. He told Fontaine that the crew shared Olivier's low opinion of her abilities. He suggested that the producer, David O. Selznick, was considering recasting her role. He ensured that she was as jittery and unsure of herself as the second Mrs de Winter. The result, for Fontaine, was weeks of misery – followed by an Oscar nomination.

BEHIND THE CAMERA

Even after the offer of a 'fancy bonus', Gregg Toland declined to accept the invitation to shoot *Rebecca*. His friend George Barnes took the job, and the famous opening sequence of *Rebecca* – in which the camera appears to squeeze through a gap in the ivy-wrapped iron gates of Manderley – might allude to a similar shot Toland created for *Citizen Kane* (1941).

76

Dir: Carol REED / UK
Released in Britain: 1968
Running Time: 146 minutes
Colour: Technicolor
Estimated Attendance: 8.9 million

Where David Lean's *Oliver Twist* was tense and harrowing 20 years earlier, Carol Reed's version of Dickens's novel (via Lionel Bart's hit stage musical) was characterised instead by joyful exuberance. It even has an exclamation mark after its title, the sure sign of a movie that just wants to be loved.

OLIVER!

Director **Carol Reed**
Producer **John Woolf**
Screenplay **Vernon Harris**, based on the musical play
   by Lionel Bart, based on the novel *Oliver Twist* by
   Charles Dickens
Director of Photography **Oswald Morris**
Editor **Ralph Kemplen**
Production Designer **John Box**
Music **Lionel Bart**

Fagin • Ron Moody
Nancy • Shani Wallis
Bill Sikes • Oliver Reed
Mr Bumble • Harry Secombe
Oliver Twist • Mark Lester
Artful Dodger • Jack Wild
The Magistrate • Hugh Griffith
Mr Brownlow • Joseph O'Conor
Mr Sowerberry • Leonard Rossiter
Mrs Sowerberry • Hylda Baker
Noah Claypole • Kenneth Cranham
Mrs Bedwin • Megs Jenkins
Mrs Bumble • Peggy Mount
Bet • Sheila White

Top *Stealing the limelight, Ron Moody (left) and Jack Wild both received Oscar nominations, as Fagin and the Artful Dodger*

THE STORY

As a punishment for requesting a second helping of gruel, Oliver Twist is evicted from the foundlings' workhouse and sold by the beadle, Mr Bumble, to Mr Sowerberry, the undertaker. Oliver runs away to seek his fortune in London. Here he meets the young Artful Dodger, who offers him lodgings in the deserted warehouse from which the elderly Fagin, a master pickpocket, supervises the activities of an assortment of young thieves. Oliver's first expedition results in his arrest for a theft committed by the Dodger; but when his accuser, Mr Brownlow, realises the boy's innocence, he takes him home and raises him like a son. Cut-throat criminal Bill Sikes, worried that Oliver will betray him and Fagin to the police, uses his girlfriend Nancy, a cheerful prostitute, to lure the trusting Oliver away from Mr Brownlow.

When Nancy understands that Sikes means to destroy the child, she contacts Mr Brownlow and promises to intervene; but Sikes clubs her to death and drags Oliver with him as he attempts a getaway over the warehouse roof. Eventually, Sikes is shot by the police while trying to leap to safety and Oliver is reunited with his benefactor, who has now confirmed his suspicion that the child is the son of his dead niece. The Dodger and Fagin, who has lost his slowly accumulated fortune in escaping from the police, set off to resume their life of larceny.

WHAT THEY SAID THEN ...

However euphemistically presented, such narrative elements as the exploitation of child labour, pimping, abduction, prostitution and murder combine to make *Oliver!* the most non-U subject so far to receive a U certificate. And an uneasy ambivalence that was already discernible on the stage in Lionel Bart's pantomimic adaptation of Dickens's moralising and melodramatic novel – child thieves zestily promising, in the spirit of some Wolf Cub initiation, to 'take the drop' for Fagin, or Fagin himself confessing in song that 'I'm finding it hard to be really as black as they paint' – is enlarged rather than diminished by Carol Reed's cinema version.

In the film that is obviously intended to become everybody's favourite Christmas outing, there is a heightened discrepancy between the romping jollity with which everyone goes about his business and the actual business being done. The workhouse of the opening sequence seems literally to spring to life from a realistic steel engraving, and John Box's splendidly designed sets – particularly the dockside tavern and the twisting, rotten stairs that lead over a fetid canal to Fagin's hide-out – create a formalised Dickensian atmosphere that is essentially at odds with the unrealistic cheeriness of the characters. Shani Wallis's bouncing Nancy seems more like a sympathetic au pair than a sorely tried prostitute and, like Ron Moody's roguish Fagin, she is only permitted to abandon this jovial mood for an even more sentimentalised lyrical one, which makes her murder all the more shocking.

The absence of realism combines with a lack of consistency, not to mention an excessively amplified soundtrack, to leave the viewer fatigued. The musical numbers remain isolated from the story – set pieces injected into the narrative without really advancing the plot. And although the number of scurrying butchers, swirling milkmaids and prancing policemen swells in infinite multiplication with each verse of

OSCARS

11 nominations, **5 winners/1 honorary award**

Best Picture
Directing: Carol Reed
Actor: Ron Moody
Actor in a Supporting Role: Jack Wild
Art Direction/Set Decoration
Cinematography: Oswald Morris
Costume Design: Phyllis Dalton
Film Editing: Ralph Kemplen
Music (Score of a Musical Picture): John Green
Sound: Shepperton Studio Sound Department
Writing (Screenplay Based on Material From Another Medium):
   Vernon Harris
Honorary Award: To Onna White for her outstanding
   choreography achievement for *Oliver!*

BAFTAS

8 nominations

Film
Direction
Actor: Ron Moody
Art Direction: John Box
Costume Design: Phyllis Dalton
Editing: Ralph Kemplen
Most Promising Newcomer to Leading Film Roles: Jack Wild
Sound Track: John Cox, Bob Jones

WHAT WON THAT YEAR?
Film: *The Graduate*
Direction: Mike Nichols *The Graduate*
Actor: Spencer Tracy *Guess Who's Coming to Dinner?*
Actress: Katharine Hepburn *The Lion in Winter/ Guess Who's
   Coming to Dinner?*

Opposite below Director Carol Reed admires Mark Lester's sombrero **Above** 'Please, sir, I want some more' **Right** Hole-in-the-wall gang leader Fagin (Ron Moody) makes a spectacular entrance

every song, the cumulative effect of Onna White's repetitive and muscular choreography is invariably more mathematical than dynamic. Ultimately, though, there is something inherently offensive in the spectacle of a chorus of pre-pubescent children swinging their arms and tapping their tiny toes in precocious imitation of Fred Astaire.

WHAT THEY SAY NOW …

Mark Lester makes a winning and understated Oliver, and Jack Wild's tireless mugging creates an Artful Dodger who is as accomplished a scene stealer as he is a pickpocket. It was inspired of Reed to partner the wet-behind-the-ears Lester with Wild, whose performance has more of the stage school about it, which seems appropriate for a street-smart young felon.

Carol Reed's nephew, Oliver Reed, was cast as Bill Sikes. Although Reed's portrayal is rather lightweight when compared with the dark and permanently scowling Robert Newton in the David Lean version of *Oliver Twist*, it can still shock at times, especially when he brutally murders Nancy in the shadow of London Bridge. Reed, legendary for his raucous off-screen lifestyle, successfully conveys a Sikes who is decisive, brutal and yet plagued by a faint sense of guilt which seems to dilute his misanthropy.

In fact, the director pulled together a quality ensemble cast, bypassing the pressure from the studio to include a star. Peter Sellers, who had wanted to play Fagin, had committed to other projects by the time production began and so Ron Moody, who had played the role on stage, reprised his performance. What is created from Reed's crafted direction and Moody's magician-like performance is a broadly enjoyable, burlesque version of the famous villain. The hard edges of Fagin, which are felt more keenly in Dickens's novel, are rounded off somewhat. Moody's interpretation makes Fagin as much a clown as a hardened criminal.

While the songs could easily prevent an audience from suspending disbelief, Reed manages to keep the artificiality in check just enough to maintain a human interest to the story. The slums and streets of London are a little too picture-book to be convincing, but the essential theatricality of this musical mean that the exuberance and brightness of the sets seems entirely in keeping with the spirit of the original stage show.

CLASSIC QUOTE

Oliver (holding out bowl): 'Please, sir, I want some more.'
Mr Bumble (roars): 'More?'

IN THE CHAIR

Carol Reed gained an international reputation as a director on the basis of three dazzling and humane post-war films – *Odd Man Out* (1947), *The Fallen Idol* (1948) and *The Third Man* (1949), all but the first from scripts by Graham Greene. But by the time Reed came to direct *Oliver!* he was considered by many to be a talent in irreversible decline. It was a riposte to the general consensus, then, when his work on the picture resulted in an Oscar.

77

Dir: Mike NEWELL / UK
Released in Britain: 1994
Running Time: 116 minutes
Colour: Eastmancolor
Estimated Attendance: 8.81 million

FOUR WEDDINGS AND A FUNERAL

Director **Mike Newell**
Producer **Duncan Kenworthy**
Screenplay **Richard Curtis**
Director of Photography **Michael Coulter**
Editor **Jon Gregory**
Production Designer **Maggie Gray**
Music **Richard Rodney Bennett**

Carrie • Andie MacDowell
Charles • Hugh Grant
Fiona • Kristin Scott Thomas
Gareth • Simon Callow
Tom • James Fleet
Matthew • John Hannah
Scarlett • Charlotte Coleman
David • David Bower
Father Gerald • Rowan Atkinson
Hamish • Corin Redgrave
Henrietta • Anna Chancellor
Best Man • Struan Rodger
Angus the Groom • Timothy Walker
Laura the Bride • Sara Crowe
Vicar • Ronald Herdman
Laura's Mother • Elspet Gray
Laura's Father • Philip Voss
George the Bore • Rupert Vansittart
Frightful Folk Duo #1 • Nicola Walker
Frightful Folk Duo #2 • Paul Stacey

As the popularity of the pretty literary adaptations that had defined British film-making in the 1980s began to wane, a new kind of home-grown cinema charmed audiences here and in the US. The first collaboration between writer Richard Curtis and actor Hugh Grant suggested they were on to something special, a suspicion confirmed by the presence on this list of all their subsequent work together.

THE STORY

Charles is a frequent wedding-goer, along with his urban haute bourgeoisie friends – the sharp-tongued Fiona and her wealthy brother Tom, his own deaf brother David, his punky flatmate Scarlett, and the effusive Gareth and his lover Matthew. At a wedding in Somerset, Charles is struck by a beautiful stranger, Carrie, who surprises him by taking him to bed. The next morning, Carrie goes back to America. At a London wedding two months later, Charles sees Carrie again, but his hopes are dashed when she introduces her new fiancé, Hamish. When Hamish leaves for a business trip, they spend a second night together.

A month later, Charles receives an invitation to Carrie's wedding. As he is buying her gift, he runs into her. Over coffee, Charles delivers a fumbling declaration of love, but nevertheless finds himself at her wedding shortly afterwards. At the party, Fiona admits to him that she has always loved him. Gareth suddenly has a heart attack. The friends reconvene at his funeral. Afterwards, moved by Matthew's speech, Charles wonders if he will ever feel that way about anyone himself. Ten months later, Charles is to marry Henrietta. As his friends, apart from Fiona, meet their ideal mates, Carrie reappears, separated from Hamish, throwing Charles into confusion. He decides to go through with the wedding anyway, but with David's encouragement he jilts Henrietta at the altar. Carrie and Charles agree not to get married till death do they part.

WHAT THEY SAID THEN …

With a wealth of easy-target caricatures to lean on (ghastly ex-girlfriends, drunken bores, senile old men – and this film doesn't miss one), a movie about a wedding can often feel like a wedding itself: two hours stuck in a crowded room with a lot of people you don't know very well and don't particularly like.

But *Four Weddings and a Funeral*, which is structured like a film student's senior project, strives to be more than that and ends up as something worse: a smarmy little fable about the magic of true love. This is a lazy, *Sleepless in*

Seattle-style romanticism, the kind that assumes that if we're told often enough that the two dull protagonists are meant for each other, we'll eventually believe it and care sufficiently to be warmed by the inevitable hearts-and-flowers finale. Of course, it would help if there were a single spark of chemistry between the two leads. Andie MacDowell looks ravishing enough for anyone to be smitten at first sight, but as a light comedienne she is disastrous. Her idea of sprightly repartee is to pronounce every syllable, and she can't quite hide the furrows of perplexity around her eyes – she doesn't seem to grasp her own witticisms. You can't help remembering how she was dubbed by Glenn Close in *Greystoke* (1984), and thinking how much livelier this film would be if she were dubbed by someone with a fundamental grasp of comic rhythm and cadence. She is not helped, either, by having to pretend she has fallen for someone who looks like a chipmunk. Hugh Grant, his hands full playing repressed and hesitant, does not exactly radiate sex appeal here (and the fact that he looks all of 22 hardly lends credence to his fretting about ending up a sad old bachelor). The fact that a post-credits photomontage shows them with a baby does little to assuage our suspicions that the affair will last six months.

The film does score points with those of the supporting cast who are graced with personalities. Kristin Scott Thomas makes a marvellously brittle Fiona; when she confesses to an elderly lady that she has never got married because she is in love with someone who never thinks of her, she makes us feel how much this admission has cost her, how morbidly proud and secretive she is beneath her icy exterior. And the film has a pleasingly matter-of-fact way of establishing Gareth and Matthew's relationship – they're a convincing couple,

OSCARS
2 nominations

Best Picture
Writing (Screenplay Written Directly for the Screen): Richard Curtis

WHAT WON THAT YEAR?
Best Picture: *Forrest Gump*
Directing: Robert Zemeckis *Forrest Gump*
Actor in a Leading Role: Tom Hanks *Forrest Gump*
Actress in a Leading Role: Jessica Lange *Blue Sky*

BAFTAS
11 nominations, **4 winners**

Film
David Lean Award for Achievement in Direction: Mike Newell
Actor in a Leading Role: Hugh Grant
Actress in a Supporting Role: Charlotte Coleman
Actress in a Supporting Role: Kristin Scott Thomas
Actor in a Supporting Role: Simon Callow
Actor in a Supporting Role: John Hannah
Anthony Asquith Award for Achievement in Film Music
Costume Design: Lindy Hemming
Editing: Jon Gregory
Original Screenplay: Richard Curtis

WHAT WON THAT YEAR?
Alexander Korda Award for Outstanding British Film: *Shallow Grave*
Actress in a Leading Role: Susan Sarandon *The Client*

Right *'Is it still raining? I hadn't noticed'*
Opposite *'Quite out of your league.' Fiona
(Kristin Scott Thomas) warns Charles off Carrie
(Andie MacDowell)*

and you wish you could see more of them, because the brief glimpses of their affectionate rapport ring true.

But too much time is taken up with the spectacle of Charles and his improbably alternative flatmate (Scarlett appears to be a 'Sarf' London punkette, so you wonder just how she got in with the independently wealthy crowd) racing to various churches, and people making boring speeches after dinner. You can feel how earnestly the film-makers tried to vary the visual aspect of the ceremonies – posh London wedding, Somerset country church, draughty Scottish castle. But the fact remains that by the time Charles's own wedding rolls around, you wish they had left it at two weddings and a funeral.

WHAT THEY SAY NOW …

Along with the books of Nick Hornby and Helen Fielding, *Four Weddings and a Funeral* – and its writer Richard Curtis and star Hugh Grant – promoted a new image of the typical modern Briton (low self-esteem, huge facility for self-deprecation, endlessly charming and bumbling). Whether it's Fielding's Bridget Jones (the movie adaptations of which both make the Ultimate Film list), Curtis's well-bred nincompoops (played by Grant here and in *Notting Hill*, 1999, and *Love Actually*, 2003 – both also on the list) or Hornby's commitment-phobic overgrown adolescents (one of whom, in the film of *About a Boy*, 2002, was also played by Grant), it seems these financially secure, emotionally shaky loser-heroes represent an internationally appealing cartoon of Britishness.

Curtis had already rehearsed his formula once before, in the 1989 comedy *The Tall Guy*, where an American buffoon (Jeff Goldblum) fell for a sarcastic nurse (Emma Thompson). The template remained intact in *Four Weddings*, with one tweak – now the buffoon and his object of desire had traded nationalities. Everything else remained: a sophisticated but boyish, bemused, self-mocking hero, a cool-cat leading lady, chums who are witty or wacky, and a romance fraught with mistiming and misunderstanding.

Four Weddings knits together superior sitcom sketches, so blithely unencumbered by back story or reason they don't bear scrutiny; yet somehow it still engages. That this good-natured jape transcends its contrivance is testimony to Curtis's fizzy take on insecure thirtysomethings, a stream of cracking exchanges, and some delightful performances.

CLASSIC QUOTE
Charles: 'Uh, in the words of David Cassidy, in fact, um, while he was still with *The Partridge Family*, uh, "I Think I Love You".'

BEHIND THE SCENES
At a time when British films succeeding internationally were almost exclusively handsome literary adaptations, along came this surprising contemporary romantic comedy. Director Mike Newell's films had met with mixed fortunes, although his period romance *Enchanted April* (1992) had tickled US critics and become a surprise art-house hit in America. *Four Weddings* was a production of modest ambition and expectations, with the cast accordingly contracted at humble British scale (about £65,000 in Hugh Grant's case). But standing out in a good ensemble turned out to be a career rocket launcher for Grant, Kristin Scott Thomas and John Hannah (as Matthew, with his show-stopping turn at the funeral reciting W. H. Auden's 'Funeral Blues': 'Stop all the clocks, cut off the telephone …').

Dir: Jerry ZUCKER / USA
Released in Britain: 1990
Running Time: 127 minutes
Colour: Technicolor
Estimated Attendance: 8.78 million

Comedy, fantasy, suspense and, above all, romance were fused seamlessly in *Ghost*, which became the most popular film of 1990 at UK cinemas. The appeal of Patrick Swayze, Demi Moore and Whoopi Goldberg may have dimmed in the intervening years, but the lure of that potter's wheel remains just as strong.

GHOST

Director **Jerry Zucker**
Producers **Howard W. Koch, Lisa Weinstein**
Screenplay **Bruce Joel Rubin**
Director of Photography **Adam Greenberg**
Editor **Walter Murch**
Production Designer **Jane Musky**
Music **Maurice Jarre**

Sam Wheat • Patrick Swayze
Molly Jensen • Demi Moore
Carl Bruner • Tony Goldwyn
Oda Mae Brown • Whoopi Goldberg
1st Elevator Man • Stanley Lawrence
2nd Elevator Man • Christopher J. Keene
Susan • Susan Breslau
Rose • Martina Degnan
1st Mover • Richard Kleber
2nd Mover • Macka Foley
Willie Lopez • Rick Aviles
Emergency Room Ghost • Phil Leeds
Surgeon • John Hugh
Minister • Sam Tsoutsouvas
Cemetery Ghost • Sharon Cornell
Subway Ghost • Vincent Schiavelli
Rosa Santiago • Angelina Estrada
Oda Mae's 1st Sister • Armelia McQueen
Oda Mae's 2nd Sister • Gail Boggs
Workman in Loft • Thom Curley

Opposite above *'You relax, you're the dead guy': Oda Mae Brown (Whoopi Goldberg) channelling Sam Wheat (Patrick Swayze)*
Opposite below *Look into my eyes: Sam Wheat works his mind magic on the cat*
Overleaf *Attendances at pottery classes soared overnight*

THE STORY

Sam Wheat, a banker, is killed by a mugger. Appalled to find himself dead but still sentient, Sam rushes to the apartment, only to realise that his grieving girlfriend Molly – fending off tentative advances from Sam's friend Carl – can neither see nor hear him. Unable to intervene physically when the same mugger invades the apartment, Sam manages to galvanise the cat into scaring the intruder away. Following the mugger, Willie Lopez, Sam overhears his telephone call to someone who had hired him. Sam impulsively interrupts fake medium Oda Mae Brown in a seance, and realises that she can hear him. The incredulous Oda Mae is badgered into visiting Molly and 'interpreting' while Sam warns her to seek police protection from Lopez. Molly consults Carl, who offers to look into it himself. Following Carl, who orders Lopez to silence Oda Mae, Sam discovers that Carl is manipulating the bank's records to launder the finance for a drugs deal, and that what he is looking for is a computer code in Sam's possession.

Going to the police anyway, Molly begins to place her trust in Carl, her confidence shaken by the information that Lopez has no record while Oda Mae has a long history of confidence trickery. Sam forces another ghost to teach him how to intervene physically in human affairs. Hurrying with Oda Mae to the apartment to protect Molly, Sam finds that he can communicate directly with her, using Oda Mae's body as a medium. When Carl arrives, Sam manages to fight him off until he is killed by a shard of broken glass. Before Sam moves on, he and Molly reaffirm their love.

WHAT THEY SAID THEN ...

From its intriguing opening credits onwards, *Ghost* is an object lesson in how to breathe new life into moribund material. But the masterstroke comes some way into the action, with the introduction of Whoopi Goldberg, perfectly cast as the very human, very fallible agency through which a mere amour achieves the status of amour fou. There are flaws. The last sight of a golden-haloed

Sam disappearing into a horizon of blinding light is too Disneyish by half; and the villain is obvious from the off. Otherwise, the unusual blend of horror, comedy and high romance is skilfully managed.

WHAT THEY SAY NOW ...

1990 was a disconcerting year for romantics. In *Pretty Woman*, impressionable young girls in the audience learned that the surest way to find Prince Charming was to become a Beverly Hills streetwalker and wait for that stretch limousine to pull over to the kerb. And in *Ghost*, true love straddled the boundaries of mortality, with Patrick Swayze and Demi Moore getting all misty-eyed about one another, despite a minor obstacle: one of them no longer had a pulse. (And no, that's not a slight on Moore's acting ability. Though it could be.)

Jerry Zucker did a good job of handling his first 'straight' movie after co-directing wacky comedies like *Airplane!* (1980) and *The Naked Gun* (1988). And though *Ghost* is pure poppycock, it's done with enough sincerity and professionalism to have retained most of its appeal today. That said, the proxy-lesbian three-way love scene, with Swayze using Whoopi Goldberg as his 'vessel' during a tryst-from-beyond-the-grave with Moore, will always be too weird for words.

SCENE STEALER

When Patrick Swayze joined Demi Moore at the potter's wheel, they had something on their minds other than bashing out a nice vase. To the accompaniment of the Righteous Brothers' 'Unchained Melody', they got awfully messy – and attendance at pottery classes soared overnight.

AT THE TYPEWRITER

The screenwriter Bruce Joel Rubin has mortality on the brain, and in every line he writes. In *Ghost*, the dead hero must help indict his own murderer before progressing to a peaceful hereafter; in *Jacob's Ladder* (1990), the hero (Tim Robbins) must make peace with his demons before being freed from limbo; and in *My Life* (1993), for which Rubin directed his own script, a man (Michael Keaton) comes to terms with his impending death by making a video for his unborn son. What a relief that Rubin failed to shoehorn such issues into his screenplay for the children's adventure *Stuart Little 2* (2002).

OSCARS
5 nominations, **2 winners**

Best Picture
Actress in a Supporting Role: Whoopi Goldberg
Film Editing: Walter Murch
Music (Original Score): Maurice Jarre
Writing (Screenplay Written Directly for the Screen): Bruce Joel Rubin

WHAT WON THAT YEAR?
Best Picture: *Dances With Wolves*
Directing: Kevin Costner *Dances With Wolves*
Actor in a Leading Role: Jeremy Irons *Reversal of Fortune*
Actress in a Leading Role: Kathy Bates *Misery*

BAFTAS
4 nominations, **1 winner**

Original Screenplay: Bruce Joel Rubin
Actress in a Supporting Role: Whoopi Goldberg
Achievement in Special Visual Effects
Make Up Artist: Ben Nye Junior

WHAT WON THAT YEAR?
Film: *Goodfellas*
Achievement in Direction: Martin Scorsese *Goodfellas*
Actor in a Leading Role: Philippe Noiret *Cinema Paradiso*
Actress in a Leading Role: Jessica Tandy *Driving Miss Daisy*

79

Dir: Richard CURTIS / UK, USA, France
Released in Britain: 2003
Running Time: 135 minutes
Colour: Deluxe
Estimated Attendance: 8.76 million

Audiences fell for *Love Actually* when it opened just before Christmas 2003; the writer Richard Curtis had earned the public's goodwill with scripts like *Four Weddings and a Funeral* (1994) and *Notting Hill* (1999). But some wondered if he had bitten off more than he could chew by opting to direct for the first time.

LOVE ACTUALLY

Director **Richard Curtis**
Producers **Tim Bevan, Eric Fellner,**
   Duncan Kenworthy
Screenplay **Richard Curtis**
Director of Photography **Michael Coulter**
Editor **Nick Moore**
Production Designer **Jim Clay**
Music **Craig Armstrong**

Harry • Alan Rickman
Billy Mack • Bill Nighy
Jamie • Colin Firth
Karen • Emma Thompson
David, The Prime Minister • Hugh Grant
Sarah • Laura Linney
Daniel • Liam Neeson
Natalie • Martine McCutcheon
Mark • Andrew Lincoln
Peter • Chiwetel Ejiofor
Joe • Gregor Fisher
Mia • Heike Makatsch
Juliet • Keira Knightley
Colin Frissell • Kristopher Marshall
Aurelia • Lucia Moniz
John • Martin Freeman
Karl • Rodrigo Santoro
Sam • Thomas Sangster
Rufus, Jewellery Salesman • Rowan Atkinson
Engineer • Rory MacGregor

THE STORY

In London, Britain's newly elected bachelor Prime Minister, David, is attracted to tea lady Natalie, and eventually declares his love for her. Fading pop star Billy Mack has a Christmas hit with a tacky single. Recently widowed Daniel struggles to connect with his 11-year-old stepson Sam, who has a crush on an American classmate; with Daniel's encouragement Sam learns the drums to impress her before dashing to Heathrow to declare his love before she leaves. Office manager Harry is seduced by his secretary. He buys her a necklace, which his wife Karen finds and thinks is for her; when she doesn't receive it she realises the situation but forgives Harry. Sarah, one of Harry's staff, has a long-standing crush on a colleague but is unable to pursue his advances because of her commitment to her mentally ill brother.

   Writer Jamie retreats to his French cottage after being jilted and falls for his Portuguese cleaner Aurelia, to whom he successfully proposes marriage. Mark does not get on with his best friend Peter's new wife Juliet; he turns out to be in love with her. Catering assistant Colin intends to go to the US to find a girlfriend; he buys a ticket to Milwaukee and within hours of landing has been picked up by three sexy girls. Two movie-set stand-ins become friendly while posing nude together and end up arranging a date. Most of the stories end at a school nativity play in south London and then at Heathrow Airport.

WHAT THEY SAY ...

Whereas previous Richard Curtis screenplays were each constructed around one blossoming relationship, Curtis has chosen for his directorial debut to juggle eight or nine plots. Instead of variations in tone, however, these strands and their characters all display the self-deprecatory affability established in Curtis's previous work; the familiarity is compounded by Hugh Grant, Emma Thompson and Colin Firth effectively reprising earlier roles. If Robert Altman's finest work – the obvious model for such multistranded parallel storytelling – convinces us

OSCARS

WHAT WON THAT YEAR?
Best Picture: *The Lord of the Rings: The Return of the King*
Directing: Peter Jackson *The Lord of the Rings: The Return of the King*
Actor in a Leading Role: Sean Penn *Mystic River*
Actress in a Leading Role: Charlize Theron *Monster*

BAFTAS

3 nominations, **1 winner**

Alexander Korda Award for the Outstanding British Film
Actor in a Supporting Role: Bill Nighy
Actress in a Supporting Role: Emma Thompson

WHAT WON THAT YEAR?
Film: *The Lord of the Rings: The Return of the King*
David Lean Award for Achievement in Direction: Peter Weir
Master and Commander: The Far Side of the World
Actor in a Leading Role: Bill Murray *Lost in Translation*
Actress in a Leading Role: Scarlett Johansson *Lost in Translation*

Far left Saying it with boards: Mark (Andrew Lincoln) declares his love
Left Natalie, the Number 10 tea lady (Martine McCutcheon) **Below** 'Love is all around': Billy Mack (Bill Nighy) and showgirls

we are eavesdropping on lived lives, here the pat dialogue and situations make engagement a real challenge.

Such vapidity is particularly damaging in a film that asks us to take seriously its presentation of love; the prologue even invokes the text and phone messages sent from victims stranded in the Twin Towers of the World Trade Center. Yet without two plausible human beings to rub together *Love Actually* can only present a succession of formulaic Mills & Boon gestures, unsubstantiated emblems of passion that the audience is expected to indulge. When Laura Linney's office worker Sarah takes to the dance floor with the object of her affections, for example, the music cuts, mid-track, to a slow song. The elision of the actual substance of romance that should underpin this moment illustrates the film's approach: cut to the smooch.

It is not simply that the characters' romantic feelings are unconvincing; often they barely know one another. The protagonists here don't so much declare love as confess crushes. Accordingly, the conclusion – a long parade of publicly staged embraces – has the unwelcome tinge of sentimental porn; the only chance of engaging with these empty gestures is to use them as springboards for one's own memories. Many of the storylines converge at Heathrow Airport, and the setting is apt given the film's confused transatlanticism. Curtis's scenic Thames shots seem to be his picture-postcard love letters to the US audiences his films have always aspired to impress. That is by far the most convincing courtship *Love Actually* has to offer.

IN THE CHAIR

Richard Curtis carved out an impressive writing career in television and theatre (mostly working with Rowan Atkinson on projects including the long-running and much-loved *Blackadder* series (1983–89)) before graduating to film with the pleasingly shambolic *The Tall Guy* (1989). But the huge success of his subsequent work, all of which appears on *The Ultimate Film* list except for *Bean* (1997), seemed to convince him that he could cut it as a director. *Love Actually* proved him wrong. It is to be hoped that he returns to the typewriter until he has learned that directing film amounts to more than just the unscrupulous pushing of emotional buttons – a technique that he has put to more productive use in his work for Comic Relief and Live8.

80

Dir: Lewis GILBERT / UK
Released in Britain: 1956
Running Time: 135 minutes
Black and white
Estimated Attendance: 8.7 million

The life story of Douglas Bader provided 1950s audiences with another opportunity to rehearse their patriotism, with the war just over a decade behind them. Some 50 years on from the release of *Reach For the Sky*, the film remains part of the fabric of post-war British cinema.

REACH FOR THE SKY

Director **Lewis Gilbert**
Producer **Daniel M. Angel**
Screenplay **Lewis Gilbert**, based on the book by
    Paul Brickhill
Director of Photography **Jack Asher**
Editor **John Shirley**
Art Director **Bernard Robinson**
Music **John Addison**

Douglas Bader • Kenneth More
Thelma Edwards Bader • Muriel Pavlow
Johnny Sanderson • Lyndon Brook
Stan Turner • Lee Patterson
Mr Joyce • Alexander Knox
Nurse Sally Brace • Dorothy Alison
Harry Day • Michael Warre
Robert Desoutter • Sydney Tafler
'Woody' Woodhall • Howard Marion-Crawford
Peel • Jack Watling
Air Vice-Marshal Halahan • Walter Hudd
Wing Commander Beiseigel • Ernest Clark
Streatfeild • Nigel Green
Sister Thornhill • Anne Leon
Air Chief Marshal Sir Hugh Dowding • Charles Carson
Air Vice-Marshal Leigh-Mallory • Ronald Adam
Crowley-Milling • Basil Appleby
Police Constable • Philip Stainton
Flight Sergeant Mills • Eddie Byrne
Sally • Beverly Brooks

THE STORY

As a young man, Douglas Bader is passionately devoted to flying. A promising career is tragically interrupted in December 1931, when a serious air accident necessitates the amputation of both his legs. Determined to live a normal life, Bader learns to walk again on artificial limbs and proves his independence by flying at the Central Flying School. He marries Thelma, a young girl he meets at a country restaurant, but suffers a temporary setback when he is grounded because regulations do not provide for a man without legs.

A monotonous civilian job is terminated by the war and Bader finds himself wanted again. His skill and powers of leadership are fully utilised in the Battle of Britain, during which he leads five squadrons of aircraft. An accident forces him to bale out, however, and he is taken prisoner. Numerous attempts at escape so enrage the Germans that, as a final resort, he is sent to Colditz. His desire for a 'last fling' at the enemy is thwarted by the end of the European war, but a moment of triumph comes in September 1945, when the victory air parade over London is led, in a Battle of Britain Spitfire, by Wing Commander Douglas Bader, D.S.O., D.F.C.

WHAT THEY SAID THEN …

A story of great human fortitude such as this can hardly fail to impress, and the integrity of the film's tribute to Douglas Bader cannot be doubted. However, good intentions are not quite enough. Lewis Gilbert's script and direction appear too dispassionate, too eager to exploit the easy laugh. Also, the attempt to combine a closely documented biography with an action-packed war story (involving some variable and complex special effects) drags out the narrative to an inordinate length.

More seriously, the central figure of Bader himself – apparently an indomitable, often irascible, personality – has been conventionalised into a slangy, headstrong British air ace and is played here, very conscientiously, by Kenneth More with his customary easy charm. But, lacking strong directorial moulding, the character rarely becomes fully or richly alive and it is only in the early scenes (such as Bader's first painful experiments with his artificial legs) that we are made to feel a genuine emotional involvement with a real person.

WHAT THEY SAY NOW ...

Kenneth More now seems to embody the values of the 1950s middle-class audiences who flocked to see his pictures. As war hero Douglas Bader, he is as Kenny More-ish as ever: hearty, bombastic, back-slapping, full of vaguely violent common-room bonhomie. He rides pillion on a motorcycle with a gang of drunken RAF recruits. He triumphs on the cricket field, rushing about with a lock of hair lapping at his wide forehead. He twinkles with insolent humour as he is upbraided by superior officers. But just as in *A Night to Remember* (1958) or *Raising a Riot* (1955), the plot conspires to kick seven shades of self-satisfaction out of him. Bader's story, of course, comes complete with a cruel reversal – an air accident which leaves him paraplegic. And from this moment in the narrative, More's trademark bloody-mindedness is more than just a form of cocky charm – it is the means of his recuperation, his success in the Battle of Britain, and his escape attempts as a prisoner of war.

CLASSIC QUOTE

Nazi officer (to Bader, after a daring escape from hospital): 'We are going to take away your legs until we are safely in the camp in Germany.'

SCENE STEALER

Determined to walk again, Bader ushers away the medical orderlies who have been helping him complete his first steps on his artificial legs. As he lurches forward, Gilbert cuts to a viewpoint from behind a set of support bars: a pair of crutches is leaning against them. More falls towards the bars, but his face is a mask of triumph: 'You know what you can do with your sticks now!'

BEHIND THE SCENES

Producer Daniel M. Angel had a personal interest in this story of disability overcome: while serving as a British soldier in Burma he contracted polio, which robbed him of the use of his legs. Shooting began initially with Richard Burton in the role of Douglas Bader. Burton pulled out of the film, forcing Gilbert to recast.

Top left Douglas Bader (Kenneth More) battles to walk again **Above left** Kenneth More replaced Richard Burton after early shooting

OSCARS

WHAT WON THAT YEAR?
Best Motion Picture: *Around the World in 80 Days*
Directing: George Stevens *Giant*
Actor: Yul Brynner *The King and I*
Actress: Ingrid Bergman *Anastasia*

BAFTAS
4 nominations, **1 winner**

British Film
British Actor: Kenneth More
British Actress: Dorothy Allison
British Screenplay: Lewis Gilbert

WHAT WON THAT YEAR?
Film: *Gervaise*
Foreign Actor: François Perier *Gervaise*
Foreign Actress: Anna Magnani *The Rose Tattoo*

Animation had been

around almost from the very beginning of cinema and, at the hands of such superb pioneers as Winsor McCay, Max Fleischer and, of course, Walt Disney, had proved a crowd-pleasing spectacle for cinema audiences. So it is surprising that it was not until 1937, well into the sound film era, that the first full-length cartoon film appeared. Yet for Disney it was a costly gamble, tying up his studio and hundreds of craftsmen who might otherwise have been engaged on profitable short subjects. *Snow White and the Seven Dwarfs* (1937) was a watershed in animation: to make it, ground-breaking techniques had to be invented, illuminating the way for countless features ever

since, most produced by Disney, among them *Fantasia* (1941), *Dumbo* (1941) and *Bambi* (1942).

Other studios, particularly Warner with *Bugs Bunny* and MGM with *Tom and Jerry*, had developed their own short-subject production lines and, as television viewing escalated and old filmgoing habits and programming died, skills were transferred to the new medium (and lost along the way, since the voracious appetite of that new medium led to some diminished quality).

Apart from the occasional full-length Disney feature, animation on the big screen felt like rather a missed opportunity, at least until the late 1980s when *Who Framed Roger Rabbit* (1988) and *The Little*

Mermaid (1989) seemed to rekindle old delights. A new burst of animated features followed, and in recent times some of the most innovative have come from non-English-speaking markets: *Belleville Rendezvous* (2002) from France, or the likes of *Akira* (1988) and *Spirited Away* (2002) from Japan.

Opposite above Mickey Mouse made an early appearance in Steamboat Willie *in 1928, but Disney's first full length feature wasn't until 1937* **Opposite below** *A scene from Disney's* Fantasia *(1941)* **Above from top** Akira, *one of the innovative animes from Japan; Bob Hoskins and Jessica Rabbit rekindling old delights; the ogre* Shrek *won DreamWorks the inaugural Academy Award for animation in 2001*

The most important development, however, was that of computer-generated imagery (CGI), initially used to create extraordinary special effects in films such as *Terminator 2: Judgement Day* (1991) and *Jurassic Park* (1993). Disney collaborated with Pixar to produce *Toy Story* (1995), the first feature wholly created by CGI, and an outstanding hit. *A Bug's Life* (1998) and *Toy Story 2* (1999) followed but Disney was at last to encounter powerful competition from other producers, especially DreamWorks, whose *Shrek* (2001) lit up the box office. Pixar's massive 2004 hit *The Incredibles* took the technique to new heights.

For a while it was as though the traditional cel-based principle of animated films would become extinct in the new age of computers, but it is too soon for obituaries. Attempts to make apparent live-action films entirely by CGI have not been entirely successful, and at best CGI characters in films such as the *Star Wars* series (the much-despised Jar Jar Binks is an example) have been neutrally received.

More promising is the notion of live actors performing against entirely animated backgrounds, and an interesting experiment in this area was *Sky Captain and the World of Tomorrow* (2004) in which the cast acted against blue-screen throughout, evoking a fantasy spectacle that would have been way beyond the budget of a conventional film.

The ultimate recognition of animation, not just as a genre but as a method of film-making in its own right, came in 2001, with the inauguration of a special Academy Award for animation, won in that first year by *Shrek*.

81

Dir: George CUKOR / USA
Released in Britain: 1965
Running Time: 172 minutes
Colour: Deluxe
Estimated Attendance: 8.6 million

Musicals are well represented on *The Ultimate Film* list, and *My Fair Lady* is one of the best loved. But despite a winning performance by Audrey Hepburn, and an Oscar-winning one by Rex Harrison, not all the critics of the day were won over by the charms of Eliza Doolittle.

MY FAIR LADY

Director **George Cukor**
Producer **Jack L. Warner**
Screenplay **Alan Jay Lerner**, based on the musical
   play by Alan Jay Lerner and Frederick Loewe,
   based on the play *Pygmalion* by George Bernard Shaw
Director of Photography **Harry Stradling**
Editor **William Ziegler**
Production Designer **Cecil Beaton**
Music **Frederick Loewe**

Eliza Doolittle • Audrey Hepburn
Professor Henry Higgins • Rex Harrison
Alfred P. Doolittle • Stanley Holloway
Colonel Hugh Pickering • Wilfrid Hyde-White
Mrs Higgins • Gladys Cooper
Freddie Eynsford-Hill • Jeremy Brett
Zoltan Karpathy • Theodore Bikel
Mrs Pearce • Mona Wasbourne
Mrs Eynsford-Hill • Isobel Elsom
Butler • John Holland
Jamie, Doolittle's Crony • John Alderson
Harry, Doolittle's Crony • John McLiam

THE STORY

A wet evening in 1912. Outside Covent Garden Opera House, Henry Higgins, professor of phonetics, is lurking with his notebook. He gets involved in an altercation with Eliza Doolittle, the flower girl whose Cockney accent he has been recording. Peace is made with the help of Colonel Pickering, late of the Indian Army, in whom Higgins is delighted to recognise a fellow enthusiast for language. Within earshot of Eliza, Higgins boasts to Pickering that he could pass her off as a duchess or shop assistant. Next morning, Eliza turns up at his Wimpole Street house, prepared to pay a shilling a lesson towards her goal of a place in a shop. But Higgins is in the grip of a grander dream, and with Pickering's help he sets about the total transformation of Eliza.

Her first public appearance, at his mother's box at Ascot, is a decidedly qualified success. Within months, however, Eliza is the rage of the season's grandest party. Returning from their triumph, Higgins and Pickering congratulate each other, and entirely ignore Eliza, who turns to Freddie Eynsford-Hill, her constant admirer. Eliza goes back to Covent Garden, to find her dustman father sinking into marriage and middle-class morality. She takes refuge with Mrs Higgins. There, Professor Higgins quarrels with her, admiring her new-found independence but still cherishing his own. Gloomily, however, he realises that he can't any longer manage without her: he has gone home, and is playing over his speech recordings of Eliza unregenerate, when she slips quietly into the room.

WHAT THEY SAID THEN ...

In one sense, it must all have been very easy: with the range of talent, taste and sheer professionalism at work, from Shaw onwards, Warners could hardly have made a film that would do less than please most of the people most of the time. Its $17 million investment looks as safe as houses. In another sense, however, George Cukor was taking on quite a job, since merely to put the stage musical safely, tastefully and even charmingly on to the screen was not quite enough. The task was to re-create it as a film. Cukor, who has achieved this in the past

with so many adaptations, here directs with great care for the values of Shaw, Beaton and Lerner and Loewe, but a rather unnecessary circumspection.

Scenes move at a steady, even pace, as though every word were worth its weight in gold (perhaps, in view of the price paid for the rights, it very nearly was). The décor tends to inhibit rather than to release the film. Cecil Beaton scores delightful effects – the stylised Ascot of black and white and grey, with even the grass faded to a silvery green; the pale blue and white of Mrs Higgins's room. You feel, however, that Beaton thinks in terms of the held stage picture, rather than the fleeting screen image. It is only in a couple of flashes during Stanley Holloway's rumbustious 'Get Me To The Church On Time' that colour comes into its own as more than a pretty adjunct to decoration. Generally, effects tend to be flat and fussy rather than light and liberating.

A stylised Ascot, but with real horses, and a stereophonic impression less of hooves than of a passing underground train; a stage Covent Garden, with road-menders and a suffragette band in attendance; 'The Street Where You Live' framed through out-of-focus window boxes – there is no stylistic coherence to hold it all together. What almost does this trick, however, is Rex Harrison's domineering, cantankerous Higgins, a performance definitive in its intelligence, bullying charm, and relish of every Shavian insult.

Audrey Hepburn can't manage the guttersnipe, and she is not the first Eliza to give the impression that it's the Cockney that has been learned from an

Above 'Wouldn't it be Lovely': Eliza Doolittle (Audrey Hepburn) with Stanley Holloway as her father *Below* Audrey Hepburn, in costume for the famous Ascot sequence, chats to designer Cecil Beaton *Overleaf* Before and after: Eliza is transformed by Higgins

OSCARS
12 nominations, **8 winners**

Best Picture
Directing: George Cukor
Actor: Rex Harrison
Actor in a Supporting Role: Stanley Holloway
Actress in a Supporting Role: Gladys Cooper
Art Direction/Set Decoration (Color): Gene Allen, Cecil Beaton,
  George James Hopkins
Cinematography (Color): Harry Stradling
Costume Design (Color): Cecil Beaton
Film Editing: William Ziegler
Music (Scoring of Music): André Previn
Sound: George R. Groves
Writing (Screenplay Based on Material From Another Medium):
  Alan Jay Lerner

WHAT WON THAT YEAR?
Actress: Julie Andrews *Mary Poppins*

BAFTAS
2 nominations, **1 winner**

Film
British Actor: Rex Harrison

WHAT WON THAT YEAR?
British Film: *The Ipcress File*
British Actor: Dirk Bogarde *Darling*
British Actress: Julie Christie *Darling*
Foreign Actor: Lee Marvin *The Killers/Cat Ballou*
Foreign Actress: Patricia Neal *In Harm's way*

elocutionist. But from the tea-table dialogue, done with deadpan precision so that every awful word strikes home, she takes a firm hold on the part. The actress has to make an impossible transition work, and Hepburn's fragile triumph and disconsolate rage are very touching. The score holds its appeal, in spite of some tinniness when the sound is at its most stereophonic. Ascot and the Embassy ball are as grand as they come, and Gladys Cooper and Stanley Holloway nobly represent the different ends of the social scale. Taste and money can go no further. Talent – and especially these talents – might have done.

WHAT THEY SAY NOW ...

With Rex Harrison repeating his Broadway role, together with Stanley Holloway as Alfred Doolittle, the dustman father of Eliza, the monumental hit stage musical was a sure-fire hit on screen. George Cukor's direction, Cecil Beaton's sumptous and striking Edwardian costumes, and André Previn's arrangements of the Lerner-Loewe score propelled the film to 12 Oscar nominations. Missing from the list was the lead, Audrey Hepburn, who had been awarded the role in defiance of the theatrical success of Julie Andrews. Officially Hepburn was cast because Andrews was untried on film. She made *Mary Poppins* (1964) for Disney as her debut instead, and won the Academy Award. Hepburn's beauty and screen presence notwithstanding, her singing voice was unimpressive and she was dubbed almost entirely by Marni Nixon. It is believed that Rex Harrison, who grew accustomed to being upstaged every night by Julie Andrews, helped to block her casting.

CLASSIC QUOTE

Shaw's Eliza shocked theatregoers in 1914 by saying, 'Not bloody likely'. Too tame for 1964. Filmgoers heard Eliza in her Ascot finery yelling at a horse: 'Come on Dover, move yer bloomin' arse!'

SCENE STEALER

So many great moments, but among the best is the triumphant jig that Higgins and Colonel Pickering (Wilfrid Hyde-White) dance around Eliza as she perfectly enunciates 'The rain in Spain stays mainly in the plain' ('By George, she's got it!').

IN THE CHAIR

George Cukor, a distinguished veteran who had directed films with Katharine Hepburn, Jean Harlow, Joan Crawford, Judy Garland and Judy Holliday, won his only Oscar for *My Fair Lady*. He expended energy rebutting the label 'women's director', yet in truth there was probably none better.

Top left Rex Harrison as latterday Pygmalion Henry Higgins *Above left* 'By George, she's got it!' Eliza celebrates her transformation with Higgins and Colonel Pickering (Wilfrid Hyde-White)

Dir: Lee TAMAHORI / UK, USA
Released in Britain: 2002
Running Time: 133 minutes
Estimated Attendance: 8.58 million

Left *'Shaken, not stirred': Bond (Pierce Brosnan) enjoys his trademark martini*

When Pierce Brosnan took over as James Bond in 1995's *GoldenEye*, his smouldering elegance and wry humour harked back to the glory years of Connery. The series has been in rude health ever since, but only one of Brosnan's outings – released on the 40th anniversary of the Bond series – makes the list.

DIE ANOTHER DAY

Director **Lee Tamahori**
Producers **Michael Wilson, Barbara Broccoli**
Screenplay **Neal Purvis, Robert Wade**
Director of Photography **David Tattersall**
Editors **Christian Wagner, Andrew MacRitchie**
Production Designer **Peter Lamont**
Music **David Arnold**

James Bond • Pierce Brosnan
Jinx • Halle Berry
Gustav Graves • Toby Stephens
Miranda Frost • Rosamund Pike
Zao • Rick Yune
General Moon • Kenneth Tsang Kong
Colonel Moon • Will Yun Lee
Raoul • Emilio Echevarría
Moneypenny • Samantha Bond
Charles Robinson • Colin Salmon
Vlad • Michael Gorevoy
Mr Kil • Lawrence Makoare
Q • John Cleese
M • Judi Dench
Falco • Michael Madsen
Snooty Desk Clerk • Ben Wee
Hotel Manager • Ho Yi
Peaceful • Rachel Grant
Creep • Ian Pirie
Dr Alvarez • Simon Andreu

THE STORY

James Bond surfs into the demilitarised zone between North and South Korea. There, the renegade North Korean Colonel Moon is laundering diamonds to buy arms. Bond disrupts Moon's operations, maiming his henchman Zao. Pursuing Bond on a hovercraft, Moon plunges over a cliff and is seemingly killed. Imprisoned by the North Korean authorities, Bond is tortured for over a year before being released in exchange for Zao, recently captured in the West.

Bond has his licence to kill revoked by his superior M, who suspects him of disclosing secrets. Determined to clear his name, Bond escapes to Cuba in search of Zao, whom he locates at a clinic undergoing treatment to change the way he looks. Bond hooks up with American agent Jinx, who is also on Zao's trail.

Reassigned the case by M, Bond is introduced to flamboyant businessman Gustav Graves, who is suspected of dealing in Moon's diamonds. Graves invites Bond to a party in an ice palace in Iceland. There Bond meets Jinx, who is also investigating Graves, and sees the unveiling of Graves's 'Icarus' project: a satellite that directs solar rays onto targets on Earth. After killing Zao, Bond rescues Jinx from the melting ice palace. The two agents sneak on board Graves's departing plane, which takes them into North Korean airspace. There Graves reveals that he is actually Colonel Moon, having changed his appearance in the Cuban clinic, and directs Icarus to set off mines in the demilitarised zone to demonstrate North Korean might. Bond kills Graves and disables Icarus.

WHAT THEY SAY ...

Celebrating the 40th anniversary of the 'official' 007 series, *Die Another Day* has been briefed to include nods to all the earlier Bonds. Perhaps the most significant is the discovery of the jet-pack from *Thunderball* (1965) in Q's arsenal, which prompts Bond to muse of the gadget, and perhaps the whole formula, 'Does this old thing still work?' Demonstrating that the film-makers aren't entirely confident of the answer, the echoes of earlier films are stirred into a remixer and overlaid with ironies. State-of-the-art gimmicks try to drag a hero into a future

OSCARS

WHAT WON THAT YEAR?
Best Picture: *Chicago*
Directing: Roman Polanski *The Pianist*
Actor in a Leading Role: Adrien Brody *The Pianist*
Actress in a Leading Role: Nicole Kidman *The Hours*

BAFTAS

WHAT WON THAT YEAR?
Film: *The Pianist*
Alexander Korda Award for Outstanding British Film:
   The Warrior
David Lean Award for Achievement in Direction:
   Roman Polanski *The Pianist*
Performance by an Actor in a Leading Role:
   Daniel Day-Lewis *Gangs of New York*
Performance by an Actress in a Leading Role:
   Nicole Kidman *The Hours*

where he has to compete with *xXx* (2002), *Austin Powers* (1997, 1999, 2002) and *The Matrix* (1999). When CG ice palaces and planes flying into death rays dominate, we have cause to wonder, like Bond, whether this old thing will work much longer.

Times have changed, and the series does a fair job of changing with them. When Halle Berry's Jinx erupts in slow motion from the Cuban surf in an echo of Ursula Andress in *Dr No* (1962), we are presented not with a Nordic sex goddess but with a woman fully qualified to be Bond's partner. Besides being a bedmate, Jinx serves the plot function fulfilled in previous films by Bond's CIA buddy Felix Leiter. The *Goldfinger* (1964) laser-torture reference is deployed against the heroine rather than the hero, and she is at least as capable as he when it comes to getting out of trouble – Berry's best action is a stunning backwards dive away from her pursuers.

But the most interesting moments direct the attention back where it ought to be: on Bond himself. Pierce Brosnan's spy goes beyond even the angst Timothy Dalton brought to the role by being clapped into a Korean hellhole for over a year and tortured by a silent Asian woman who favours alternating doses of scorpion venom and antidote (a touch Ian Fleming might have liked). Escaping from his own boss (M 'disavows' him on the assumption he has talked), Bond shambles bare-chested, full-bearded and in pyjamas into the Hong Kong Yacht Club. There, he is greeted by an obsequious manager who treats him with all the deference accorded Sean Connery as he strolled into tropical hotels back when pre-package-holiday UK audiences found Bond's travel habits as beyond their means as his tastes in liquor and women.

BEHIND THE SCENES

Madonna, who sings the title song, makes a cameo appearance as a fencing instructor.

IN THE CHAIR

New Zealander Lee Tamahori first attracted attention with the fierce drama *Once Were Warriors* (1994), about a Maori family headed by a brutal patriarch. Following that film's success, he did an efficient job directing Hollywood thrillers such as *The Edge* (1997) and *Along Came a Spider* (2001), none of which displayed the urgency of the picture that made his name.

Above left *Verity (Madonna): 'I see you handle your weapon well.' Bond: 'I have been known to keep my tip up.' Gustav Graves (Toby Stephens), Miranda Frost (Rosamund Pike) and Bond receive instruction on the noble art of fencing* ***Below*** *Jinx (Halle Berry) in* that *bikini*

Dir: George LUCAS / USA
Released in Britain: 2005
Running Time: 139 minutes
Colour: Deluxe
Estimated Attendance: 8.57 million

The final *Star Wars* movie clocked up almost nine million UK admissions in less than two months, thereby ensuring that every episode figures in the Ultimate Film top 100. And while the dialogue still betrayed George Lucas's cloth ear, his eye for spectacle was in evidence once again.

STAR WARS EPISODE III: REVENGE OF THE SITH

Director **George Lucas**
Producer **Rick McCallum**
Screenplay **George Lucas**
Director of Photography **David Tattersall**
Editors **Roger Barton, Ben Burtt**
Production Designer **Gavin Bocquet**
Music **John Williams**

Obi-Wan Kenobi • Ewan McGregor
Senator Padmé Amidala • Natalie Portman
Anakin Skywalker • Hayden Christensen
Supreme Chancillor Palpatine • Ian McDiarmid
Yoda • Frank Oz
Senator Bail Organa • Jimmy Smits
Chewbacca • Peter Mayhew
Jar Jar Binks • Ahmed Best
Sio Bibble • Oliver Ford Davies
Commander Cody • Temuera Morrison
C-3PO • Anthony Daniels
R2-D2 • Kenny Baker
Ki-Adi-Mundi/Nute Gunray • Silas Carson
Jedi Knight Mace Windu • Samuel L. Jackson
Count Dooku • Christopher Lee
Queen of Naboo • Keisha Castle-Hughes
Captain Typho • Jay Laga'aia
Tion Medon • Bruce Spence
Governor Tarkin • Wayne Pygram
Mas Amedda • David Bowers

Top *The man behind the mask: Anakin Skywalker (Hayden Christensen), barely alive, is reborn as Darth Vadar*

THE STORY

Supreme Chancellor Palpatine has apparently been kidnapped by the droid General Grievous and Count Dooku – but Palpatine is also Darth Sidious, a Sith lord who keeps the Clone Wars going to serve his own ends. Anakin Skywalker and Obi-Wan Kenobi effect a rescue mission and save Palpatine. Urged on by Palpatine, Anakin overcomes his conscience and executes the unarmed Dooku, unseen by Obi-Wan.

Anakin is secretly married to Padmé, Queen of Naboo. When she tells him she is pregnant, he has visions of her dying in childbirth. While the Republic continues its battles with Grievous and the separatists, an enmity grows between Palpatine and the suspicious Jedi Council, each of whom pressures Anakin to spy on the other. Palpatine tells Anakin that followers of the Sith can confer immortality onto their loved ones. Palpatine persuades Anakin to pledge allegiance to the Dark Side and confers upon him the name Lord Vader.

After Vader wipes out the separatists, Palpatine abandons democracy, transforming the Republic into the First Galactic Empire with himself as Emperor. He institutes a programme of assassinations in an attempt to wipe out the entire Jedi Council. As the Emperor battles with Yoda, Obi-Wan duels with Vader on Mustafar, a planet rife with volcanic upheavals. Vader is horribly injured. Obi-Wan flees with Padmé, who is so distressed that she dies – after giving birth to twins she names Luke and Leia. Leia is adopted by Bail Organa, who promises to raise her as a princess in Alderaan; Luke is taken to Tattooine and placed with his uncle on a farm. Anakin is repaired by surgery and robed and masked as the Emperor's chief minion, Darth Vader.

Above Director George Lucas frames a scene while Samuel L. Jackson looks on **Below** Palpatine (Ian McDiarmid) turns Anakin (Hayden Christensen) to the dark side

WHAT THEY SAY ...

The stated aim of *Star Wars Episode III: Revenge of the Sith* – or *Star Wars 6*, as it might be labelled – is to join up the two trilogies, taking the characters, and that long-ago and far-away galaxy, to a point that sets the scene for the opening of *Star Wars*. This is a dramatic challenge for Lucas, whose abilities as a writer lag notably behind his skills as a director, which in turn plod behind his genius as the creator-producer-owner of his own universe.

As in the 1969 Bond entry *On Her Majesty's Secret Service*, another atypical 'Part Six', darker matter necessitates a reordering of the formula. Lucas has been roundly criticised since the Ewoks of *Jedi* (1983), but more pointedly in the case of Jar-Jar Binks of *Phantom Menace* (1999), for the fact that the childish humour – which began with the droids of the original – has become embarrassing. Here Jar-Jar has no dialogue, the robots have little to do and none of the new characters is remotely cute or humorous. For the first time, the series' overall title makes sense – here the stars are finally at war. We are shown a leader who has manipulated democracy to the point where he can invoke a paper tiger of an external threat to justify the suspension of the democratic process.

This is good stuff, but Lucas's characters still remind one of the cursed fairytale princess who can't open her mouth without a frog leaping out: every line of dialogue in the film falls dead, and none of the distinguished cast can do a thing about it. Whenever the space opera pauses, the characters (and Natalie Portman's Padmé suffers most) stand in big rooms telling other characters things they've said before and will say again. Each time Lucas cuts away from a battle or a duel to politics, or (worst of all) Anakin's home life, there is a sense that he'd like to draw out the resonances Francis Ford Coppola finds in moving between public rituals and the mass murders of the Corleone enemies in the *Godfather* trilogy. Instead, he succeeds only in stopping the film for mind-numbing minutes as he labours over such obvious ironies as the fact that Anakin's terror of losing his wife in childbirth leads to the circumstances where this is exactly what happens.

When the characters shut up and are in action (or even in tableau) *Revenge of the Sith* can claim to be the best-looking *Star Wars* episode of all. The opening shot, which needs to top the beginning of *Star Wars*, is a fully realised depiction of something that even a few years ago would have been an inconceivable special-effects scene – two tiny ships threading through a vast, screen-filling space battle. *Revenge of the Sith* is packed with equally astounding, equally beautiful shots and sequences, especially the many duels. For the first time since the best moments of *The Empire Strikes Back* (1980), a *Star Wars* film looks as good as the lavish production art displayed in the tie-in coffee-table books.

BEHIND THE SCENES

George Lucas's 'original' plan – which seems to have been hatched somewhere after the break-out success of *Star Wars*

in 1977 but before the development of its immediate sequels *The Empire Strikes Back* and *Return of the Jedi* – was to make a 'trilogy of trilogies'. This required the first three films to be retroactively reconfigured as Episodes IV to VI of the saga in re-release versions that tinker slightly or massively to smooth over inconsistencies. Poor old Sebastian Shaw, once a ghostly Anakin, has been digitally exorcised from *Jedi* on DVD and replaced by Hayden Christensen, who plays the character in Episodes II and III of the second-wave trilogy.

This set of three prequels, which begin with *The Phantom Menace* (1999) and *Attack of the Clones* (2002) and follow the transformation of Anakin, Luke Skywalker's father, from 'good' Jedi knight to the sinister Darth Vader, definitively incorporate their status as Episodes I to III in their official titles. Things seem to have gone quiet on the possibility of the third trilogy, although ongoing spin-offs in other media (comics, TV animation, books, computer games) zip around the films like the tiny, buzzing vehicles that are perpetually on the move in the background of Lucas's stately vistas of outer space or alien worlds. So, we must assume that this concludes the saga.

OSCARS & BAFTAS
Not known at time of publication

Below About time: C-3PO (Anthony Davies) watches Padmé (Natalie Portman) and Anakin get together

Steven Spielberg's fourth movie, made in 1977, is also his fourth to feature on *The Ultimate Film* list. It may be his best, too – a thoroughly beguiling fairy tale that manages to address the child within whilst never being anything less than grown-up.

Dir: Steven SPIELBERG / USA
Released in Britain: 1978
Running Time: 135 minutes
Colour: Metrocolor
Estimated Attendance: 8.54 million

Director **Steven Spielberg**
Producers **Julia Phillips, Michael Phillips**
Screenplay **Steven Spielberg**
Director of Photography **Vilmos Zsigmond**
Editor **Michael Kahn**
Production Designer **Joe Alves**
Music **John Williams**

Roy Neary • Richard Dreyfuss
Claude Lacombe • François Truffaut
Ronnie Neary • Teri Garr
Jillian Guiler • Melinda Dillon
Barry Guiler • Cary Guffey
David Laughlin • Bob Balaban
Farmer • Roberts Blossom
Team Leader • Merrill Connally
Major Benchley • George DiCenzo
Robert • Lance Henriksen
Wild Bill • Warren Kemmerling
Project Leader • J. Patrick McNamara
Jean Claude • Philip Dodds
Brad Neary • Shawn Bishop
Silvia Neary • Adrienne Campbell
Toby Neary • Justin Dreyfuss
Implantee • Amy Douglass
Implantee • Alexander Lockwood
Ike • Gene Dynarski
Mrs Harris • Mary Gafrey

CLOSE ENCOUNTERS OF THE THIRD KIND

THE STORY

After a massive power blackout hits large areas of Indiana, workman Roy Neary is sent out to investigate and is flabbergasted when his truck is suddenly caught in a cone of intense light and shaken by tremors. He follows what appear to be strange craft in the sky, and on the way encounters other people similarly affected, including Jillian Guiler, whose small son Barry ran from the house in delighted pursuit of these uncanny presences. Meanwhile, Claude Lacombe, an international researcher into UFO phenomena, has discovered that the craft may be transmitting a musical signal, which translates mathematically into the map co-ordinates of a site in Wyoming.

Having already been fired from his job, Roy's increasingly strange behaviour, particularly his obsession with sculpting models of a mountain, upsets his wife Ronnie and their children. They finally leave when he begins constructing a giant model in the living room. Roy at last realises (as does Jillian Guiler, who has had similar visions and lost her son to the alien presences) that the real mountain is the Devil's Tower in Wyoming, where Lacombe and his team have created a nerve-gas scare to clear the area. In an effort to reach the Tower, Roy and Jillian find the secret landing site prepared by Lacombe and his men for the aliens. The latter finally arrive and, after an exchange of musical messages, release the humans (including Barry) who they have 'borrowed' at different times for study; Roy leaves on a mission with the clearly benevolent extra-terrestrials.

WHAT THEY SAID THEN …

Before it succumbs in the second half to a tone of awed, quasi-religious uplift, *Close Encounters of the Third Kind* is a startlingly innovative blockbuster. Tone, as it happens, is all important, for in no real sense does the film have a theme – or, rather, its theme is its plot mechanism, the means by which Everyman, power-worker Roy Neary, is sucked into a transcendental experience. The

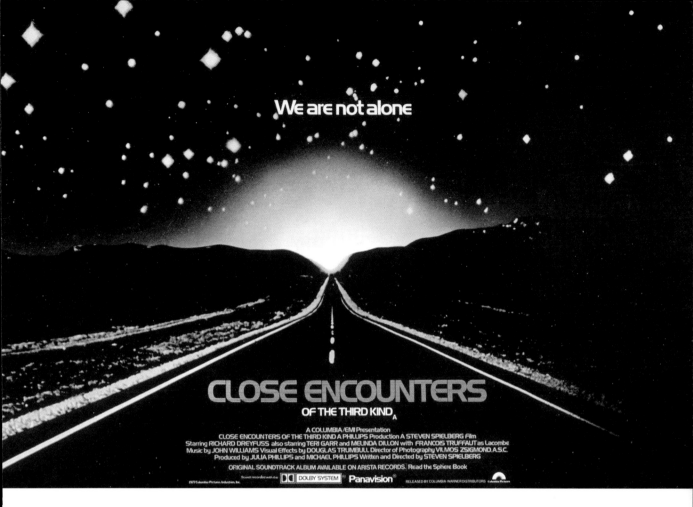

We are not alone

CLOSE ENCOUNTERS
OF THE THIRD KIND A

A COLUMBIA/EMI Presentation
CLOSE ENCOUNTERS OF THE THIRD KIND A PHILLIPS Production A STEVEN SPIELBERG Film
Starring RICHARD DREYFUSS also starring TERI GARR and MELINDA DILLON with FRANCOIS TRUFFAUT as Lacombe
Music by JOHN WILLIAMS Visual Effects by DOUGLAS TRUMBULL Director of Photography VILMOS ZSIGMOND, A.S.C.
Produced by JULIA PHILLIPS and MICHAEL PHILLIPS Written and Directed by STEVEN SPIELBERG
ORIGINAL SOUNDTRACK ALBUM AVAILABLE ON ARISTA RECORDS. Read the Sphere Book
1977 Columbia Pictures Industries, Inc.   Sound recorded with the   DOLBY SYSTEM   Panavision   RELEASED BY COLUMBIA-WARNER DISTRIBUTORS Columbia Pictures

Below Roy Neary (Richard Dreyfuss) willingly
goes with the aliens

mechanism is the same that draws audiences into the film, inviting them to become Everyman – although they are really offered a double identification figure, with Neary as the ordinary mortal who is suddenly seized with the intensity of Van Gogh, and Claude Lacombe as the scientist/intellectual also invested with a generous dose of Gallic humanity.

The film adroitly sidesteps the need to suggest possible explanations and never allows the audience's scepticism to gain a foothold. Having cleared (or bypassed) the rational ground, Spielberg is free to concentrate on the magic. And at this level, the film is a joy to watch, anchoring its unimaginable events in the most ordinary settings imaginable, producing a peculiar frisson that is part poetic, part comic. In one of the earliest manifestations of the aliens' presence, a child wakes at night to find all his mechanical toys coming to life and scuttling about the floor (even so simple an identification has a fairly complex reflexive function: a childish innocence distinguishes those who will be touched by the aliens' message, such as Neary, first seen playing with an electric train, but the aliens are also, of course, simply the toys of the special effects department). Running outside after his night-visitors, the boy is spotted by his bleary-eyed mother giggling on the lawn in a pale circle of light – an exquisite shot, capped by a later moment when the child rounds a bend on a lonely country road, now palely lit by the moon, to confront a silent, stolid group of farmers waiting for the lights to reappear.

Neary's excited attempts to tell his wife about the extra-terrestrials prompts some puzzled discussion as to whether their craft are shaped more like ice-cream

Above Roy Neary (Richard Dreyfuss) wins the most untidy living room competition *Below* Little boy lost: Barry (Cary Guffey) is drawn to the light *Opposite* Small alien ships fly over the landing site

cones or some variety of Sara Lee cookie, and Spielberg brilliantly intertwines both the pathos and bathos of this working-class family man's plight. In his first scene, Neary's visionary role is anticipated by the sight of *The Ten Commandments* flickering on a television; later, when he wakes to the realisation that he must turn his whole house into a receptacle for his vision. Daffy Duck is duelling on the small screen with a Martian, and the subsequent scene, of Neary frantically filling his house with materials for his mountain, is properly cartoon-like in its manic action and cacophony of bangs and crashes.

As the terrestrial power that shares the aliens' ability to implant images in the minds of millions, it is fittingly television that finally draws Neary and his fellow visionaries to the Devil's Tower. But it is also about here that the plot begins to go into overdrive, with the Hitchcockian flavour of Spielberg's tricks of audience control coyly emphasised by the Bernard Herrmann-esque tones of John Williams's score. For all its hesitations and insufficiencies, however, *Close Encounters of the Third Kind* is the first of the new breed of science fiction film which approaches the best in the literature.

WHAT THEY SAY NOW ...

Close Encounters incorporates themes that recur throughout Steven Spielberg's work. His staple characters and elements (the lonely quest, the sympathetic mother, the lost boy, the untrustworthy authorities) convene, as in *E.T.* (1982), in a transforming experience. There is rescue, redemption and affirmation of an individual's worth. Take away the spectacular sound and light show, and what remains is a compassionate human story of an ordinary man in extraordinary circumstances. Running parallel with the main protagonists' intimate experiences of frustration and fear are the intriguing globetrotting efforts of the hopeful Claude Lacombe. Remarkably, this tender performance by François Truffaut marks the only showing on the Ultimate Film list for this masterful French auteur. Without him, Spielberg's work would be the poorer – his handling of child actors in films like *The 400 Blows* (1959) and *Small Change* (1976) influenced the US director, while it was Truffaut who encouraged Spielberg to make 'a film about kids' (this was to become *E.T.*).

Released a few months after *Star Wars* (1977), *Close Encounters* was a different matter entirely – euphoric where Lucas's film was brittle, and alive to possibilities (of cinema, of mankind) where *Star Wars* was, emotionally at least, dead in the water. In its director's oeuvre, it is matched only by *Jaws* (1975) in its orchestration of childlike pleasure, and by *E.T.* in its harmonious marriage of the intimate and the intergalactic. The passage of time has only enhanced its wonders.

CLASSIC QUOTE

Roy: 'This *means* something.'

SCENE STEALER

The abduction of young Barry Guiler – a scene so meticulously constructed, and so suspenseful, that it withstands comparison with the best of Hitchcock's set pieces. There is genius in every shot, no matter how trivial – screws unfastening themselves from an air-vent grille, household appliances miraculously springing into life. It all ends horribly with Barry's mother and the unseen alien forces playing tug-of-war with the poor child's body.

BEHIND THE SCENES

For Spielberg, who wrote *Close Encounters* himself after passing on Paul Schrader's overly dark first draft (other uncredited work was done by Walter Hill, Matthew Robbins, Hal Barwood and others), this remains the film he can't leave behind. Since its original release, he has re-edited it into 1980's *Special Edition* (tightened middle section of Neary's crisis, extended alien climax) and 1997's *Collector's Edition* (digitally remastered, snippets reinstated, the unnecessary sequence inside the mother ship sensibly deleted).

OSCARS
9 nominations, **2 winners**

Directing: Steven Spielberg
Actress in a Supporting Role: Melinda Dillon
Art Direction/Set Decoration: Joe Alves, Dan Lomino, Phil Abramson
Cinematography: Vilmos Zsigmond
Film Editing: Michael Kahn
Music (Original Score): John Williams
Sound
Visual Effects
**Special Achievement Award (Sound Effects Editing):
    Frank E. Warner**

WHAT WON THAT YEAR?
Best Picture: *Annie Hall*
Directing: Woody Allen *Annie Hall*
Actor in a Leading Role: Richard Dreyfuss *The Goodbye Girl*
Actress in a Leading Role: Diane Keaton *Annie Hall*

BAFTAS
9 nominations, **1 winner**

Film
Direction: Steven Spielberg
Anthony Asquith Award for Original Film Music: John Williams
Cinematography: Vilmos Zgismond
Film Editing: Michael Kahn
Production Design: Joe Alves
Screenplay: Steven Spielberg
Sound Track
Supporting Actor: François Truffaut

WHAT WON THAT YEAR?
Film: *Julia*
Direction: Alan Parker *Midnight Express*
Actor: Richard Dreyfuss *The Goodbye Girl*
Actress: Jane Fonda *Julia*

Dir: King VIDOR / UK
Released in Britain: 1939
Running Time: 110 minutes
Black and white
Estimated Attendance: 8.5 million

The directing career of Hollywood legend King Vidor ran from 1913 to the late 1950s, but he made just one film in Britain – this well-regarded drama about a doctor who finds his ideals receding as comfort and complacency take hold.

THE CITADEL

Director **King Vidor**
Producer **Victor Saville**
Screenplay **Ian Dalrymple, Frank Wead, Elizabeth Hill**, based on the novel by A. J. Cronin
Director of Photography **Harry Stradling**
Editor **Charles Frend**
Art Directors **Lazare Meerson, Alfred Junge**
Music **Louis Levy**

Andrew • Robert Donat
Denny • Ralph Richardson
Christine • Rosalind Russell
Dr Lawford • Rex Harrison
Owen • Emlyn Williams
Toppy Leroy • Penelope Dudley Ward
Ben Chenkin • Francis L. Sullivan
Dr A. H. Llewellyn • Joss Ambler
Mr Boon • Felix Aylmer
Nurse Sharp • Joyce Bland
Joe Morgan • Edward Chapman
Mrs Orlando • Mary Clare
Charles Every • Cecil Parker
Mrs Thornton • Nora Swinburne
Lady Raeburn • Athene Seyler
Mr Stillman • Percy Parsons
Mrs Page • Dilys Davies
Dr Page • Basil Gill

THE STORY

Andrew Manson, an enthusiastic young doctor, begins work in a Welsh mining village, where his research into the cause of tuberculosis among the miners arouses intense opposition. Eventually he and his wife are driven from the locality and they seek their fortune in London. Here, his idealism fades before the lure of easy money obtained from wealthy women with imaginary complaints. It is only when his best friend is killed, through the incompetence of one of his 'specialist' colleagues, that Manson realises that he has betrayed his profession. His subsequent work, in co-operation with a non-qualified doctor, to save the life of a child, brings him into conflict with the General Medical Council, after which he gives a moving appeal.

WHAT THEY SAID THEN ...

Robert Donat gives a magnificent performance as the young doctor. Rosalind Russell is perfect as his wife, while Ralph Richardson is his usual competent, good-humoured self as Manson's friend. The settings, particularly those of Welsh life and scenery, are convincing, while the direction has avoided the pitfalls of emotionalism and dry-as-dust propaganda.

The picture is a forceful attack on certain abuses which, it is claimed, exist in medical life today. In spite of this, however, it never loses its interest as a story, and some of the passages, notably when Manson is fighting for the life of a new-born child in the Welsh village, and the last scene before the council of doctors, are probably among the most moving to have been seen on the screen.

WHAT THEY SAY NOW ...

This was the only film that King Vidor directed in Britain (as part of MGM's short-lived UK operation of the late 1930s), and it is rather more sober in style and mood than most of his American work. Only occasionally does Vidor's usual expressionist intensity show through. It makes an interesting comparison with Carol Reed's *The Stars Look Down*, made a couple of years later in 1940 from another A. J. Cronin novel. Both are set partly in Welsh mining communities

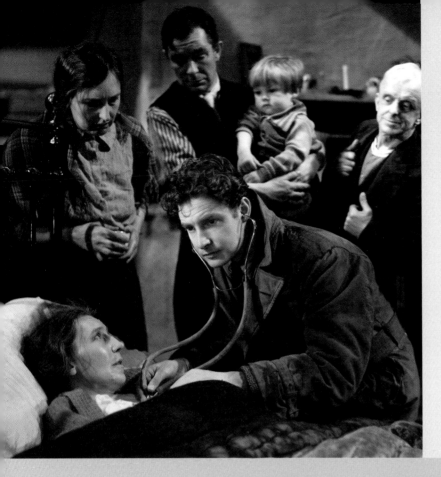

OSCARS
4 nominations

Outstanding Production
Directing: King Vidor
Actor: Robert Donat
Writing (Screenplay): Ian Dalrymple, Frank Wead, Elizabeth Hill

WHAT WON THAT YEAR?
Outstanding Production: *You Can't Take It with You*
Directing: Frank Capra *You Can't Take It with You*
Actor: Spencer Tracy *Boys Town*
Actress: Bette Davis *Jezebel*

BAFTAS NOT AWARDED UNTIL 1947

Opposite Dirty Denny (Ralph Richardson) proposes to young doctor Andrew Manson (Robert Donat) that they blow up a sewer
Left 'Say "aah".' Andrew makes a house call

and feature – as must almost any movie that deals with coal mining – a cave-in down the pit. But there's more of a Metro glossiness to Vidor's picture, and the implausible upbeat ending is pure Hollywood – Manson loftily denounces the General Medical Council set up to investigate him and, his wife beaming supportively at his side, strides from the room without waiting for their response.

Vidor finds sly humour in the episodes where Manson is seduced from his idealism by the fat pickings to be made in London. There's a particularly choice scene where Vidor's camera tracks steadily backwards before Manson and three fellow medics as they play out a round of golf while coolly discussing how best to fleece their spoilt, hypochondriac patients. Humour of a more idiosyncratic sort enters with Ralph Richardson's boozy, scurrilous Denny, with Richardson as usual effortlessly walking off with every scene in which he appears.

As often with Vidor's movies, *The Citadel*'s politics are a touch confused. Denny's plot to blow up the disease-spreading sewer is right-wing anarchism – rather like Gary Cooper blowing up a building of which he disapproves in Vidor's later *The Fountainhead* (1949). Yet his scheme for an East End 'co-operative' to tackle ill health foreshadows the NHS. And where *The Stars Look Down* openly called for nationalisation of the mines, Manson's alternative to the self-serving smugness of the medical profession involves rich industrialist backers and an eccentric, unqualified American genius – a rather precarious solution.

CLASSIC QUOTE
Manson (to Dr Every, whose incompetence on the operating table has caused Denny's death): 'This wasn't surgery. It was murder.'

SCENE STEALER
Recently arrived in the poverty-stricken Welsh mining village, and still unsure of himself, Manson is called to attend a woman having a difficult labour. It's her first child, long awaited by its parents. Despite Manson's best efforts the child – a boy – is born dead. As he slumps despondently the grandmother pats him gently on the shoulder and murmurs, 'She wanted a boy.' Suddenly resolute, Manson calls urgently for basins of water, picks up the infant and massages it vigorously, dowsing it in water and blowing into its mouth. The grandmother and nurse look on in amazement as the baby stirs and cries. Handing the child to its mother, Manson leaves the house, pausing to congratulate the anxious father, then walks on, exultantly saying to himself, 'Thank God – I'm a doctor!'

86

Dirs: Ben **SHARPSTEEN**, Hamilton **LUSKE** / USA
Released in Britain: 1940
Running Time: 88 minutes
Colour: Technicolor
Estimated Attendance: 8.5 million

One of the world's most cherished fairy tales became one of the most popular films of all time, as well as a symbol of Walt Disney's Golden Age. And despite being more than 60 years old now, Pinocchio is still looking light on his pins.

PINOCCHIO

Directors **Ben Sharpsteen, Hamilton Luske**
Producer **Walt Disney**
Screenplay **Aurelius Battaglia, William Cottrell, Otto Englander, Edrman Penner, Joseph Sabo, Ted Sears, Webb Smith**, based on *The Adventures of Pinocchio* by Carlo Collodi
Art Direction **Ken Anderson**
Music **Leigh Harline, Paul J. Smith**

THE STORY

The woodcarver Gepetto makes a new marionette, Pinocchio, and prays on the wishing star that the little wooden figure may be given life. The Blue Fairy grants his wish and appoints the tiny Jiminy Cricket as Pinocchio's conscience. Jiminy has to rescue Pinocchio first from the clutches of Stromboli, a rascally puppet-master, and then from Pleasure Island, a funfair to which naughty little boys are enticed in order to be turned into donkeys for sale to the mines. When Jiminy finally gets Pinocchio home, it is only to find that Gepetto – who has set out to search for him – has been eaten by a whale. Pinocchio and Jiminy rescue him. For his unselfish courage the Blue Fairy rewards Pinocchio by turning him into a real boy.

WHAT THEY SAID THEN …

This film is the most perfect example of cartoon work ever seen on the screen, and is a great advance on *Snow White and the Seven Dwarfs* (1937). The characters, to all intents and purposes, live and breathe, and, with very rare exceptions, there is none of the jerky flicker in their movement that has hitherto been characteristic of such pictures. From the first, it is difficult to realise that the scenes on the screen – with their delicate nuances of shade and their illusion of depth – are only drawings. Only in the music, which, with the exception of a cheerful marching song 'Hi-Diddle-De-Dee, an Actor's Life for Me', seems pedestrian and uninspired, does *Pinocchio* fail to surpass Disney's best work to date.

Jiminy Cricket, with his matter-of-fact humour and resourcefulness, earns his place as one of the immortal screen drawings. Figaro the cat and Cleo the goldfish follow him closely, while the three stages in Pinocchio's life – puppet, living doll and little boy – are cleverly contrasted. In technique, wit, humour and poetry it is difficult to see how this adaptation of a fairy story could have been bettered.

WHAT THEY SAY NOW …

There are no signs that the status of *Pinocchio* as one of the shining examples of movie animation is under threat. The characterisation is as affectionately detailed as the animation, the humour and wonder balanced expertly with the darkness –

and what darkness: the Pleasure Island sequence remains as disturbing today as ever. Many film-makers have been bewitched by the story: Roberto Benigni made his own version and Steven Spielberg's *AI: Artificial Intelligence* (2001) drew heavily on it, even accommodating a Blue Fairy voiced by Meryl Streep.

CLASSIC QUOTE

The Blue Fairy: 'A lie keeps growing and growing until it's as plain as the nose on your face.'

SCENE STEALER

On Pleasure Island, Pinocchio is shooting pool with his new pal, Lampwick. To the consternation of Jiminy Cricket, the boys have been dragging on cigars; Pinocchio has inhaled so deeply that he is unable even to grasp his cue as the eight-ball swims before his rattling eyes. Then the real horrors begin. Lampwick sprouts first a pair of long ears, then a tail: he is turning into a donkey. Until he hears his own hee-hawing guffaw, he is oblivious to the metamorphosis. But then he staggers to a full-length mirror, beholds himself as a donkey in boys' clothing – and goes crazy. He cries out, releasing an agonising, bestial roar at the top of his lungs, and kicks out with his hooves at the mirror, shattering it. It's one of those moments of intense, otherworldly horror that the best Disney films handle so brilliantly. Unlike modern Disney, or the family entertainments made by, say, Spielberg or Robert Rodriguez, there is no rush here to diffuse the tension with humour: our fear and disbelief are left to linger.

BEHIND THE SCENES

The 'rotoscope' technique of animating on top of an actor's movements was used for the Blue Fairy, as it had been for the Prince in *Snow White and the Seven Dwarfs*. In recent years, the technique has been favoured by the director Richard Linklater in his movies *Waking Life* (2001) and *A Scanner Darkly* (2006).

Opposite Pinocchio seems interested but there are strings attached *Below* It's not cricket: Pinocchio's conscience Jiminy gets a leg up

OSCARS

2 nominations, **2 winners**

**Music (Original Score): Leigh Harline,
   Paul J. Smith, Ned Washington
Music (Song): 'When You Wish upon a Star'
   Music by Leigh Harline, Lyrics by
   Ned Washington**

WHAT WON THAT YEAR?
Outstanding Production: *Rebecca*
Directing: John Ford *The Grapes of Wrath*
Actor: James Stewart *The Philadelphia Story*
Actress: Ginger Rogers *Kitty Foyle*

BAFTAS NOT AWARDED UNTIL 1947

Dir: John LASSETER / USA
Released in Britain: 1999
Running Time: 96 minutes
Colour: Monaco colour
Estimated Attendance: 8.41 million

Four out of the six Pixar movies released at the time of writing have been successful enough to figure in *The Ultimate Film* list. That's quite a strike rate. And no wonder, when the wit, imagination and loving attention to detail found in *A Bug's Life* are typical of that studio's output.

A BUG'S LIFE

Director **John Lasseter**
Producers **Darla Anderson, Kevin Reher**
Screenplay **Donald McEnery, Bob Shaw**, based on a story by John Lasseter, Andrew Stanton, Joe Ranft
Director of Photography **Sharon Calahan**
Editor **Lee Unkrich**
Production Designer **William Cone**
Music **Randy Newman**

Voice of Flik, the Hero Ant • David Foley
Voice of Hopper, Badass Grasshopper • Kevin Spacey
Voice of Princess Atta, a She-Ant • Julia Louis-Dreyfus
Voice of Princess Dot • Hayden Panettiere
Voice of the Queen • Phyllis Diller
Voice of Molt • Richard Kind
Voice of Slim, a Walking Stick • David Hyde Pierce
Voice of Heimlich • Joe Ranft
Voice of Francis, a Male Lady Bug • Denis Leary
Voice of Manny, the Praying Mantis • Jonathan Harris
Voice of Gypsy, a Moth • Madeline Kahn
Voice of Rosie, a Black Widow Spider • Bonnie Hunt
Voice of Tuck/Roll, Hungarian Pillbugs • Mike McShane
Voice of P. T. Flea • John Ratzenberger
Voice of Dim, a Not-So-Bright Beetle • Brad Garrett
Voice of Mr Soil • Roddy McDowall
Voice of Doctor Flora • Edie McClurg
Voice of Thorny • Alex Rocco
Voice of Cornelius • David Ossman
Additional Voice • Carlos Alazraqui

THE STORY

On a tiny island, a colony of ants gathers its yearly midsummer grain offering to appease a marauding grasshopper gang led by the ferocious Hopper. Worker ant Flik, while demonstrating his new grain-harvesting contraption, accidentally dumps the offering into deep water. An incensed Hopper demands the ants provide twice their usual offering. Flik volunteers to get help from bigger bugs in the mainland city (a rubbish pile). Princess Atta, training to take over from her mother the Queen, agrees to let him go.

In the city, a troupe of circus bugs is fired by its ringmaster, P. T. Flea, after a disastrous performance. Flik sees them fighting with some flies and mistakes them for warriors, while they mistake him for a talent scout. Flik leads them back to the island. When the misunderstanding is clarified, the circus bugs try to leave, but stop to help save Atta's sister Dot from a hungry bird. Flik is inspired: he persuades the colony and the bugs to build a fake bird to scare off the grasshoppers, but when he realises that no one expected him to succeed, he leaves with the circus bugs whom Flea has rehired. The grasshoppers arrive, intending to squash the Queen. Dot finds Flik and persuades him to return. The fake-bird plan partly succeeds until the bird catches fire. Flik stands up to Hopper and the ants attack en masse; Hopper is tricked into falling into the clutches of a real bird and meets his demise. The circus bugs set off, leaving behind Flik, now considered a hero by the colony.

WHAT THEY SAY ...

A Bug's Life is a far lighter film than the DreamWorks production *Antz* (1998), which preceded it into British cinemas by several months. That lightness is literal, with much more of its action taking place above ground rather than inside the ant hill.

It is no accident, though, that an Anglepoise (star of award-winning short *Luxo Jr*, 1986) is Pixar's mascot. Subtle use of light and colour has emerged as director John Lasseter and co.'s trademark, and their deployment of these elements in *A Bug's Life* is quite astounding. Where the last film, *Toy Story* (1995), was set mainly indoors and afforded opportunities to mimic incandescent lighting and sunlight filtered through windows, *A Bug's Life* goes for an even more complex palette of effects. As the summer wanes and autumn kicks in, the shades darken and the angles of illumination change almost imperceptibly. In this arena, computers really can achieve things cel animation would struggle to get right.

Nonetheless, the film's makers are canny enough to realise the value of stylisation. *A Bug's Life* really has the edge over *Antz* in the graphic simplicity of its characterisation. Where *Antz* made things harder for itself with anatomically correct six-legged ants given almost human-proportioned faces, Pixar's film takes an opposite strategy, reducing faces to huge, white-filled eyes and giving the ant bodies only four limbs. Meanwhile, the grasshoppers (their relentless leader Hopper wittily voiced by Kevin Spacey) have a lobster-shell texture, their joints constantly clicking menacingly, forming a sharp contrast with the soft, incandescent burnish on the pastel-coloured ants. Little of it will wash with entomologists,

but *A Bug's Life* achieves the aim of reducing the squirm factor inherent in having insect protagonists.

Nevertheless, the script has fun playing with our common knowledge of insects. The film's best line comes from a bored fly at the circus dismissing the bugs' performance with, 'I only have 24 hours to live and I'm not wasting it on this.' This fly would be less likely to say this of *A Bug's Life*. Indeed, the rest of the film has similar fun joyfully mixing bug-world givens with anthropomorphism.

CLASSIC QUOTE

Mosquito: 'Bartender. Bloody Mary, O-positive.'

SCENE STEALER

The death of Hopper, the tyrannical grasshopper. Having already survived an attack by a fake bird, piloted by ants, he doesn't flinch when a real one swoops down towards him, believing it to be just another mock-up. But this time Hopper is plucked up and swept away to face his doom in the beaks of some adorable fluffy yellow chicks unexpectedly transformed into objects of terror.

OSCARS
1 nomination

Music (Original Musical or Comedy Score): Randy Newman

WHAT WON THAT YEAR?
Best Picture: *Shakespeare in Love*
Directing: Steven Spielberg *Saving Private Ryan*
Actor in a Leading Role: Roberto Benigni *Life is Beautiful*
Actress in a Leading Role: Gwyneth Paltrow *Shakespeare in Love*

BAFTAS
1 nomination

Achievement in Visual Special Effects

WHAT WON THAT YEAR?
Film: *American Beauty*
Alexander Korda Award for Outstanding British Film: *East is East*
David Lean Award for Achievement in Direction: Pedro Almodovar
   All About My Mother
Actor: Kevin Spacey *American Beauty*
Actress: Annette Bening *American Beauty*

Above left *Flik (voiced by David Foley) makes a telescope for Princess Atta (voiced by Julia Louis-Dreyfus)* **Left** *Flik addresses a gathering of the bugs*

Dir: David LEAN / UK
Released in Britain: 1962
Running Time: 207 minutes
Colour: Technicolor
Estimated Attendance: 8.4 million

The popularity of David Lean's self-consciously vast epics is demonstrated by the appearance on *The Ultimate Film* list of *Lawrence of Arabia*, the third of his works to feature here. In its day, the picture was both controversial and frustrating in its reluctance to investigate its hero's motives and persona. Do the doubts about it persist?

LAWRENCE OF ARABIA

Director **David Lean**
Producer **Sam Spiegel**
Screenplay **Robert Bolt, Michael Wilson**
Director of Photography **Freddie Young**
Editor **Anne V. Coates**
Production Designer **John Box**
Music **Maurice Jarre**

T. E. Lawrence • Peter O'Toole
Prince Feisal • Alec Guinness
Auda Abu Tayi • Anthony Quinn
General Allenby • Jack Hawkins
Turkish Bey • Jose Ferrer
Colonel Harry Brighton • Anthony Quayle
Mr Dryden • Claude Rains
Jackson E. Bentley • Arthur Kennedy
Gasim • I. S. Johar
Majid • Gamil Ratib
Tafas • Zia Mohyeddin
General Murray • Donald Wolfit
Sherif Ali ibn el Kharish • Omar Sharif
Farraj • Michel Ray
Daud • John Dimech
Medical Officer • Howard Marion-Crawford
Club Secretary • Jack Gwillim
RAMC Colonel • Hugh Miller
Vicar at St Paul's • Noel Howlett
Reporter at St Paul's • Jack Hedley

THE STORY

T. E. Lawrence is an untidy, disgruntled young lieutenant on the staff in Cairo, wanting only to get out into the desert. This he achieves through Mr Dryden of the Arab Bureau, who arranges for him to be seconded for special duty, to make contact with Prince Feisal and check on the progress of the Arab Revolt. In the desert, Lawrence's guide is shot down at a water hole by Sherif Ali. Feisal is philosophically resigned to the absorption of his guerrilla army into the regular British forces. A miracle is needed to sustain the independent spirit of the Arab Revolt, and Lawrence provides it, crossing the Nefud Desert with Sherif Ali and a small force, and capturing the Turkish port of Aqaba. To halt another tribal quarrel, Lawrence has to shoot down one of his own men. His realisation that he enjoys the act of killing sends him back to Cairo in a mood of remorseful self-doubt. But General Allen offers arms and money, and Lawrence goes back to a period of triumphant guerrilla warfare, hero-worshipped by his own men and made a world hero through the dispatches of the American journalist Jackson Bentley.

On a scouting expedition with Ali into the Turkish-held town of Deraa, Lawrence is picked up by the Turks and savagely beaten. The discovery that he is not invincible persuades him that he should throw up his command. But he is again sent back to the desert. Lawrence's attack on a Turkish column becomes a needlessly brutal massacre. He leads his force into Damascus, sets up an Arab Council to run the city, and sees it collapse under the strain of tribal divisions. The politicians are left to come to a settlement, while the idealist, Lawrence, rides away from Damascus.

WHAT THEY SAID THEN ...

It is clear from the outset that T. E. Lawrence remains an enigma, and we should not look here for a solution. But to build a blockbuster lasting nearly four hours around a character about whose motives and drives the film admits its own

Opposite The iconic headdress *Above left* Cue Lawrence! Peter O'Toole relaxes on set by playing snooker *Above right* David Lean stands firm while the film blew everyone else away *Below* 'They went that-a-way' David Lean (right) with Anthony Quinn (centre) and Peter O'Toole

uncertainty is already to take a sizeable risk. The story is by its nature episodic, despite the script's obvious determination to supply action climaxes at suitable intervals. Lawrence himself must hold the thing together; and before Lawrence the film in effect retires defeated, while Peter O'Toole's likeable performance lacks that ultimate star quality which would lift the film along with it.

Breaking its character portrait down into a series of episodes, David Lean's film does better with Lawrence the exhibitionist, capering about the desert in his new Arab robes or parading on the roof of a newly captured train, than with the introvert. When it comes to the massacre of the Turks, the film is not close enough to its central character to communicate a human rather than a spectacular experience.

The strength of *Lawrence* lies in the fact that its makers have obviously felt the enormous fascination of the desert. Even if the camera offers too many slow stares at corrugated landscapes, too many mesmerised panning shots, at its best the film is trying not just to engineer a response, but to communicate something strongly felt. The most hauntingly effective moment is the first sight of Sherif Ali, the black dot riding out of the mirage. This is wonderful; and there are fine scenes of preparation for battle. Any amount of production intelligence has gone into *Lawrence*, at all levels, but it is intelligence of the rule-book rather than the sweepingly inventive order. (The long sequence, for instance, in which Lawrence rides back into the desert for the man he will later have to execute has been built by Lean into an over-immaculate exercise in crosscutting.)

Imagination is let down with a thud by the score, with its insistent themes, and picked up again by much of the playing (Jack Hawkins's bluffly ruthless Allenby, Alec Guinness's impeccably intelligent if oddly accented Feisal, Omar Sharif's admirably straightforward Sherif Ali). *Lawrence* is not, as has been made clear, a biography: inventions in the script have been severely criticised.

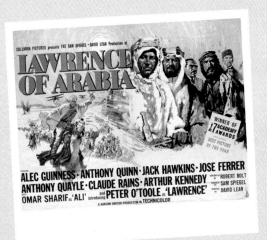

OSCARS
10 nominations, **7 winners**

Best Picture
Directing: David Lean
Actor: Peter O'Toole
Actor in a Supporting Role: Omar Sharif
**Art Direction/Set Decoration (Color): John Box, John Stoll,
   Dario Simoni**
Cinematography (Color): Fred A. Young
Film Editing: Anne Coates
Music (Music Score – Substantially Original): Maurice Jarre
Sound: John Cox
Writing (Screenplay – based on material from Another Medium):
   Robert Bolt, Michael Wilson

WHAT WON THAT YEAR?
Actor: Gregory Peck *To Kill a Mockingbird*
Actress: Anne Bancroft *The Miracle Worker*

BAFTAS
4 nominations, **3 winners**

Film and British Film
British Actor: Peter O'Toole
Foreign Actor: Anthony Quinn
British Screenplay: Robert Bolt

WHAT WON THAT YEAR?
British Actress: Leslie Caron *The L-Shaped Room*
Foreign Actor: Burt Lancaster *Birdman of Alcatraz*
Foreign Actress: Anne Bancroft *The Miracle Worker*

Yet the fault is not that they are inventions but that they seem to belong to script conventions rather than taking us closer to the subject. This is part of the problem for a film that is trying to be everything at once; a film in which grandeur of conception is not up to grandeur of setting.

WHAT THEY SAY NOW ...

David Lean's mythic blockbuster is both a stunning epic and a sensitive portrait of one of the great romantic legends of the 20th century. Lawrence's tormented psyche and the political and cultural turmoil of the time and place are picked out against a spectacular backdrop.

Inspired and influential moments have the feel of classic silent-film storytelling spiced with delicate technical invention. Action in *Lawrence* is not confined to battle sequences, railway explosions and whooping Arabs charging down sand dunes – Lean was anxious to avoid *Desert Song* (1953) clichés. Truly remarkable scenes empty the screen of extras and noise, and what combat there is illustrates the concept of literate action. The berserk blood bath in which retreating Turks are hacked to death is practically discreet by today's explicit standards, but it has not lost its power to shock; the quivering, bloodied Lawrence has visibly snapped and the action is accordingly chaotic and ugly, his boyish adventure blurred into inglorious, masochistic madness. For the generations born long after the 'real' Lawrence of the newsreels was every schoolboy's hero, *Lawrence of Arabia* honours him with a more complex but still compelling fame.

SCENE STEALER

In the most coolly audacious and entrancing of character introductions, cinematographer Freddie Young redefined the term 'long shot' with his miraculous mirage of a quivering dark speck on the white horizon slowly taking shape as camel and rider, *finally* revealed as the murderously proud Ali. Nine minutes were shot; Lean later said he 'lost his nerve'" and cut to under three.

BEHIND THE SCENES

With several rival productions foiled over the years, two years of laborious preparation were followed by 14 dust-choked months of location shooting in Spain, Morocco and Jordan (where King Hussein's hospitality culminated in his marrying the production office switchboard supervisor, Toni Gardiner). This was longer than it took the real Lawrence, from lieutenant to colonel, to see the desert tribes unite under Prince Faisal and tip the balance for the Allies against the Turks in the First World War.

Producer Sam Spiegel's choice for Lawrence, Marlon Brando, dropped out and 24-year-old Albert Finney (whose *Lawrence* screen tests in Arab costume are the most requested viewing item in Britain's National Film Archive) turned it down. Lean fixed on 28-year-old O'Toole, the right age and with the same Irish heritage as Lawrence (though many inches taller than the diminutive T. E.). When the film premiered, Noel Coward famously quipped that if O'Toole had been any prettier the film would have had to be called *Florence of Arabia*. He is pretty indeed, and the arresting image of his pale blue eyes staring intensely from under the white headdress became iconic.

Above Noel Coward quipped that 'if O'Toole had been any prettier, the film would have to be called Florence of Arabia.' *Below* Making an entrance: the far-off speck that will become Sherif Ali (Omar Sharif) *Opposite* Three minutes later (though nine were shot) Sherif Ali finally arrives

89

Dir: Michael ANDERSON / UK
Released in Britain: 1955
Running Time: 124 minutes
Black and white
Estimated Attendance: 8.4 million

A true story provided the basis for this rousing wartime drama that had more than 8 million British cinemagoers gasping and goose-pimpling. But it is the film's dramatic subtlety, its refusal to trade authenticity for cheap jingoism, that has helped it stand the test of time.

THE DAM BUSTERS

Director **Michael Anderson**
Producer **Robert Clark**
Screenplay **R. C. Sherriff**, based on the book by
　Paul Brickhill and Guy Gibson
Director of Photography **Erwin Hillier**
Editor **Richard Best**
Art Director **Robert Jones**
Music **Leighton Lucas**

Wing Commander Guy Gibson • Richard Todd
Dr Barnes N. Wallis • Michael Redgrave
Group Captain J. N. H. Whitworth • Derek Farr
Mrs Wallis • Ursula Jeans
Air Chief Marshal Sir Arthur Harris • Basil Sydney
Captain Joseph 'Mutt' Summers • Patrick Barr
Air Vice Marshal the Hon. Ralph Cochrane • Ernest Clark
Flight Lieutenant J. V. Hopgood • John Fraser
Flying Officer F. M. Spafford • Nigel Stock
Flight Lieutenant H. B. Martin • Bill Kerr
Flight Lieutenant D. J. H. Maltby • George Baker
Flight Sergeant J. Pulford • Robert Shaw
Flight Lieutenant R. E. G. Hutchison • Tony Doonan
Crosby • Harold Goodwin
Farmer • Laurence Naismith

THE STORY

In order to paralyse the German industrial potential in the Ruhr, it is decided that the Ruhr dams must be destroyed by some foolproof method. Dr Barnes Wallis, a scientist engaged in 'back room' research, is working to perfect a special bomb powerful enough to breach the dams. Despite official scepticism and several technical setbacks, the explosive (designed to ricochet across the water towards its target) is finally tested and proves to be effective. The preparatory work completed, the responsibility for organising the raid is given to Wing Commander Guy Gibson, who proceeds to form and train a hand-picked squadron of experienced flyers.

After several weeks of secret training and technical revision, the operation is set in motion. Flying at tree-top level, the three waves of aircraft concentrate their attack despite heavy opposition, and the pilots are rewarded by the sight of their bombs exploding on the Moehne and Eder dams. Widespread flooding follows, causing great damage to the industrial areas in the vicinity. The depleted squadron returns to base and Gibson is met by Wallis, who has been following the raid from the Ops Room. Although cheered by the success of the mission, the scientist's first thoughts are for the 56 men who have not come back.

WHAT THEY SAID THEN ...

Although the story development and general background of this ambitious production are based firmly on the conventions built up over the years by the British war film, there are, in *The Dam Busters*, indications of an added recognition of some of the realities of war, and an attempt (albeit rather tentative, at times) to express a more deeply felt emotion than one has come to expect. R. C. Sherriff's script and Michael Anderson's direction work up a mood of cumulative tension which successfully suggests something of the nervous strain and the personal comradeship of those involved in this dangerous operation and, in the scenes immediately before and after the raid itself, communicates an awareness of what 'pressing home the attack' meant in terms of human lives.

The closely documented scenes of preparation (Wallis's experiments and his conflict with officialdom and the training of Gibson's aircrew in low-level flying) are convincingly presented, and the brilliantly photographed aerial sequences include an extensive (and for the most part, realistic) use of models and special effects. Apart from the central figures of Wallis and Gibson, there is little attempt at individual characterisation. The bomber crews are viewed objectively as a group of eager, earnest young men, and there is a welcome absence of the more irksome type of Service humour. Michael Redgrave as Wallis does his utmost to turn the conventional 'boffin' into a warm and recognisably human figure and, apart from a few early scenes, his playing is quietly persuasive.

On the other hand, Richard Todd's Guy Gibson is rather mannered and lacking in authority; there is little variety of mood in the performance, and his final scene with Redgrave (in itself quite pointed) is made to sound trite and false. The film is over-long (the flying sequences include some repetition) and the music score is, regrettably, very blatant. Despite these drawbacks a mood of sober respect is maintained.

WHAT THEY SAY NOW ...

Adapted from Guy Gibson's own book *Enemy Coast Ahead*, Michael Anderson's 1954 docudrama captures the tension and bravery of this audacious raid on the centre of Nazi Germany's industrial complex, and the quintessentially English

Above *Back to school: Barnes Wallis (Michael Redgrave) explains the theory behind the bouncing bomb* **Below** *Wing Commander Gibson (Richard Todd, right) defers to Barnes Wallis*

Associated British Presents

RICHARD
TODD · MICHAEL
REDGRAVE

THE DAM BUSTERS

URSULA JEANS · BASIL SYDNEY · PATRICK BARR · ERNEST CLARK
and DEREK FARR   Screenplay by R. C. Sherriff   Directed by Michael Anderson

RELEASED THROUGH WARNER-PATHE

This page The dam is well and truly bust
Opposite Formation flying: the Lancaster bombers weave their way through German searchlights

combination of inventiveness and dogged determination. Split into two distinct sections, it deals first with the fraught, but ultimately successful development of a new weapon. The second and pacier section deals with the mission itself, and its associated costs for the enemy and for the British airmen.

Anderson had made his name as an assistant director, and had directed only a few small features before being offered *The Dam Busters*. With key actors in place, he spent two years researching the story and the principal characters. This approach explains the documentary feel of much of the film, especially in the detail of the bureaucratic obstacles to Barnes Wallis's plan. The decision was made to shoot the film in black and white, in order to allow the integration of original footage of the bomb trails, and to preserve a 'gritty', documentary-style reality.

The actual raid occupies surprisingly little screen time, with Barnes Wallis, his invention and his determined pursuit of the idea making up the bulk of the film. Anderson's clear intention is to celebrate the unsung heroes of the wartime period, and to highlight one facet of Britain's national identity. In demonstrating the way in which Barnes Wallis's inventions are routinely confronted by bureaucratic negativity, Anderson passes critical comment on Britain's dismal tendency to stifle genius.

It is testament to Anderson's authoritative, quiet guidance that the performances are largely realistic, and multi-dimensional. The end of the film might, in other hands, be an opportunity for jingoistic flag-waving, but instead Anderson emphasises the human cost of war without falling into sentimentality. Similarly, Eric Coates's eminently hummable and much-loved 'Dam Busters March' is used more judiciously than is sometimes remembered.

CLASSIC QUOTE

Gibson: 'Well, the training's over. For obvious reasons, you've had to work without knowing your target, or even your weapon. You've to put up with a good deal from other people who think you've been having a soft time. But, tonight, you're going to have a chance to hit the enemy harder, and more destructively, than any small force has ever done before. You're going to attack the great dams of western Germany!'

BEHIND THE SCENES

By good fortune, the Ruhr was in flood at the time of shooting, allowing the crew to film the flooded towns and valleys and incorporate this into the closing scenes. The model work was completed prior to principal shooting to ensure the climax of the film was right, and to allow the flight scenes to be built around this. Five Lancaster bombers had to be rebuilt for the film, with a special studio aircraft mounted on a mechanism designed to allow it to bank and tilt.

OSCARS

1 nomination

Special Effects

WHAT WON THAT YEAR?
Best Motion Picture: *Marty*
Directing: Delbert Mann *Marty*
Actor: Ernest Borgnine *Marty*
Actress: Anna Magnani *The Rose Tattoo*

BAFTAS

2 nominations

Film and British Film
British Screenplay

WHAT WON THAT YEAR?
Film and British Film: *Richard III*
British Actor: Laurence Olivier *Richard III*
British Actress: Katie Johnson *The Ladykillers*
Foreign Actor: Ernest Borgnine *Marty*
Foreign Actress: Betsy Blair *Marty*

90

Dir: Richard MARQUAND / USA
Released in Britain: 1983
Running Time: 132 minutes
Colour: Rankcolor
Estimated Attendance: 8.35 million

All six *Star Wars* movies have earned a place in *The Ultimate Film* list. *Return of the Jedi*, made in 1983, but chronologically the final chapter, is the lowest-ranking, perhaps reflecting its status as the worst-regarded of the series. Blame the Ewoks.

RETURN OF THE JEDI

Director **Richard Marquand**
Producer **Howard G. Kazanjian**
Screenplay **Lawrence Kasdan, George Lucas**
Director of Photography **Alan Hume**
Editors **Sean Barton, Marcia Lucas, Duwayne Dunham**
Production Designer **Norman Reynolds**
Music **John Williams**

Luke Skywalker • Mark Hamill
Han Solo • Harrison Ford
Princess Leia • Carrie Fisher
Lando Calrissian • Billy Dee Williams
C-3PO • Anthony Daniels
Chewbacca • Peter Mayhew
Anakin Skywalker • Sebastian Shaw
Emperor Palpatine • Ian McDiarmid
Yoda • Frank Oz
Darth Vader • David Prowse
Voice of Darth Vader • James Earl Jones
Ben Obi-Wan Kenobi • Alec Guinness
R2-D2 • Kenny Baker
Moff Jerjerrod • Michael Pennington
Admiral Piett • Kenneth Colley
Bib Fortuna • Michael Carter
Wedge • Denis Lawson
Admiral Ackbar • Tim Rose
General Madine • Dermot Crowley
Mon Mothma • Caroline Blakiston

Opposite top Hide and seek: Princess Leia (Carrie Fisher) and an Ewok keep watch for Imperial stormtroopers *Opposite middle* Bait: Ewoks were used to secure the interest of younger viewers *Opposite below* Princess Leia held captive by Jabba the Hutt

THE STORY

As Darth Vader supervises the construction of a new improved Death Star, Luke Skywalker, Lando Calrissian, Princess Leia, R2-D2 and C-3PO rescue Han Solo from Jabba the Hutt. As his friends make plans with the Rebel Alliance, Luke visits his ancient teacher Yoda, who confirms that Darth Vader is his father. Luke also learns that Leia is his twin sister. He travels with her and the others to destroy the deflector-shield installation that protects the Death Star, so that Calrissian and the rebel fleet can demolish the Empire's forces. Luke allows himself to be captured by Vader and is taken to the Emperor Palpatine, who reveals that the rebels are flying into a trap and, eager to recruit Luke to the 'dark side' of the Force, urges him to duel with his ruthless father.

As the Death Star unleashes unsuspected fire power at the rebels, Luke nearly kills Vader but recovers his self-control; in turn, his father destroys the Emperor at the cost of his own life. With the help of the Ewoks, furry inhabitants of Endor, Leia and Han at last accomplish their mission and Calrissian blows up the Death Star. Han and Leia are reunited with Luke, and the friends join the Ewoks in celebration.

WHAT THEY SAID THEN ...

Once threatening us with at least nine episodes of his saga, Lucas offers in *Return of the Jedi* an obvious conclusion to a trilogy, and has stated his interest in retirement. Han and Leia are conveniently paired off – and a nicely understated job has been achieved with the romantic stuff – while Luke has succeeded in dispatching his father to the Jedi equivalent of Nirvana, with Viking funeral thrown in. The completion of Luke's hunt for his parent, the struggle to win over (in both senses) his father, seems a tempting point of justification for the whole *Star Wars* quest.

If the revels are indeed now ended, *Jedi* couldn't have been a better resolution for them. Self-effacingly directed by Richard Marquand, who wisely makes no attempt to compete with Lucas's dominating magic, the film sparkles crisply from one peak of action to the next. The acrobatic struggle in midair over

OSCARS
4 nominations, **1 winner**

Art Direction
Music (Original Score): John Williams
Sound
Sound Effects Editing: Ben Burtt
Special Achievement Award (Visual Effects)

WHAT WON THAT YEAR?
Best Picture: *Terms of Endearment*
Directing: James L. Brooks *Terms of Endearment*
Actor in a Leading Role: Robert Duvall *Tender Mercies*
Actress in a Leading Role: Shirley MacLaine *Terms of Endearment*

BAFTAS
4 nominations, **1 winner**

Make-Up Artist: Phil Tippett, Stuart Freeborn
Production Design: Norman Reynolds
Sound: Ben Burtt, Tony Dawe, Gary Summers
Special Visual Effects

WHAT WON THAT YEAR?
Film: *Educating Rita*
Direction: Bill Forsyth *Local Hero*
Actor: Michael Caine *Educating Rita*, Dustin Hoffman *Tootsie*
Actress: Julie Walters *Educating Rita*

the lethal creature in its sand pit, with Luke doing a Fairbanks with his light-sabre, has no equivalent in excitement this side of Tarzan creator Edgar Rice Burroughs. The sequence is then smartly outpaced by the vertiginous pursuits through the forest of Endor. The Ewoks steal much of the thunder in the final battles, and but for their tendency to sound like a chorus from *Oklahoma!* could replace E.T. and teddies in the world's nurseries. We shall, of course, be seeing their like again, as a fresh crop of imitations swarms in the wake of Lucas's film. But Luke himself now seems destined for a new universe.

WHAT THEY SAY NOW ...

After the triumph of *The Empire Strikes Back* (1980), it was reasonable to expect that George Lucas would step up the suspense and excitement for what is (at least for the foreseeable future) the final instalment of the *Star Wars* series. But instead, *Return of the Jedi* is a muddle. After an impressively outlandish encounter with Jabba the Hutt and his rubbery cronies, the picture decamps for large periods of time to a forest populated by rat-faced teddy bears (the Ewoks). A more pertinent question even than 'What was Lucas on?' would be 'How did he think he could get away with it?'

But get away with it he did. *Empire* had been witty, thrilling and even poignant. *Jedi*, blandly directed by Marquand but with Lucas's thumbprints all over it, severely infantilised promising material. It has been said that Lucas used the Ewoks as bait to secure the interest of younger viewers, who would then pester their parents for the merchandise. That sounds consistent with this film-maker, whose entrepreneurial skill far outweighs his artistic abilities. But in the process, he alienated many older viewers. It is hard now, more than two decades after the release of *Jedi*, to find anyone who does not rank it as the worst of the series.

SCENE STEALER

The hair-raising chase through the forests of Endor at breakneck speed – a rare example of undiluted pleasure in this most calculated of movies.

The roster of UK 100

top box-office films takes in a wide range of styles and genres: science fiction and musicals, animation and war movies, comedy, drama, romance, period movies, fantasy and satire. Some are black and white; some are in colour. They range from the 1930s to the opening decade of the 21st century. But they have one thing in common: they're all English-language movies. No foreign film makes it into the list.

This is probably due not so much to the dominance of Hollywood product in the UK film market, but because Britain, alone among the larger European countries, prefers to show foreign-language films subtitled rather than dubbed. In France, Germany, Italy and Spain, countries where the size of the market makes the more expensive process of dubbing financially viable, the vast majority of foreign movies are revoiced. Many actors in these countries make a very comfortable living in the dubbing studios, rarely appearing on screen at all.

Prior to the advent of sound, films really could be universal in their appeal. All producers needed to do was to slot in new intertitles, often renaming the characters to make them seem

indigenous – John and Mary became Jean-Pierre and Anne-Marie, or Fritz and Gretchen. When sound arrived film-makers tried to retain this international scope by shooting multiple versions of a film, wheeling in new sets of actors to speak the dialogue in their native tongue. Some films were simultaneously shot in as many as seven different language versions. But the cost was prohibitive, and by the end of the 1930s this practice had largely died out. Dubbing or subtitling became the only viable options.

Since in the UK the majority of mass-market movies were already in English, Britain increasingly tended to favour subtitling. Foreign-language films were in any case seen as something of a highbrow taste, full of Swedish gloom or outré sex and generally hived off into the art-house circuit. Subtitling confirmed that status. Over recent decades dubbing has become increasingly rare in the UK, except for exploitation fare like spaghetti westerns and Hong Kong chopsocky movies. Even films like *La Dolce Vita* (1960), which attracted widespread attention in the British press, were shown subtitled. Occasional exceptions, such as Lucchino Visconti's *Il Gattopardo* (*The Leopard*, 1963), only seemed to confirm the trend; the English-language dubbed version was condemned by many reviewers, and disowned by Visconti himself.

Opposite above Zhang Ziyi in Wong Kar-Wai's 2046 *Opposite below* Despite widespread press attention, Fellini's La Dolce Vita failed to make the list *Top* House of Flying Daggers, one of the new breed of subtitled hits from the Far East *Above* Director Luchino Visconti himself condemned the dubbed version of Il Gattopardo (The Leopard)

These days only animated films are usually dubbed, and not always then. Hayao Miyazaki's *Spirited Away* (2001) was distributed in both subtitled and dubbed versions, and did equally well in both. The dubbed-exploitation rule seems to be weakening: latter-day martial-arts movies like *Crouching Tiger, Hidden Dragon* (2000) or Zhang Yimou's *Hero* (2002) are released with subtitles. Stephen Chow's *Shaolin Soccer* (2001) was a recent exception, but there again reviewers expressed disapproval, and his subsequent hit, *Kung Fu Hustle* (2004), was subtitled.

All this will please the purists, to whom dubbing is an abomination. But given that the majority of UK cinemagoers still find subtitles off-putting (or even are unable to read them), it means that no foreign-language movie is ever likely to make the box-office top 100.

91

Dir: Frank CAPRA / USA
Released in Britain: 1936
Running Time: 115 minutes
Black and white
Estimated Attendance: 8.3 million

MR DEEDS GOES TO TOWN

Director/Producer **Frank Capra**
Screenplay **Robert Riskin**, based on the story by
    Clarence Budington Kelland
Director of Photography **Joseph Walker**
Editor **Gene Havlick**
Production Designer **Stephen Goosson**
Music **Howard Jackson**

Longfellow Deeds • Gary Cooper
Louise 'Babe' Bennett • Jean Arthur
MacWade • George Bancroft
Cornelius Cobb • Lionel Stander
John Cedar • Douglass Dumbrille
Walter, The valet • Raymond Walburn
Judge May • H. B. Warner
Mabel Dawson • Ruth Donnelly
Morrow • Walter Catlett
Farmer • John Wray
Anderson • Harry C. Bradley
James Cedar • Stanley Andrews

The second Frank Capra title on The Ultimate Film list is a charming fable about an Ordinary Joe from Nowhereville who inherits a fortune and winds up in New York. Gary Cooper and Jean Arthur are delightful, and Capra pulls off the blend of frothy screwball and social commentary with matchless ease.

THE STORY

Mr Deeds, who has never stirred from the backwoods town in which he was born and where he makes a reasonable living writing poetry for postcards, inherits a fortune of $20 million from an uncle he has never met. He is sought out and brought to New York and is immediately surrounded by crooks and parasites; his common sense, however, prevents him from tumbling into their clutches. Naturally, he becomes 'news' and a star reporter, Mary – AKA Louise 'Babe' Bennett – is dispatched to write him up. By a ruse she gains his confidence and day after day fills the front page with the comic and sometimes extraordinary antics of the Cinderella-Man, as she dubs him.

Quite unsuspecting that Mary is the author of the articles that hurt him so much, he continues to go out with her daily and eventually falls in love with her. She tells her editor that she will not go on writing him up any longer and makes up her mind to tell Deeds the truth about herself, but the news is broken to him from another source that his Mary is the author of the articles. The shock of this final disillusionment is so great that he decides to give away all his money and use it to bring happiness to those who are suffering from the Slump and poverty. He devises a scheme to put farmers back on the land in smallholdings and works feverishly at it himself.

Meanwhile, other relatives of the dead man and their lawyers have Deeds arrested on the ground of insanity, in order to get the money for themselves. He is now so disgusted with everything that he meekly goes to the asylum, refuses to have counsel at his examination or even, at the start, to plead. Witness after witness comes forward for the plaintiffs, but after Mary has publicly declared her love for him, Deeds makes up his mind to plead and goes into the witness box. There, he puts up such a spirited defence that he is triumphantly acquitted and all ends happily.

WHAT THEY SAID THEN …

Frank Capra has made an excellent job of a good story that is allowed to unfold itself in a restrained manner. Exaggeration has been carefully avoided. Gary Cooper as Mr Longfellow Deeds never becomes a simpleton or a buffoon and

the gradual ripening of Jean Arthur's affection is excellently done. The smaller parts are allowed to be strongly enough characterised to stand out. The only time that interest seems to flag is during the trial scene, when the final denouement is obvious, and it is but a question of how it will be encompassed.

WHAT THEY SAY NOW ...

Frank Capra's talent for combining screwball comedy with social fable reached its apogee with this film in which Gary Cooper turns the tables on mocking city types by deciding to give it all away to those whose lives have been wrecked by the Depression. Cooper gives a classic, commanding portrayal; his solid, integrity-laden performance as an individual who demonstrates that the world is out of step with him can be seen as being directly related to another of his roles – Marshal Will Kane in *High Noon* (1952). Jean Arthur as the newswoman initially engaged in a sneering game falls in love affectingly, in the role that made a star of her, but which was originally intended for Carole Lombard. The film's charms have not been dimmed either by the years or by a misguided 2002 remake with the gurning comedian Adam Sandler in the lead, opposite Winona Ryder.

CLASSIC QUOTE

Louise 'Babe' Bennett: That guy is either the dumbest, stupidest, most imbecilic idiot in the world, or else he's the grandest thing alive. I can't make him out.'

SCENE STEALER

After making sure that nobody's looking, Longfellow slides down the banister of the grand staircase of his newly acquired mansion, as though injecting his own idiosyncratic personality into his new-found surroundings of wealth and abundance.

Above *It's a shoe-in for Walter the valet (Raymond Walburn) and a grumpy Longfellow Deeds (Gary Cooper)* **Below** *Mary's love conquers all when Deeds' sanity is questioned in court* **Overleaf** *Longfellow Deeds leaves town with a rousing send off*

OSCARS
5 nominations, **1 winner**

Outstanding Production
Directing: Frank Capra
Actor: Gary Cooper
Sound Recording: John Livadary
Writing (Screenplay): Robert Riskin

WHAT WON THAT YEAR?
Outstanding Production: *The Great Ziegfeld*
Actor: Paul Muni *The Story of Louis Pasteur*
Actress: Luise Rainer *The Great Ziegfeld*

BAFTAS NOT AWARDED UNTIL 1947

92

Dir: Ken ANNAKIN / UK, USA
Released in Britain: 1960
Running Time: 126 minutes
Colour: Technicolor
Estimated Attendance: 8.3 million

There is no shortage of Disney movies in *The Ultimate Film* list. In fact, that studio's output accounts for more than 10 per cent of the titles collected here. But what a surprise to find *The Swiss Family Robinson* among them. It is scarcely mentioned now, and was in no sense influential – so what exactly was its special appeal?

THE SWISS FAMILY ROBINSON

Director **Ken Annakin**
Producer **Bill Anderson**
Screenplay **Lowell S. Hawley**, based on the novel by
    Johann David Wyss
Director of Photography **Harry Waxman**
Editor **Peter Boita**
Production Designer **John Howell**
Music **William Alwyn**

Father • John Mills
Mother • Dorothy McGuire
Fritz • James MacArthur
Roberta • Janet Munro
Pirate Chief • Sessue Hayakawa
Ernst • Tommy Kirk
Francis • Kevin Corcoran
Captain Moreland • Cecil Parker
Pirate • Andy Ho
Pirate • Milton Reid
Pirate • Larry Taylor

THE STORY

Mr and Mrs Robinson, with their sons Fritz, Ernst and Francis, are emigrating from Basle to New Guinea when they are shipwrecked after fleeing from pirates. They manage to reach land on a raft and to bring ashore animals and provisions of all kinds from the wrecked ship. Feeling that their stay may be a long one, they build a comfortable house in the tree tops and settle down to an idyllic life. But Fritz and Ernst set out in a home-made boat to explore the island. They are driven ashore on the other side of the island where they encounter the pirate crew and two captives, an English sea captain and his granddaughter Roberta, disguised as a cabin boy. They rescue Roberta and take her back with them across country. The pirates pursue them and besiege the fortified hill on which the family has taken refuge. After a long fight Roberta's grandfather arrives in his ship and drives the pirates away. He arranges to take Ernst back to Europe, but Fritz and Roberta decide to stay on the island with Mr and Mrs Robinson.

WHAT THEY SAID THEN ...

A film that exactly achieves its aim deserves credit even when the target is relatively easy. Ken Annakin and the Disney team were out to make an entertaining adventure film for children and they have hit the bull's-eye. Shot on location in Tobago, it has enormous zest and humour, splendid colour, and even several oddly touching moments. There are faults, of course. Certain situations are either too easily sorted out or go on too long, but the resultant longueurs never upset the film's essential buoyancy. The entire cast, including an arkful of assorted wild animals, play with just the right high-minded seriousness. And the high spots – a race with the entire family mounted on animals and a battle with pirates which is as funny as it is furious – aptly underline the story's glorious absurdity.

WHAT THEY SAY NOW ...

The Swiss Family Robinson provides pleasant, unexceptional entertainment of the kind routinely available in the live-action confections released by Disney in between their better-regarded animated spectaculars. In the main, these pictures never achieved the success of their animated stable mates, but then they weren't meant to; they were usually cheap and quick to make, and could be relied upon to turn a profit when released to coincide with school holidays. The list runs on and on, from the well-liked (*Herbie* series) to the justly forgotten (*Hill's Angels*, 1979). But only *The Swiss Family Robinson* did well enough to make it onto *The Ultimate Film* list.

It is hard to see now what gave this inconsequential movie such a mighty commercial boost, but then the sanctity of genuinely family-oriented films should not be underestimated; and this is certainly well-packaged stuff with maximum appeal. Adult viewers could admire that good egg John Mills, gamely allowing himself to be upstaged by a spider monkey here, an ostrich there; or Dorothy McGuire, languishing beneath a pink parasol, looking almost indistinguishable from the flamingos lazily picking through the undergrowth. Adolescent girls dragged along by their parents to a Sunday afternoon at the pictures could feast their eyes on the teenage sons who disrobe at every opportunity, and who turn to bickering once a young female enters the vicinity. For the very young, there is endless tomfoolery with the wildlife – a galumphing elephant, a sneaky tiger, and a giant sea turtle happy to give piggybacks.

Despite the appearance of some snarling pirates, there is little to suggest that being shipwrecked isn't a jolly nice alternative to the daily grind. The picture's sincerity looks quaint and funny now. As the camera regards the majestic tree house that Mills has knocked together, apparently without disturbing a hair on his head, the score (which, in true Disney style, never lets up for a second) swells with a fervour that suggests he has just polished off the ceiling of the Sistine Chapel.

CLASSIC QUOTE

Father Robinson: 'The world is full of nice, ordinary little people who live in nice, ordinary little houses on the ground. But didn't you ever dream of a house up on a tree top?'

*This page Armed and dangerous: John Mills and Dorothy McGuire prepare for the fight as Mr and Mrs Robinson **Right** Speed king: Fritz (James MacArthur) rides a turtle*

OSCARS

WHAT WON THAT YEAR?
Best Motion Picture: *The Apartment*
Directing: Billy Wilder *The Apartment*
Actor: Burt Lancaster *Elmer Gantry*
Actress: Elizabeth Taylor *Butterfield 8*

BAFTAS

WHAT WON THAT YEAR?
Film: *The Apartment*
British Film: *Saturday Night, Sunday Morning*
British Actor: Peter Finch *The Trials of Oscar Wilde*
British Actress: Rachel Roberts *Saturday Night, Sunday Morning*
Foreign Actor: Jack Lemmon *The Apartment*
Foreign Actress: Shirley MacLaine *The Apartment*

93

Dir: Lewis GILBERT / UK
Released in Britain: 1967
Running Time: 116 minutes
Colour: Technicolor
Estimated Attendance: 8.3 million

Yes, it's that man again. Two years later, he would pass the torch, albeit briefly, to George Lazenby. But for now it was Sean Connery as 007: his third Bond movie on the list is a riot of gadgets and glamour that boasts one of the series' most memorable villains (plus cat).

YOU ONLY LIVE TWICE

Director **Lewis Gilbert**
Producers **Albert R. Broccoli, Harry Saltzman**
Screenplay **Roald Dahl**, based on the novel by
 Ian Fleming
Director of Photography **Freddie Young**
Editor **Thelma Connell**
Production Designer **Ken Adam**
Music **John Barry**

James Bond • Sean Connery
Aki • Akiko Wakabayashi
Tiger Tanaka • Tetsuro Tanba
Kissy Suzuki • Mie Hama
Osato • Teru Shimada
Helga Brandt • Karin Dor
Miss Moneypenny • Lois Maxwell
Q • Desmond Llewelyn
Henderson • Charles Gray
M • Bernard Lee
Ernst Stavro Blofeld • Donald Pleasance
Ling • Ts'ai Chin
Car Driver • Peter Fanene Maivia
SPECTRE No. 3 • Burt Kwouk
SPECTRE No. 4 • Michael Chow
Blofeld's Bodyguard • Ronald Rich
Bond's Masseuse • Jeanne Roland
Assassin in Bedroom • David Toguri
Submarine Captain • John Stone
Astronaut, 1st US Spacecraft • Norman Jones

THE STORY

When an American space capsule is intercepted and vanishes after landing somewhere in Japan, the Russians are blamed and an international incident seems likely. The real culprit is SPECTRE, and after an elaborate charade designed to make the enemy think he is dead, James Bond swims ashore in Japan to investigate. His contact in Tokyo, Henderson, is promptly murdered. Bond kills the assailant, takes his place in the getaway car, and is driven to the Osato Chemical Engineering Company. Surviving an attempt to kill him as he cracks the safe, he escapes with the aid of Aki, secretary to Tiger Tanaka, head of the Japanese secret service. Returning to the Osato warehouses, Bond finds a ship being loaded with liquid nitrogen, is captured and left trapped in a pilotless aircraft by Osato's sadistic aide, Helga Brandt. He survives.

Meanwhile, Tanaka has traced the ship to a remote part of the Japanese coastline. Reconnoitring in a miniature helicopter, Bond places the centre of operations in the vicinity of an extinct volcano. Disguised as a Japanese fisherman and provided with a 'wife', Kissy Suzuki, Bond moves into the area, while Tanaka holds his Ninja Commandos in readiness. Gaining entrance to the well-armoured volcano, Bond finds SPECTRE arch-villain Ernst Stavro Blofeld — who has just fed Helga to his piranha fish — preparing to follow up his success with a Russian capsule by seizing an American one. Bond is captured, but with the aid of Tanaka and his Ninjas manages to foil Blofeld just in time and blow up his entire HQ.

WHAT THEY SAID THEN ...

Really no better and no worse than its predecessors, the fifth James Bond is rather less enjoyable mainly because the formula has become so completely mechanical (and Bond himself so predictably indestructible) without any compensation in other directions. Beautiful but disposable women, fiendish devices and expendable opponents duly make their appearance at carefully regulated intervals; all are handled with the same expressionless competence by Bond. It would be hard to care less.

Below *Evil genius Ernst Stavro Blofeld
(Donald Pleasence) with feline friend*

It would be different if *You Only Live Twice* revealed some of the elegance and imagination in direction which gives such a lift to a film like *Modesty Blaise* (1966). But in this series money flows like water to ensure a glossy, well-oiled operation where no touch of individuality is allowed to upset the applecart. Still, whatever else one can say about the Bond films, their mechanical gimmicks run rings round anything offered by most of the other spy and secret-agent films. *You Only Live Twice* has its generous share, including a helicopter fitted with an electromagnet for removing unwanted pursuing cars from the highway, a desk with a built-in X-ray machine for seeing if your client is carrying a gun, and a do-it-yourself miniature helicopter kit complete with supply of machine guns, missiles and aerial mines.

The dialogue also has its moments, mainly risqué, but it is perhaps symptomatic of the film that the machines don't give the humans a look in. Even Donald Pleasence – scar-faced, sneering and fondling a supercilious cat – as the chief villain, seems diminished.

WHAT THEY SAY NOW ...
Roald Dahl wrote the screenplay for this entertaining yarn and freely admitted it was hokum. The producers told him, 'You can come up with anything you like as far as the story goes.' But they warned him there were two elements he must not mess with, 'The first is the character of Bond. That's fixed. The second is the girl formula. That is also fixed.' When he asked what 'the girl formula' was, Dahl was told: 'You use three different girls and Bond has them all.' 'Separately or en masse?' he asked.

This has emerged as one of the better Bonds. Donald Pleasence makes a memorably creepy Blofeld, a part that fits him like a glove. Ken Adam's production design of Spectre's secret base in the mouth of a volcano is awe-inspiring. Sean Connery was bellyaching off-set about playing Bond, but on camera, he is still the same saturnine and mischievous presence. Audiences couldn't get enough of him.

94

Dir: **William FRIEDKIN / USA**
Released in Britain: **1974**
Running Time: **122 minutes**
Colour: **Metrocolor**
Estimated Attendance: **8.3 million**

The scariest movie of all time? Or a recruitment film for the Catholic Church? One thing's for sure: as the only horror title on the list, *The Exorcist* is still the head-spinning, vomit-spouting phenomenon that it was on its first release.

THE EXORCIST

Director **William Friedkin**
Producer **William Peter Blatty**
Screenplay **William Peter Blatty**, based on his novel
Director of Photography **Owen Roizman**
Editor **Evan Lottman, Norman Gay**
Production Designer **Bill Malley**
Music **Jack Nitzsche**

Chris MacNeil • Ellen Burstyn
Father Lancaster Merrin, S.J. • Max Von Sydow
Father Damien Karras, S.J. • Jason Miller
Regan Theresa MacNeil • Linda Blair
Lt William Kinderman • Lee J. Cobb
Sharon Spencer • Kitty Winn
Burke Dennings • Jack MacGowran
Father Dyer, S.J. • William O'Malley
Dr Klein • Barton Heyman
Clinic Director • Peter Masterson
Karl • Rudolf Schundler
Willie • Gina Petrushka
Dr Tanney • Robert Symonds
Psychiatrist • Arthur Storch
President of University • Thomas Bermingham
Karras's Mother • Vasiliki Maliaros
Karras's Uncle • Titos Vandis
Bishop Michael • Wallace Rooney
Assistant Director • Ron Faber
Mary Jo Perrin • Donna Mitchell

THE STORY

In Iraq, Father Merrin, an elderly Jesuit archaeologist, has a premonition of evil while examining artefacts found in his excavations. In Georgetown, Washington, DC, Chris MacNeil, an actress filming on location at the Jesuit college, is troubled by noises in the house she has taken with her 12-year-old daughter Regan, who is behaving oddly. Panic-stricken when she finds Regan's bed bucking uncontrollably one night, Chris seeks medical advice. Diagnosing brain disturbance, the doctors are puzzled when exhaustive tests reveal nothing wrong with Regan. Meanwhile, Regan becomes possessed of a demonic strength, speaks with an alien voice and seems to be undergoing physical deformation.

In the college chapel, a statue of the Virgin is found desecrated. Burke Dennings, the director of Chris's film, is found dead outside Regan's window after being alone with the child. When a detective, Kinderman, concludes that Dennings was murdered, the distraught Chris – realising that Regan must have killed him – begs the college's psychiatric counsellor, Father Karras, to perform an exorcism. Karras, troubled by loss of faith, is sceptical. But when he sees Regan, now unrecognisable as a child, he secures permission for an exorcism. Since Karras is inexperienced, Father Merrin is summoned. Recognising the evil within Regan, Merrin embarks on a lengthy battle with the demon, and seems to be winning when he dies of a heart attack. In despair, Karras calls upon the demon to enter his body, then jumps to his death from the window, freeing Regan.

WHAT THEY SAID THEN ...

The dispiriting thing about *The Exorcist* is not so much that it expects to be taken seriously, as the fact that it has been. In fact, it is no more nor less than a blood-and-thunder horror movie, foundering heavily on the rocks of pretension. In the more leisurely space of his novel, William Peter Blatty had time to build up the gradual sense of malaise overtaking Georgetown, and to develop convincingly within that general malaise the more private torment of Father Karras's loss of faith. The film, however, offers little more than a perfunctory acknowledgement of the community (one Jesuit party, one shot of a desecrated church, one

Above *Regan (Linda Blair) isn't a normal 12-year-old girl, as the demon within makes an early, fleeting physiognomic appearance*
Right *Turning point: Regan's head goes round and round and round*

unhappy priest), and the crosscutting between the discovery of Regan's possession and Karras's spiritual torment is all too clearly designed to establish a significant (but in fact quite empty) parallel between the two kinds of 'possession' or loss of purity.

In addition, the whole Karras subplot has become embarrassingly perfunctory, with poor old white-haired momma languishing in the workhouse while darkly brooding son works off his guilt on a punchball. It is symptomatic of what is wrong with the film that in adapting his novel Blatty has simply thinned it out, leaving in characters who now have no function whatsoever or are there merely as convenient plot hooks, wasting time with them that would have been better spent exploring atmosphere and motivations.

Predictably, perhaps, the film is at its best in the centre section where it can forget about significance and concentrate on the chills. Even more horrifying, perhaps, than the sensationalist sections involving head-turning, profanity and vomit are the elaborate and endless medical tests to which the unfortunate child

WILLIAM PETER BLATTY'S

THE EXORCIST.

Directed by WILLIAM FRIEDKIN

10 ACADEMY AWARD NOMINATIONS INCLUDING
BEST PICTURE

ELLEN BURSTYN · MAX VON SYDOW · LEE J. COBB · KITTY WINN · JACK MacGOWRAN

JASON MILLER as Father Karras · LINDA BLAIR as Regan · Produced by WILLIAM PETER BLATTY · Executive Producer NOEL MARSHALL · Screenplay by WILLIAM PETER BLATTY based on

From Warner Bros. A Warner Communications Company · Released by Columbia-Warner Distributors · Hear The Theme Song Mike Oldfield's "Tubular Bells"

is submitted, with the ghastly ritual of encephalograms and spinals shot to look like a refined form of torture. Beside these scenes, the messier aspects of the possession (the vomited bile, the self-inflicted wounds) look all too much like routine paint and make-up jobs.

Still, with Mercedes McCambridge doing sterling work on the demon's hoarsely mocking voice, the film does build up a fair tension – and an expectation all the more dashed when the Merrin-Devil confrontation promised in the (much too) exquisitely shot prologue turns out to be a mumble of oaths and prayers which doesn't even attempt the dialectic it had in the novel.

WHAT THEY SAY NOW ...

In some quarters *The Exorcist* is reckoned the scariest horror film of all time, and some critics have rated it even higher, calling it the 'the greatest film ever made'. Such claims seem hard to sustain. The scary moments are potently orchestrated, and the central concept of a sweet, sunny-natured 12-year-old girl being transformed into an obscene, foul-mouthed monster has enough shock-value to hold the attention. Perhaps Catholics – or lapsed Catholics – can take the theological content seriously, and certainly the Church is presented in a flatteringly heroic light. (Pauline Kael described the movie as 'the biggest recruiting poster the Catholic Church has had since the sunnier days of *Going My Way* [1944] and *The Bells of St Mary's* [1945].') For the more sceptical among us, *The Exorcist* is Hammer-horror stuff with a bigger budget, slam-bang special effects and added blasphemy. When it comes to demonic possession, *Rosemary's Baby* (1968) does the whole thing far more subtly – and hence far more chillingly.

SCENE STEALER

Alerted by her daughter's screams, Chris rushes to her room to find objects hurtling wildly about the air and Regan masturbating with a crucifix. When Chris tries to stop her, Regan first forces her mother's head down into her bloody crotch, then hits her in the face, knocking her across the room. Next, Regan turns her head to look at Chris – and the head just keeps on turning, beyond human possibility, until it has twisted completely around.

BEHIND THE SCENES

Several prominent directors turned down *The Exorcist*, among them Stanley Kubrick, Arthur Penn, Mike Nichols and John Boorman. The latter did agree to direct the ill-fated sequel, *Exorcist II: The Heretic* (1977) – a decision he came to regret.

Mercedes McCambridge, who provided the rasping voice of the demon, had to sue Warner Brothers to gain proper credit. A fellow litigant was stunt double Eileen Smith, who performed the projectile-vomiting scenes (which used pea soup). Smith also sued Warner Brothers to get the credit she felt she deserved.

OSCARS
10 nominations, **2 winners**

Best Picture
Directing: William Friedkin
Actress: Ellen Burstyn
Actor in a Supporting Role: Jason Miller
Actress in a Supporting Role: Linda Blair
Art Direction: Bill Malley, Jerry Wunderlich
Cinematography: Owen Roizman
Film Editing
Sound: Robert Knudson, Chris Newman
Writing (Screenplay Based on Material from Another Medium):
  William Peter Blatty

WHAT WON THAT YEAR?
Best Picture: *The Sting*
Directing: George Roy Hill *The Sting*
Actor: Jack Lemmon *Save the Tiger*
Actress: Glenda Jackson *A Touch of Class*

BAFTAS
1 nomination

Sound Track

WHAT WON THAT YEAR?
Film: *Lacombe Lucien*
Direction: Roman Polanski *Chinatown*
Actor: Jack Nicholson *The Last Detail/Chinatown*
Actress: Joanne Woodward *Summer Wishes, Winter Dreams*

95

Dir: Walter LANG / USA
Released in Britain: 1956
Running Time: 132 minutes
Colour: DeLuxe
Estimated Attendance: 8.2 million

The third movie on the list to be adapted from a Rodgers and Hammerstein musical is a spectacular feast of song and dance that seduced millions of British cinemagoers. Some, though, were left wondering what happened to the serious undertones in this story about an English governess and the King of Siam.

THE KING AND I

Director **Walter Lang**
Producers **Darryl F. Zanuck, Charles Brackett**
Screenplay **Ernest Lehman**, based on the musical play by Richard Rodgers and Oscar Hammerstein II, based on the novel by Margaret Landon
Director of Photography **Leon Shamroy**
Editor **Robert Simpson**
Production Designers **Lyle Wheeler, John F. DeCuir**
Music **Richard Rodgers**

Anna Leonowens • Deborah Kerr
King Mongkut • Yul Brynner
Tuptim • Rita Moreno
Kralahome • Martin Benson
Louis Leonowens • Rex Thompson
Prince Chulalongkorn • Patrick Adiarte
Lady Thiang • Terry Saunders
Lun Tha • Carlos Rivas
British Ambassador • Alan Mowbray
Sir Edward Ramsay • Geoffrey Toone
Eliza in Ballet • Yuriko
Simon Legree in Ballet • Marion Jim
Keeper of the Dogs • Robert Banas

Opposite 'Shall we dance?' The King (Yul Brynner) and Anna (Deborah Kerr)

THE STORY

In 1862 Anna Leonowens, widow of a British army officer, arrives in Bangkok as governess to the children of the King of Siam. Her independent spirit at first angers the King, who repudiates his agreement to provide her with a house of her own outside the palace walls. Gradually, however, the King begins to depend on her advice and Anna increasingly sympathises with him in his attempts to 'civilise' himself and his people and come to terms with Western habits and ideas.

Afraid that the British may regard him as a barbarian, the King enlists Anna's help in organising a state banquet on the occasion of the British Ambassador's visit. But Anna's affection for the King is shattered when he threatens to brutally flog one of his wives, who has been recaptured after escaping from the palace with her lover. She intervenes, saving the girl, but the incident breaks the King's spirit. Anna is preparing to leave Bangkok when she learns that the King is dying. She agrees to remain to instruct the new ruler of Siam, the young crown prince.

WHAT THEY SAID THEN ...

The King and I follows the pattern established by Carousel (1956). The trend now is away from the film musical in its own right, as developed by Minnelli, Gene Kelly and others, and towards productions that are essentially screen versions of successful stage shows. The conception is static, the numbers are used to punctuate the action rather than as a natural extension of it, and the emphasis is on elaborate décor. Much of The King and I is agreeable to look at, in a style that might perhaps be described as Far Eastern wedding cake, and the costumes, by Irene Sharaff, are rich and ripe. The material itself wears well, exhibiting the customary Rodgers and Hammerstein flair for exploiting the unlikely scene and situation, and the story of the Victorian lady and the sympathetic barbarian, though sentimentalised in this version, still has its charm.

In these musicals, songs count for more than dances. The ballet set piece, the Siamese interpretation of Uncle Tom's Cabin, is intermittently inventive in choreography and design; two numbers, the first entry of the Siamese royal children and the captivating 'Shall We Dance?' are handled with a pleasantly light sentiment. But the film, like its predecessor, is in the long run simply too large and weighty for its material: gaiety has something of a struggle to survive.

WHAT THEY SAY NOW ...

This lavish film version of the Rodgers and Hammerstein Broadway musical enabled Yul Brynner to reprise his charismatic performance as the polygamous, bald-pated Siamese king introduced to the ways of the West by the hoop-skirted, mid-Victorian English governess engaged as tutor for his many children. She had been played on stage by Gertrude Lawrence in her last role before her death in 1952, then by Deborah Kerr on screen. The result was dazzling, with the costume designs by Irene Sharaff counting among its five Oscars.

The teaming of Brynner and Kerr works well, although the actress's singing voice was not considered adequate, and she was almost entirely dubbed by Marni Nixon (as Audrey Hepburn would be in *My Fair Lady* in 1964). Many of the Rodgers-Hammerstein songs have become standards, and are staged with great charm. Consequently, serious undertones dealing with the confrontation of alien cultures tend to be submerged in delightful sweetness, in contrast with the abrasive dramatic versions of the same story, *Anna and the King of Siam* (1946) and the later *Anna and the King* (1999). The film was banned outright in Thailand, where it was regarded as a travesty of history – with some justification, as the real Anna Leonowens never enjoyed such an exalted friendship with the monarch.

CLASSIC QUOTE

The King's command of English is persistently eccentric, and often when uttering a royal pronouncement he adds by way of reinforcement, 'et cetera, et cetera, et cetera'.

SCENE STEALER

A classic ice-melting moment is the 'Shall We Dance?' number when Brynner gets the hang of western-style ballroom technique and extends his hand to grasp Kerr's tightly-corseted waist before whirling her frenziedly around his grand salon.

IN THE CHAIR

Walter Lang, a reliable Fox contract director and veteran of silent movies, had in the 1940s made several Betty Grable musicals. His career ended with *Snow White and the Three Stooges* in 1961.

OSCARS
9 nominations, **5 winners**

Best Motion Picture
Directing: Walter Lang
Actor: Yul Brynner
Actress: Deborah Kerr
Art Direction (Color)
Cinematography (Color): Leon Shamroy
Costume Design (Color): Irene Sharaff
Music (Scoring of a Musical Picture): Alfred Newman, Ken Darby
Sound Recording: Carl Faulkner

WHAT WON THAT YEAR?
Best Motion Picture: *Around the World in 80 Days*
Directing: George Stevens *Giant*
Actress: Ingrid Bergman *Anastasia*

BAFTAS

WHAT WON THAT YEAR?
Film: *Gervaise*
British Film: *Reach for the Sky*
British Actor: Peter Finch *A Town Like Alice*
British Actress: Virginia McKenna *A Town Like Alice*
Foreign Actor: François Perier *Gervaise*
Foreign Actress: Anna Magnani *The Rose Tattoo*

96

Dirs: Peter LORD, Nick PARK / UK, USA
Released in Britain: 2000
Running Time: 84 minutes
Estimated Attendance: 8.12 million

After taking Wallace and Gromit to its collective heart, the British public had high expectations for the feature debut from Bristol-based Aardman Animations. And *Chicken Run* didn't disappoint, with its pleasingly silly plot, inventiveness to spare *and* a guest spot for a genuine action hero.

CHICKEN RUN

Directors **Peter Lord, Nick Park**
Producers **Peter Lord, David Sproxton, Nick Park**
Screenplay **Karey Kirkpatrick**, based on a story by
    Peter Lord and Nick Park
Director of Photography **Tristan Oliver**
Editor **Mark Solomon**
Production Designer **Phil Lewis**
Music **John Powell, Harry Gregson-Williams**

Voice of Rocky • Mel Gibson
Voice of Ginger • Julia Sawalha
Voice of Babs • Jane Horrocks
Voice of Mrs Tweedy • Miranda Richardson
Voice of Nick • Timothy Spall
Voice of Bunty • Imelda Staunton
Voice of Fetcher • Phil Daniels
Voice of Mac • Lynn Ferguson
Voice of Mr Tweedy • Tony Haygarth
Voice of Fowler • Benjamin Whitrow
Voice of Circus Man • John Sharian
Voice of Additional Chicken • Jo Allen
Voice of Additional Chicken • Lisa Kay
Voice of Additional Chicken • Laura Strachan

Above 'This ain't no chick flick!' *Opposite* Up
on the roof: Rocky (voiced by Mel Gibson) and
Ginger (Julia Sawalha)

THE STORY

Ginger, a hen, plans a series of escape attempts from Tweedy's Chicken Farm, but all are thwarted. Rocky, a rooster who has escaped from a circus, flies into the farm. Ginger enlists him to teach the chickens how to fly. Mrs Tweedy, tired of low-profit egg fanning, orders a new machine that kills chickens to produce ready-made pies. After installing it, Mr Tweedy singles out Ginger to test the machine. During his rescue attempt, Rocky unwittingly joins Ginger inside the contraption. Before sabotaging the device and breaking free, Ginger and Rocky realise that all the farm's chickens are slated for slaughter.

Despite winning the admiration of the chickens, Rocky slips away, leaving behind proof that he was only able to fly when shot out of a cannon. Ginger calls on Fowler, an aged cockerel, to supervise the construction of an ornithopter out of odds and ends. Having fixed the pie machine, the Tweedys chance upon the chickens as they prepare for their escape bid; the chickens take to the ornithopter. With the help of Rocky, the chickens at last complete a successful escape.

WHAT THEY SAY …

Chicken Run is a prisoner-of-war film featuring grimacing Plasticine chickens in place of Richard Attenborough, John Mills or any other persistent screen escapee. To underline this, there are quotes from *The Great Escape* (1963), the only POW film likely to be familiar to an international audience. After each failed escape attempt, Ginger, the mastermind behind the chickens' plans, is confined to a coal bunker where she bounces a Brussels sprout, just as 'cooler king' Steve McQueen did a baseball in solitary confinement. The finale of the film also sees a tricycling Rocky pull off a version of the wire-jumping motorcycle stunt that was McQueen's finest moment in *The Great Escape*.

The chickens' construction of a home-made flying machine has a stylistic predecessor in the elaborate contraptions that featured in co-director Nick Park's award-winning *Wallace and Gromit* short films. Though the characters in *Chicken Run* are well defined and have their share of memorable moments, no cast members quite match up to Wallace and Gromit's inspired inventor-dog double-act. The added length of a feature doesn't help: some of the minor players – wartime bore Fowler, aggressive hen Bunty – are one-joke creations who repeat their routines two or three times with little development and diminishing effect.

Pitched almost as a UK answer to *Toy Story* (1995), *Chicken Run* offers a specific British setting and employs animation techniques that are (ostensibly) as old-fashioned and hand-crafted as *Toy Story*'s CGI imagery is high-tech and virtual. Like *Toy Story*, the tale hinges on bickering between two characters, replacing the past/future opposition of Woody and Buzz with the Brit/Yank opposition of Ginger and Rocky. Ginger, voiced with spirit by Julia Sawalha, is a British escape-film officer incarnate, not satisfied unless the whole prison population can head for freedom, while Rocky, drawled to near-creepy perfection by Mel Gibson, is the hollow blowhard hero who pulls through in the end. But it is the model work and animation that make these creatures so vivid. With wide eyes and broad grins (hen's teeth are not rare hereabouts), the poultry cast are capable of an extraordinary range of expression, especially during the sad or mildly scary scenes.

SCENE STEALER

Taking a sequence almost at random and breaking it down to its components, you realise just how much physical and emotional texture Nick Park and Peter Lord have achieved. The scene in which Ginger discovers the truth about Rocky, for instance, features an inspired narrative device as she joins together two halves of a poster that reveal the rooster can only fly by being shot from a cannon. It's a small masterpiece of cinematic storytelling: as tear-like raindrops fall all around, a thunderclap erupts in the distance, acting as a literal burst of understanding and an imagined, mocking echo of Rocky's impression of flight.

BEHIND THE SCENES

At the time of *Chicken Run*'s release, Nick Park was working on a version of the *The Tortoise and the Hare*. But in fact the next Aardman film – *Wallace & Gromit: The Curse of the Were-Rabbit*, directed by Park and Steve Box – came five years later.

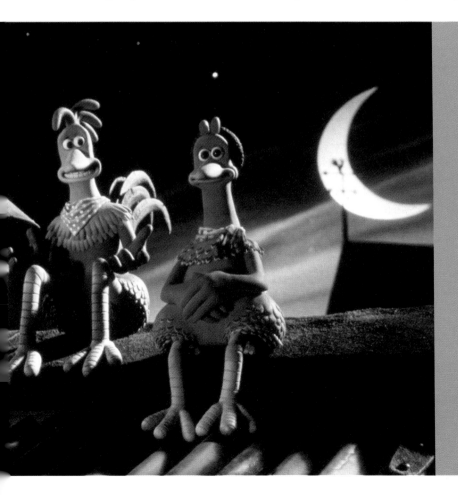

OSCARS

WHAT WON THAT YEAR?
Best Picture: *Gladiator*
Directing: Steven Soderbergh *Traffic*
Actor in a Leading Role: Russell Crowe *Gladiator*
Actress in a Leading Role: Julia Roberts *Erin Brockovich*

BAFTAS
1 nomination

Alexander Korda Award for Outstanding British Film
Achievement in Visual Special Effects: Paddy Eason,
  Mark Nelmes, Dave Alex Riddett

WHAT WON THAT YEAR?
Film: *Gladiator*
Alexander Korda Award for Outstanding British Film:
  Billy Elliot
David Lean Award for Achievement in Direction:
  Ang Lee *Crouching Tiger, Hidden Dragon*
Actor in a Leading Role: Jamie Bell *Billy Elliot*
Actress in a Leading Role: Julia Roberts *Erin Brockovich*

97

Dirs: Roger ALLERS, Rob MINKOFF / USA
Released in Britain: 1994
Running Time: 87 minutes
Colour: Technicolor
Estimated Attendance: 8.08 million

THE LION KING

Directors **Roger Allers, Rob Minkoff**
Producer **Don Hahn**
Screenplay **Irene Mecchi, Jonathan Roberts,**
  Linda Woolverton
Editor **Ivan Bilancio**
Production Designer **Chris Sanders**
Music **Hans Zimmer**

Voice of Mufasa • James Earl Jones
Voice of Scar • Jeremy Irons
voice of Shenzi • Whoppi Goldberg
Voice of Rafiki • Robert Guillaume
Voice of Simba • Matthew Broderick
Voice of Timon • Nathan Lane
Voice of Banzai • Cheech Marin
Voice of Zazu • Rowan Atkinson
Voice of Nala • Moira Kelly
Voice of Pumbaa • Ernie Sabella
Voice of Sarabi • Madge Sinclair
Voice of Young Simba • Jonathan Taylor Thomas
Voice of Young Nala • Niketa Calame
Voice of Ed • Jim Cummings

'Hakuna Matata.' It means 'Don't worry'. And Disney didn't. The decline of its animated output was arrested in the late 1980s and early 1990s by hits like *The Little Mermaid* (1989) and *Beauty and the Beast* (1991). But while *The Lion King* restored the studio's prestige, not everyone thought it was deserved.

THE STORY

At Pride Rock in the African plains, Mufasa, the king of the lions, presents his new-born heir Simba. Everyone is happy except for Scar, Mufasa's embittered younger brother, who burns with thwarted political ambition. As the months pass, Simba grows into a mischievous cub. But Scar is waiting to make his move to be king. Enlisting the help of the hyenas, Scar lures the unsuspecting Simba into the path of a wildebeest stampede; Mufasa is killed trying to save his son. Scar then convinces the shocked Simba that the tragedy was his fault, and that he should go into exile. Narrowly escaping Scar's hyena henchmen, Simba collapses in the desert. There he is found by Pumbaa, a friendly wart hog, and his wisecracking meerkat sidekick Timon. Adopting their laid-back philosophy, Simba grows into a bug-eating slacker.

One day, he saves Pumbaa from being eaten by a lioness; it turns out to be his childhood friend Nala, who brings bad news from Pride Rock. Scar's reign has brought famine and devastation to the plain, and she urges Simba to return and put things right. He returns to do battle with Scar and learns the truth about his father's death. Galvanised with righteous anger, Simba saves himself but lets Scar be torn to pieces by the hyenas. A year later, the ecological balance is restored; Nala gives birth to her and Simba's son – the future lion king.

WHAT THEY SAID THEN …

Disney's first cartoon feature to be based on an original story purports to be no less than 'a unique allegory about each new generation being a torchbearer for its ancestors'. Since Disney have always been at their best when bastardising well-loved children's stories, it seems a shame that they have suddenly felt the need to start weaving unique allegories. From the opening scene, the film clearly aspires to a kind of Shakespearian grandeur. It begins with the hordes of furry faithful applauding the arrival of Simba to a song entitled 'Circle of Life'. (Just what are the gazelles and zebras so happy about? There's a new predator in town.) The *Hamlet* parallel is earnestly laboured, and there's a bizarre moment when Scar, like a hairier Richard III, sings of his *coup d'état* while his cave sprouts the phallic towers of fascist architecture and the hyenas start goose-stepping.

There is a jolly interlude (as well as a jarring change of pace) with the fast-talking meerkat Timon, but the fun loses out to the portentousness. And despite all the money lavished on it, the stylisation looks cheap and rather nasty – the lions are peaky, the zebras beaky, and the wart hog has a nose like an electrical socket. Nonetheless, *The Lion King* has been so popular that Disney are pulling it out of US theatres so that they can re-release it for Thanksgiving – the kind of shameless marketing exercise that only this studio can get away with.

WHAT THEY SAY NOW …

Now that the premature rejoicing about the arrival of a modern Disney masterpiece – engineered largely by Disney itself – has died down, it is possible to see *The Lion King* for what it truly is: a cynical hotchpotch, sewn together from ill-fitting segments designed to maximise box-office appeal at the cost of coherence. There is the horror of Mustafa's death, manufactured to provoke undeserved comparisons with *Bambi* (1942); the tomfoolery of Timon and Pumbaa for the youngsters; the hysterical menace posed to the family unit by closet-case Scar for the Christian Right; and high-kicking, big, emoting Elton John/Tim Rice show tunes that impose cosmetic gaudiness on the whole sorry affair. However, the voice work – particularly from Jeremy Irons as Scar and Nathan Lane as Timon – is first-rate.

CLASSIC QUOTE

Mustafa's ghost: 'You have forgotten who you are and so have forgotten me. Look inside yourself, Simba. You are more than what you have become. You must take your place in the Circle of Life.'

BEHIND THE SCENES

Two straight-to-video sequels followed. So far, so exploitative. But check out the second one, *Lion King 3: Hakuna Matata!* (2004). This witty postmodern comedy, clearly influenced by Tom Stoppard's *Rosencrantz and Guildenstern Are Dead* (1990), picks over the first film from the skew-whiff perspective of Timon and Pumbaa. Streets ahead of the original.

OSCARS
4 nominations, **2 winners**

Music (Original Score): Hans Zimmer
Music (Original Song): 'Can You Feel the Love Tonight'
   Music by Elton John, Lyrics by Tim Rice
Music (Original Song): 'Circle of Life' Music by Elton John,
   Lyrics by Tim Rice
Music (Original Song): 'Hakuna Matata' Music by Elton John,
   Lyrics by Tim Rice

WHAT WON THAT YEAR?
Best Picture: *Forrest Gump*
Directing: Robert Zemeckis *Forrest Gump*
Actor in a Leading Role: Tom Hanks *Forrest Gump*
Actress in a Leading Role: Jessica Lange *Blue Sky*

BAFTAS
2 nominations

Anthony Asquith Award for Achievement in Film Music: Hans Zimmer
Sound

WHAT WON THAT YEAR?
Film: *Four Weddings and a Funeral*
Alexander Korda Award for Outstanding British Film: *Shallow Grave*
David Lean Award for Achievement in Direction: Mike Newell
   Four Weddings and a Funeral
Actor in a Leading Role: Hugh Grant *Four Weddings and a Funeral*
Actress in a Leading Role: Susan Sarandon *The Client*

Left Lion fodder: the cubs sing and dance with a plentiful supply of zebra meat at hand *Above* King of the Jungle: Simba returns to Pride Rock

Dir: Roger MICHELL / UK, USA
Released in Britain: 1999
Running Time: 124 minutes
Colour: Deluxe
Estimated Attendance: 8.05 million

Another year, another role for Hugh Grant as a lovable fool winning the woman of his dreams through concentrated self-deprecation. And another box-office smash. The Richard Curtis formula showed no sign of wearing thin; in fact, it was only bolstered by having the world's highest-paid actress along for the ride.

NOTTING HILL

Director **Roger Michell**
Producer **Duncan Kenworthy**
Screenplay **Richard Curtis**
Director of Photography **Michael Coulter**
Editor **Nick Moore**
Production Designer **Stuart Craig**
Music **Trevor Jones**

Anna Scott • Julia Roberts
William Thacker • Hugh Grant
Bernie • Hugh Bonneville
Honey • Emma Chambers
Martin • James Dreyfus
Spike • Rhys Ifans
Max • Tim McInnerny
Bella • Gina McKee
Tony • Richard McCabe
Rufus the Thief • Dylan Moran
Annoying Customer • Roger Frost
Time Out Journalist • Julian Rhind-Tutt
Anna's Publicist • Lorelei King
PR Chief • John Shrapnel
Helix Lead Actor • Clarke Peters
Foreign Actor • Arturo Venegas
Interpreter • Yolanda Vasquez
Ten-Year-Old Actress • Mischa Barton
Ritz Concierge • Henry Goodman
Loud Man in Restaurant • Dorian Lough

THE STORY

Divorcee William Thacker owns an ailing bookshop in Notting Hill, London. One day a film star, Anna Scott, buys a book from him. Shortly afterwards, they messily collide in the street. William invites Anna back to his house to clean up, where impulsively she kisses him. Some days later, the couple arrange a date – it's William's sister Honey's birthday, so they all meet at William's friends Bella and Max's house. Afterwards, Anna invites William up to her hotel room but they find Anna's boyfriend there on a surprise visit. William beats a swift retreat.

Salacious shots of Anna appear in the newspapers, and she seeks refuge at William's house where they have sex. The following morning, the press are at the door. Furious, Anna accuses William of setting her up, although it was his flatmate Spike who accidentally tipped off the press. Seasons pass. Filming a Henry James adaptation in London, Anna invites William to meet her on the set. She seems pleased to see him, but William overhears her dismissing him to a fellow actor, so he sidles away. A contrite Anna appears at the bookshop, but William rejects her. Realising his mistake, he chases after her. He arrives at her press conference and declares his love. Some time later, Anna is pregnant with William's child.

WHAT THEY SAY …

Unlike *Four Weddings and a Funeral* (1994), where 'vulgar' America is in thrall to cultured, wealthy Britain, there's no contest in *Notting Hill*. Big, bold, glamorous America is on top; Britain has banana-slipped from importance to impotence. America is shown to have a clear identity, while Britain is all at sea. Anna the actress is a somebody; William the bookseller (mistaken first for a journalist, then a hotel employee) could be anybody. Hugh Grant makes the most of his role, the perfectly pained martyr to comic calamity.

It is the emphasis on William and Britain's high-brow 'crapness' that fails to convince, because *Notting Hill* – a British film, after all – is obsessed with money and success. Henry James – that great chronicler of doomed Anglo-American relations – would have been horrified by this film's disingenuous attitude to economics (we never find out where William gets the money to afford such a posh address). Nor would James have understood the presentation of the British as 'innocents'. Each time we are asked to watch William the Non-Conqueror, all we can think is how well his tribe has colonised Notting Hill. That's why the US has to appear so dominant and knowing. Who else could make William seem like an underdog? In *Four Weddings*, we enjoyed cheering on the British rich. Now we have to be tricked into it.

The film is also intent on reminding us of the duplicity of actors, not least Anna. But Grant's public image and charm are inextricably tied to his unreliability. In the homage to his personality that was *Four Weddings*, his character's bitchy indiscretion was intriguingly turned into a virtue. In this film, when asked why his wife left him, he winces and says, 'She saw through me'. We are meant to see this as marvellous self-deprecation, but it's one of the few lines that ring true. Anna is the official actor in this relationship, but William – an instinctive actor – appears equally untrustworthy.

Messages sent out by the film seem so mixed, as well as so loaded, that it's no wonder the audience warms to the simplest pleasures on offer, such as the reliably comical sight of the film's chief clown (Rhys Ifans) posing unselfconsciously in his grimy underwear.

SCENE STEALER

The one visually ravishing moment in a humdrum looking film: William walks through Portobello Road market while the seasons change around him: snow falls, spring blossoms, and a pregnant woman is suddenly accompanied by her baby. It sure beats a 'Nine months later' on-screen caption.

IN THE CHAIR

Roger Michell drops a clue to what was scheduled to be his next assignment in the last shot of *Notting Hill*, in which a copy of *Captain Corelli's Mandolin* is glimpsed. Michell was set to direct the adaptation of Louis de Bernières' novel, but suffered a heart attack. After recovering, he made the excellent Hollywood thriller *Changing Lanes* (2002) and has since returned to British cinema.

OSCARS
Best Picture: *American Beauty*
Directing: Sam Mendes *American Beauty*
Actor in a Leading Role: Kevin Spacey *American Beauty*
Actress in a Leading Role: Hilary Swank *Boys Don't Cry*

BAFTAS
2 nominations

Alexander Korda Award for Outstanding British Film
Actor in a Supporting Role: Rhys Ifans

WHAT WON THAT YEAR?
Film: *American Beauty*
Alexander Korda Award for Outstanding British Film: *East is East*
David Lean Award for Achievement in Direction: Pedro Almodovar
 All About My Mother
Actor in a Leading Role: Kevin Spacey *American Beauty*
Actress in a Leading Role: Annette Bening *American Beauty*

Opposite Anna Scott (Julia Roberts) keeping a low profile **Left** Honey (Emma Chambers) and Spike (Rhys Ifans) at the climactic press conference

99

Dir: Beeban KIDRON / USA, France,
    UK, Ireland
Released in Britain: 2004
Running Time: 107 minutes
Colour: Technicolor
Estimated Attendance: 8.02 million

It is rumoured that several members of the production team involved on both *Bridget Jones* movies can actually distinguish between the two films. But for the rest of us, the sequel looked suspiciously like a case of 'If it ain't broke, don't fix it'. Not that this stopped it romping to box-office glory.

BRIDGET JONES: THE EDGE OF REASON

Director **Beeban Kidron**
Producers **Tim Bevan, Eric Fellner, Jonathan Cavendish**
Screenplay **Andrew Davies, Helen Fielding, Richard Curtis, Adam Brooks**, adapted from the novel by Helen Fielding
Director of Photography **Adrian Biddle**
Editor **Greg Hayden**
Production Designer **Gemma Jackson**
Music **Harry Gregson-Williams**

Bridget Jones • Renée Zellweger
Daniel Cleaver • Hugh Grant
Mark Darcy • Colin Firth
Bridget's Dad • Jim Broadbent
Bridget's Mum • Gemma Jones
Rebecca • Jacinda Barrett
Tom • James Callis
Jude • Shirley Henderson
Shazzer • Sally Phillips
Richard Finch • Neil Pearson
Magda • Jessica Stevenson
Uncle Geoffrey • James Faulkner
Una Alconbury • Celia Imrie
Bernard • Dominic McHale
Admiral Darcy • Donald Douglas
Mrs Darcy • Shirley Dixon
Receptionist • Rosalind Halstead
Mexican Ambassador • Luis Soto
Production Assistant • Tom Brooke
Girl in Rome • Alba Fleming Furlan

THE STORY

Formerly frustrated singleton Bridget Jones basks in the joy of her fledgling affair with lawyer Mark Darcy, but her suspicious jealousy of Mark's close colleague, Rebecca, creates rifts. One evening, a catty acquaintance tells Bridget that she spotted Rebecca at Mark's flat; Bridget investigates but merely finds an innocent work-related meeting. At a lawyers' function, Rebecca inadvertently embarrasses Bridget during a quiz, but Mark saves the night by telling Bridget he loves her. When Mark tells Bridget's parents they're not yet considering marriage, Bridget breaks off the relationship.

Bridget's ex-flame Daniel Cleaver now hosts a television travel programme and wants Bridget as his counterpart. They journey to Thailand on assignment with Bridget's chum Shazzer in tow. Bridget and Daniel nearly have sex, but are interrupted by a prostitute whose appointment Daniel has neglected to cancel. Shazzer meets a handsome young man who gives her a 'fertility snake bowl', which Bridget offers to carry home. At the airport, drug-sniffing dogs detect the cocaine inside, and the authorities throw Bridget into jail. Weeks later, Mark arrives to tell Bridget her release is imminent.

Back home, Bridget's friends tell her of the extraordinary legal efforts Mark made on her behalf while she was imprisoned. Bridget seeks out Mark to apologise; Mark proposes to her.

WHAT THEY SAY...

In *Bridget Jones's Diary* (2001), a bumbling, gaffe-prone but essentially decent and sympathetic young woman searching for true love, negotiates an obstacle course of minor humiliations. The film's sequel, *The Edge of Reason*, improbably ups the ante on its predecessor's comedy-of-embarrassment quotient. Bridget skydives into a pigpen. Bridget arrives at a party unaccountably slathered in blusher. And so on. None of her faux pas or slapstick blundering can darken Mark Darcy's fond gaze, so the script contrives to separate them by other, implausible means: Bridget breaks things off when Mark admits to their respective parents that, no, after less than two months together, they're not planning to marry just yet. According to the bizarre logic of the rom-com, Mark's remark means that he will, in Bridget's words, 'never muster the strength to fight' for her.

That's rubbish, of course – Darcy ends up sparring with erstwhile rival Daniel Cleaver, as he did in the first film, and *Edge of Reason* ends like any Shakespeare comedy, albeit one crowded with mallet-to-skull song cues ('Everlasting Love', 'I'm Not in Love', 'Crazy in Love'). Here and elsewhere, the film bears only essential resemblances to Helen Fielding's novel; we can breathe a sigh of relief, for instance, that the script (compiled by four familiar names, including Fielding herself and the omnipresent Richard Curtis) mostly eschews Fielding's regrettable predilection for exotic encounters with the Other. It wisely excises Bridget's mum's horizon-expanding dalliance with a Kenyan tourist, but unfortunately retains the heroine's ill-starred sojourn to Thailand, where she lands in jail. Upon hearing of her fellow prisoners' travails with boyfriends who beat them up and pimp them out, Bridget comes to the hard-earned realisation that her romance with Mark can't be so very bad after all.

Then she conducts the jailbirds, funny accents and all, in a rendition of 'Like a Virgin' – because Bridget, beneath her rumpled, blushing façade, is a born leader. Everybody loves Bridget. Cleaver says she's the best shag ever. Mark's colleague Rebecca has the hots for her. Her friends Shazzer, Jude and Tom circle like moons around her sun, emitting lunar beams of admiration and encouragement. Zellweger's sheepish, crinkly-eyed charms and vanity-free knack for physical comedy can inspire affectionate sympathy in even worse straits than this, but the actress can't fill the void at the centre of *Edge of Reason*'s known universe.

CLASSIC QUOTE

Bridget Jones: 'I truly believe that happiness is possible … even when you're 33 and have a bottom the size of two bowling balls.'

IN THE CHAIR

British director Kidron made a lasting impression early in her career with her work on the BBC adaptation of Jeanette Winterson's novel *Oranges Are Not the Only Fruit* (1990). Since then her career has been unpredictable, taking in Hollywood curiosities, such as the drag queen comedy *To Wong Foo Thanks for Everything, Julie Newmar* (1995) and interesting television projects – *Great Moments in Aviation* (1993) and the BBC series *Murder* (2002).

OSCARS

WHAT WON THAT YEAR?
Best Picture: *Million Dollar Baby*
Directing: Clint Eastwood *Million Dollar Baby*
Actor in a Leading Role: Jamie Foxx *Ray*
Actress in a Leading Role: Hilary Swank *Million Dollar Baby*

BAFTAS

WHAT WON THAT YEAR?
Film: *The Aviator*
Alexander Korda Award for Outstanding British Film:
    My Summer of Love
David Lean Award for Achievement in Direction: Mike Leigh
    Vera Drake
Actor in a Leading Role: Jamie Foxx *Ray*
Actress in a Leading Role: Imelda Staunton *Vera Drake*

Top *Girl Power: Bridget (Renée Zellwegger) leads her Thai jailmates in a rendition of 'Like a Virgin'* **Above** *Free falling: ace reporter Bridget skydives into a pigpen*

100

Dirs: Andy WACHOWSKI, Larry
    WACHOWSKI / USA, Australia
Released in Britain: 2003
Running Time: 138 minutes
Colour: Technicolor
Estimated attendance: 7.96 million

The first of two sequels to the fantasy thriller *The Matrix* (1999) offered technology so cutting edge it was in danger of drawing blood, combined with unwieldy dialogue delivered in hilariously sombre tones. (At times the cast sounded like a company of undertakers reading from a computer manual.) Business as usual, then.

THE MATRIX RELOADED

Directors/Screenplay **Andy Wachowski, Larry Wachowski**
Producer **Joel Silver**
Director of Photography **Bill Pope**
Editor **Zack Staenberg**
Production Designer **Owen Paterson**
Music **Don Davis**

Thomas 'Neo' Anderson • Keanu Reeves
Morpheus • Laurence Fishburne
Trinity • Carrie-Anne Moss
Agent Smith • Hugo Weaving
Niobe • Jada Pinkett
The Oracle • Gloria Foster
Link • Harold Perrineau Jr
Persephone • Monica Bellucci
Commander Lock • Harry J. Lennix
Merovingian • Lambert Wilson
Agent Jackson • David A. Kilde
Zee • Nona Gaye
Councillor Hamann • Anthony Zerbe
Power Station Guard • Ray Anthony
Kali • Christine Anu
Police 2 • Andy Arness
Girl, Link's Niece • Alima Ashton-Sheibu
The Architect • Helmut Bakaitis
Soren • Steve Bastoni
Vector • Don Batte

THE STORY

Poisoned and derelict, Earth is controlled by the Matrix, a computer-generated intelligence feeding off the human race. Hidden underground, the city of Zion is the only haven for those who have escaped Matrix programming. But when the Matrix unleashes machines to destroy Zion within 72 hours, the city's Council must decide its best defence. According to prophecy, the war can be ended by a super-human 'One', but although this role appears to fit Neo, recently wrested from Matrix control by Zion's militant visionary Morpheus, he has no idea how to proceed.

Consulting the Oracle, Neo describes his recurring nightmare in which Trinity, the girl to whom he owes his life, is shot by a Matrix agent. The Oracle indicates that the solution to this and other possible futures can only be unlocked by the Keymaker, held captive by the Merovingian, a dissolute consumer of Matrix luxuries. After fighting off a horde of cloned Agent Smiths (a Matrix assassin), Neo teams up with Morpheus and Trinity to bargain for the Keymaker's release. The Merovingian refuses, but his wife Persephone, for the price of a kiss from Neo, hands the Keymaker over. In a ferocious motorway struggle, they at last get him to safety.

The Keymaker reports that only the 'One' can open the door leading to the source of knowledge, and only at a precise time.

As they approach the required location, they are attacked by more Agent Smiths, and both Trinity and the Keymaker, who passes the vital key to Neo, are mortally wounded. Through the door, Neo meets the Architect, designer of the Matrix, who comments that this is the sixth time Zion has been under threat and offers two further doors, one leading to Zion's defence, the other to Trinity's rescue. Neo selects the route to Trinity, and restores her to life. As Zion faces destruction, its defenders fear that the prophecy was a lie.

WHAT THEY SAY ...

Like George Lucas with *Star Wars*, the Wachowski Brothers got hung up on the idea of a trilogy after their first, enjoyably enigmatic *Matrix* film proved hugely popular. But the two sequels – *Reloaded* and *Revolutions* (2003), filmed back-to-back and released six months apart – lacked the focus and surprise of that opening instalment.

Conforming to producer Joel Silver's 'action-beat' strategy (jolts of excitement every ten minutes), the Wachowski Brothers compiled their first *Matrix* sequel from scenes of exuberant overkill. Open to everything from postmodern theorist Jean Baudrillard to Superman, the Wachowskis can also be briskly perfunctory, as if to check we've been paying attention. Apparently random details abound. No context is given in *Reloaded* for the glimpse of an Armoured Personnel Unit, while the significance of a power struggle between the Councillors or an abortive assassination attempt seem similarly set aside for some other occasion.

Those deadly Wachowski dialogues sometimes carry an unpredictable edge, like the 'sweet dreams' wished by Morpheus on the citizens of Zion, overlooking the irony that this is precisely what they would receive from the Matrix. It's clearly not a phrase to be trusted, any more than the evident silliness of the agreement between Neo and Councillor Hamann that some machines are more reliable than others, or Niobe's confident announcement that 'Some things never change,' (pause) 'and some do'.

But the text, of course, is wholly secondary to the image, beginning as in the first *Matrix* with Trinity's spectacular escape bid, fully good enough for the encore it duly gets. That Neo versus a hundred Agent Smiths, innumerable high-speed duels and the great motorway car chase are enthralling to watch for their technical ingenuity cannot quite prevent a certain fatigue by the time the Architect reveals it has all happened five times already. No reflection on the cast, who are immensely watchable (with particular zest from Lambert Wilson and Hugo Weaving), but once more will probably be about enough. Perhaps the Wachowskis can then extricate themselves from their private Matrix and, with another bound, set themselves free.

CLASSIC QUOTE

Agent Smith (just before introducing his clones): 'The best thing about being me: there are so many "me"s.'

SCENE STEALER

The astonishing highway chase sequence took three months to film, and was shot on a mile-long, three-lane loop of road specially built on a decommissioned navy base.

OSCARS

WHAT WON THAT YEAR?
Best Picture: *The Lord of the Rings: The Return of the King*
Directing: Peter Jackson *The Lord of the Rings: The Return of the King*
Actor in a Leading Role: Sean Penn *Mystic River*
Actress in a Leading Role: Charlize Theron *Monster*

BAFTAS

WHAT WON THAT YEAR?
Film: *The Lord of the Rings: The Return of the King*
David Lean Award for Achievement in Direction: Peter Weir *Master and Commander: The Far Side of the World*
Actor in a Leading Role: Bill Murray *Lost in Translation*
Actress in a Leading Role: Scarlett Johansson *Lost in Translation*

Top Motorway mayhem: Keymaker Randall Duk Kim rides pillion behind Trinity (Carrie-Anne Moss) *Above* Playschool? Morpheus (Laurence Fishburne, centre) leads Trinity and Neo (Keanu Reeves) through the arched window *Left* Seeing double? Multiple Agent Smiths (Hugo Weaving) prepare to fire *Overleaf* Don't look back in anger: is it the end of the road for Morpheus (Laurence Fishburne)?

RESEARCHING THE ULTIMATE FILM

At BFI Information Services we receive all sorts of questions about the cinema. Sometimes answering these takes us deep into uncharted research territory, and such was the case with *The Ultimate Film* project. It began when North One Television approached us to provide a definitive list of the most popular films of all-time at the British cinema for a two-part Channel 4 programme. The brief spanned all feature films released, with the exception of silent films and documentaries. This request seems straightforward, but has never been successfully undertaken before now.

The truth is that the film industry can be a secretive business; commercial information has rarely been shared between industry competitors or with the wider world. Before the 1970s the recording and publicising of cinema admissions or ticket sales was haphazard at best. Listings of all-time hits have traditionally been based on box office income, but such rankings are heavily distorted by inflation, inevitably favouring recent releases over old. Compiling a list based instead on estimated 'bums on seats' it was felt would give us a much more consistent picture of popularity over time. Older hits must in reality often outrank their modern counterparts; after all, in the 1940s annual cinema admissions were well over 1000 million, falling to 54 million in 1984 and remaining below 200 million today.

So without comprehensive data how did we do it? Researching *The Ultimate Film* meant combing the BFI National Library's extensive collections in a hunt for evidence with which to formulate a Top 100. It wasn't straightforward, but we do feel that this list is as accurate a record as possible of the films that the British public have flocked to see.

We looked at annual round-ups of hits in trade magazines of the past, press reports, and press releases from film distributors. By matching the information gleaned with known data on the total number of cinema visits per year, estimates for the numbers of people likely to have seen older films were produced. For the newer titles, we used the average ticket price at the time of a film's release to convert its box office into a proverbial 'bums on seats' estimate. So there you have it? There were further factors to take into account; for instance lower priced children's tickets mean that more people see a family film than an '18'-certificate title for the equivalent box office takings. Changing industry practices also have an influence. In the 1950s and 1960s epics and musicals such as *South Pacific* sometimes had 'Roadshow' releases – meaning they played (sometimes for years) at a single big city cinema at top prices before later touring the country's 'fleapits'.

Digging into our cinema past threw up surprises, even for the seasoned researcher. It was heartening to find so many British films making the chart (aided for a time by British film quotas for cinemas) and younger readers may be bemused by the huge popularity of now unfamiliar films or stars, such as Anna Neagle. Through this list we see more than just movies – we get a picture of British society, our tastes, and how they have changed.

PHIL WICKHAM AND MATT KER

LIST OF CONTRIBUTORS

Contributors

The Editor and the Publisher would like to thank the following people who have contributed to entries within the book:

Angie Errigo
Philip Kemp
Ed Lawrenson
Geoffrey Macnab
George Perry
Tim Robey
Matthew Sweet

Original Reviewers

The Editor and the Publisher would also like to acknowledge the contribution of the original reviewers of the films within this book. Due to limitations of space these reviews have been edited, but every effort has been made to retain the sense of the original. Not all the reviewers are known. Those who can be identified are:

José Arroyo
Nina Caplan
Manohla Dargis
Leslie Felperin
Mark Kermode
Matthew Leyland
Laura Miller
Caren Myers
Kim Newman
Andrew O'Hehir
Charlotte O'Sullivan
Philip Strick
Ben Walters
Rob White
Vicky Wilson
Jessica Winter

Screen Online
Material from www.screenonline.org.uk has occasionally been used within the book. The Editor and the Publisher would like to acknowledge the contribution of the original authors of this material. They are:

Sergio Angelini
Michael Brooke
Mark Duguid
Janet Moat
David Parker
Tom Ryall
Mike Sutton
Rob White

UK CINEMA
ADMISSIONS BY YEAR

Figures are given in millions of attendees

Year	Admissions	Year	Admissions	Year	Admissions	Year	Admissions
		1940	1027.0	1950	1395.0	1960	500.8
		1941	1309.0	1951	1365.0	1961	449.1
		1942	1494.0	1952	1312.1	1962	395.0
		1943	1541.0	1953	1284.5	1963	357.2
		1944	1575.0	1954	1275.8	1964	342.8
1935	912.3	1945	1585.0	1955	1181.8	1965	326.6
1936	917.0	1946	1635.0	1956	1100.8	1966	288.8
1937	946.0	1947	1462.0	1957	915.2.0	1967	264.8
1938	987.0	1948	1514.0	1958	754.7.0	1968	237.3
1939	990.0	1949	1430.0	1959	581.0	1969	214.9

Year	Admissions	Year	Admissions	Year	Admissions	Year	Admissions
1970	193.0	1980	101.0	1990	97.4	2000	142.5
1971	176.0	1981	86.0	1991	100.3	2001	155.9
1972	156.6	1982	64.0	1992	103.6	2002	176.0
1973	134.2	1983	65.7	1993	114.4	2003	167.3
1974	138.5	1984	54.0	1994	123.5	2004	171.3
1975	116.3	1985	72.0	1995	114.6		
1976	103.9	1986	75.5	1996	123.8		
1977	103.5	1987	78.5	1997	139.3		
1978	126.1	1988	84.0	1998	135.5		
1979	111.9	1989	94.5	1999	139.7		

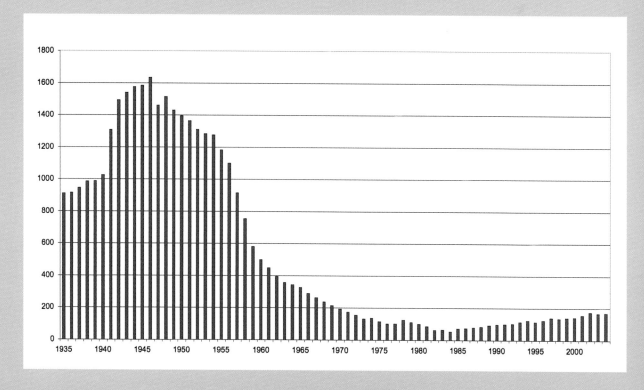

THE ULTIMATE FILM ALPHABETICALLY

THE ULTIMATE FILM BY DECADE

1930s
1936	91	Mr Deeds Goes to Town
1937	66	Lost Horizon
1938	3	Snow White and the Seven Dwarfs
1939	85	The Citadel

1940s
1940	1	Gone with the Wind
	75	Rebecca
	86	Pinocchio
1941	65	49th Parallel
	72	The Great Dictator
1942	52	Mrs Miniver
	7	Bambi
1943	38	Random Harvest
1944	41	Fanny by Gaslight
	60	For Whom the Bell Tolls
1945	10	The Seventh Veil
	51	I Live in Grosvenor Square
1946	9	The Wicked Lady
	20	The Bells of St Mary's
	43	Piccadilly Incident
1947	6	The Best Years of Our Lives
	17	The Courtneys of Curzon Street
	42	The Jolson Story
1948	5	Spring in Park Lane
1949	26	The Third Man

1950s
1950	29	The Blue Lamp
1951	35	The Great Caruso
1952	32	The Greatest Show on Earth
1954	36	Doctor in the House
1955	89	The Dam Busters
1956	62	High Society
	80	Reach for the Sky
	95	The King and I
1957	21	The Ten Commandments
	33	The Bridge on the River Kwai
1958	13	South Pacific
	73	The Big Country
1959	50	Carry on Nurse
	64	I'm All Right Jack

1960s
1960	30	Ben-Hur
	92	The Swiss Family Robinson
1961	44	The Guns of Navarone
	68	One Hundred and One Dalmatians
1962	88	Lawrence of Arabia
1964	25	Mary Poppins
	27	Goldfinger
1965	2	The Sound of Music
	81	My Fair Lady
1966	18	Thunderball
1967	46	Doctor Zhivago
	93	You Only Live Twice
1968	7	The Jungle Book
	76	Oliver!

1970s
1972	48	The Godfather
	56	A Clockwork Orange
1973	71	Live and Let Die
1974	47	The Sting
	94	The Exorcist
1975	40	The Towering Inferno
1976	14	Jaws
	61	One Flew over the Cuckoo's Nest
1977	34	The Spy Who Loved Me
1978	4	Star Wars
	12	Grease
	70	Saturday Night Fever
	84	Close Encounters of the Third Kind
1979	53	Superman
	63	Moonraker

1980s
1980	69	The Empire Strikes Back
1983	31	E.T. The Extra-Terrestrial
	90	Return of the Jedi
1987	57	'Crocodile' Dundee

1990s
1990	78	Ghost
1993	15	Jurassic Park
1994	77	Four Weddings and a Funeral
	97	The Lion King
1996	49	Independence Day
1997	23	The Full Monty
	59	Men in Black
1998	8	Titanic
1999	28	Star Wars Episode I: The Phantom Menace
	87	A Bug's Life
	98	Notting Hill

2000s
2000	37	Toy Story 2
	96	Chicken Run
2001	11	Harry Potter and the Philosopher's Stone
	16	The Lord of the Rings: The Fellowship of the Ring
	54	Bridget Jones's Diary
2002	22	The Lord of the Rings: The Two Towers
	24	Harry Potter and the Chamber of Secrets
	55	Monsters, Inc.
	67	Star Wars Episode II: Attack of the Clones
	82	Die Another Day
2003	19	The Lord of the Rings: The Return of the King
	58	Finding Nemo
	79	Love Actually
	100	The Matrix Reloaded
2004	39	Shrek 2
	45	Harry Potter and the Prisoner of Azkaban
	99	Bridget Jones: The Edge of Reason
2005	83	Star Wars Episode III: Revenge of the Sith

THE ULTIMATE FILM MOST POPULAR ACTORS

The list of actors with four or more appearances in the chart makes interesting reading. It is dominated by character actresses in successful franchises (notably Bond or *Star Wars* films), with only occasional appearances from the Hollywood 'A' list. As well as featuring in earlier British classics, Bernard Lee played 'M' in several Bond films to make him a clear leader in the list. He is joined here by Lois Maxwell (Miss Moneypenny) and Desmond Llewellyn ('Q'). With all six *Star Wars* episodes in the list it's not surprising to see appearances from Kenny Baker (R2-D2), Anthony Daniels (C-3PO), Frank Oz (the voice of Yoda), Peter Mayhew (Chewbacca), Ian McDiarmid (Palpatine) and also James Earl Jones as the voice of Darth Vadar. Alec Guinness benefits from the first three *Star Wars* films to be highly placed, but the fastest rising box office star is clearly Hugh Grant with five films in the list already under his belt.

9

Bernard Lee

6

Kenny Baker
Anthony Daniels
Alec Guinness
Lois Maxwell
Frank Oz

5

Hugh Grant
Desmond Llewelyn

4

John Cleese
Charlton Heston
James Earl Jones
Ian McDiarmid
Peter Mayhew
Anna Neagle
Alan Rickman

CREDITS AND ACKNOWLEDGMENTS
Original sources for the 'Story' and 'What they said...' sections

The *Monthly Film Bulletin* was published by the British Film Institute between 1934 and 1991. Initially aimed at distributors and exhibitors as well as filmgoers, it carried reviews and details of all UK film releases. In 1991, the Bulletin was incoporated into *Sight and Sound* magazine.

1   Gone with the Wind: *Monthly Film Bulletin*, Vol. 7 No. 76, April 1940, p. 56
2   The Sound of Music: *Monthly Film Bulletin*, Vol. 32 No. 376, May 1965, p. 72
3   Snow White and the Seven Dwarfs: *Monthly Film Bulletin*, Vol. 5 No. 50, February 1938, p. 44
4   Star Wars: *Monthly Film Bulletin*, Vol. 44 No. 526, November 1977, pp. 243–4
5   Spring in Park Lane: *Monthly Film Bulletin*, Vol. 15 No. 172, April 1948, p. 48
6   The Best Years of Our Lives: *Monthly Film Bulletin*, Vol. 14 No. 160, April 1947, p. 148
7   The Jungle Book: *Monthly Film Bulletin*, Vol. 35 No. 408, January 1968, p. 10
8   Titanic: *Sight and Sound*, Vol. 8 No. 2, February 1998, pp. 50–2 (Laura Miller)
9   The Wicked Lady: *Monthly Film Bulletin*, Vol. 12 No. 143, November 1945, p. 130
10 The Seventh Veil: *Monthly Film Bulletin*, Vol. 12 No. 142, October 1945, p. 118
11 Harry Potter and the Philosopher's Stone: *Sight and Sound*, Vol. 12 No. 1, January 2002, pp. 43–4 (Rob White)
12 Grease: *Monthly Film Bulletin*, Vol. 45 No. 536, September 1978, pp. 175–6
13 South Pacific: *Monthly Film Bulletin*, Vol. 25 No. 293, June 1958, p. 73
14 Jaws: *Monthly Film Bulletin*, Vol. 42 No. 503, December 1975, pp. 263–4
15 Jurassic Park: *Sight and Sound*, Vol. 3 No. 8, August 1993, pp. 44–5 (Kim Newman)
16 Lord of the Rings: The Fellowship of the Ring: *Sight and Sound*, Vol. 12 No. 2, February 2002, pp. 49–50, 52 (Andrew O'Hehir)
17 The Courtneys of Curzon Street: *Monthly Film Bulletin*, Vol. 14 No. 161, May 1947, p. 61
18 Thunderball: *Monthly Film Bulletin*, Vol. 33 No. 385, February 1966, p. 20
19 Lord of the Rings: Return of the King: *Sight and Sound*, Vol. 14 No. 2, February 2004, pp. 52–4 (Kim Newman)
20 The Bells of St.Mary's: *Monthly Film Bulletin*, Vol. 13 No 151, July 1946, p. 95
21 The Ten Commandments: *Monthly Film Bulletin*, Vol. 25 No. 288, January 1958, p. 4
22 Lord of the Rings: The Two Towers: *Sight and Sound*, Vol. 13 No. 2, February 2003, pp. 48, 50–51 (Kim Newman)
23 The Full Monty: *Sight and Sound*, Vol. 7 No. 9.September 1997, p. 43 (Nina Caplan)
24 Harry Potter and the Chamber of Secrets: *Sight and Sound*, Vol. 13 No. 1, January 2003, pp. 47–9 (Leslie Felperin)
25 Mary Poppins: *Monthly Film Bulletin*, Vol. 32 No. 373, February 1965, p. 20
26 The Third Man: *Monthly Film Bulletin*, Vol. 16 No. 189, September 1949, p.159
27 Goldfinger: *Monthly Film Bulletin*, Vol. 31 No. 370 November 1964, p. 161
28 Star Wars Episode I: The Phantom Menace: *Sight and Sound*, Vol. 9 No. 7, July 1999, pp. 34–5, 54–5 (Andrew O'Hehir)
29 The Blue Lamp: *Monthly Film Bulletin*, Vol. 17 No. 193, Jan–Feb 1950, p. 2
30 Ben-Hur: *Monthly Film Bulletin*, Vol. 27 No. 313, February 1960, p. 18
31 E.T.: *Monthly Film Bulletin*, Vol. 49 No. 587, December 1982, pp. 282–3
32 The Greatest Show on Earth: *Monthly Film Bulletin*, Vol. 19 No. 218, March 1952, p. 29
33 The Bridge on the River Kwai: *Monthly Film Bulletin*, Vol. 24 No. 286 November 1957, p. 134
34 The Spy Who Loved Me: *Monthly Film Bulletin*, Vol. 44 No. 523, August 1977, p. 176
35 The Great Caruso: *Monthly Film Bulletin*, Vol. 18 No. 209, June 1951, p. 280
36 Doctor in the House: *Monthly Film Bulletin*, Vol. 21 No. 244, May 1954, p. 73
37 Toy Story 2: *Sight and Sound*, Vol. 10 No. 3, March 2000, pp. 56–7 (Kim Newman)
38 Random Harvest: *Monthly Film Bulletin*, Vol. 10 1943, p. 6
39 Shrek 2: *Sight and Sound*, Vol. 14 No. 8, August 2004, pp. 64–6 (Matthew Leyland)
40 The Towering Inferno: *Monthly Film Bulletin*, Vol. 42 No. 493, February 1975, p. 41
41 Fanny by Gaslight: *Monthly Film Bulletin*, Vol. 11 No. 125, May 1944, p. 53
42 The Jolson Story: *Monthly Film Bulletin*, Vol. 13 No. 155 1946, p. 151
43 Piccadilly Incident: *Monthly Film Bulletin*, Vol. 13 No 153 1946, p. 122
44 The Guns of Navarone: *Monthly Film Bulletin*, Vol. 28 No. 329, June 1961, p. 75
45 Harry Potter and the Prisoner of Azkaban: *Sight and Sound*, Vol. 14 No. 8, August 2004, pp. 51–2, 54 (Vicky Wilson)
46 Doctorr Zhivago: *Monthly Film Bulletin*, Vol. 33 No. 389, June 1966, p. 86
47 The Sting: *Monthly Film Bulletin*, Vol. 41 No. 480, January 1974, pp. 14–15
48 The Godfather: *Monthly Film Bulletin*, Vol. 39 No. 464, September 1972, p. 190
49 Independence Day: *Sight and Sound*, Vol. 6 No. 8, August 1996, pp. 53–4 (Manohla Dargis)
50 Carry on Nurse: *Monthly Film Bulletin*, Vol. 26 No. 303, April 1959, p. 45
51 I Live in Grosvenor Square: *Monthly Film Bulletin*, Vol. 12 No. 138, June 1945, p. 69

52 Mrs Miniver: *Monthly Film Bulletin*, Vol. 9 No. 103 1942, p. 89

53 Superman: *Monthly Film Bulletin*, Vol. 46 No. 541, February 1979, pp. 33–4

54 Bridget Jones's Diary: *Sight and Sound*, Vol. 11 No. 4, April 2001, pp. 36–7, 39–40 (Leslie Felperin)

55 Monsters Inc: *Sight and Sound*, Vol. 12 No. 2, February 2002, pp. 54–5 (Matthew Leyland)

56 A Clockwork Orange: *Monthly Film Bulletin*, Vol. 39 No. 457, February 1972, pp. 28–9

57 Crocodile Dundee: *Monthly Film Bulletin*, Vol. 53 No. 635, December 1986, p. 367

58 Finding Nemo: *Sight and Sound*, Vol. 13 No. 11 November 2003, pp. 43–4 (Leslie Felperin)

59 Men in Black: *Sight and Sound*, Vol. 7 No. 8, August 1997, pp. 47–8 (Mark Kermode)

60 For Whom the Bell Tolls: *Monthly Film Bulletin*, Vol. 11 No. 123, March 1944, p. 29

61 One Flew over the Cuckoo's Nest: *Monthly Film Bulletin*, Vol. 43 No. 505, February 1976, pp. 32–3

62 High Society: *Monthly Film Bulletin*, Vol. 23 No. 275, December 1956, p. 150

63 Moonraker: *Monthly Film Bulletin*, Vol. 46 No. 547, August 1979, pp. 179–80

64 I'm All Right Jack: *Monthly Film Bulletin*, Vol. 26 No. 309, October 1959, p. 133

65 49th Parallel: *Monthly Film Bulletin*, Vol. 8 No. 94, October 1941, p. 129

66 Lost Horizon: *Monthly Film Bulletin*, Vol. 4 No. 40, April 1937, p. 82

67 Star Wars Episode II: Attack of the Clones: *Sight and Sound*, Vol. 12 No. 7, July 2002, pp. 54–5 (Andrew O'Hehir)

68 One Hundred and One Dalmatians: *Monthly Film Bulletin*, Vol. 28 No. 328, May 1961, p. 61

69 The Empire Strikes Back: *Monthly Film Bulletin*, Vol. 47 No. 558, July 1980, pp. 129–30

70 Saturday Night Fever: *Monthly Film Bulletin*, Vol. 45 No. 531, April 1978, pp. 68–9

71 Live and Let Die: *Monthly Film Bulletin*, Vol. 40 No. 475, August 1973, pp. 171–2

72 The Great Dictator: *Monthly Film Bulletin*, Vol. 7 No. 84, December 1940, p. 184

73 The Big Country: *Monthly Film Bulletin*, Vol. 26 No. 301, February 1959, p. 14

74 Bambi: *Monthly Film Bulletin*, Vol. 15 No. 171, March 1948, pp. 31–2

75 Rebecca: *Monthly Film Bulletin*, Vol. 7 No 79 1940, p. 115

76 Oliver!: *Monthly Film Bulletin*, Vol. 35 No. 418 November 1968, p. 172

77 Four Weddings and a Funeral: *Sight and Sound*, Vol. 4 No. 6, June 1994, p. 46 (Caren Myers)

78 Ghost: *Monthly Film Bulletin*, Vol. 57 No. 681, October 1990, pp. 295–6

79 Love Actually: *Sight and Sound*, Vol. 13 No. 12, December 2003, pp. 44, 46 (Ben Walters)

80 Reach for the Sky: *Monthly Film Bulletin*, Vol. 23 No. 270, July 1956, p. 87

81 My Fair Lady: *Monthly Film Bulletin*, Vol. 32 No. 374, March 1965, p. 35

82 Die Another Day: *Sight and Sound*, Vol. 13 No. 1, January 2003, pp. 41–2 (Kim Newman)

83 Star Wars Episode III: Revenge of the Sith: *Sight and Sound*, Vol. 15 No. 7, July 2005, pp. 38–9, 75 (Kim Newman)

84 Close Encounters of the Third Kind: *Monthly Film Bulletin*, Vol. 45 No. 531, April 1978, pp. 63–4

85 The Citadel: *Monthly Film Bulletin*, Vol. 5 No 60 1938, p. 276

86 Pinocchio: *Monthly Film Bulletin*, Vol. 7 No 75 1940, p. 41

87 A Bug's Life: *Sight and Sound*, Vol. 9 No. 2, February 1999, pp. 39–40 (Leslie Felperin)

88 Lawrence of Arabia: *Monthly Film Bulletin*, Vol. 30 No. 349, February 1963, p. 17

89 The Dam Busters: *Monthly Film Bulletin*, Vol. 22 No. 257, June 1955, p. 82

90 Return of the Jedi: *Monthly Film Bulletin*, Vol. 50 No. 594, July 1983, pp. 181–3

91 Mr Deeds Goes to Town: *Monthly Film Bulletin*, Vol. 3 No. 32, August 1936, p. 133

92 The Swiss Family Robinson: *Monthly Film Bulletin*, Vol. 28 No. 325, February 1961, p. 24

93 You Only Live Twice: *Monthly Film Bulletin*, Vol. 34 No. 403, August 1967, p. 122

94 The Exorcist: *Monthly Film Bulletin*, Vol. 41 No. 483, April 1974, p.71

95 The King and I: *Monthly Film Bulletin*, Vol. 23 No. 272, September 1956, p. 114

96 Chicken Run: *Sight and Sound*, Vol. 10 No. 8, August 2000, pp. 41–2 (Kim Newman)

97 The Lion King: *Sight and Sound*, Vol. 4 No. 10, October 1994, pp. 47–8 (Caren Myers)

98 Notting Hill: *Sight and Sound*, Vol. 9 No. 6, June 1999, pp. 49–50 (Charlotte O'Sullivan)

99 Bridget Jones: The Edge of Reason: *Sight and Sound*, Vol. 14 No. 12, December 2004, pp. 40–41 (Jessica Winter)

100 The Matrix Reloaded: *Sight and Sound*, Vol. 13 No. 7, July 2003, pp. 50, 52–3 (Philip Strick)

IMAGE CREDITS

While considerable effort has been made to identify the copyright holders correctly, this may not have been possible in all cases. We apologise for any apparent negligence. Omissions or corrections brought to our attention will be remedied in any future editions.

Introduction: Jonathan Ross courtesy of Open Mike Productions; **1.** Gone with the Wind: Warner Bros./Turner; **2.** The Sound of Music: 20th Century Fox; **3.** Snow White and the Seven Dwarfs: Buena Vista International; **4.** Star Wars: Lucasfilm; **5.** Spring in Park Lane: Canal + Image UK; **6.** The Best Years of Our Lives: MGM/Sony; **7.** The Jungle Book: Buena Vista International; **8.** Titanic: 20th Century Fox; **9.** The Wicked Lady: Granada International; **10.** The Seventh Veil: Granada International; **Picture Palaces:** Cinema images pp. 46–7 courtesy of Alan Eyles; **11.** Harry Potter and the Philosopher's Stone: Warner Bros.; **12.** Grease: Paramount Pictures; **13.** South Pacific: MGM/Sony; **14.** Jaws: Universal Studios; **15.** Jurassic Park: Universal Studios; **16.** The Lord of the Rings: The Fellowship of the Ring: New Line Cinema; **17.** The Courtneys of Curzon Street: Canal + Image UK; **18.** Thunderball: MGM/Sony; **19.** The Lord of the Rings: The Return of the King: New Line Cinema; **20.** The Bells of St Mary's: BBC Worldwide Motion Gallery (UK); Warner Bros./Turner (Rest of the World); **Leading Ladies:** Sandra Bullock (Columbia Tristar); Katharine Hepburn (Leow's Inc.); **21.** The Ten Commandments: Paramount Pictures; **22.** The Lord of the Rings: The Two Towers: New Line Cinema; **23.** The Full Monty: 20th Century Fox; **24.** Harry Potter and the Chamber of Secrets: Warner Bros.; **25.** Mary Poppins: Buena Vista International; **26.** The Third Man: Canal + Image UK; **27.** Goldfinger: MGM/Sony; **28.** Star Wars Episode I: The Phantom Menace: Lucasfilm; **29.** The Blue Lamp: Canal + Image UK; **30.** Ben-Hur: Warner Bros./Turner; **His Name's Bond:** MGM/Sony; **30.** E.T. The Extra-Terrestrial: Universal Studios; **32.** The Greatest Show on Earth: Paramount Pictures; **33.** The Bridge on the River Kwai: Columbia Tristar; **34.** The Spy Who Loved Me: MGM/Sony; **35.** The Great Caruso: Warner Bros./Turner; **36.** Doctor in the House: Granada International; **37.** Toy Story 2: Buena Vista International; **38.** Random Harvest: Warner Bros./Turner; **39.** Shrek 2: Dreamworks; **40.** The Towering Inferno: The Estate of Irwin Allen; 20th Century Fox (North American Rights); Warner Bros., (Rest of the World); **Film at War:** London Can Take It!, Listen to Britain (both Crown Film Unit); Millions Like Us (Granada International); The Life and Death of Colonel Blimp (Carlton International); . The Foreman Went to France (Ealing Studios); **41.** Fanny by Gaslight: Granada International; **42.** The Jolson Story: Columbia Tristar; **43.** Piccadilly Incident: Canal + Image UK; **44.** The Guns of Navarone: Columbia Tristar; **45.** Harry Potter and the Prisoner of Azkaban: Warner Bros.; **46.** Doctor Zhivago: Warner Bros./Turner; **47.** The Sting: Universal Studios; **48.** The Godfather: Paramount Pictures; **49.** Independence Day: 20th Century Fox; **50.** Carry on Nurse: Canal + Image UK; **Missing Men:** James Dean (Warner Bros.); Montgomery Clift (Paramount Pictures); Cary Grant (Leow's Inc.); **51.** I Live in Grosvenor Square: Canal + Image UK; **52.** Mrs Miniver: Warner Bros./Turner; **53.** Superman: Warner Bros.; **54.** Bridget Jones's Diary: Universal Studios; **55.** Monsters Inc: Buena Vista International; **56.** A Clockwork Orange: Warner Bros.; **57.** 'Crocodile' Dundee: 20th Century Fox; **58.** Finding Nemo: Buena Vista International; **59.** Men in Black: Columbia Tristar; **60.** For Whom the Bell Tolls: Universal Studios; **That's (Home) Entertainment:** Betamax VCR (Sony); HD DVD disks and player (Toshiba); **61.** One Flew over the Cuckoo's Nest: MGM/Sony; **62.** High Society: Warner Bros./Turner; **63.** Moonraker: MGM/Sony; **64.** I'm All Right Jack: Canal + Image UK; **65.** 49th Parallel: Granada International; **66.** Lost Horizon: Columbia Tristar; **67.** Star Wars Episode II: Attack of the Clones: Lucasfilm; **68.** One Hundred and One Dalmatians: Buena Vista International; **69.** The Empire Strikes Back: Lucasfilm; **70.** Saturday Night Fever: Paramount Pictures; **Ones that Got Away:** Citizen Kane (RKO Pictures); Casablanca (Warner Bros.); Psycho (Buena Vista International); The Magnificent Seven (MGM/Sony); The Terminator (Cinema '84); **71.** Live and Let Die: MGM/Sony; **72.** The Great Dictator: Roy Export Company Establishment; **73.** The Big Country: MGM/Sony; **74.** Bambi: Buena Vista International; **75.** Rebecca: Buena Vista International; **76.** Oliver!: Columbia Tristar; **77.** Four Weddings and a Funeral: Universal Studios; **78.** Ghost: Paramount Pictures; **79.** Love Actually: Universal Studios; **80.** Reach for the Sky: Granada International; **Drawing the Crowds:** Steamboat Willie, Fantasia, Who Framed Roger Rabbit (all Buena Vista International); Akira (Akira Committee); Shrek (Dreamworks); **81.** My Fair Lady: Warner Bros.; **82.** Die Another Day: MGM/Sony; **83.** Star Wars Episode III: Revenge of the Sith: Lucasfilm; **84.** Close Encounters of the Third Kind: Columbia Tristar; **85.** The Citadel: Warner Bros./Turner; **86.** Pinocchio: Buena Vista International; **87.** A Bug's Life: Buena Vista International; **88.** Lawrence of Arabia: Columbia Tristar; **89.** The Dam Busters: Canal + Image UK; **90.** Return of the Jedi: Lucasfilm; **Foreign Bodies:** 2046 (Block 2 Pictures); La Dolce Vita (Riama Film); House of Flying Daggers (Elite Group Enterprises); Il Gattopardo (Titanus); **91.** Mr Deeds Goes to Town: Columbia Tristar; **92.** The Swiss Family Robinson: Buena Vista International; **93.** You Only Live Twice: MGM/Sony; **94.** The Exorcist: Warner Bros.; **95.** The King and I: 20th Century Fox; **96.** Chicken Run: Dreamworks; **97.** The Lion King: Buena Vista International; **98.** Notting Hill: Universal Studios; **99.** Bridget Jones: The Edge of Reason: Universal Studios; **100.** The Matrix Reloaded: Warner Bros.

INDEX